AMERICAN PRAVDA

JEWS, NAZIS, AND ISRAEL

GRASPING THE "THIRD RAIL" OF JOURNALISTS AND HISTORIANS

AMERICAN PRAVDA
JEWS, NAZIS, AND ISRAEL
GRASPING THE "THIRD RAIL" OF JOURNALISTS AND HISTORIANS

Unz Review Press

Copyright © 2022 by Ron Unz

Published by The Unz Review Press
555 Bryant St. #371
Palo Alto, California 94301

All rights reserved. Printed in the United States of America. No part of this book may be reproduced in any manner whatsoever without written permission except in the case of brief quotations embodied in critical articles and reviews.

ISBN: 979-8-84-10330-9-7

Designed by Anthony Mioni (www.anthonymioni.com)
Cover photo of rabbi praying by David Cohen from Shutterstock

*To the Memory of Israel Shahak,
Who Began Opening My Eyes Nearly Forty Years Ago*

CONTENTS

Introduction ix

Sharonism vs. Building a Wall
The Sacramento Bee, April 28, 2002 1

The Remarkable Historiography of David Irving
The Unz Review, June 4, 2018 6

Oddities of the Jewish Religion
The Unz Review, July 16, 2018 12

The Bolshevik Revolution and Its Aftermath
The Unz Review, July 23, 2018 33

The Nature of Anti-Semitism
The Unz Review, July 30, 2018 51

Jews and Nazis
The Unz Review, August 6, 2018 66

Holocaust Denial
The Unz Review, August 27, 2018 85

The ADL in American Society
The Unz Review, October 15, 2018 136

Amazon Book Censorship
The Unz Review, March 11, 2019 156

Secrets of Military Intelligence
The Unz Review, June 10, 2019 178

The Power of Organized Crime
The Unz Review, July 15, 2019 215

Mossad Assassinations
The Unz Review, January 27, 2020 251

Seeking 9/11 Truth After Twenty Years
The Unz Review, September 7, 2021 330

Remembering the Liberty
The Unz Review, October 18, 2021 356

Introduction

In today's Western world, the touchiest of all touchy subjects are those involving the interrelated topics of Jews, Nazis, and Israel. Journalists and academics recognize that these constitute the deadly "third rail" of their professions.

The resulting pattern of avoidance has produced enormous omissions and distortions in our established narrative history. As a consequence, these issues have become a major focus of my own American Pravda series, and the resulting essays are collected together in this book.

All of the articles contained in this volume are also available online or in freely downloadable eBook formats. The numerous reference links are indicated by boldface text and may be accessed in those latter versions.

- **Jews, Nazis, and Israel Articles**
  https://www.unz.com/page/jews-nazis-and-israel-articles/

AMERICAN PRAVDA
Jews, Nazis, and Israel"
Grasping the "Third Rail" of Journalists and Historians

Sharonism vs. Building a Wall
The Sacramento Bee, April 28, 2002

Any attempt to resolve the crisis in the Middle East forces us — the American people and American Jewry — to appraise the motives and the ultimate goals of the leaders involved.

Endless disputes have raged over whether Yasser Arafat and the other Arab leaders merely seek a Palestinian state living peacefully alongside Israel or whether they continue to harbor the ultimate goal of exterminating what they once derided as the "Zionist entity."

But just as important, perhaps even more so, is reaching an understanding of the true goals of Israel's current Prime Minister Ariel Sharon and his close associates. They—even more than their Arab opponents—hold the fate of the Israeli people in their hands.

Consider the facts. Over the past 18 months, Israel has suffered over 400 civilian dead and thousands more wounded, primarily from the suicide-bombings that have so horrified the world. These losses are the per capita equivalent of over 100,000 American civilian casualties.

During nearly all previous wars, danger in Israel had been largely confined to those in the military or civilians living on the border. Now all patrons of a pizza parlor or disco are suddenly on the front lines. This change is inflicting terrible damage to Israeli morale. By any reasonable standard, Israel now faces the gravest threat to its survival since 1967, perhaps even since 1948.

Israel's leaders have certainly recognized this threat by their rhetoric and by their actions, launching punishing military strikes against the Palestinian organizations and towns whence the suicide-bombers have issued. Faced with resulting criticism from various world quarters, the Sharonists have defended themselves as the security-conscious guardians of a small, embattled nation, unwilling to take risks with their people's very survival. They have reasonably asked how America itself would have responded to waves of attacks that together completely dwarf those of Sept. 11 in relative terms.

But perhaps this is the exact question that we ourselves should be asking. Suppose that over the past year and a half, over 100,000 American civilians had been killed or grievously injured by Mexican terrorists who crossed our border and filled our cities from Los Angeles to New York with daily explosions.

Certainly, we would have taken punitive military actions against the terrorist organizations claiming responsibility and also against any Mexican government that we judged complicit in these massacres. But surely the first and most obvious response on our part would have been — NAFTA or no — to completely fortify our Mexican border with the best possible safeguards, perhaps an electrified security fence studded with machine-gun turrets.

Israel has not. Today, America's long border with Mexico is far better defended against the dire threat of Mexican nannies and gardeners than Israel's own border is secured against suicide bombers. An unknown number of these recent attackers, perhaps even including the bomber who killed over two dozen at their Passover seder, simply walked across an unguarded frontier into Israel or else drove to their targets using well-known but unpatrolled back roads. This is madness, pure and simple.

Why have the Sharonists suffered through 18 months of terrorist incursions without building a simple fence? Such a fence would have provided much greater security than endless attacks on Ramallah and Nablus.

By all accounts, the Palestinians of Gaza are considerably more militant in their anti-Israel Islamic fervor than those of the West Bank, yet Gaza's simple existing fence has prevented the infiltration of even a single suicide-bomber and also kept ordinary terrorist attacks to a negligible level. If a border fence has worked so well in Gaza, why have the Sharonists not considered one for the West Bank as well?

Consider the above analogy. Perhaps an American president would have similarly done nothing if he and his close political allies firmly believed that God had granted them the land of Mexico, and that any American fence along that border would be a dangerous concession to the border's legal validity.

Israel's ruling Likud coalition contains a powerful political strain of individuals who fervently believe that the Palestinian territories of the West Bank — Judea and Samaria to them — are incontestable portions of the once and future homeland of the Jews, granted them by the One Himself. A fence would be a huge step backwards from achieving that dream of a Greater Israel.

In support of this dream, Israeli governments have for decades encouraged some 200,000 Jewish settlers to make their homes in these Palestinian territories, and the ultimate disposition of these settlers is regularly cited as the most nettlesome part of any future peace agreement.

Most of these settlers are peaceable Israeli suburbanites, lured to the West Bank environs of Jerusalem by heavy government housing subsidies, many of which were established by Ariel Sharon in his past role as housing minister of the Begin government, and whose costs are ultimately paid by the American taxpayer.

But a hard core of these settlers, perhaps up to 50,000, are messianic and militant Jews, often from around the world, who are absolutely convinced that God has commanded them to settle and thus control this portion of Eretz Yisrael, whether or not Palestinians have lived there for hundreds or even thousands of years. Although less than 1 percent of Israel's population, these determined individuals are a powerful force within the Sharonist coalition, many of whose leaders publicly or privately share their views.

And these Jewish militants in their hundreds of small settlements do not merely restrict themselves to lobbying. A few years ago, Israeli Prime Minister and Nobel Peace Prize Laureate Yitzhak Rabin became the first Middle Eastern leader in years to fall to an assassin's bullet, killed by a Jewish militant for his impious desire to make peace with the Palestinians.

A year earlier, a Brooklynite settler named Baruch Goldstein massacred dozens of peaceful Muslim worshippers kneeling at prayer in their mosque, before he himself was overpowered and killed. Random acts of senseless violence occur throughout the world, but Goldstein's grave is still venerated as the tomb of a holy martyr by thousands of other Jewish settlers, who treat it as a pilgrimage site.

Some of these Jewish militants possess beliefs that would strike most Americans as strange and extreme even by the standards of the Middle East.

For example, over the years Israeli security forces have discovered and thwarted various militant plots to destroy by explosives the Muslim world's holiest mosques in Jerusalem, an action intended to help ensure the outbreak of the biblical battle of Armageddon and thereby the ultimate restoration of the Kingdom of David. And just recently, the birth of a red heifer has been widely heralded by some of these militant leaders as a divine portent instructing them to redouble their efforts to cleanse Jerusalem of its defiling Muslim religious presence.

By any reasonable criteria, many of these 50,000 militant settlers — and they include at least some of my own relatives — are best understood as being bearded, Jewish Taliban, as uncompromising and difficult as their Islamic counterparts in Afghanistan.

Yet they are also the heart and soul of the Sharonist movement, and while an Israeli border fence might effectively protect close to 99 percent of Israel's population from terrorism, it would also leave these militant settlers on what was obviously the wrong side of the eventual border. This terrible dilemma between protecting Israeli lives and preserving messianic Greater Israel ideology has so far been resolved entirely in favor of the latter.

And this ideology represents an almost complete abandonment of traditional Zionism. The modern state of Israel was founded by secular socialists from Eastern Europe, men whose own attitude toward Judaism ranged from mild distaste to deepest hostility.

Israel was intended to be a national homeland for a long-persecuted people, a place of refuge and safety for Jews threatened everywhere else. Yet today, in part because of the policies of men like Sharon, Jews enjoy less physical security in their own country than perhaps anywhere else in the world, certainly far less than in our own America. The founders of the Jewish national movement would surely regard a successor who sacrificed Jewish lives and safety to his dreams of a Greater Israel as an absolute traitor to Zionist principles.

They would not be the only ones. For decades, numerous rabbinical scholars, of the deepest Talmudic learning, have regularly denounced the supporters of Greater Israel as individuals who have disgustingly perverted their Jewish faith into a nationalist Golden Calf that they worship in place of the Almighty. For centuries, such false Jewish prophets have periodically arisen and invariably led their misguided followers into disaster.

If the current leaders of Israel are indeed willing to continue sacrificing the lives of their own people — including those of young, innocent children — to their imperial dreams of expansion and glory, then according to these learned Jews they are committing sins on a truly biblical scale.

How would Americans view a president who regarded over 100,000 dead and injured American civilians merely as unavoidable collateral damage toward his ultimate goal of annexing Mexico? We would view him as a madman.

If Ariel Sharon continues to wantonly sacrifice the lives of his people for messianic expansionism, then his arms are the ones elbow-deep in the blood of innocent Jews. He faces the world not as a David Ben Gurion or as our own Washington or Lincoln, but instead as someone whose extremism leads his own followers to their doom.

This article is available online at:
https://www.unz.com/runz/sharonism-vs-building-a-wall/

The Remarkable Historiography of David Irving
The Unz Review, June 4, 2018

I'm very pleased to announce that our selection of **HTML Books** now contains works by renowned World War II historian David Irving, including his magisterial *Hitler's War*, named by famed military historian Sir John Keegan as one of the most crucial volumes for properly understanding that conflict.

- **Hitler's War**
  David Irving • 1991 • 397,000 Words

With many millions of his books in print, including a string of best-sellers translated into numerous languages, it's quite possible that the eighty-year-old Irving today ranks as the most internationally-successful British historian of the last one hundred years. Although I myself have merely read a couple of his shorter works, I found these absolutely outstanding, with Irving regularly deploying his remarkable command of the primary source documentary evidence to totally demolish my naive History 101 understanding of major historical events. It would hardly surprise me if the huge corpus of his writings eventually constitutes a central pillar upon which future historians seek to comprehend the catastrophically bloody middle years of our hugely destructive twentieth century even after most of our other chroniclers of that era are long forgotten.

Carefully reading a thousand-page reconstruction of the German side of the Second World War is obviously a daunting undertaking, and his remaining thirty-odd books would probably add at least another 10,000 pages to that Herculean task. But fortunately, Irving is also a riveting speaker, and several of his extended lectures of recent decades are conveniently available on YouTube, as given below. These effectively present many of his most remarkable revelations concerning the wartime policies of both Winston Churchill and Adolf Hitler, as well as sometimes recounting the challenging personal situation he himself faced. Watching these lectures may consume several hours, but that is still a trivial investment compared to the many weeks it would take to digest the underlying books themselves.

- *Churchill's War - David Irving* • 1:48:26
  https://www.bitchute.com/video/C9z1fCgUn5If/

- *David Irving - the Manipulation of History* • 1:53:10
  https://www.bitchute.com/video/bNmOZGlGnbCC/

When confronted with astonishing claims that completely overturn an established historical narrative, considerable skepticism is warranted, and my own lack of specialized expertise in World War II history left me especially cautious. The documents Irving unearths seemingly portray a Winston Churchill so radically different from that of my naive understanding as to be almost unrecognizable, and this naturally raised the question of whether I could credit the accuracy of Irving's evidence and his interpretation. All his material is massively footnoted, referencing copious documents in numerous official archives, but how could I possibly muster the time or energy to verify them?

Rather ironically, an extremely unfortunate turn of events seems to have fully resolved that crucial question.

Irving is an individual of uncommonly strong scholarly integrity, and as such he is unable to see things in the record that do not exist, even if it were in his considerable interest to do so, nor to fabricate non-existent evidence. Therefore, his unwillingness to dissemble or pay lip-service to various widely-worshiped cultural totems eventually provoked an outpouring of vilification by a swarm of ideological fanatics drawn from a particular ethnic persuasion. This situation was rather similar to the troubles my old Harvard professor E.O. Wilson had experienced around that same time upon publication of his own masterwork *Sociobiology: The New Synthesis*, the book that helped launch the field of modern human evolutionary psychobiology.

These zealous ethnic-activists began a coordinated campaign to pressure Irving's prestigious publishers into dropping his books, while also disrupting his frequent international speaking tours and even lobbying countries to bar him from entry. They maintained a drumbeat of media vilification, continually blackening his name and his research skills, even going so far as to denounce him as a "Nazi" and a "Hitler-lover," just as had similarly been done in the case of Prof. Wilson.

During the 1980s and 1990s, these determined efforts, sometimes backed by considerable physical violence, increasingly bore fruit, and Irving's career was severely impacted. He had once been feted by the world's leading publishing houses and his books serialized and reviewed in Britain's most august newspapers; now he gradually became a marginalized figure, almost a pariah, with enormous damage to his sources of income.

In 1993, Deborah Lipstadt, a rather ignorant and fanatic professor of Theology and Holocaust Studies (or perhaps "Holocaust Theology") ferociously attacked him **in her book** as being a "Holocaust Denier," leading Irving's timorous publisher to suddenly cancel the contract for his major new historical volume. This development eventually sparked a rancorous lawsuit in 1998, which resulted in a celebrated 2000 libel trial held in British Court.

That legal battle was certainly a David-and-Goliath affair, with wealthy Jewish movie producers and corporate executives providing a huge war-chest of $13 million to Lipstadt's side, allowing her to fund a veritable army of 40 researchers and legal experts, captained by one of Britain's most successful Jewish divorce lawyers. By contrast, Irving, being an impecunious historian, was forced to defend himself without benefit of legal counsel.

In real life unlike in fable, the Goliaths of this world are almost invariably triumphant, and this case was no exception, with Irving being driven into personal bankruptcy, resulting in the loss of his fine central London home. But seen from the longer perspective of history, I think the victory of his tormenters was a remarkably Pyrrhic one.

Although the target of their unleashed hatred was Irving's alleged "Holocaust denial," as near as I can tell, that particular topic was almost entirely absent from all of Irving's dozens of books, and exactly that very silence was what had provoked their spittle-flecked outrage. Therefore, lacking such a clear target, their lavishly-funded corps of researchers and fact-checkers instead spent a year or more apparently performing a line-by-line and footnote-by-footnote review of everything Irving had ever published, seeking to locate every single historical error that could possibly cast him in a bad professional light. With almost limitless money and manpower, they even utilized the process of legal discovery to subpoena and read the thousands of pages in his bound personal diaries and correspondence, thereby hoping to find some evidence of his "wicked thoughts." ***Denial***, a 2016 Hollywood film co-written by Lipstadt, may provide a reasonable outline of the sequence of events as seen from her perspective.

Yet despite such massive financial and human resources, they apparently came up almost entirely empty, at least if Lipstadt's triumphalist 2005 book ***History on Trial*** may be credited. Across four decades of research and writing, which had produced numerous controversial historical claims of the most astonishing nature, they only managed to find a couple of dozen rather minor alleged errors of fact or interpretation, most of these ambiguous or disputed. And the worst they discovered after reading every page of the many linear meters of Irving's personal diaries was that he had once composed a short "racially insensitive" ditty for his infant daughter, a trivial item which they naturally then trumpeted as proof that he was a "racist." Thus, they seemingly admitted that Irving's enormous corpus of historical texts was perhaps 99.9% accurate.

I think this silence of "the dog that didn't bark" echoes with thunderclap volume. I'm not aware of any other academic scholar in the entire history of the world who has had all his decades of lifetime work subjected to such painstakingly exhaustive hostile scrutiny. And since Irving apparently passed that test with such flying colors, I think we can regard almost every astonishing claim in all of his books—as recapitulated in his videos—as absolutely accurate.

Aside from this important historical conclusion, I believe that the most recent coda to Irving's tribulations tells us quite a lot about the true nature of "Western liberal democracy" so lavishly celebrated by our media pundits, and endlessly contrasted with the "totalitarian" or "authoritarian" characteristics of its ideological rivals, past and present.

In 2005, Irving took a quick visit to Austria, having been invited to speak before a group of Viennese university students. Shortly after his arrival, he was arrested at gunpoint by the local Political Police on charges connected with some historical remarks he had made 16 years earlier on a previous visit to that country, although those had apparently been considered innocuous at the time. Initially, his arrest was kept secret and he was held completely incommunicado; for his family back in Britain, he seemed to have disappeared off the face of the earth, and they feared him dead. More than six weeks were to pass before he was allowed to communicate with either his wife or a lawyer, though he managed to provide word of his situation earlier through an intermediary.

And at the age of 67 he was eventually brought to trial in a foreign courtroom under very difficult circumstances and given a three-year prison sentence. An interview he gave to the BBC about his legal predicament resulted in possible additional charges, potentially carrying a further twenty-year sentence, which probably would have ensured that he died behind bars. Only the extremely good fortune of a successful appeal, partly on technical grounds, allowed him to depart the prison grounds after spending more than 400 days under incarceration, almost entirely in solitary confinement, and he escaped back to Britain.

His sudden, unexpected disappearance had inflicted huge financial hardships upon his family, and they lost their home, with most of his personal possessions being sold or destroyed, including the enormous historical archives he had spent a lifetime accumulating. He later recounted this gripping story in **Banged Up**, a slim book published in 2008, as well as in a video interview available on YouTube.

- *David Irving - Jailed and Beaten for Telling Truth of 2nd World War* • **2:16:36**
  https://www.bitchute.com/video/DTizLU1nLl4d/

Perhaps I am demonstrating my ignorance, but I am not aware of any similar case of a leading international scholar who suffered such a dire fate for quietly stating his historical opinions, even during in darkest days of Stalinist Russia or any of the other totalitarian regimes of the twentieth century. Although this astonishing situation taking place in a West European democracy of the "Free World" did receive considerable media exposure within Europe, coverage in our own country was so minimal that I doubt that today even one well-educated American in twenty is even aware it ever happened.

One reason that most of us still believe that the West remains a free society is that **Our American Pravda** works so hard to conceal the important exceptions.

- **Introduction to HITLER'S WAR**
  David Irving • 1991 • 11,000 Words

This article is available online at:
https://www.unz.com/runz/the-remarkable-historiography-of-david-irving/

Oddities of the Jewish Religion
The Surprising Elements of Talmudic Judaism
The Unz Review, July 16, 2018

Israel Shahak and the Middle East

About a decade ago, I happened to be talking with an eminent academic scholar who had become known for his sharp criticism of Israeli policies in the Middle East and America's strong support for them. I mentioned that I myself had come to very similar conclusions some time before, and he asked when that had happened. I told him it had been in 1982, and I think he found my answer quite surprising. I got the sense that date was decades earlier than would have been given by almost anyone else he knew.

Sometimes it is quite difficult to pinpoint when one's world view on a contentious topic undergoes sharp transformation, but at other times it is quite easy. My own perceptions of the Middle East conflict drastically shifted during Fall 1982, and they have subsequently changed only to a far smaller extent. As some might remember, that period marked the first Israeli invasion of Lebanon, and culminated in the notorious Sabra-Shatila Massacre during which hundreds or even thousands of Palestinians were slaughtered in their refugee camps. But although those events were certainly major factors in my ideological realignment, the crucial trigger was actually a certain letter to the editor published around that same time.

A few years earlier, I had discovered *The London Economist*, as it was then called, and **it had quickly become my favorite publication**, which I religiously devoured cover-to-cover every week. And as I read the various articles about the Middle East conflict in that publication, or others such as the *New York Times*, the journalists occasionally included quotes from some particularly fanatic and irrational Israeli Communist named Israel Shahak, whose views seemed totally at odds with those of everyone else, and who was consequently treated as a fringe figure. Opinions that seem totally divorced from reality tend to stick in one's mind, and it took only one or two appearances from that apparently die-hard and delusional Stalinist for me to guess that he would always take an entirely contrary position on every given issue.

In 1982 Israel Defense Minister Ariel Sharon launched his massive invasion of Lebanon using the pretext of the wounding of an Israeli diplomat in Europe at the hands of a Palestinian attacker, and the extreme nature of his action was widely condemned in the media outlets I read at the time. His motive was obviously to root out the PLO's political and military infrastructure, which had taken hold in many of Lebanon's large Palestinian refugee camps. But back in those days invasions of Middle Eastern countries on dubious prospects were much less common than they have subsequently become, after our recent American wars killed or displaced so many millions, and most observers were horrified by the utterly disproportionate nature of his attack and the severe destruction he was inflicting upon Israel's neighbor, which he seemed eager to reduce to puppet status. From what I recall, he made several entirely false assurances to top Reagan officials about his invasion plans, such that they afterward called him the worst sort of liar, and he ended up besieging the Lebanese capital of Beirut even though he had originally promised to limit his assault to a mere border incursion.

The Israeli siege of the PLO-controlled areas of Beirut lasted some time, and negotiations eventually resulted in the departure of the Palestinian fighters to some other Arab country. Shortly afterward, the Israelis declared that they were moving into West Beirut in order to better assure the safety of the Palestinian women and children left behind and protect them from any retribution at the hands of their Christian Falangist enemies. And around that same time, I noticed a long letter in *The Economist* by Shahak which seemed to me the final proof of his insanity. He claimed that it was obvious that Sharon had marched to Beirut with the intent of organizing a massacre of the Palestinians, and that this would shortly take place. When the slaughter indeed occurred not long afterward, apparently with heavy Israeli involvement and complicity, I concluded that if a crazy Communist fanatic like Shahak had been right, while apparently every mainstream journalist had been so completely wrong, my understanding of the world and the Middle East required total recalibration. Or at least that's how I've always remembered those events from a distance of over thirty-five years.

During the years that followed, I still periodically saw Shahak's statements quoted in my mainstream publications, which sometimes suggested that he was a Communist and sometimes not. Naturally enough, his ideological extremism made him a prominent opponent of the 1991 Oslo Peace Agreement between Israel and the occupied Palestinians, which was otherwise supported by every sensible person, though since Oslo ended up being entirely a failure, I couldn't hold it too strongly against him. I stopped paying much attention to foreign policy issues during the 1990s, but I still read my *New York Times* every morning and would occasionally see his quotes, inevitably contrarian and irredentist.

Then the 9/11 attacks returned foreign policy and the Middle East to the absolute center of our national agenda, and I eventually read somewhere or other that Shahak had died at age 68 only a few months earlier, though I hadn't noticed any obituary. Over the years, I'd seen some vague mention that during the previous decade he'd published a couple of stridently anti-Jewish and anti-Zionist books, just as might be expected from a hard-line Communist fanatic, and during the early 2000s I started seeing more and more references to these works, ironically coming from fringe sources of the anti-Semitic Far Right, thereby once again proving that extremists flock together. Finally, about a decade ago, my curiosity got the better of me and clicking a few buttons on Amazon.com, I ordered copies of his books, all of which were quite short.

The Unusual Doctrines of Traditional Judaism

My first surprise was that Shahak's writings included introductions or glowing blurbs by some of America's most prominent public intellectuals, including Christopher Hitchens, Gore Vidal, Noam Chomsky, and Edward Said. Praise also came from quite respectable publications such as *The London Review of Books*, *Middle East International*, and *Catholic New Times* while Allan Brownfeld of *The American Council for Judaism* had published **a very long and laudatory obituary**. And I discovered that Shahak's background was very different than I had always imagined. He had spent many years as an award-winning Chemistry professor at Hebrew University, and was actually anything but a Communist. Whereas for decades, Israel's ruling political parties had been Socialist or Marxist, his personal doubts about Socialism had left him politically in the wilderness, while his relationship with Israel's tiny Communist Party was solely because they were the only group willing to stand up for the basic human rights issues that were his own central focus. My casual assumptions about his views and background had been entirely in error.

Once I actually began reading his books, and considering his claims, my shock increased fifty-fold. Throughout my entire life, there have been very, very few times I have ever been so totally astonished as I was after I digested ***Jewish History, Jewish Religion: The Weight of Three Thousand Years***, whose text runs barely a hundred pages. In fact, despite his solid background in the academic sciences and the glowing endorsements provided by prominent figures, I found it quite difficult to accept the reality of what I was reading. As a consequence, I paid a considerable sum to a young graduate student I knew, tasking him to verify the claims in Shahak's books, and as far as he could tell, all of the hundreds of references he checked seemed to be accurate or at least found in other sources.

Even with all of that due diligence, I must emphasize that I cannot directly vouch for Shahak's claims about Judaism. My own knowledge of that religion is absolutely negligible, mostly being limited to my childhood, when my grandmother occasionally managed to drag me down to services at the local synagogue, where I was seated among a mass of elderly men praying and chanting in some strange language while wearing various ritualistic cloths and religious talismans, an experience that I always found much less enjoyable than my usual Saturday morning cartoons.

Although Shahak's **books are quite short**, they contain such a density of astonishing material, it would take many, many thousands of words to begin to summarize them. Almost everything I had known—or thought I had known—about the religion of Judaism, at least in its zealously Orthodox traditional form, was utterly wrong.

For example, traditionally religious Jews pay little attention to most of the Old Testament, and even very learned rabbis or students who have devoted many years to intensive study may remain largely ignorant of its contents. Instead, the center of their religious world view is the Talmud, an enormously large, complex, and somewhat contradictory mass of secondary writings and commentary built up over many centuries, which is why their religious doctrine is sometimes called "Talmudic Judaism." Among large portions of the faithful, the Talmud is supplemented by the Kabala, another large collection of accumulated writings, mostly focused on mysticism and all sorts of magic. Since these commentaries and interpretations represent the core of the religion, much of what everyone takes for granted in the Bible is considered in a very different manner.

Given the nature of the Talmudic basis of traditional Judaism and my total previous ignorance of the subject, any attempt on my part of summarize some of the more surprising aspects of Shahak's description may be partially garbled, and is certainly worthy of correction by someone better versed in that dogma. And since so many parts of the Talmud are highly contradictory and infused with complex mysticism, it would be impossible for someone like me to attempt to disentangle the seeming inconsistencies that I am merely repeating. I should note that although Shahak's description of the beliefs and practices of Talmudic Judaism provoked a fire-storm of denunciations, few of those harsh critics seem to have denied his very specific claims, including the most astonishing ones, which would seem to strengthen his credibility.

On the most basic level, the religion of most traditional Jews is actually not at all monotheistic, but instead contains a wide variety of different male and female gods, having quite complex relations to each other, with these entities and their properties varying enormously among the numerous different Jewish sub-sects, depending upon which portions of the Talmud and the Kabala they place uppermost. For example, the traditional Jewish religious cry "The Lord Is One" has always been interpreted by most people to be an monotheistic affirmation, and indeed, many Jews take exactly this same view. But large numbers of other Jews believe this declaration instead refers to achievement of sexual union between the primary male and female divine entities. And most bizarrely, Jews having such radically different views see absolutely no difficulty in praying side by side, and merely interpreting their identical chants in very different fashion.

Furthermore, religious Jews apparently pray to Satan almost as readily as they pray to God, and depending upon the various rabbinical schools, the particular rituals and sacrifices they practice may be aimed at enlisting the support of the one or the other. Once again, so long as the rituals are properly followed, the Satan-worshippers and the God-worshippers get along perfectly well and consider each other equally pious Jews, merely of a slightly different tradition. One point that Shahak repeatedly emphasizes is that in traditional Judaism the nature of the ritual itself is absolutely uppermost, while the interpretation of the ritual is rather secondary. So perhaps a Jew who washes his hands three times clockwise might be horrified by another who follows a counter-clockwise direction, but whether the hand-washing were meant to honor God or to honor Satan would be hardly be a matter of much consequence.

Strangely enough, many of the traditional rituals are explicitly intended to fool or trick God or His angels or sometimes Satan, much like the mortal heroes of some Greek legend might seek to trick Zeus or Aphrodite. For example, certain prayers must be uttered in Aramaic rather than Hebrew on the grounds that holy angels apparently don't understand the former language, and their confusion allows those verses to slip by unimpeded and take effect without divine interference.

Furthermore, since the Talmud represents a massive accretion of published commentary built up over more than a millennium, even the most explicit mandates have sometimes been transformed into their opposites. As an example, Maimonides, one of the highest rabbinical authorities, absolutely prohibited rabbis from being paid for their religious teaching, declaring that any rabbi who received a salary was an evil robber condemned to everlasting torment; yet later rabbis eventually "reinterpreted" this statement to mean something entirely different, and today almost all rabbis collect salaries.

Another fascinating aspect is that up until very recent times, the lives of religious Jews were often dominated by all sorts of highly superstitious practices, including magical charms, potions, spells, incantations, hexes, curses, and sacred talismans, with rabbis often having an important secondary role as sorcerers, and this even remains entirely true today among the enormously influential rabbis of Israel and the New York City area. Shahak's writings had not endeared him to many of these individuals, and for years they constantly attacked him with all sorts of spells and fearful curses aimed at achieving his death or illness. Many of these traditional Jewish practices seem not entirely dissimilar to those we typically associate with African witch-doctors or Voodoo priests, and indeed, the famous legend of the Golem of Prague described the successful use of rabbinical magic to animate a giant creature built of clay.

The Attitude of Judaism Towards Non-Jews

If these ritualistic issues constituted the central features of traditional religious Judaism, we might regard it as a rather colorful and eccentric survival of ancient times. But unfortunately, there is also a far darker side, primarily involving the relationship between Jews and non-Jews, with the highly derogatory term *goyim* frequently used to describe the latter. To put it bluntly, Jews have divine souls and *goyim* do not, being merely beasts in the shape of men. Indeed, the primary reason for the existence of non-Jews is to serve as the slaves of Jews, with some very high-ranking rabbis occasionally stating this well-known fact. In 2010, Israel's top Sephardic rabbi **used his weekly sermon to declare** that the only reason for the existence of non-Jews is to serve Jews and do work for them. The enslavement or extermination of all non-Jews seems an ultimate implied goal of the religion.

Jewish lives have infinite value, and non-Jewish ones none at all, which has obvious policy implications. For example, in a published article a prominent Israeli rabbi explained that if a Jew needed a liver, it would be perfectly fine and indeed obligatory, to kill an innocent Gentile and take his. Perhaps we should not be too surprised that today Israel is widely regarded as **one of the world centers of organ-trafficking**.

As a further illustration of the seething hatred traditional Judaism radiates towards all those of a different background, saving the life of a non-Jew is generally considered improper or even prohibited, and taking any such action on the Sabbath would be an absolute violation of religious edict. Such dogmas are certainly ironic given the widespread presence of Jews in the medical profession during recent centuries, but they came to the fore in Israel when a religiously-minded military doctor took them to heart and his position was supported by the country's highest religious authorities.

And while religious Judaism has a decidedly negative view towards all non-Jews, Christianity in particular is regarded as a total abomination, which must be wiped from the face of the earth.

Whereas pious Muslims consider Jesus as the holy prophet of God and Muhammed's immediate predecessor, according to the Jewish Talmud, Jesus is perhaps the vilest being who ever lived, condemned to spend eternity in the bottommost pit of Hell, immersed in a boiling vat of excrement. Religious Jews regard the Muslim Quran as just another book, though a totally mistaken one, but the Christian Bible represents purest evil, and if circumstances permit, burning Bibles is a very praiseworthy act. Pious Jews are also enjoined to always spit three times at any cross or church they encounter, and direct a curse at all Christian cemeteries. Indeed, many deeply religious Jews utter a prayer each and every day for the immediate extermination of all Christians.

Over the years prominent Israeli rabbis have sometimes publicly debated whether Jewish power has now become sufficiently great that all the Christian churches of Jerusalem, Bethlehem, and other nearby areas can finally be destroyed, and the entire Holy Land completely cleansed of all traces of its Christian contamination. Some have taken this position, but most have urged prudence, arguing that Jews needed to gain some additional strength before they should take such a risky step. These days, many tens of millions of zealous Christians and especially Christian Zionists are enthusiastic advocates for Jews, Judaism, and Israel, and I strongly suspect that at least some of that enthusiasm is based upon ignorance.

For the last two thousand years, Jews have almost invariably existed as small, relatively weak minorities living in the lands of others, whether Christian or Muslim, so a religious doctrine so unswervingly hostile to outsiders has naturally presented considerable obstacles for peaceful co-existence. The solution to this dilemma has been based on the divine mandate to preserve Jewish life and well-being above all else, superseding almost all other religious considerations. Thus, if any of the behaviors discussed above are considered likely to stir up resentment from powerful Gentile groups and put Jews at risk, they must be avoided.

For example, the prohibition against Jewish physicians treating the illnesses of non-Jews is waived in the case of powerful non-Jews, especially national leaders, whose favor might provide benefits to the Jewish community. And even ordinary non-Jews may be aided unless some persuasive excuse can be found to explain such lack of assistance since otherwise the vengeful hostility of their friends and relatives might cause difficulties for other Jews. Similarly, it is permissible to exchange gifts with non-Jews but only if such behavior can be justified in strictly utilitarian terms, with any simple expression of friendship towards a non-Jew being a violation of holy principles.

If the Gentile population became aware of these Jewish religious beliefs and the behaviors they promote, major problems for Jews might develop, so an elaborate methodology of subterfuge, concealment, and dissimulation has come into being over the many centuries to minimize this possibility, especially including the mistranslation of sacred texts or the complete exclusion of crucial sections. Meanwhile, the traditional penalty for any Jew who "informs" to the authorities on any matter regarding the Jewish community has always been death, often preceded by hideous torture.

Much of this dishonesty obviously continues down to recent times since it seems very unlikely that Jewish rabbis, except perhaps for those of the most *avant garde* disposition, would remain totally unaware of the fundamental tenets of the religion that they claim to lead, and Shahak is scathing toward their apparent self-serving hypocrisy, especially those who publicly express strongly liberal views. For example, according to mainstream Talmudic doctrine, black Africans are traditionally placed somewhere between people and monkeys in their intrinsic nature, and surely all rabbis, even liberal ones, would be aware of this religious dogma. But Shahak notes that the numerous American rabbis who so eagerly worked with Martin Luther King, Jr. and other black Civil Rights leaders during the 1950s and 1960s strictly concealed their religious beliefs while denouncing American society for its cruel racism, presumably seeking to achieve a political *quid pro quo* beneficial to Jewish interests with America's substantial black population.

Shahak also emphasizes the utterly totalitarian nature of traditional Jewish society, in which rabbis held the power of life and death over their congregants, and often sought to punish ideological deviation or heresy using those means. They were often outraged that this became difficult as states grew stronger and increasingly prohibited such private executions. Liberalizing rabbis were sometimes murdered and Baruch Spinoza, the famous Jewish philosopher of the Age of Reason, only survived because the Dutch authorities refused to allow his fellow Jews to kill him.

Given the complexity and exceptionally controversial nature of this subject matter, I would urge readers who find this topic of interest to spend three or four hours reading Shahak's very short book, and then decide for themselves whether his claims seem plausible and whether I may have inadvertently misunderstood them. Aside from the copies on Amazon, the work may also be found at **Archive.org** and **a very convenient HTML copy is also freely available on the Internet.**

The Historical Role of Jews in Western Societies

My encounter a decade ago with Shahak's candid description of the true doctrines of traditional Judaism was certainly one of the most world-altering revelations of my entire life. But as I gradually digested the full implications, all sorts of puzzles and disconnected facts suddenly became much more clear. There were also some remarkable ironies, and not long afterward I joked to a (Jewish) friend of mine that I'd suddenly discovered that Nazism could best be described as "Judaism for Wimps" or perhaps Judaism as practiced by Mother Teresa of Calcutta.

There may actually be a deeper historical truth behind that irony. I think I've read here and there that some scholars believe that Hitler may have modeled certain aspects of his racially-focused National Socialist doctrine upon the Jewish example, which really makes perfect sense. After all, he saw that despite their small numbers Jews had gained enormous power in the Soviet Union, Weimar Germany, and numerous other countries throughout Europe, partly due to their extremely strong ethnic cohesion, and he probably reasoned that his own Germanic people, being far greater in numbers and historical achievements could do even better if they adopted similar practices.

It's also interesting to note that quite a number of the leading racialist pioneers of 19th century Europe came from a particular ethnic background. For example, my history books had always disapprovingly mentioned Germany's Max Nordau and Italy's Cesare Lombroso as two of the founding figures of European racism and eugenics theories, but it was only very recently that I discovered that Nordau had also been the joint founder with Theodor Herzl of the world Zionist movement, while his major racialist treatise **Degeneration**, was dedicated to Lombroso, his Jewish mentor.

Even as late as the 1930s and afterward, international Zionist groups closely cooperated with the Third Reich on their economic projects, and during the world war itself one of the smaller rightwing factions, led by future Israeli Prime Minister Yizhak Shamir, actually offered a military alliance to the Axis Powers, denouncing the decadent Western democracies and hoping to collaborate against their mutual British enemies. *The Transfer Agreement* by Edwin Black, *51 Documents* by Lenni Brenner, and other writings have documented all these facts in detail, though for obvious reasons they have generally been ignored or mischaracterized by most of our media outlets.

Obviously the Talmud is hardly regular reading among ordinary Jews these days, and I would suspect that except for the strongly Orthodox and perhaps most rabbis, barely a sliver are aware of its highly controversial teachings. But it is important to keep in mind that until just a few generations ago, almost all European Jews were deeply Orthodox, and even today I would guess that the overwhelming majority of Jewish adults had Orthodox grand-parents. Highly distinctive cultural patterns and social attitudes can easily seep into a considerably wider population, especially one that remains ignorant of the origin of those sentiments, a condition enhancing their unrecognized influence. A religion based upon the principal of "Love Thy Neighbor" may or may not be workable in practice, but a religion based upon "Hate Thy Neighbor" might have long-term cultural ripple effects that extend far beyond the direct community of the deeply pious. If nearly all Jews for a thousand or two thousand years were taught to feel a seething hatred toward all non-Jews and also developed an enormous infrastructure of cultural dishonesty to mask that attitude, it is difficult to believe that such an unfortunate history has had absolutely no consequences for our present-day world, or that of the relatively recent past.

Furthermore, Jewish hostility toward non-Jews may often have served the interests of others, and helped determine the economic role that the group filled, especially in European countries, with this factor having been obscured by widespread ignorance of the underlying religious tenets. As most of us know from our history books, political rulers who harshly exploit their subjects sometimes restrict military power to a relatively small group of well-rewarded mercenaries, often of foreign origins so that they will have little sympathy for the population they harshly repress. I strongly suspect that some of the most common traditional economic niches of European Jews, such as tax-farming and the *arrenda* estate-management system of Eastern Europe, should be best understood in a similar light, with Jews being more likely to extract every last penny of value from the peasants they controlled for the benefit of their local king or lords, and their notorious antipathy for all non-Jews ensuring that such behavior was minimally tempered by any human sympathy. Thus, we should not be surprised that Jews first entered England in the train of William the Conqueror, in order to help him and his victorious Norman lords effectively exploit the subjugated Anglo-Saxon population they now ruled.

But states in which the vast majority of the population is oppressed and dominated by a thin slice of rulers and their mercenary enforcers tend to be much weaker and more brittle than those in which rulers and ruled share common interests, and I believe this is just as true for economic enforcers as for military ones. In many cases, lands reliant upon Jewish economic intermediaries, notably Poland, never successfully developed a native middle class, and often later fared quite poorly against their nationally-unified competitors. Spain was actually one of the last countries in Europe to expel its Jews, and over the next century or two reached the peak of its military and political glory. Prof. Kevin MacDonald's controversial books on Judaism have also extensively argued that rulers who seem to have been more concerned for the well-being of their subjects also tend to be the ones more likely to be labeled "anti-Semitic" in modern history books, and his volumes are now easily available in my selection of HTML Books:

- **A People That Shall Dwell Alone**
  Judaism as a Group Evolutionary Strategy
  Kevin MacDonald • 1994 • 168,000 Words

- **Separation and Its Discontents**
  Toward an Evolutionary Theory of Anti-Semitism
  Kevin MacDonald • 1998 • 168,000 Words

In 2009, Gene Expression blogger Razib Khan interviewed eminent evolutionary theorist David Sloan Wilson on the group selection ideas that have been his major focus. During this hour-long discussion, the theories of MacDonald became a major topic, with Wilson seeming to take them quite seriously, and pointing out that within the scientific framework "parasitism" has a simple technical definition, namely the exploitation of the large by the small. Unsurprisingly, the video record of such extremely touchy subject matter was quickly truncated to just the first 11 minutes, and eventually completely removed from both YouTube and **BloggingHeadsTV**. But it still at least partially survives **in archived form**:

In recent years, the history of Jewish expulsions from various European societies over the last thousand years has received considerable attention. The total number is somewhat disputed but almost certainly in excess of 100, with the 1930s policies of Hitler's Germany being merely the most recent example, and *Wired Magazine* provided **an interesting graphical presentation** of this large dataset in 2013. Given these unfortunate facts, it may be difficult to point to any other group so consistently at bitter odds with its local neighbors, and the religious details provided by Shahak certainly make this remarkable historical pattern far less inexplicable.

A very even-handed but candid description of the behavior pattern of Jewish newcomers to America was provided in a chapter of a 1914 book on immigration groups by E.A. Ross, one of America's greatest early sociologists. Ross had been among of the towering Progressive intellectuals of his era, widely quoted by Lothrop Stoddard on the Right while still so highly regarded by the Left that he was named to the Dewey Commission to adjudicate the conflicting accusations of Trotsky and Stalin and also received **glowing praise** in the pages of the Communist *New Masses*. His dismissal on political grounds from Stanford University led to the formation of the American Association of University Professors. Yet his name had so totally vanished from our history books I had never even encountered it until beginning work on my content-archiving project, and I would not be surprised if that single chapter from one of his many books played a major role in his disappearance.

- **The Old World in the New**
  The Eastern European Hebrews
  E.A. Ross • 1914 • 5,000 Words

Jews spent two thousand years living as a diaspora people, and their tightly-bound trans-national colonies provided them with a uniquely effective international trading network. Since their religious traditions regarded slavery as the natural and appropriate lot of all non-Jews, both ideological and practical factors combined to apparently make them some of the leading slave-traders of Medieval Europe, though this is hardly emphasized in our histories. Closer to home, in 1991 the Black Nationalists of The Nation of Islam published ***The Secret Relationship Between Blacks and Jews, Volume One***, which seemed to persuasively document the enormous role Jews had played in the American slave-trade. In 1994, Harold Brackman published a short attempted rebuttal entitled ***Ministry of Lies*** under the auspices of the Simon Wiesenthal Center, but I found his denials much less compelling. I very much doubt that most Americans are aware of these historical facts.

Throughout most of my life, Nobel Laureate Alexander Solzhenitsyn was generally regarded as the greatest Russian literary figure of our modern era, and after reading all of his works, including *The First Circle, Cancer Ward,* and *The Gulag Archipelago*, I certainly concurred with this assertion, and eagerly absorbed Michael Scammell's brilliant thousand page biography. Although Russian himself, many of his closest friends were Jewish, but during the 1980s and 1990s, whispers of his supposed anti-Semitism began floating around, probably because he had sometimes hinted at the very prominent role of Jews in both financing and leading the Bolshevik Revolution, and afterward staffing the NKVD and administering the Gulag labor camps. Late in his life, he wrote a massive two-volume history of the tangled relationship between Jews and Russians under the title *Two Hundred Years Together*, and although that work soon appeared in Russian, French, and German, after nearly two decades, no English translation has ever been authorized. His literary star also seems to have greatly waned in America since that time, and these days I only very rarely see his name mentioned in any of my regular newspapers.

Samizdat versions of major sections of his final work may easily be located on the Internet, and a few years ago Amazon temporarily sold a 750 page hard copy edition, which I ordered and lightly skimmed. Everything seemed quite innocuous and factual, and nothing new jumped out at me, but perhaps the documentation of the very heavy Jewish role in Communism was considered inappropriate for American audiences, as was the discussion of the extremely exploitative relationship between Jews and Slavic peasants in pre-revolutionary times, based on liquor-dealing and money-lending, which the Czars had often sought to mitigate.

When a ruling elite only has a limited connection to the population it controls, benevolent behavior is far less likely to occur, and those problems are magnified when that elite has a long tradition of ruthlessly extractive behavior. Enormous numbers of Russians suffered and died in the aftermath of the Bolshevik Revolution, and given the overwhelmingly Jewish composition of the top leadership during much of that period, it is hardly surprising that "anti-Semitism" was deemed a capital offense. Kevin MacDonald may have been the one who coined the term "hostile elite," and discussed the unfortunate consequences when a country comes under such control.

After the collapse of the Soviet Union in 1991, reborn Russia soon fell under the overwhelming domination of a small group of Oligarchs, almost entirely of Jewish background, and a decade of total misery and impoverishment for the general Russian population soon followed. But once an actual Russian named Vladimir Putin regained control, these trends reversed and the lives of Russians have enormously improved since that time. America's media organs were overwhelmingly friendly toward Russia when it was under Jewish Oligarchic rule, while Putin has been demonized in the press more ferociously than any world leader since Hitler. Indeed, our media pundits regularly identify Putin as "the new Hitler" and I actually think the analogy might be a reasonable one, but just not in the way they intend.

Sometimes it is much easier to notice obvious patterns in a foreign country than in one's own. In the early 2000s I read ***The Master Switch***, a widely-praised history of modern communications technology by Columbia University professor Tim Wu, who has subsequently become a leading Internet-rights activist. I found the account fascinating, with so many stories never before known to me. However, I couldn't help but notice that all the powerful mass-media technologies of our modern world–film, radio, and television–had been invented and pioneered by Gentiles, mostly of Anglo-Saxon origin, but in each case control was seized by ruthless Jewish businessmen, who sometimes destroyed the lives and careers of those creators. By the 1950s, nearly all of America's leading concentrations of electronic media power—with the sole major exception of Disney Studios—were solidly in Jewish hands. In an open society such as ours, these are the central levers of political influence, and over the next generation or so, America's long-dominant and heavily Anglo-Saxon ruling elite was replaced by a mostly Jewish one, a development I alluded to in my long **Meritocracy article** of a few years ago.

Critics today of all backgrounds bemoan the total impoverishment of so much of America's once comfortably affluent middle class, noting that some **sixty percent of the American population today possesses less than $500** in readily available savings. A younger generation has been reduced to permanent debt-servitude by ruinous student loans, while the the newspapers report that the opioid drug epidemic has claimed a dreadful toll in lives and family-breakdown even while Wall Street and other elite sectors of the financialized economy are richer than they have ever been before. There are certainly many different explanations for this sad economic trajectory, including technological change, growing international competition, and shifts of political power in the American system of government. But it does sometimes seem like a substantial fraction of our population has been reduced to a 21st century version of the drunken, ignorant, exploited, indebted, impoverished, and immiserated Slavic peasantry of the Jewish-dominated Pale of Settlement, and a striking graph produced by the Economic Policy Institute demonstrates that a very sharp economic inflection point occurred in the early 1970s, right around the time that the aforementioned ethnic transformation of our ruling elites was fully under way.

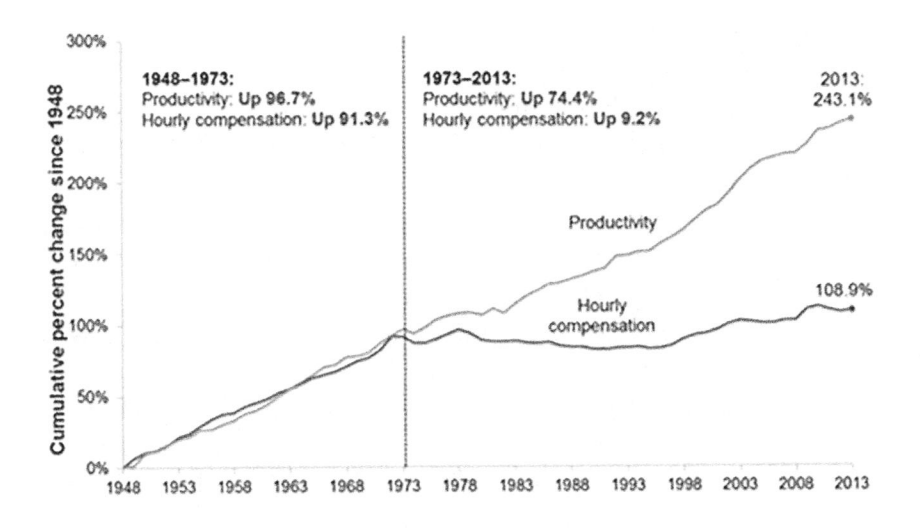

1948–1973:
Productivity: Up 96.7%
Hourly compensation: Up 91.3%

1973–2013:
Productivity: Up 74.4%
Hourly compensation: Up 9.2%

2013:
243.1%

108.9%

Contrary to widespread popular belief, it is not actually illegal to be a "Nazi" in America, nor are Nazis prohibited from owning property, even including media outlets. But suppose that the overwhelming majority of America's major media concentrations were owned and controlled by Nazis of a particularly fanatical type. Surely that might have serious consequences for the course of our society, and especially that fraction of the population viewed with considerable disfavor under Nazi doctrine.

One important point to consider in the abbreviated history of Hitler's Third Reich was that although the ruling Nazi elite was often quite harsh and extreme in its behavior, well over 98% of the population it ruled prior to the outbreak of war consisted of Germans, the particular group which that ruling elite most sought to benefit and uplift in all possible ways, and despite the obscuring cloud of retrospective propaganda, this goal seems to have largely been achieved. In 2004, *Counterpunch* published **a column** by the late Alexander Cockburn, its redoubtable editor, noting the tremendous success of Hitler's peacetime economic policies, and in 2013 that same webzine carried **a much longer column focused entirely on this same subject**, citing **the analysis of Henry C.K. Liu**, whose Chinese background provided him greater critical distance. Indeed, during most of the 1930s Hitler received widespread international praise for the great success of his domestic economic and social achievements, making the cover of *Time Magazine* on numerous occasions and even being named its Man of the Year for 1938. By contrast, I suspect that a population that was some 98% non-German but ruled by those same fanatically pro-German leaders might have fared far worse.

Most of these disheartening facts that have so completely upended my understanding of reality over the last decade could not possibly have come to my attention until the rise of the Internet, which partially broke centralized control over the distribution of information. But many other people must surely have known large portions of this important story long before that, and recognized the very serious consequences these matters might have for the future of our society. Why has there been so little public discussion?

I believe one factor is that over the years and the decades, our dominant media organs of news and entertainment have successfully conditioned most Americans to suffer a sort of mental allergic reaction to topics sensitive to Jews, which leads to all sorts of issues being considered absolutely out of bounds. And with America's very powerful Jewish elites thereby insulated from almost all public scrutiny, Jewish arrogance and misbehavior remain largely unchecked and can increase completely without limit.

I've also sometimes suggested to people that one under-emphasized aspect of a Jewish population, greatly magnifying its problematical character, is the existence of what might be considered a biological sub-morph of exceptionally fanatical individuals, always on hair-trigger alert to launch verbal and sometimes physical attacks of unprecedented fury against anyone they regard as insufficiently friendly towards Jewish interests. Every now and then, a particularly brave or foolhardy public figure challenges some off-limits topic and is almost always overwhelmed and destroyed by a veritable swarm of these fanatical Jewish attackers. Just as the painful stings of the self-sacrificing warrior caste of an ant colony can quickly teach large predators to go elsewhere, fears of provoking these "Jewish berserkers" can often severely intimidate writers or politicians, causing them to choose their words very carefully or even completely avoid discussing certain controversial subjects, thereby greatly benefiting Jewish interests as a whole. And the more such influential people are thus intimidated into avoiding a particular topic, the more that topic is perceived as strictly taboo, and avoided by everyone else as well.

For example, about a dozen years ago I was having lunch with an especially eminent Neoconservative scholar with whom I'd become a little friendly. We were bemoaning the overwhelmingly leftward skew among America's intellectual elites, and I suggested it largely seemed a function of our most elite universities. Many of our brightest students from across the nation entered Harvard and the other Ivies holding a variety of different ideological perspectives, but after four years departed those halls of learning overwhelmingly in left-liberal lock-step. Although he agreed with my assessment, he felt I was missing something important. He nervously glanced to both sides, shifted his head downward, and lowered his voice. "It's the Jews," he said.

The Controversial Scholarship of Ariel Toaff

I do not doubt that much of the candid analysis provided above will be quite distressing to many individuals. Indeed, some may believe that such material far exceeds the boundaries of mere "anti-Semitism" and easily crosses the threshold into constituting an actual "blood libel" against the Jewish people. That extremely harsh accusation, widely used by stalwart defenders of Israeli behavior, refers to the notorious Christian superstition, prevalent throughout most of the Middle Ages and even into more modern times, that Jews sometimes kidnapped small Christian children in order to drain their blood for use in various magic rituals, especially in connection with the Purim religious holiday. One of my more shocking discoveries of the last dozen years is that there is a fairly strong likelihood that these seemingly impossible beliefs were actually true.

I personally have no professional expertise whatsoever in Jewish ritual traditions, nor the practices of Medieval Jewry. But one of the world's foremost scholars in that field is Ariel Toaff, professor of Jewish Renaissance and Medieval Studies at Bar-Ilan University near Tel Aviv, and himself the son of the Chief Rabbi of Rome.

In 2007, he published the Italian edition of his academic study **Blood Passovers**, based on many years of diligent research, assisted by his graduate students and guided by the suggestions of his various academic colleagues, with the initial print run of 1,000 copies selling out on the first day. Given Toaff's international eminence and such enormous interest, further international distribution, including an English edition by a prestigious American academic press would normally have followed. But the ADL and various other Jewish-activist groups regarded such a possibility with extreme disfavor, and although these activists lacked any scholarly credentials, they apparently applied sufficient pressure to cancel all additional publication. Although Prof. Toaff initially attempted to stand his ground in stubborn fashion, he soon took the same course as Galileo, and his apologies naturally became the basis of the always-unreliable Wikipedia entry on the topic.

Eventually, an English translation of his text turned up on the Internet in a PDF format and was also placed for sale on Amazon.com, where I purchased a copy and eventually read it. Given those difficult circumstances, this work of 500 pages is hardly in ideal form, with most of the hundreds of footnotes disconnected from the text, but it still provides a reasonable means of evaluating Toaff's controversial thesis, at least from a layman's perspective. He certainly seems an extremely erudite scholar, drawing heavily upon the secondary literature in English, French, German, and Italian, as well as the original documentary sources in Latin, Medieval Latin, Hebrew, and Yiddish. Indeed, despite the shocking nature of the subject matter, this scholarly work is actually rather dry and somewhat dull, with very long digressions regarding the particular intrigues of various obscure Medieval Jews. My own total lack of expertise in these areas must be emphasized, but overall I thought Toaff made a quite persuasive case.

It appears that a considerable number of Ashkenazi Jews traditionally regarded Christian blood as having powerful magical properties and considered it a very valuable component of certain important ritual observances at particular religious holidays. Obviously, obtaining such blood in large amounts was fraught with considerable risk, which greatly enhanced its monetary value, and the trade in the vials of that precious commodity seems to have been widely practiced. Toaff notes that since the detailed descriptions of the Jewish ritualistic murder practices are very similarly described in locations widely separated by geography, language, culture, and time period, they are almost certainly independent observations of the same rite. Furthermore, he notes that when accused Jews were caught and questioned, they often correctly described obscure religious rituals which could not possibly have been known to their Gentile interrogators, who often garbled minor details. Thus, these confessions were very unlikely to have been concocted by the authorities.

Furthermore, as extensively discussed by Shahak, the world-view of traditional Judaism did involve a very widespread emphasis on magical rituals, spells, charms, and similar things, providing a context in which ritualistic murder and human sacrifice would hardly be totally unexpected.

Obviously, the ritual murder of Christian children for their blood was viewed with enormous disfavor by the local Gentile population, and the widespread belief in its existence remained a source of bitter tension between the two communities, flaring up occasionally when a Christian child mysteriously disappeared at a particular time of year, or when a body was found that exhibited suspicious types of wounds or showed a strange loss of blood. Every now and then, a particular case would reach public prominence, often leading to a political test of strength between Jewish and anti-Jewish groups. During the mid-19th century, there was one such famous case in French-dominated Syria, and just before the outbreak of the First World War, Russia was wracked by a similar political conflict in the 1913 Beilis Affair in the Ukraine.

I first encountered these very surprising ideas almost a dozen years ago in a long article by Israel Shamir that was referenced in *Counterpunch*, and this would definitely be worth reading as **an overall summary**, together with **a couple** of his **follow-up columns**, while writer Andrew Hamilton offers **the most recent 2012 overview** of the controversy. Shamir also helpfully provides **a free copy of the book in PDF form**, an updated version with the footnotes properly noted in the text. Anyway, I lack the expertise to effectively judge the likelihood of the Toaff Hypothesis, so I would invite those interested to read Toaff's book or better yet the related articles and decide for themselves.

The notion that the world is not only stranger than we imagine, it is stranger than we can imagine has often been misattributed to the British astronomer Sir Arthur Eddington, and over the last fifteen-odd years I've sometimes begun to believe that the historical events of our own era could be considered in a similar light. I've also sometimes joked with my friends that when the true history of our last one hundred years is finally written and told—probably by a Chinese professor at a Chinese university—none of the students in his lecture hall will ever believe a word of it.

This article is available online at:
https://www.unz.com/runz/american-pravda-oddities-of-the-jewish-religion/

The Bolshevik Revolution and Its Aftermath
The Unz Review, July 23, 2018

Although I always had a great interest in history, **I naively believed what I read in my textbooks**, and therefore regarded American history as just too bland and boring to study.

By contrast, one land I found especially fascinating was China, the world's most populous country and its oldest continuous civilization, with a tangled modern history of revolutionary upheaval, then suddenly reopened to the West during the Nixon Administration and under Deng's economic reforms starting to reverse decades of Maoist economic failure.

In 1978 I took a UCLA graduate seminar on the rural Chinese political economy, and probably read thirty or forty books during that semester. E.O. Wilson's seminal ***Sociobiology: The New Synthesis*** had just been published a couple of years earlier, reviving that field after decades of harsh ideological suppression, and with his ideas in the back of my mind, I couldn't help noticing the obvious implications of the material I was reading. The Chinese had always seemed a very smart people, and the structure of China's traditional rural peasant economy produced Social Darwinist selective pressure so thick that you could cut it with a knife, thus providing a very elegant explanation of how the Chinese got that way. A couple of years later in college, I wrote up my theory while studying under Wilson, and then decades afterward dug it out again, finally publishing my analysis as **How Social Darwinism Made Modern China**.

With the Chinese people clearly having such tremendous inherent talent and their potential already demonstrated on a much smaller scale in Hong Kong, Taiwan, and Singapore, I believed there was an excellent chance that Deng's reforms would unleash enormous economic growth, and sure enough, **that was exactly what happened**. In the late 1970s, China was poorer than Haiti, but I always told my friends that it might come to dominate the world economically within a couple of generations, and although most of them were initially quite skeptical of such an outrageous claim, every few years they became a little less so. For years *The Economist* **had been my favorite magazine**, and in 1986 they published an especially long **letter of mine** emphasizing the tremendous rising potential of China and urging them to expand their coverage with a new Asia Section; the following year, they did exactly that.

These days I feel tremendous humiliation for having spent most of my life being so totally wrong about so many things for so long, and I cling to China as a very welcome exception. I can't think of a single development during the last forty years that I wouldn't have generally expected back in the late 1970s, with the only surprise having been the total lack of surprises. About the only "revision" I've had to make in my historical framework is that I'd always casually accepted the ubiquitous claim that Mao's disastrous Great Leap Forward of 1959-61 had caused 35 million or more deaths, but **I've recently encountered some serious doubts**, suggesting that such a total could be considerably exaggerated, and today I might admit the possibility that only 15 million or fewer had died.

But although I always had a great interest in China, European history was even more fascinating to me, with the political interplay of so many conflicting states and the huge ideological and military upheavals of the twentieth century.

In my unjustified arrogance, I also sometimes relished a sense of seeing obvious things that magazine or newspaper journalists got so completely wrong, mistakes which often slipped into historical narratives as well. For example, discussions of the titanic 20th century military struggles between Germany and Russia quite often made casual references to the traditional hostility between those two great peoples, who for centuries had stood as bitter rivals, representing the eternal struggle of Slav against Teuton for dominion over Eastern Europe.

Although the bloodstained history of the two world wars made that notion seem obvious, it was factually mistaken. Prior to 1914, those two great peoples had not fought against each other for the previous 150 years, and even the Seven Years' War of the mid-18th century had involved a Russian alliance with Germanic Austria against Germanic Prussia, hardly amounting to a conflict along civilizational lines. Russians and Germans had been staunch allies during the endless Napoleonic wars and closely cooperated during the Metternich and Bismarck eras that followed, while even as late as 1904, Germany had supported Russia in its unsuccessful war against Japan. During the 1920s, Weimar Germany and Soviet Russia had a period of close military cooperation, the Hitler-Stalin Pact of 1939 marked the beginning of the Second World War, and throughout the long Cold War, the USSR had no more loyal a satellite than East Germany. Perhaps two dozen years of hostility over the last three centuries, with good relations or even outright alliance during most of the remainder, hardly suggested that Russians and Germans were hereditary enemies.

Moreover, during much of that period, Russia's ruling elite had had a considerable Germanic tinge. Russia's legendary Catherine the Great had been a German princess by birth, and over the centuries so many Russian rulers had taken German wives that the later Czars of the Romanov dynasty were usually more German than Russian. Russia itself had a substantial but heavily assimilated German population, which was very well represented in elite political circles, with German names being quite common among government ministers and sometimes found among important military commanders. Even a top leader of the Decembrist revolt of the early 19th century had had German ancestry but was a zealous Russian-nationalist in his ideology.

Under the governance of this mixed Russian and German ruling class, the Russian Empire had steadily risen to become one of the world's foremost powers. Indeed, given its vast size, manpower, and resources, combined with one of the fastest economic growth rates and a natural increase in total population that was not far behind, a 1914 observer might have easily pegged it to soon dominate the European continent and perhaps even much of the world, just as Tocqueville had famously prophesized in the early decades of the 19th century. A crucial underlying cause of the First World War was Britain's belief that only a preventative war could forestall a rising Germany, but I suspect that an important secondary cause was the parallel German notion that similar measures were necessary against a rising Russia.

Obviously, this entire landscape was totally transformed by the Bolshevik Revolution of 1917, which swept the old order from power, massacring much of its leadership and forcing the remainder to flee, thereby ushering in the modern world era of ideological and revolutionary regimes. I grew up during the final decades of the long Cold War, when the Soviet Union stood as America's great international adversary, so the history of that revolution and its aftermath always fascinated me. During college and graduate school I probably read at least one hundred books in that general topic, devouring the brilliant works of Solzhenistyn and Sholokhov, the thick historical volumes of mainstream academic scholars such as Adam Ulam and Richard Pipes, as well as the writings of leading Soviet dissidents such as Roy Medvedev, Andrei Sakharov, and Andrei Amalrik. I was fascinated by the tragic story of how Stalin outmaneuvered Trotsky and his other rivals, leading to the massive purges of the 1930s as Stalin's growing paranoia produced such gigantic loss of life.

I was not so totally naive that I did not recognize some of the powerful taboos surrounding discussion of the Bolsheviks, particularly regarding their ethnic composition. Although most of the books hardly emphasized the point, anyone with a careful eye for the occasional sentence or paragraph would surely know that Jews were enormously over-represented among the top revolutionaries, with three of Lenin's five potential successors— Trotsky, Zinoviev, and Kamenev—all coming from that background, along with many, many others within the top Communist leadership. Obviously, this was wildly disproportionate in a country having a Jewish population of perhaps 4%, and surely helped explain the large spike in worldwide hostility towards Jews soon afterward, which sometimes took the most deranged and irrational forms, such as the popularity of *The Protocols of the Learned Elders of Zion* and Henry Ford's notorious publication of *The International Jew*. But with Russian Jews so much more likely to be educated and urbanized, and suffering from fierce anti-Semitic oppression under the Czars, everything seemed to make reasonable sense.

Then perhaps fourteen or fifteen years ago, I encountered a rip in my personal space-time continuum, among the first of many to come.

In this particular instance, an especially rightwing friend of evolutionary theorist Gregory Cochran had been spending long days browsing the pages of *Stormfront*, a leading Internet forum for the Far Right, and having come across a remarkable factual claim, asked me for my opinion. Allegedly Jacob Schiff, America's leading Jewish banker, had been the crucial financial supporter of the Bolshevik Revolution, providing the Communist revolutionaries with $20 million in funding.

My first reaction was that such a notion was utterly ridiculous since a fact so enormously explosive could not have been ignored by the many dozens of books I had read on the origins of that revolution.

But the source seemed extremely precise. The *Knickerbocker* columnist in the February 3, 1949 edition of *The New York Journal-American*, then one of the leading local newspapers, wrote that "Today it is estimated by Jacob's grandson, John Schiff, that the old man sank about 20,000,000 dollars for the final triumph of Bolshevism in Russia."

Once I checked around a little, I discovered that numerous mainstream accounts described the enormous hostility of Schiff towards the Czarist regime for its ill-treatment of Jews, and these days even so establishmentarian a source as Wikipedia's entry on Jacob Schiff notes that he played a major role financing the Russian Revolution of 1905, as was revealed in the later memoirs of one of his key operatives. And if you run a search on "jacob schiff bolshevik revolution" numerous other references come up, representing a wide variety of different positions and degrees of credibility. One very interesting statement appears in **the memoirs of Henry Wickham Steed**, editor of *The Times of London* and one of the foremost international journalists of his era. He very matter-of-factly mentioned that Schiff, Warburg and the other top Jewish international bankers were among the leading backers of the Jewish Bolsheviks, through whom they hoped to gain an opportunity for the Jewish exploitation of Russia, and he described their lobbying efforts on behalf of their Bolshevik allies at the 1919 Paris Peace Conference following the end of the First World War.

Even the very recent and highly skeptical analysis in Kenneth D. Ackerman's 2016 book *Trotsky in New York, 1917* notes that U.S. Military Intelligence reports of the period directly made that astonishing claim, pointing to Trotsky as the conduit for the heavy financial backing of Schiff and numerous other Jewish financiers. In 1925 this information was published in the British *Guardian* and was widely discussed and accepted throughout the 1920s and 1930s by numerous major media publications, long before Schiff's own grandson provided a direct confirmation of those facts in 1949. Ackerman rather cavalierly dismisses all of this considerable contemporaneous evidence as "anti-Semitic" and a "conspiracy story," arguing that since Schiff was a notorious conservative who had never shown any sympathy for socialism in his own American milieu, he surely would not have funded the Bolsheviks.

Now admittedly, a few details might easily have gotten somewhat garbled over time. For example, although Trotsky quickly became second only to Lenin in the Bolshevik hierarchy, in early 1917 the two men were still bitterly hostile over various ideological disputes, so he certainly was not then considered a member of that party. And since everyone today acknowledges that Schiff had heavily financed the failed 1905 Revolution in Russia, it seems perfectly possible that the $20 million figure mentioned by his grandson refers to the total invested over the years supporting all the different Russian revolutionary movements and leaders, which together finally culminated in the establishment of Bolshevik Russia. But with so many seemingly credible and independent sources all making such similar claims, the basic facts appear almost indisputable.

Consider the implications of this remarkable conclusion. I would assume that most of Schiff's funding of revolutionary activities was spent on items such as stipends for activists and bribes, and adjusted for the average family incomes of that era, $20 million would be as much as $2 billion in present-day money. Surely without such enormous financial support, the likelihood of any Bolshevik victory would have been far lower, perhaps almost impossible.

When people casually used to joke about the total insanity of "anti-Semitic conspiracy theories" no better example was ever tossed around than the self-evidently absurd notion that the international Jewish bankers had created the worldwide Communist movement. And yet by any reasonable standard, this statement appears to be more or less true, and apparently was widely known at least in rough form for decades after the Russian Revolution, but had never been mentioned in any of the numerous more recent histories that shaped my own knowledge of those events. Indeed, none of these very comprehensive sources had ever even mentioned Schiff's name, although it was universally acknowledged that he had funded the 1905 Revolution, which was often discussed in enormous detail in many of those very weighty books. What other astonishing facts might they similarly be concealing?

When someone encounters remarkable new revelations in an area of history in which his knowledge was rudimentary, being little more than introductory textbooks or History 101 courses, the result is a shock and an embarrassment. But when the same situation occurs in an area in which he had read tens of thousands of pages in the leading authoritative texts, which seemingly explored every minor detail, surely his sense of reality begins to crumble.

In 1999, Harvard University published the English edition of *The Black Book of Communism*, whose six co-authors devoted 850 pages to documenting the horrors inflicted upon the world by that defunct system, which had produced a total death toll they reckoned at 100 million. I have never read that book and I have often heard that the alleged body-count has been widely disputed. But for me the most remarkable detail is that when I examine the 35 page index, I see a vast profusion of entries for totally obscure individuals whose names are surely unknown to all but the most erudite specialist. But there is no entry for Jacob Schiff, the world-famous Jewish banker who apparently financed the creation of the whole system in the first place. Nor one for Olaf Aschberg, the powerful Jewish banker in Sweden, **who played such an important role** in providing the Bolsheviks a financial life-line during the early years of their threatened regime, and even founded **the first Soviet international bank**.

When one discovers a tear in the fabric of reality, there is a natural tendency to nervously peer inside, wondering what mysterious objects might dwell within. The Ackerman book denounced the notion of Schiff having funded the Bolsheviks as "a favorite trope of Nazi anti-Jewish propaganda" and just prior to those words he issued a similar denunciation of Henry Ford's *Dearborn Independent*, a publication which once would have meant almost nothing to me. Although Ackerman's particular book had not yet been published when I first began considering the Schiff story a dozen years ago, many other writers had similarly conjoined those two topics, so I decided to explore the matter.

Ford himself was a very interesting individual, and his world-historical role certainly received very scanty coverage in my basic history textbooks. Although the exact reasons for his decision **to raise his minimum wage to $5 per day in 1914**—double the existing average pay for industrial workers in America—can be disputed, it certainly seems to have played a huge role in the creation of our middle class. He also adopted a highly paternalistic policy of providing good company housing and other amenities to his workers, a total departure from the "Robber Baron" capitalism so widely practiced at that time, thereby establishing himself as a world-wide hero to industrial workers and their advocates. Indeed, Lenin himself had regarded Ford as a towering figure in the world's revolutionary firmament, glossing over his conservative views and commitment to capitalism and instead focusing on his remarkable achievements in worker productivity and economic well-being. It is a forgotten detail of history that even after Ford's considerable hostility to the Russian Revolution became widely known, the Bolsheviks still described their own industrial development policy as "Fordism." Indeed, it was not unusual to see **portraits of Lenin and Ford hanging side-by-side in Soviet factories**, representing the two greatest secular saints of the Bolshevik pantheon.

As for *The Dearborn Independent*, Ford had apparently launched his newspaper on a national basis not long after the end of the war, intending to focus on controversial topics, especially those related to Jewish misbehavior, whose discussion he believed was being ignored or suppressed by nearly all mainstream media outlets. I had been aware that he had long been one of the wealthiest and most highly-regarded individuals in America, but I was still astonished to discover that his weekly newspaper, previously almost unknown to me, had reached a total national circulation of 900,000 by 1925, ranking it as the second largest in the country and by far the biggest with a national distribution. I found no easy means of examining the contents of a typical issue, but apparently the anti-Jewish articles of the first couple of years had been collected and published as short books, together constituting the four volumes of ***The International Jew: The World's Foremost Problem***, a notoriously anti-Semitic work occasionally mentioned in my history textbooks. Eventually my curiosity got the best of me, so I clicked a few buttons on Amazon.com, bought the set, and wondered what I would discover.

Based on all my pre-suppositions, I expected to read some foaming-at-the-mouth screed, and doubted I would be able to get past the first dozen pages before losing interest and consigning the volumes to gather dust on my shelves. But what I actually encountered was something entirely different.

Over the last couple of decades, the enormous growth in the power of Jewish and pro-Israel groups in America has occasionally led writers to cautiously raise certain facts regarding the untoward influence of those organizations and activists, while always carefully emphasizing that the vast majority of ordinary Jews do not benefit from these policies and actually might be harmed by them, even leaving aside the possible risk of eventually provoking an anti-Jewish backlash. To my considerable surprise, I found that the material in Ford's 300,000 word series seemed to follow this exact same pattern and tone.

The individual 80 chapter-columns of Ford's volumes generally discuss particular issues and events, some of which were well-known to me, but with most totally obscured by the passage of almost a hundred years. However, as far as I could tell, almost all the discussions seemed quite plausible and factually-oriented, even sometimes overly cautious in their presentation, and with one possible exception I can't recall anything that seemed fanciful or unreasonable. As an example, there was no claim that Schiff or his fellow Jewish bankers had funded the Bolshevik Revolution since those particular facts had not yet come out, only that he had seemed to be strongly supportive of the overthrow of Czarism, and had worked toward that end for many years, motivated by what he regarded as the hostility of the Russian Empire towards its Jewish subjects. This sort of discussion is not all that different from what one might find in a modern Schiff biography or in his Wikipedia entry, though many of the important details presented in the Ford books have disappeared from the historical record.

Although I somehow managed to plow through all four volumes of *The International Jew*, the unrelenting drum-beat of Jewish intrigue and misbehavior became somewhat soporific after a while, especially since so many of the examples provided may have loomed quite large in 1920 or 1921 but were almost totally forgotten today. Most of the content was a collection of rather monotonous complaints regarding Jewish malfeasance, scandals, or clannishness, the sort of mundane matters which might have normally appeared in the pages of an ordinary newspaper or magazine, let alone one of the muckraking type.

However, I cannot fault the publication for having such a narrow focus. A consistent theme was that because of the intimidating fear of Jewish activists and influence, virtually all of America's regular media outlets avoided discussion of any of these important matters, and since this new publication was intended to fill that void, it necessarily provided coverage overwhelmingly skewed toward that particular subject. The articles were also aimed at gradually expanding the window of public debate and eventually shaming other periodicals into discussing Jewish misbehavior. When leading magazines such as *The Atlantic*

Monthly and *Century Magazine* began running such articles, this result was hailed as a major success.

Another important goal was to make ordinary Jews more aware of the very problematical behavior of many of their community leaders. Occasionally, the publication received a letter of praise from a self-proclaimed "proud American Jew" commending the series and sometimes including a check to purchase subscriptions for other members of his community, and this achievement might become the subject of an extended discussion.

And although the details of these individual stories differed considerably from those of today, the pattern of behavior being criticized seemed remarkably similar. Change a few facts, adjust the society for a century of change, and many of the stories might be exactly the same ones that well-meaning people concerned about the future of our country are quietly discussing today. Most remarkably, there were even a couple of columns about the troubled relationship between the earliest Zionist settlers in Palestine and the surrounding native Palestinians, and deep complaints that under Jewish pressure the media often totally misreported or hid some of the outrages suffered by the latter group.

I cannot vouch for the overall accuracy of the contents of these volumes, but at the very least they would constitute an extremely valuable source of "raw material" for further historical investigation. So many of the events and incidents they recount seem to have been entirely omitted from the major media publications of that day, and certainly were never included in later historical narratives, given that even such widely known stories as Schiff's major financial backing for the Bolsheviks were completely tossed down George Orwell's "memory hole."

With the volumes long out of copyright, I have added the set to my collection of HTML Books, and those so interested may read the text and decide for themselves.

- **The International Jew**
  The World's Foremost Problem
  Henry Ford • 1920 • 323,000 Words

As mentioned, the overwhelming majority of *The International Jew* seemed a rather bland recitation of complaints about Jewish misbehavior. But there was one major exception, which has a very different impact upon our modern mind, namely that the writer took quite seriously ***The Protocols of the Learned Elders of Zion***. Probably no "conspiracy theory" in modern times has been subjected to such immense vilification and ridicule as the *Protocols*, but a voyage of discovery often acquires a momentum of its own, and I became curious about the nature of that infamous document.

Apparently, the *Protocols* first came to light during the last decade of the 19th century, and the British Museum stored a copy in 1906, but it attracted relatively little attention at the time. However, all this changed after the Bolshevik Revolution and toppling of many other long-standing governments at the end of the First World War led many people to seek a common cause behind so many enormous political upheavals. From my distance of many decades, the text of the *Protocols* strikes me as rather bland and even dull, describing in rather long-winded fashion a plan of secret subversion aimed at weakening the bonds of the social fabric, setting groups against each other, gaining control over political leaders by bribery and blackmail, and eventually restoring society along rigidly hierarchical lines with an entirely new group in control. Admittedly, there were many shrewd insights into politics or psychology, notably the enormous power of the media and the benefits of advancing political front-men who were deeply compromised or incompetent and hence easily controllable. But nothing else really jumped out at me.

Perhaps one reason I found the text of the *Protocols* so uninspiring is that over the century since its publication, these notions of diabolical plots by hidden groups have become such a common theme in our entertainment media, with countless thousands of spy novels and science fiction stories presenting something similar, though these usually involve far more exciting techniques, such as a super-weapon or a powerful drug. If some Bond villain proclaimed his intent to conquer the world merely through simple political subversion, I suspect that such a film would immediately die at the box office.

But back one hundred years ago, these were apparently exciting and novel notions, and I actually found the discussion of the *Protocols* in many of the chapters of *The International Jew* far more interesting and informative than reading the text itself. The author of the Ford books appropriately treated it as any other historical document, dissecting its content, speculating on its provenance, and wondering whether or not it was what it purported to be, namely an approximate record of the statements of a group of conspirators pursuing mastery over the world, with those conspirators seeming to be an elite fraternity of international Jews.

Other contemporaries took the *Protocols* very seriously as well. The august *Times of London* fully endorsed it, before later retracting that position under heavy pressure, and I've read that more copies were published and sold in the Europe of that era than any other book save the Bible. The Bolshevik government of Russia paid the volume its own sort of deep respect, with mere possession of the *Protocols* warranting immediate execution.

Although *The International Jew* concludes that the *Protocols* were probably genuine, I doubt that likelihood based upon the style and presentation. Browsing around on the Internet a dozen years ago, I discovered quite a variety of different opinions even within the precincts of the Far Right, where such matters were freely discussed. I remember some forum writer somewhere characterizing the *Protocols* as "based upon a true story," suggesting that someone who was generally familiar with the secretive machinations of elite international Jews against the existing governments of Czarist Russia and other countries had drafted the document to outline his view of their strategic plans, and such an interpretation seems perfectly plausible to me.

Another reader somewhere claimed that the *Protocols* were pure fiction but quite significant nonetheless. He argued that the very keen insights into the methods by which a small conspiratorial group can quietly corrupt and overthrow powerful existing regimes arguably ranked the work alongside Plato's *The Republic* and Machiavelli's *The Prince* as one of the three great classics of Western political philosophy, earning it a place on the required reading list of every Political Science 101 course. Indeed, the author of Ford's books emphasizes that there are very few mentions of Jews anywhere in the *Protocols*, and all the implied connections to Jewish conspirators could be completely struck from the text without affecting its content whatsoever.

In any event, this short work is now available as one of my HTML Books, making it quite convenient for reading and text-search.

- **The Protocols of the Learned Elders of Zion**
  Anonymous • 1903 • 28,000 Words

Some ideas have consequences and others do not. Although my introductory history textbooks had often mentioned Henry Ford's anti-Semitic activities, his publication of *The International Jew*, and the concurrent popularity of the *Protocols*, they never suggested any lasting political legacy, or at least I don't recall such a claim. However, once I actually read the contents and also discovered the enormous contemporary popularity of those writings and the huge national circulation of *The Dearborn Independent*, I quickly came to a very different conclusion.

For decades pro-immigration liberals, many of them Jewish, have suggested that anti-Semitism was a major factor behind the 1924 Immigration Act that drastically reduced European immigration for the next forty years, while anti-immigration activists have always heatedly denied this. The documentary evidence from that era certainly favors the position of the latter, but I really do wonder what important private discussions may not have been set down in print and entered into the *Congressional Record*. The overwhelming popular support for immigration restriction had been successfully blocked for decades by powerful business interests, which greatly benefited from the reduced wages resulting from fierce labor-competition, but now matters had suddenly changed, and surely the Bolshevik Revolution in Russia must have had been a powerful influence.

Russia, overwhelmingly populated by Russians, had been governed for centuries by a Russian ruling elite. Then, heavily Jewish revolutionaries, drawn from a group amounting to just 4% of the population had taken advantage of military defeat and unsettled political conditions to seize control of the country, butchering those previous elites or forcing them to desperately flee abroad as penniless refugees.

Trotsky and a large fraction of the leading Jewish revolutionaries had been living as exiles in New York City, and now many of their Jewish cousins still resident in America began loudly proclaiming that a similar revolution would soon follow here as well. Huge waves of recent immigration, mostly from Russia, had increased the Jewish fraction of the national population to 3%, not far below the figure for Russia itself on the eve of its revolution. If the Russian elites who ruled Russia had been suddenly overthrown by Jewish revolutionaries, is it not obvious that the Anglo-Saxon elites who ruled Anglo-Saxon America feared suffering the same fate?

The "Red Scare" of the 1919 was one response, with numerous immigrant radicals such as Emma Goldman rounded up and summarily deported. The Sacco-Vanzetti murder trial in 1921 Boston captured the attention of the nation, suggesting that other immigrant groups were violent radicals as well, and might ally themselves with the Jews in a revolutionary movement, just like the Letts and other disgruntled Russian minorities had done during the Bolshevik Revolution. But drastically reducing the inflow of these dangerous foreigners was absolutely essential since otherwise their numbers might easily grow by hundreds of thousands each year, increasing their already huge presence in our largest cities of the East Coast.

Sharply reducing immigration would certainly cause a rise in worker wages and hurt business profits. But considerations of profits are secondary if you fear that you and your family might eventually end up facing a Bolshevik firing squad or fleeing to Buenos Aires with just the clothes on your backs and a few hurriedly-packed suitcases.

A noteworthy bit of evidence in support of this analysis was the subsequent failure of Congress to enact similar restrictive legislation curtailing immigration from Mexico or the rest of Latin America. The local business interests of Texas and the Southwest argued that continuation of unrestricted Mexican immigration was important for their economic success, with Mexicans being good people, politically docile workers, and no threat to stability of the country. This was a clear contrast with the Jews and some other European immigrant groups.

The much less familiar early 1920s battle over restricting Jewish enrollment in the Ivy League may have been another consequence. In his magisterial 2005 volume *The Chosen*, Jerome Karabel documents how the very rapid growth in Jewish numbers at Harvard, Yale, Princeton, and other Ivy League colleges had by the early 1920s become an enormous concern to the Anglo-Saxon elites which had established those institutions and always dominated their student bodies.

As a result, a quiet war over admissions broke out, involving both political and media influence, with the reigning WASPs seeking to reduce and restrict Jewish numbers and the Jews struggling to maintain or expand them. Although there seems no paper-trail of any direct references to the enormously popular national newspaper and books published by Henry Ford or any similar material, it is difficult to believe that the academic combatants were not at least somewhat aware of the theories of a Jewish assault on Gentile society then being so widely promoted. It is easy to imagine that a respectable Boston Brahmin such as Harvard President A. Lawrence Lowell regarded his own moderate "anti-Semitism" as a very reasonable middle-ground between the lurid claims promoted by Ford and others and the demands for unlimited Jewish enrollment made by his opponents. Indeed, Karabel himself points to the social impact of Ford's publications as a significant background factor to this academic conflict.

At this point in time, the Anglo-Saxon elites still held the upper hand in the media. The very heavily Jewish film industry was only in its infancy and the same was true for radio, while the vast majority of major print outlets were still in Gentile hands, so the descendants of America's original settlers won this round of the admissions war. But when the battle was rejoined a couple of decades later, the strategic political and media landscape had completely shifted, with Jews having achieved near-parity in print influence and overwhelming dominance in the more powerful electronic media formats such as film, radio, and nascent television, and this time they were victorious, easily breaking the hold of their longtime ethnic rivals, and eventually achieving **almost complete dominance over those elite institutions**.

And ironically enough, the most lasting cultural legacy of the widespread anti-Jewish agitation of the 1920s may be the least recognized. As mentioned above, modern readers might find the text of the Protocols rather boring and bland, almost like they had been cribbed from the extremely long-winded monologue of one of the diabolical villains of a James Bond story. But it wouldn't surprise me if there were actually an arrow of causality in the opposite direction. Ian Fleming created this genre in the early 1950s with his string of international best-sellers, and it is interesting to speculate about the source of his ideas.

Fleming had spent his youth during the 1920s and 1930s when the *Protocols* were among the most widely read books in much of Europe and leading British newspapers of the highest credibility were recounting the successful plots of Schiff and other international Jewish bankers to overthrow the government of Britain's Czarist ally and replace it with Jewish Bolshevik rule. Moreover, his later service in an arm of British Intelligence would surely have made him privy to details of that history that went far beyond those public headlines. I think it is more than pure coincidence that two of his most memorable Bond villains, **Goldfinger** and Blofeld, had distinctly Jewish-sounding names, and that so many of the plots involve schemes of world-conquest by *Spectre*, a secretive and mysterious international organization hostile to all existing governments. The *Protocols* themselves may be half-forgotten today, but their cultural influence probably survives in the Bond films, whose $7 billion of aggregate box-office gross ranks them as the most successful movie series in history when adjusted for inflation.

The extent to which established historical facts can appear or disappear from the world should certainly force all of us to become very cautious in believing anything we read in our standard textbooks, let alone what we absorb from the more transient electronic media.

In the early years of the Bolshevik Revolution, almost no one questioned the overwhelming role of Jews in that event, nor their similar preponderance in the ultimately unsuccessful Bolshevik takeovers in Hungary and parts of Germany. For example, former British Minister **Winston Churchill in 1920** denounced the "terrorist Jews" who had seized control of Russia and other parts of Europe, noting that "the majority of the leading figures are Jews" and stating that "In the Soviet institutions the predominance of Jews is even more astonishing," while lamenting the horrors these Jews had inflicted upon the suffering Germans and Hungarians.

Similarly, journalist Robert Wilton, former Russia correspondent of the *Times of London*, provided a very detailed summary of the enormous Jewish role in his 1918 book *Russia's Agony* and 1920 book *The Last Days of the Romanovs*, although one of the most explicit chapters of the latter **was apparently excluded from the English language edition**. Not long afterward, the facts regarding the enormous financial support provided to the Bolsheviks by international Jewish bankers such as Schiff and Aschberg were widely reported in the mainstream media.

Jews and Communism were just as strongly tied together in America, and for years **the largest circulation Communist newspaper in our country was published in Yiddish**. When they were finally released, the Venona Decrypts demonstrated that even as late as the

1930s and 1940s, a remarkable fraction of America's Communist spies came from that ethnic background.

A personal anecdote tends to confirm these dry historical records. During the early 2000s I once had lunch with an elderly and very eminent computer scientist, with whom I'd become a little friendly. While talking about this and that, he happened to mention that both his parents had been zealous Communists, and given his obvious Irish name, I expressed my surprise, saying that I'd thought almost all the Communists of that era were Jewish. He said that was indeed the case, but although his mother had such an ethnic background, his father did not, which made him a very rare exception in their political circles. As a consequence, the Party had always sought to place him in as prominent a public role as possible just to prove that not all Communists were Jews, and although he obeyed Party discipline, he was always irritated at being used as such a "token."

However, once Communism sharply fell out of favor in 1950s America, nearly all of the leading "Red Baiters" such as Sen. Joseph McCarthy went to enormous lengths to obscure the ethnic dimension of the movement they were combatting. Indeed, many years later **Richard Nixon casually spoke in private** of the difficulty he and other anti-Communist investigators had faced in trying to focus on Gentile targets since nearly all of the suspected Soviet spies were Jewish, and when this tape became public, his alleged anti-Semitism provoked a media firestorm even though his remarks were obviously implying the exact opposite.

This last point is an important one, since once the historical record has been sufficiently whitewashed or rewritten, any lingering strands of the original reality that survive are often perceived as bizarre delusions or denounced as "conspiracy theories." Indeed, even today the ever-amusing pages of Wikipedia provides an entire 3,500 word article attacking the notion of "**Jewish Bolshevism**" as an "antisemitic canard."

I remember in the 1970s the enormous gusts of American praise for Solzhenitysn's three volume Gulag Archipelago suddenly encountered a temporary headwind when someone noticed that his 2,000 pages had included a single photograph depicting many of the leading Gulag administrators, along with a caption revealing their unmistakably Jewish names. This detail was treated as serious evidence of the great author's possible anti-Semitism since the actual reality of the enormously large role of Jews in the NKVD and the Gulag system had long since disappeared from all the standard history books.

As another example, the Rev. Pat Robertson, a leading Christian televangelist, published *The New World Order* in 1991, his fiery attack on the "godless globalists" whom he considered his greatest enemy, and it quickly became a massive national best-seller. He happened to include a couple of brief, somewhat garbled mentions of the $20 million which Wall Street banker Jacob Schiff had provided to the Communists, carefully avoiding any suggestion of a Jewish angle and providing no reference for that claim. His book quickly provoked a vast outpouring of denunciation and ridicule across the elite media, with the Schiff story seen as conclusion proof of **Robertson's delusional anti-Semitism**. I cannot really fault these critics since in pre-Internet days they could only consult the indexes of a few standard histories of the Bolshevik Revolution, and finding no mention of Schiff or his money, naturally assumed that Robertson or his source had simply invented the bizarre story. I myself had had exactly the same reaction at the time.

Only after Soviet Communism had died in 1991 and no longer was perceived as a hostile force were academic scholars in America once again able to publish mainstream books that gradually restored the true picture of that past era. In many respects, a widely praised work such as **The Jewish Century** by Yuri Slezkine, published in 2004 by Princeton University Press, provides a narrative quite consistent with the long-forgotten works by Robert Wilton but marks a very sharp departure from the largely obfuscatory histories of the intervening eighty-odd years.

Until about a dozen years ago, I had always vaguely assumed that Henry Ford's *The International Jew* was a work of political lunacy and the *Protocols* a notorious hoax. Yet today, I would probably consider the former as a potentially useful source of possible historical events otherwise excluded from most standard accounts, while at least recognize why some would think the latter should deserve a place alongside Plato and Machiavelli as a great classic of Western political thought.

This article is available online at:
https://www.unz.com/runz/american-pravda-the-bolshevik-revolution-and-its-aftermath/

The Nature of Anti-Semitism
The Unz Review, July 30, 2018

I recently published a couple of long essays, and although they primarily focused on other matters, the subject of anti-Semitism was a strong secondary theme. In that regard, I mentioned my shock at discovering a dozen or more years ago that several of the most self-evidently absurd elements of anti-Semitic lunacy, which I had always dismissed without consideration, were probably correct. It does seem likely that a significant number of traditionally-religious Jews did indeed occasionally commit **the ritual murder of Christian children** in order to use their blood in certain religious ceremonies, and also that powerful Jewish international bankers did play **a large role in financing the establishment of Bolshevik Russia.**

When one discovers that matters of such enormous moment not only apparently occurred but that they had been successfully excluded from nearly all of our histories and media coverage for most of the last one hundred years, the implications take some time to properly digest. If the most extreme "anti-Semitic canards" were probably true, then surely the whole notion of anti-Semitism warrants a careful reexamination.

All of us obtain our knowledge of the world by two different channels. Some things we discover from our own personal experiences and the direct evidence of our senses, but most information comes to us via external sources such as books and the media, and a crisis may develop when we discover that these two pathways are in sharp conflict. The official media of the old USSR used to endlessly trumpet the tremendous achievements of its collectivized agricultural system, but when citizens noticed that there was never any meat in their shops, "Pravda" became a watchword for "Lies" rather than "Truth."

Now consider the notion of "anti-Semitism." Google searches for that word and its close variants reveal over 24 million hits, and over the years I've surely seen that term tens of thousands of times in my books and newspapers, and heard it endlessly reported in my electronic media and entertainment. But thinking it over, I'm not sure I can ever recall a single real-life instance that I've personally encountered, nor have I heard of almost any such cases from my friends or acquaintances. Indeed, the only persons I've ever come across making such claims were individuals who bore unmistakable signs of serious psychological imbalance. When the daily newspapers are brimming with lurid tales of hideous demons walking among us and attacking people on every street corner, but you yourself have never actually seen one, you may gradually grow suspicious.

Over the years some of my own research has uncovered a sharp contrast between image and reality. As recently as the late 1990s, leading mainstream media outlets such as *The New York Times* were still **denouncing a top Ivy League school such as Princeton** for the supposed anti-Semitism of its college admissions policy, but a few years ago when I carefully investigated that issue in quantitative terms for my lengthy **Meritocracy analysis** I was very surprised to reach a polar-opposite conclusion. According to the best available evidence, white Gentiles were over 90% less likely to be enrolled at Harvard and the other Ivies than were Jews of similar academic performance, a truly remarkable finding. If the situation had been reversed and Jews were 90% less likely to be found at Harvard than seemed warranted by their test scores, surely that fact would be endlessly cited as the absolute smoking-gun proof of horrendous anti-Semitism in present-day America.

It has also become apparent that a considerable fraction of what passes for "anti-Semitism" these days seems to stretch that term beyond all recognition. A few weeks ago an unknown 28-year-old Democratic Socialist named Alexandria Ocasio-Cortez scored a stunning upset primary victory over a top House Democrat in New York City, and naturally received a blizzard of media coverage as a result. However, when it came out that she had denounced the Israeli government for its recent massacre of over 140 unarmed Palestinian protesters in Gaza, cries of "anti-Semite" soon appeared, and according to Google there are now over 180,000 such hits combining her name and that harsh accusatory term. Similarly, just a few days ago the *New York Times* ran **a major story** reporting that all of Britain's Jewish newspapers had issued an "unprecedented" denunciation of Jeremy Corbyn's Labour Party, describing it as an "existential threat" to the Jewish community for the anti-Semitism it was fostering; but this apparently amounted to nothing more than its willingness to sharply criticize the Israeli government for its long mistreatment of the Palestinians.

One plausible explanation of the strange contrast between media coverage and reality might be that anti-Semitism once did loom very large in real life, but dissipated many decades ago, while the organizations and activists focused on detecting and combating that pernicious problem have remained in place, generating public attention based on smaller and smaller issues, with the zealous Jewish activists of the Anti-Defamation League (ADL) representing a perfect example of this situation. As an even more striking illustration, the Second World War ended over seventy years ago, but what historian Norman Finkelstein has so aptly labeled "**the Holocaust Industry**" has grown ever larger and more entrenched in our academic and media worlds so that scarcely a day passes without one or more articles relating to that topic appearing in my major morning newspapers. Given this situation, a serious exploration of the true nature of anti-Semitism should probably avoid the mere media phantoms of today and focus on the past, when the condition might still have been widespread in daily life.

Many observers have pointed to the aftermath of the Second World War as marking a huge watershed in the public acceptability of anti-Semitism both in America and Europe, so perhaps a proper appraisal of that cultural phenomenon should focus on the years before that global conflict. However, the overwhelming role of Jews in the Bolshevik Revolution and other bloody Communist seizures of power quite naturally made them objects of considerable fear and hatred throughout the inter-war years, so the safest course might be to push that boundary back a little further and confine our attention to the period prior to the outbreak of the First World War. The pogroms in Czarist Russia, the Dreyfus Affair in France, and the lynching of Leo Frank in the American South come to mind as some of the most famous examples from that period.

In 1991 Cambridge University Press published *The Jew Accused* by Albert Lindemann, a noted scholar of European ideological movements, and his book focused on exactly that era and those sorts of incidents. Although the text is quite short, running less than 300 pages, Lindemann built his discussion upon a huge foundation of secondary literature, with his footnotes drawn from the 200 works included in his extensive bibliography. As far as I could tell, he seems a very scrupulous scholar, generally providing the multiple, often conflicting accounts of a given incident, and coming to his own conclusions with considerable hesitation.

This approach is certainly demonstrated in the first of his major cases, the notorious Dreyfus affair of late 19th century France, probably one of history's most famous anti-Semitic incidents. Although he concludes that Captain Alfred Dreyfus was very likely innocent of the charge of espionage, he notes the seemingly strong evidence that initially led to his arrest and conviction and finds—contrary to myth-making by numerous later writers—absolutely no indications that his Jewish origins played any role whatsoever in his predicament.

However, he does note some of the underlying social context to this fierce political battle. Although only one Frenchman in a thousand was Jewish, just a few years earlier a group of Jews had been the leading culprits behind several huge financial scandals that had impoverished large numbers of small investors, and the swindlers afterward escaped any punishment by means of political influence and bribery. Given this history, much of the outrage of the anti-Dreyfusards probably arose from their fears that a Jewish military spy from a very wealthy family might be able to walk free using similar tactics, and the public claims that Dreyfus's brother was offering enormous bribes to win his brother's release certainly strengthened this concern.

Lindemann's discussion of the 1913 Leo Frank Affair, in which a wealthy Northern Jew working in Atlanta was accused of sexually-assaulting and murdering a young girl, is even more interesting. Once again, he notes that contrary to the traditional narrative, there seems absolutely no hint that Frank's Jewish background played any role in his arrest or conviction. Indeed, at his trial it was instead his very highly-paid defense attorneys who unsuccessfully sought to "play the race card" with the jurors by crudely attempting to deflect suspicion upon a local black worker by means of racially-charged invective.

Although Lindemann regards Frank as probably innocent, my own reading of the evidence he presents suggests the overwhelming likelihood of his guilt. Meanwhile, it seems undeniable that the outpouring of popular anger against Frank was produced by the vast ocean of outside Jewish money—at least $15 million or more in present-day dollars—that was committed to the legal efforts to save the life of someone widely regarded as a brutal murderer. There are strong suggestions that far more improper means were also employed, including bribery and influence-peddling, so that after Frank was convicted by a jury of his peers and thirteen separate legal appeals were denied, a governor with strong personal ties to the defense lawyers and Jewish interests chose to spare Frank's life a few months before leaving office. Under these circumstances, the lynch-mob that hung Frank was viewed by the community as merely enforcing his official death sentence by extra-judicial means.

I also discovered that the leading figures in the anti-Frank movement had views far nuanced than I had expected. For example, populist writer Tom Watson had previously been a strong defender of Jewish anarchist Emma Goldman, while ferociously denouncing the Rockefellers, Morgans, and Goulds as the "true destroyers" of Jeffersonian democracy, so his outrage that Frank might escape punishment for murder seemed motivated by the extreme wealth of Frank's family and his supporters rather than any pre-existing anti-Semitic sentiments.

The unmistakable conclusion of Lindemann's analysis is that if the defendants in both the Dreyfus and Frank cases had not been Jewish, they would have suffered identical arrests and convictions, but lacking any wealthy and politically mobilized Jewish community to rally around them, they would have received their punishments, just or unjust, and immediately been forgotten. Instead, Theodor Herzl, the founding father of Zionism, later claimed that the massive anti-Semitism revealed by the Dreyfus Affair was the basis of his personal ideological awakening, while the Frank Affair led to the establishment of America's Anti-Defamation League. And both these cases have entered our history books as among the most notorious examples of pre-World War I anti-Semitism.

Lindemann's discussion of the often difficult relations between Russia's restive Jewish minority and its huge Slavic majority is also quite interesting, and he provides numerous instances in which major incidents, supposedly demonstrating the enormously strong appeal of vicious anti-Semitism, were quite different than has been suggested by the legend. The famous Kishinev Pogrom of 1903 was obviously the result of severe ethnic tension in that city, but contrary to the regular accusations of later writers, there seems absolutely no evidence of high-level government involvement, and the widespread claims of 700 dead that so horrified the entire world were grossly exaggerated, with only 45 killed in the urban rioting. Chaim Weizmann, the future president of Israel, later promoted the story that he himself and some other brave Jewish souls had personally defended their people with revolvers in hand even as they saw the mutilated bodies of 80 Jewish victims. This account was totally fictional since Weizmann happened to have been be hundreds of miles away when the riots occurred.

Although a tendency to lie and exaggerate was hardly unique to the political partisans of Russian Jewry, the existence of a powerful international network of Jewish journalists and Jewish-influenced media outlets ensured that such concocted propaganda stories might receive enormous worldwide distribution, while the truth followed far behind, if at all.

For related reasons, international outrage was often focused on the legal confinement of most of Russia's Jews to the "Pale of Settlement," suggesting some sort of tight imprisonment; but that area was the traditional home of the Jewish population and encompassed a landmass almost as large as France and Spain combined. The growing impoverishment of Eastern European Jews during that era was often assumed to be a consequence of hostile government policy, but the obvious explanation was extraordinary Jewish fecundity, which far outstripped that of their Slavic fellow countrymen, and quickly led them to outgrow the available spots in any of their traditional "middleman" occupations, a situation worsened by their total disinclination to engage in agriculture or other primary-producer activities. Jewish communities expressed horror at the risk of losing their sons to the Czarist military draft, but this was simply the flip-side of the full Russian citizenship they had been granted, and no different from what was faced by their non-Jewish neighbors.

Certainly the Jews of Russia suffered greatly from widespread riots and mob attacks in the generation prior to World War I, and these did sometimes have substantial government encouragement, especially in the aftermath of the very heavy Jewish role in the 1905 Revolution. But we should keep in mind that a Jewish plotter had been implicated in the killing of Czar Alexander II, and Jewish assassins had also struck down several top Russian ministers and numerous other government officials. If the last decade or two had seen American Muslims assassinate a sitting U.S. President, various leading Cabinet members, and a host of our other elected and appointed officials, surely the position of Muslims in this country would have become a very uncomfortable one.

As Lindemann candidly describes the tension between Russia's very rapidly growing Jewish population and its governing authorities, he cannot avoid mentioning the notorious Jewish reputation for bribery, corruption, and general dishonesty, with numerous figures of all political backgrounds noting that the remarkable Jewish propensity to commit perjury in the courtroom led to severe problems in the effective administration of justice. The eminent American sociologist E.A. Ross, writing in 1913, characterized **the regular behavior of Eastern European Jews in very similar terms**.

Lindemann also allocates a short chapter to discussing the 1911 Beilis Affair, in which a Ukrainian Jew was accused of the ritual murder of a young Gentile boy, an incident that generated a great deal of international attention and controversy. Based on the evidence presented, the defendant seems likely to have been innocent, although the obvious lies he repeatedly told police interrogators hardly helped foster that impression, and "the system worked" in that he was ultimately found innocent by the jurors at his trial. However, a few pages are also given to a much less well-known ritual murder case in late 19th century Hungary, in which the evidence of Jewish guilt seemed far stronger, though the author hardly accepted the possible reality of such an outlandish crime. Such reticence was quite understandable since the publication of **Ariel Toaff's remarkable volume on the subject** was still a dozen years in the future.

Lindemann subsequently expanded his examination of historical anti-Semitism into a much broader treatment, *Esau's Tears*, which appeared in 1997. In this volume, he added comparative studies of the social landscape in Germany, Britain, Italy, and several other European countries, and demonstrated that the relationship between Jews and non-Jews varied greatly across different locations and time periods. But although I found his analysis quite useful and interesting, the extraordinarily harsh attacks his text provoked from some outraged Jewish academics seemed even more intriguing.

For example, Judith Laikin Elkin opened her discussion in *The American Historical Review* by describing the book as a "545-page polemic," a strange characterization of a book so remarkably even-handed and factually-based in its scholarship. Writing in *Commentary*, Robert Wistrich was even harsher, stating that merely reading the book had been a painful experience for him, and his review seemed filled with spittle-flecked rage. Unless these individuals had somehow gotten copies of a different book, I found their attitudes simply astonishing.

I was not alone in such a reaction. Richard S. Levy of the University of Illinois, a noted scholar of anti-Semitism, expressed amazement at Wistrich's seemingly irrational outburst, while Paul Gottfried, writing in *Chronicles*, mildly suggested that Lindemann had "touched raw nerves." Indeed, Gottfried's own evaluation quite reasonably criticized Lindemann for perhaps being a little too even-handed, sometimes presenting numerous conflicting analyzes without choosing between them. For those interested, a good discussion of the book by Alan Steinweis, a younger scholar specializing in the same topic, **is conveniently available online**.

The remarkable ferocity with which some Jewish writers attacked Lindemann's meticulous attempt to provide an accurate history of anti-Semitism may carry more significance than merely an exchange of angry words in low-circulation academic publications. If our mainstream media shapes our reality, scholarly books and articles based upon them tend to set the contours of that media coverage. And the ability of a relatively small number of agitated and energetic Jews to police the acceptable boundaries of historical narratives may have enormous consequences for our larger society, deterring scholars from objectively reporting historical facts and preventing students from discovering them.

The undeniable truth is that for many centuries Jews usually constituted a wealthy and privileged segment of the population in nearly all the European countries in which they resided, and quite frequently they based their livelihood upon the heavy exploitation of a downtrodden peasantry. Even without any differences in ethnicity, language, or religion, such conditions almost invariably provoke hostility. The victory of Mao's Communist forces in China was quickly followed by the brutal massacre of a million or more Han Chinese landlords by the Han Chinese poor peasants who regarded them as cruel oppressors, with William Hinton's classic ***Fanshen*** describing the unfortunate history that unfolded in one particular village. When similar circumstances led to violent clashes in Eastern Europe between Slavs and Jews, does it really make logical sense to employ a specialized term such as "anti-Semitism" to describe that situation?

Furthermore, some of the material presented in Lindemann's rather innocuous text might also lead to potentially threatening ideas. Consider, for example, the notorious *Protocols of the Learned Elders of Zion*, almost certainly fictional, but hugely popular and influential during the years following World War I and the Bolshevik Revolution. The fall of so many longstanding Gentile dynasties and their replacement by new regimes such as Soviet Russia and Weimar Germany, which were heavily dominated by their tiny Jewish minorities, quite naturally fed suspicions of a worldwide Jewish plot, as did the widely discussed role of Jewish international bankers in producing those political outcomes.

Over the decades, there has been much speculation about the possible inspiration for the *Protocols*, but although Lindemann makes absolutely no reference to that document, he does provide a very intriguing possible candidate. Jewish-born British Prime Minister Benjamin Disraeli certainly ranked as one of the most influential figures of the late 19th century, and in his novel *Coningsby*, he has the character representing Lord Lionel Rothschild boast about **the existence of a vast and secret network of powerful international Jews**, who stand near the head of almost every major nation, quietly controlling their governments from behind the scenes. If one of the world's most politically well-connected Jews eagerly promoted such notions, was Henry Ford really so unreasonable in doing the same?

Lindemann also notes Disraeli's focus on the extreme importance of race and racial origins, a central aspect of traditional Jewish religious doctrine. He reasonably suggests that this must surely have had a huge influence upon the rise of those political ideas, given that Disraeli's public profile and stature were so much greater than the mere writers or activists whom our history books usually place at center stage. In fact, Houston Stewart Chamberlain, a leading racial theorist, actually cited Disraeli as a key source for his ideas. Jewish intellectuals such as Max Nordau and Cesare Lombroso are already widely recognized as leading figures in the rise of the racial science of that era, but Disraeli's under-appreciated role may have actually been far greater. The deep

Jewish roots of European racialist movements are hardly something that many present-day Jews would want widely known.

One of the harsh Jewish critics of *Esau's Tears* denounced Cambridge University Press for even allowing the book to appear in print, and although that major work is easily available in English, there are numerous other cases where an important but discordant version of historical reality has been successfully blocked from publication. For decades most Americans would have ranked Nobel Laureate Alexander Solzhenitsyn as among the world's greatest literary figures, and his *Gulag Archipelago* alone sold over 10 million copies. But his last work was a massive **two-volume account** of the tragic 200 years of shared history between Russians and Jews, and despite its 2002 release in Russian and numerous other world languages, there has yet to be an authorized English translation, though various partial editions have circulated on the Internet in *samizdat* form.

At one point, a full English version was briefly available for sale at Amazon.com and I purchased it. Glancing through a few sections, the work appeared quite even-handed and innocuous to me, but it seemed to provide a far more detailed and uncensored account than anything else previously available, which obviously was the problem. The Bolshevik Revolution resulted in the deaths of many tens of millions of people worldwide, and the overwhelming Jewish role in its leadership would become more difficult to erase from historical memory if Solzhenitsyn's work were easily available. Also, his candid discussion of the economic and political behavior of Russian Jewry in pre-revolutionary times directly conflicted with the hagiography widely promoted by Hollywood and the popular media. Historian Yuri Slezkine's award-winning 2004 book ***The Jewish Century*** provided many similar facts, but his treatment was far more cursory and his public stature not remotely the same.

Near the end of his life, Solzhenitsyn gave his political blessing to Russian President Vladimir Putin, and Russia's leaders honored him upon his death, while his *Gulag* volumes are now enshrined as mandatory reading in the standard high school curriculum of today's overwhelmingly Christian Russia. But even as his star rose again in his own homeland, it seems to have sharply fallen in our own country, and his trajectory may eventually relegate him to nearly un-person status.

A couple of years after the release of Solzhenitsyn's controversial final book, an American writer named Anne Applebaum published a thick history bearing the same title *Gulag*, and her work received enormously favorable media coverage and won her a Pulitzer Prize; I have even heard claims that her book has been steadily replacing that earlier *Gulag* on many college reading lists. But although Jews constituted a huge fraction of the top leadership of the Soviet Gulag system during its early decades, as well as that of the dreaded NKVD which supplied the inmates, nearly her entire focus on her own ethnic group during Soviet times is that of victims rather than victimizers. And by a remarkable irony of fate, she shares a last name with one of the top Bolshevik leaders, Hirsch Apfelbaum, who concealed his own ethnic identity by calling himself Grigory Zinoviev.

The striking decline in Solzhenitsyn's literary status in the West came just a decade or two after **an even more precipitous collapse in the reputation of David Irving**, and for much the same reason. Irving probably ranked as the most internationally successful British historian of the last one hundred years and a renowned scholar of World War II, but his extensive reliance on primary source documentary evidence posed an obvious threat to the official narrative promoted by Hollywood and wartime propaganda. When he published his magisterial *Hitler's War*, this conflict between myth and reality came into the open, and an enormous wave of attacks and vilification was unleashed, gradually leading to his purge from respectability and eventually even his imprisonment.

Similarly, Israeli academic Ariel Toaff, son of the chief rabbi of Rome, was regarded as one of the world's leading scholarly authorities on Medieval Jewry. But when he published his remarkable 2004 analysis suggesting the likely reality of the Jewish ritual murders of Christian children throughout history, **the resulting media firestorm forced the cancellation of the book's publication**, and the work only survives in *samizdat* **form**, while there were even calls for his arrest and incarceration.

In other cases, pressure from the ADL and similar Jewish activist groups have led Amazon to completely eliminate entire categories of historical analysis and ban those publishers who produce such works, which drastically reduces their availability to the reading public.

All of these cases were the sort of high-profile examples which are well-known to anyone who pays attention to such matters. But surely there must have been many other incidents, involving far less prominent authors, which never received any significant media coverage, and also a vastly larger universe of cases in which writers have self-censored their texts in order to avoid such controversies. Over the decades, I have gradually discovered through sad experience that I must exercise extreme caution whenever I read anything relating to the subjects of Jews, Judaism, or Israel.

These important examples may help to explain the puzzling contrast between the behavior of Jews in the aggregate and Jews as individuals. Observers have noticed that even fairly small Jewish minorities may often have a major impact upon the far larger societies that host them. But on the other hand, in my experience at least, a large majority of individual Jews do not seem all that different in their personalities or behavior than their non-Jewish counterparts. So how does a community whose individual mean is not so unusual generate what seems to be such a striking difference in collective behavior? I think the answer may involve the existence of information choke-points, and the role of relatively small numbers of particularly zealous and agitated Jews in influencing and controlling these.

We live our lives constantly immersed in media narratives, and these allow us to decide the rights and wrongs of a situation. The vast majority of people, Jew and Gentile alike, are far more likely to take strong action if they are convinced that their cause is a just one. This is obviously the basis for war-time propaganda.

Now suppose that a relatively small number of zealous Jewish partisans are known to always attack and denounce journalists or authors who accurately describe Jewish misbehavior. Over time, this ongoing campaign of intimidation may cause many important facts to be left on the cutting-room floor, or even gradually expel from mainstream respectability those writers who refuse to conform to such pressures. Meanwhile, similar small numbers of Jewish partisans frequently exaggerate the misdeeds committed against Jews, sometimes piling their exaggerations upon past exaggerations already produced by a previous round of such zealots.

Eventually, these two combined trends may take a complex and possibly very mixed historical record and transform it into a simple morality-play, with innocent Jews tremendously injured by vicious Jew-haters. And as this morality-play becomes established it deepens the subsequent intensity of other Jewish-activists, who redouble their demands that the media "stop vilifying Jews" and covering up the supposed evils inflicted upon them. An unfortunate circle of distortion following exaggeration following distortion can eventually produce a widely accepted historical account that bears little resemblance to the reality of what actually happened.

So as a result, the vast majority of quite ordinary Jews, who would normally behave in quite ordinary ways, are misled by this largely fictional history, and rather understandably become greatly outraged at all the horrible things that had been done to their suffering people, some of which are true and some of which are not, while remaining completely ignorant of the other side of the ledger.

Furthermore, this situation is exacerbated by the common tendency of Jews to "cluster" together, perhaps representing just one or two percent of the total population, but often constituting 20% or 40% or 60% of their immediate peer-group, especially in certain professions. Under such conditions, the ideas or emotional agitation of some Jews probably permeates others around them, often provoking additional waves of indignation.

As a rough analogy, a small quantity of uranium is relatively inert and harmless, and entirely so if distributed within low-density ore. But if a significant quantity of weapons-grade uranium is sufficiently compressed, then the neutrons released by fissioning atoms will quickly cause additional atoms to undergo fission, with the ultimate result of that critical chain-reaction being a nuclear explosion. In similar fashion, even a highly agitated Jew may have no negative impact, but if the collection of such agitated Jews becomes too numerous and clusters together too closely, they may work each other into a terrible frenzy, perhaps with disastrous consequences both for themselves and for their larger society. This is especially true if those agitated Jews begin to dominate certain key nodes of top-level control, such as the central political or media organs of a society.

Whereas most living organisms exist solely in physical reality, human beings also occupy an ideational space, with the interaction of human consciousness and perceived reality playing a major role in shaping behavior. Just as the pheromones released by mammals or insects can drastically affect the reactions of their family members or nest-mates, the ideas secreted by individuals or the media-emitters of a society can have an enormous impact upon their fellows.

A cohesive, organized group generally possesses huge advantages over a teeming mass of atomized individuals, much like a disciplined Macedonian Phalanx could easily defeat a vastly larger body of disorganized infantry. Many years ago, on some website somewhere I came across a very insightful comment regarding the obvious connection between "anti-Semitism" and "racism," which our mainstream media organs identify as two of the world's greatest evils. Under this analysis, "anti-Semitism" represents the tendency to criticize or resist Jewish social cohesion, while "racism" represents the attempt of white Gentiles to maintain a similar social cohesion of their own. To the extent that the ideological emanations from our centralized media organs serve to strengthen and protect Jewish cohesion while attacking and dissolving any similar cohesion on the part of their Gentile counterparts, the former will obviously gain enormous advantages in resource-competition against the latter.

Religion obviously constitutes an important unifying factor in human social groups and we cannot ignore the role of Judaism in this regard. **Traditional Jewish religious doctrine seems to consider Jews as being in a state of permanent hostility with all non-Jews**, and the use of dishonest propaganda is an almost inevitable aspect of such conflict. Furthermore, since Jews have invariably been a small political minority, maintaining such controversial tenets required the employment of a massive framework of subterfuge and dissimulation in order to conceal their nature from the larger society surrounding them. It has often been said that truth is the first casualty in war, and surely the cultural influences of over a thousand years of such intense religious hostility may continue to quietly influence the thinking of many modern Jews, even those who have largely abandoned their religious beliefs.

The notorious Jewish tendency to shamelessly lie or wildly exaggerate has sometimes had horrifying human consequences. I very recently discovered a fascinating passage in Peter Moreira's 2014 book ***The Jew***

Who Defeated Hitler: Henry Morgenthau Jr., FDR, and How We Won the War, focused on the important political role of that powerful Secretary of the Treasury.

A turning point in Henry Morgenthau Jr.'s relationship with the Jewish community came in November 1942, when Rabbi Stephen Wise came to the corner office to tell the secretary what was happening in Europe. Morgenthau knew of the millions of deaths and the lampshades made from victims' skin, and he asked Wise not to go into excessive details. But Wise went on to tell of the barbarity of the Nazis, how they were making soap out of Jewish flesh. Morgenthau, turning paler, implored him, "Please, Stephen, don't give me the gory details." Wise went on with his list of horrors and Morgenthau repeated his plea over and over again. Henrietta Klotz was afraid her boss would keel over. Morgenthau later said the meeting changed his life.

It is easy to imagine that Morgenthau's gullible acceptance of such obviously ridiculous war-time atrocity stories played a major role when he later lent his name and support to remarkably brutal American occupation policies that **probably led to the postwar deaths of many millions of innocent German civilians.**

This article is available online at:
https://www.unz.com/runz/american-pravda-anti-semitism-a-century-ago/

Jews and Nazis
The Hidden History of the 1930s and 1940s
The Unz Review, August 6, 2018

Israeli Leaders and Nazi Germany

Around 35 years ago, I was sitting in my college dorm-room closely reading the *New York Times* as I did each and every morning when I noticed an astonishing article about the controversial new Israeli Prime Minister, Yitzhak Shamir.

Back in those long-gone days, the Gray Lady was strictly a black-and-white print publication, lacking the large color photographs of rap stars and long stories about dieting techniques that fill so much of today's news coverage, and it also seemed to have a far harder edge in its Middle East reporting. A year or so earlier, Shamir's predecessor Menacham Begin had allowed his Defense Minister Ariel Sharon to talk him into invading Lebanon and besieging Beirut, and the subsequent massacre of Palestinian women and children in the Sabra and Shatila refugee camps had outraged the world and angered America's government. This eventually led to Begin's resignation, with Shamir, his Foreign Minister, taking his place.

Prior to his surprising 1977 election victory, Begin had spent decades in the political wilderness as an unacceptable right-winger, and Shamir had an even more extreme background, with the American mainstream media freely reporting his long involvement in all sorts of high-profile assassinations and terrorist attacks during the 1940s, painting him as a very bad man indeed.

Given Shamir's notorious activities, few revelations would have shocked me, but this one did. Apparently, during the late 1930s, Shamir and his small Zionist faction had become great admirers of the Italian Fascists and German Nazis, and after World War II broke out, they had made repeated attempts to contact Mussolini and the German leadership in 1940 and 1941, hoping to enlist in the Axis Powers as their Palestine affiliate, and undertake a campaign of attacks and espionage against the local British forces, then share in the political booty after Hitler's inevitable triumph.

Now the *Times* clearly viewed Shamir in a very negative light, but it seemed extremely unlikely to me that they would have published such a remarkable story without being absolutely sure of their facts. Among other things, there were long excerpts from the official letters sent to Mussolini ferociously denouncing the "decadent" democratic systems of Britain and France that he was opposing, and assuring *Il Duce* that such ridiculous political notions would have no future place in the totalitarian Jewish client state they hoped to establish under his auspices in Palestine.

As it happens, both Germany and Italy were preoccupied with larger geopolitical issues at the time, and given the small size of Shamir's Zionist faction, not much seems to have ever come of those efforts. But the idea of the sitting Prime Minister of the Jewish State having spent his early wartime years as an unrequited Nazi ally was certainly something that sticks in one's mind, not quite conforming to the traditional narrative of that era which I had always accepted.

Most remarkably, the revelation of Shamir's pro-Axis past seems to have had only a relatively minor impact upon his political standing within Israeli society. I would think that any American political figure found to have supported a military alliance with Nazi Germany during the Second World War would have had a very difficult time surviving the resulting political scandal, and the same would surely be true for politicians in Britain, France, or most other western nations. But although there was certainly some embarrassment in the Israeli press, especially after the shocking story reached the international headlines, apparently most Israelis took the whole matter in stride, and Shamir stayed in office for another year, then later served a second, much longer term as Prime Minister during 1986-1992. The Jews of Israel apparently regarded Nazi Germany quite differently than did most Americans, let alone most American Jews.

Around that same time, a second intriguing example of this quite different Israeli perspective towards the Nazis also came to my attention. In 1983, Amoz Oz, often described as Israel's greatest novelist, had published ***In the Land of Israel*** to glowing reviews. This book was a collection of lengthy interviews with various representative figures in

Israeli society, both moderate and extreme, as well as some coverage of the Palestinians who also lived among them.

Of these ideological profiles, one of the shortest but most widely discussed was that of an especially hard-line political figure, unnamed but almost universally believed to be Ariel Sharon, a conclusion certainly supported by the personal details and physical description provided. Near the very beginning, that figure mentioned that people of his ideological ilk had recently been denounced as "Judeo-Nazis" by a prominent liberal Israeli academic, but rather than reject that label, he fully welcomed it. So the subject generally became known in public discussions as the "Judeo-Nazi."

That he described himself in such terms was hardly an exaggeration, since he rather gleefully advocated the slaughter of millions of Israel's enemies, and the vast expansion of Israeli territory by conquest of neighboring lands and expulsion of their populations, along with the free use of nuclear weapons if they or anyone else too strongly resisted such efforts. In his bold opinion, the Israelis and Jews in general were just too soft and meek, and needed to regain their place in the world by once again becoming a conquering people, probably hated but definitely feared. To him, the large recent massacre of Palestinian women and children at Sabra and Shatila was of no consequence whatsoever, and the most unfortunate aspect of the incident was that the killers had been Israel's Christian Phalangist allies rather than Israeli soldiers themselves.

Now rhetorical excess is quite common among politicians and a shroud of pledged anonymity will obviously loosen many tongues. But can anyone imagine an American or other Western public figure talking in such terms, let alone someone who moves in higher political circles? These days, Donald Trump sometimes Tweets out a crude misspelled insult at 2am, and the American media is aghast in horror. But given that his administration leaks like a sieve, if he routinely boasted to his confidants about possibly slaughtering millions, we surely would have heard about it. For that matter, there seems not the slightest evidence that the original German Nazis ever spoke in such ways privately, let alone while a journalist was carefully taking notes. But the "Judeo-Nazis" of Israel are another story.

As near as I can recall, the last even slightly prominent figure in American public life who declared himself a "Nazi" was George Lincoln

Rockwell during the 1960s, and he was much more of a political performance artist than an actual political leader. Even as marginalized a figure as David Duke has always hotly denied such an accusation. But apparently politics in Israel is played by different rules.

In any event, Sharon's purported utterances seem to have had little negative impact upon his subsequent political career, and after spending some time in the political wilderness after the Lebanon disaster, he eventually served five years as Prime Minister during 2001-2006, although by that later date his views were regularly denounced as too soft and compromising due to the steady rightward drift of the Israeli political spectrum.

Zionism in the Age of the Dictators

Over the years I've occasionally made half-hearted attempts to locate the *Times* article about Shamir that had long stuck in my memory, but have had no success, either because it was removed from the *Times* archives or more likely because my mediocre search skills proved inadequate. But I'm almost certain that the piece had been prompted by the 1983 publication of **Zionism in the Age of the Dictators** by Lenni Brenner, an anti-Zionist of the Trotskyite persuasion and Jewish origins. I only very recently discovered that book, which really tells an extremely interesting story.

Brenner, born in 1937, has spent his entire life as an unreconstructed hard-core leftist, with his enthusiasms ranging from Marxist revolution to the Black Panthers, and he is obviously a captive of his views and his ideology. At times, this background impairs the flow of his text, and the periodic allusions to "proletarian," "bourgeoisie," and "capitalist classes" sometimes grow a little wearisome, as does his unthinking acceptance of all the shared beliefs common to his political circle. But surely only someone with that sort of fervent ideological commitment would have been willing to devote so much time and effort to investigating that controversial subject and ignoring the endless denunciations that resulted, which even included physical assaults by Zionist partisans.

In any event, his documentation seems completely airtight, and some years after the original appearance of his book, he published a companion volume entitled **51 Documents: Zionist Collaboration**

with the Nazis, which simply provides English translations of all the raw evidence behind his analytical framework, allowing interested parties to read the material and draw their own conclusions.

Among other things, Brenner provides considerable evidence that the larger and somewhat more mainstream right-wing Zionist faction later led by future Israeli Prime Minister Menachem Begin was almost invariably regarded as a Fascist movement during the 1930s, even apart from its warm admiration for Mussolini's Italian regime. This was hardly such a dark secret in that period given that its main Palestine newspaper carried a regular column by a top ideological leader entitled "Diary of a Fascist." During one of the major international Zionist conferences, factional leader Vladimir Jabotinsky entered the hall with his brown-shirted followers in full military formation, leading the chair to ban the wearing of uniforms in order to avoid a riot, and his faction was soon defeated politically and eventually expelled from the Zionist umbrella organization. This major setback was largely due to the widespread hostility the group had aroused after two of its members were arrested by British police for the recent assassination of Chaim Arlosoroff, one of the highest-ranking Zionist officials based in Palestine.

Indeed, the inclination of the more right-wing Zionist factions toward assassination, terrorism, and other forms of essentially criminal behavior was really quite remarkable. For example, in 1943 Shamir **had arranged the assassination of his factional rival**, a year after the two men had escaped together from imprisonment for a bank robbery in which bystanders had been killed, and he claimed he had acted to avert the planned assassination of David Ben-Gurion, the top Zionist leader and Israel's future founding-premier. Shamir and his faction certainly continued this sort of behavior into the 1940s, successfully assassinating Lord Moyne, the British Minister for the Middle East, and Count Folke Bernadotte, the UN Peace Negotiator, though they failed in their other attempts to kill **American President Harry Truman** and **British Foreign Minister Ernest Bevin**, and **their plans to assassinate Winston Churchill** apparently never moved past the discussion stage. His group also **pioneered the use of terrorist car-bombs and other explosive attacks against innocent civilian targets,** all long before any Arabs or Muslims had **ever thought of using similar tactics**; and Begin's larger and more "moderate" Zionist faction did much the same. Given that background, it was hardly surprising that Shamir later served as director of assassinations at the Israeli Mossad during 1955-1965, so if the **Mossad did indeed play a major role in the assassination of President John F. Kennedy**, he was very likely involved.

The Nazi-Zionist Economic Partnership of the 1930s

The cover of the 2014 paperback edition of Brenner's book displays the commemorative medal struck by Nazi Germany to mark its Zionist alliance, with a Star-of-David on the front face and a Swastika on the obverse. But oddly enough, this symbolic medallion actually had absolutely no connection with the unsuccessful attempts by Shamir's small faction to arrange a Nazi military alliance during World War II.

Although the Germans paid little attention to the entreaties of that minor organization, the far larger and more influential mainstream Zionist movement of Chaim Weizmann and David Ben-Gurion was something else entirely. And during most of the 1930s, these other Zionists had formed an important economic partnership with Nazi Germany, based upon an obvious commonality of interests. After all, Hitler regarded Germany's one percent Jewish population as a disruptive and potentially dangerous element which he wanted gone, and the Middle East seemed as good a destination for them as any other. Meanwhile, the Zionists had very similar objectives, and the creation of their new national homeland in Palestine obviously required both Jewish immigrants and Jewish financial investment.

After Hitler had been named Chancellor in 1933, outraged Jews worldwide had quickly launched an economic boycott, hoping to bring Germany to its knees, with London's *Daily Express* famously running the banner headline "Judea Declares War on Germany." Jewish political and economic influence, then just like now, was very considerable, and in the depths of the Great Depression, impoverished Germany needed to export or die, so a large scale boycott in major German markets posed a potentially serious threat. But this exact situation provided Zionist groups with an excellent opportunity to offer the Germans a means of breaking that trade embargo, and they demanded favorable terms for the export of high-quality German manufactured goods to Palestine, together with accompanying German Jews. Once word of this major *Ha'avara* or "Transfer Agreement" with the Nazis came out at a 1933 Zionist Convention, many Jews and Zionists were outraged, and it led to various splits and controversies. But the economic deal was too good to resist, and it went forward and quickly grew.

> **Daily Express**
>
> **JUDEA DECLARES WAR ON GERMANY**
> *Jews Of All The World Unite In Action*
>
> **BOYCOTT OF GERMAN GOODS**
>
> MASS DEMONSTRATIONS IN MANY DISTRICTS
>
> DRAMATIC ACTION

The importance of the Nazi-Zionist pact for Israel's establishment is difficult to overstate. According to a 1974 analysis in *Jewish Frontier* cited by Brenner, between 1933 and 1939 over 60% of all the investment in Jewish Palestine came from Nazi Germany. The worldwide impoverishment of the Great Depression had drastically reduced ongoing Jewish financial support from all other sources, and Brenner reasonably suggests that without Hitler's financial backing, the nascent Jewish colony, so tiny and fragile, might easily have shriveled up and died during that difficult period.

Such a conclusion leads to fascinating hypotheticals. When I first stumbled across references to the *Ha'avara* Agreement on websites here and there, one of the commenters mentioning the issue half-jokingly suggested that if Hitler had won the war, statues would surely have been built to him throughout Israel and he would today be recognized by Jews everywhere as the heroic Gentile leader who had played the central role in reestablishing a national homeland for the Jewish people in Palestine after almost 2000 years of bitter exile.

This sort of astonishing counter-factual possibility is not nearly as totally absurd as it might sound to our present-day ears. We must recognize that our historical understanding of reality is shaped by the media, and media organs are controlled by the winners of major wars and their allies, with inconvenient details often excluded to avoid confusing the public. It is undeniably true that in his 1924 book *Mein Kampf*,

Hitler had written all sorts of hostile and nasty things about Jews, especially those who were recent immigrants from Eastern Europe, but when I read the book back in high school, I was a little surprised to discover that these anti-Jewish sentiments hardly seemed central to his text. Furthermore, just a couple of years earlier, a vastly more prominent public figure such as British Minister Winston Churchill had **published sentiments nearly as hostile and nasty**, focusing on the monstrous crimes being committed by Bolshevik Jews. In Albert Lindemann's *Esau's Tears*, I was surprised to discover that the author of the famous Balfour Declaration, the foundation of the Zionist project, was apparently also quite hostile to Jews, with an element of his motivation probably being his desire to exclude them from Britain.

Once Hitler consolidated power in Germany, he quickly outlawed all other political organizations for the German people, with only the Nazi Party and Nazi political symbols being legally permitted. But a special exception was made for German Jews, and Germany's local Zionist Party was accorded complete legal status, with Zionist marches, Zionist uniforms, and Zionist flags all fully permitted. Under Hitler, there was strict censorship of all German publications, but the weekly Zionist newspaper was freely sold at all newsstands and street corners. The clear notion seemed to be that a German National Socialist Party was the proper political home for the country's 99% German majority, while Zionist National Socialism would fill the same role for the tiny Jewish minority.

In 1934, Zionist leaders invited an important SS official to spend six months visiting the Jewish settlement in Palestine, and upon his return, his very favorable impressions of the growing Zionist enterprise were published as a massive 12-part series in Joseph Goebbel's *Der Angriff*, the flagship media organ of the Nazi Party, bearing the descriptive title "A Nazi Goes to Palestine." In his very angry 1920 critique of Jewish Bolshevik activity, Churchill had argued that Zionism was locked in a fierce battle with Bolshevism for the soul of European Jewry, and only its victory might ensure amicable future relations between Jew and Gentile. Based on available evidence, Hitler and many of the other Nazi leaders seemed to have reached a somewhat similar conclusion by the mid-1930s.

During that era extremely harsh sentiments regarding Diaspora Jewry were sometimes found in rather surprising quarters. After the controversy surrounding Shamir's Nazi ties erupted into the headlines, Brenner's material became the grist for an important article by Edward Mortimer, the longtime Middle East expert at the august *Times of London*, and the 2014 edition of the book includes some choice extracts from Mortimer's February 11, 1984 *Times* piece:

> Who told a Berlin audience in March 1912 that "each country can absorb only a limited number of Jews, if she doesn't want disorders in her stomach. Germany already has too many Jews"?
>
> No, not Adolf Hitler but Chaim Weizmann, later president of the World Zionist Organization and later still the first president of the state of Israel.
>
> And where might you find the following assertion, originally composed in 1917 but republished as late as 1936: "The Jew is a caricature of a normal, natural human being, both physically and spiritually. As an individual in society he revolts and throws off the harness of social obligation, knows no order nor discipline"?
>
> Not in *Der Sturmer* but in the organ of the Zionist youth organization, Hashomer Hatzair.
>
> As the above quoted statement reveals, Zionism itself encouraged and exploited self-hatred in the Diaspora. It started from the assumption that anti-Semitism was inevitable and even in a sense justified so long as Jews were outside the land of Israel.
>
> It is true that only an extreme lunatic fringe of Zionism went so far as to offer to join the war on Germany's side in 1941, in the hope of establishing "the historical Jewish state on a national and totalitarian basis, and bound by a treaty with the German Reich." Unfortunately this was the group which the present Prime Minister of Israel chose to join.

The very uncomfortable truth is that the harsh characterizations of Diaspora Jewry found in the pages of *Mein Kampf* were not all that different from what was voiced by Zionism's founding fathers and its subsequent leaders, so the cooperation of those two ideological movements was not really so totally surprising.

However, uncomfortable truths do remain uncomfortable. Mortimer had spent nineteen years at the *Times*, the last dozen of them as the foreign specialist and leader-writer on Middle Eastern affairs. But the year after he wrote that article including those controversial quotations, **his career at that newspaper ended**, leading to an unusual gap in his employment history, and that development may or may not be purely coincidental.

Also quite ironic was the role of Adolf Eichmann, whose name today probably ranks as one of the most famous half-dozen Nazis in history, due to his postwar 1960 kidnapping by Israeli agents, followed by his public show-trial and execution as a war-criminal. As it happens, Eichmann had been a central Nazi figure in the Zionist alliance, even studying Hebrew and apparently becoming something of a philo-Semite during the years of his close collaboration with top Zionist leaders.

Brenner is a captive of his ideology and his beliefs, accepting without question the historical narrative with which he was raised. He seems to find nothing so strange about Eichmann being a philo-Semitic partner of the Jewish Zionists during the late 1930s and then suddenly being transformed into a mass-murderer of the European Jews in the early 1940s, willingly committing the monstrous crimes for which the Israelis later justly put him to death.

This is certainly possible, but I really wonder. A more cynical observer might find it a very odd coincidence that the first prominent Nazi the Israelis made such an effort to track down and kill had been their closest former political ally and collaborator. After Germany's defeat, Eichmann had fled to Argentina and lived there quietly for a number of years until his name resurfaced in a celebrated mid-1950s controversy surrounding one of his leading Zionist partners, then living in Israel as a respected government official, who was denounced as a Nazi collaborator, eventually ruled innocent after a celebrated trial, but later assassinated by former members of Shamir's faction.

Following that controversy in Israel, Eichmann supposedly gave a long personal interview to a Dutch Nazi journalist, and although it wasn't published at the time, perhaps word of its existence may have gotten into circulation. The new state of Israel was just a few years old at that time, and very politically and economically fragile, desperately dependent upon the goodwill and support of America and Jewish donors worldwide. Their remarkable former Nazi alliance was a deeply-suppressed secret, whose public release might have had absolutely disastrous consequences.

According to the version of the interview later published as a two-part story in *Life Magazine*, Eichmann's statements seemingly did not touch upon the deadly topic of the 1930s Nazi-Zionist partnership. But surely Israeli leaders must have been terrified that they might not be so lucky the next time, so we may speculate that Eichmann's elimination suddenly became a top national priority, and he was tracked down and captured in 1960. Presumably, harsh means were employed to persuade him not to reveal any of these dangerous pre-war secrets at his Jerusalem trial, and one might wonder if the reason he was famously kept in an enclosed glass booth was to ensure that the sound could quickly be cut off if he started to stray from the agreed upon script. All of this analysis is purely speculative, but Eichmann's role as a central figure in the 1930s Nazi-Zionist partnership is undeniable historical fact.

Just as we might imagine, America's overwhelmingly pro-Israel publishing industry was hardly eager to serve as a public conduit for Brenner's shocking revelations of a close Nazi-Zionist economic partnership, and he mentions that his book agent uniformly received rejections from each firm he approached, based on a wide variety of different excuses. However, he finally managed to locate an extremely obscure publisher in Britain willing to take on the project, and his book was released in 1983, initially receiving no reviews other than a couple of harsh and perfunctory denunciations, though Soviet *Izvestia* took some interest in his findings until they discovered that he was a hated Trotskyite.

His big break came when Shamir suddenly became Israel's Prime Minister, and he brought his evidence of former Nazi ties to the English-language Palestinian press, which put it into general circulation. Various British Marxists, including the notorious "Red Ken" Livingstone of London, organized a speaking tour for him, and when a group of right-wing Zionist militants attacked one of the events and inflicted injuries, the story of the brawl caught the attention of the mainstream newspapers. Soon afterward the discussion of Brenner's astonishing discoveries appeared in the *Times of London* and entered the international media. Presumably, the *New York Times* article that had originally caught my eye ran sometime during this period.

Public relations professionals are quite skilled at minimizing the impact of damaging revelations, and pro-Israel organizations have no shortage of such individuals. Just before the 1983 release of his remarkable book, Brenner suddenly discovered that a young pro-Zionist author named Edwin Black was furiously working on a similar project, apparently backed by sufficient financial resources that he was employing an army of fifty researchers to allow him to complete his project in record time.

Since the entire embarrassing subject of a Nazi-Zionist partnership had been kept away from the public eye for almost five decades, this timing surely seems more than merely coincidental. Presumably word of Brenner's numerous unsuccessful efforts at securing a mainstream publisher during 1982 had gotten around, as had as his eventual success in locating a tiny one in Britain. Having failed to prevent publication of such explosive material, pro-Israel groups quietly decided that their next best option was trying to seize control of the topic themselves, allowing disclosure of those parts of the story that could not be concealed but excluding items of greatest danger, while portraying the sordid history in the best possible light.

Black's book, *The Transfer Agreement*, may have arrived a year later than Brenner's but was clearly backed by vastly greater publicity and resources. It was released by Macmillan, a leading publisher, ran nearly twice the length of Brenner's short book, and carried powerful endorsements by leading figures from the firmament of Jewish activism, including the Simon Weisenthal Center, the Israel Holocaust Memorial, and the American Jewish Archives. As a consequence, it received long if not necessarily favorable reviews in influential publications such as *The New Republic* and *Commentary*.

In all fairness, I should mention that in the Foreword to his book, Black claims that his research efforts had been totally discouraged by nearly everyone he approached, and as a consequence, he had been working on the project with solitary intensity for many years. This implies the near-simultaneous release of the two books was purely due to chance. But such a picture is hardly consistent with his glowing testimonials from so many prominent Jewish leaders, and personally I find Brenner's claim that Black was assisted by fifty researchers far more convincing.

Since both Black and Brenner were describing the same basic reality and relying upon many of the same documents, in most respects the stories they tell are generally similar. But Black carefully excludes any mention of offers of Zionist military cooperation with the Nazis, let alone the repeated attempts by Shamir's Zionist faction to officially join the Axis Powers after the war had broken out, as well as numerous other details of a particularly embarrassing nature.

Assuming Black's book was published for the reasons I suggested, I think that the strategy of the pro-Israel groups largely succeeded, with his version of the history seeming to have quickly supplanted Brenner's except perhaps in strongly leftist or anti-Zionist circles. Googling each combination of the title and author, Black's book gets eight times as many hits, and his Amazon sales ranks and numbers of reviews are also larger by roughly that same factor. Most notably, neither the Wikipedia articles on "**The Transfer Agreement**" and "**The *Ha'avara* Agreement**" contain any mention of Brenner's research whatsoever, even though his book was published earlier, was far broader, and only he provided the underlying documentary evidence. As a personal example of the current situation, I was quite unaware of the entire *Ha'avara* history until just a few years ago when I encountered some website comments mentioning Black's book, leading me to purchase and read it. But even then, Brenner's far more wide-ranging and explosive volume remained totally unknown to me until very recently.

Hitler's Jewish Soldiers

Once World War II began, this Nazi-Zionist partnership quickly lapsed for obvious reasons. Germany was now at war with the British Empire, and financial transfers to British-run Palestine were no longer possible. Furthermore, the Arab Palestinians had grown quite hostile to the Jewish immigrants whom they rightfully feared might eventually displace them, and once the Germans were forced to choose between maintaining their relationship with a relatively small Zionist movement or winning the political sympathy of a vast sea of Middle Eastern Arabs and Muslims, their decision was a natural one. The Zionists faced a similar choice, and especially once wartime propaganda began so heavily blackening the German and Italian governments, their long previous partnership was not something they wanted widely known.

However, at exactly this same moment a somewhat different and equally long-forgotten connection between Jews and Nazi Germany suddenly moved to the fore.

Like most people everywhere, the average German, whether Jewish or Gentile, was probably not all that political, and although Zionism had for years been accorded a privileged place in German society, it is not entirely clear how many ordinary German Jews paid much attention to it. The tens of thousands who emigrated to Palestine during that period were probably motivated as much by economic pressures as by ideological commitment. But wartime changed matters in other ways.

This was even more true for the German government. The outbreak of a world war against a powerful coalition of the British and French empires, later augmented by both Soviet Russia and the United States, imposed the sorts of enormous pressures that could often overcome ideological scruples. A few years ago, I discovered a fascinating 2002 book by Bryan Mark Rigg, **Hitler's Jewish Soldiers**, a scholarly treatment of exactly what the title implies. The quality of this controversial historical analysis is indicated by the glowing jacket-blurbs from numerous academic experts and an extremely favorable treatment by an eminent scholar in *The American Historical Review*.

Obviously, Nazi ideology was overwhelmingly centered upon race and considered racial purity a crucial factor in national cohesion. Individuals possessing substantial non-German ancestry were regarded with considerable suspicion, and this concern was greatly amplified if that admixture was Jewish. But in a military struggle against an opposing coalition possessing many times Germany's population and industrial resources, such ideological factors might be overcome by practical considerations, and Rigg persuasively argues that some 150,000 half-Jews or quarter-Jews served in the armed forces of the Third Reich, a percentage probably not much different than their share of the general military-age population.

Germany's long-integrated and assimilated Jewish population had always been disproportionately urban, affluent, and well-educated. As a consequence it is not entirely surprising that a large proportion of these part-Jewish soldiers who served Hitler were actually combat officers rather than merely rank-and-file conscripts, and they included at least 15 half-Jewish generals and admirals, and another dozen quarter-Jews holding those same high ranks. The most notable example was Field Marshal Erhard Milch, Hermann Goering's powerful second-in-command, who played such an important operational role in creating the Luftwaffe. Milch certainly had a Jewish father, and according to some much less substantiated claims, perhaps even a Jewish mother as well, while his sister was married to an SS general.

Admittedly, the racially-elite SS itself generally had far stricter ancestry standards, with even a trace of non-Aryan parentage normally seen as disqualifying an individual from membership. But even here, the situation was sometimes complicated, since there were widespread rumors that Reinhard Heydrich, the second-ranking figure in that very powerful organization, actually had considerable Jewish ancestry. Rigg investigates that claim without coming to any clear conclusions, though he does seem to think that the circumstantial evidence involved may have been used by other high-ranking Nazi figures as a point of leverage or blackmail against Heydrich, who stood as one of the most important figures in the Third Reich.

As a further irony, most of these individuals traced their Jewish ancestry through their father rather than their mother, so although they were not Jewish according to rabbinical law, their family names often reflected their partly Semitic origins, though in many cases Nazi authorities attempted to studiously overlook this glaringly obvious situation. As an extreme example noted by an academic reviewer of the book, a half-Jew bearing the distinctly non-Aryan name of Werner Goldberg actually had his photograph prominently featured in a 1939 Nazi propaganda newspaper, with the caption describing him as the "The Ideal German Soldier."

The author conducted more than 400 personal interviews of the surviving part-Jews and their relatives, and these painted a very mixed picture of the difficulties they had encountered under the Nazi regime, which varied enormously depending upon particular circumstances and the personalities of those in authority over them. One important source of complaint was that because of their status, part-Jews were often denied the military honors or promotions they had rightfully earned. However, under especially favorable conditions, they might also be legally reclassified as being of "German Blood," which officially eliminated any taint on their status.

Even official policy seems to have been quite contradictory and vacillating. For example, when the civilian humiliations sometimes inflicted upon the fully Jewish parents of serving half-Jews were brought to Hitler's attention, he regarded that situation as intolerable, declaring that either such parents must be fully protected against those indignities or all the half-Jews must be discharged, and eventually in April 1940 he issued a decree requiring the latter. However, this order was largely ignored by many commanders, or implemented through a honor-system that almost amounted to "Don't Ask, Don't Tell," so a considerable fraction of half-Jews remained in the military if they so wished. And then in July 1941, Hitler somewhat reversed himself, issuing a new decree that allowed "worthy" half-Jews who had been discharged to return to the military as officers, while also announcing that after the war, all quarter-Jews would be reclassified as fully "German Blood" Aryan citizens.

It has been said that after questions were raised about the Jewish ancestry of some of his subordinates, Goering once angrily responded "I will decide who is a Jew!" and that attitude seems to reasonably capture some of the complexity and subjective nature of the social situation.

Interestingly enough, many of part-Jews interviewed by Rigg recalled that prior to Hitler's rise to power, the intermarriage of their parents had often provoked much greater hostility from the Jewish rather than the Gentile side of their families, suggesting that even in heavily-assimilated Germany, the traditional Jewish tendency toward ethnic exclusivity had still remained a powerful factor in that community.

Although the part-Jews in German military service were certainly subject to various forms of mistreatment and discrimination, perhaps we should compare this against the analogous situation in our own military in those same years with regard to America's Japanese or black minorities. During that era, racial intermarriage was legally prohibited across a large portion of the US, so the mixed-race population of those groups was either almost non-existent or very different in origin. And when Japanese-Americans were allowed to leave their wartime concentration camps and enlist in the military, they were entirely restricted to segregated all-Japanese units, but with the officers generally being white. Meanwhile, blacks were almost entirely barred from combat service, though they sometimes served in strictly-segregated support roles. The notion that an American with any appreciable trace of African, Japanese, or for that matter Chinese ancestry might serve as a general or even an officer in the U.S. military and thereby exercise command authority over white American troops would have been almost unthinkable. The contrast with the practice in Hitler's own military is quite different than what Americans might naively believe.

The Racial Focus of Traditional Judaism

This paradox is not nearly as surprising as one might assume. The non-economic divisions in European societies had almost always been along lines of religion, language, and culture rather than racial ancestry, and the social tradition of more than a millennium could not easily be swept away by merely a half-dozen years of National Socialist ideology. During all those earlier centuries, a sincerely-baptized Jew, whether in Germany or elsewhere, was usually considered just as good a Christian as any other. For example, Tomas de Torquemada, the most fearsome figure of the dreaded Spanish Inquisition, actually came from a family of Jewish converts.

Even wider racial differences were hardly considered of crucial importance. Some of the greatest heroes of particular national cultures, such as Russia's Alexander Pushkin and France's Alexandre Dumas, had been individuals with significant black African ancestry, and this was certainly not considered any sort of disqualifying characteristic.

By contrast, American society from its inception had always been sharply divided by race, with other differences generally constituting far smaller impediments to intermarriage and amalgamation. I've seen widespread claims that when the Third Reich devised its 1935 Nuremberg Laws restricting marriage and other social arrangements between Aryans, non-Aryans, and part-Aryans, its experts drew upon some of America's long legal experience in similar matters, and this seems quite plausible. Under that new Nazi statute, pre-existing mixed-marriages received some legal protection, but henceforth Jews and half-Jews could only marry each other, while quarter-Jews could only marry regular Aryans. The obvious intent was to absorb that latter group into mainstream German society, while isolating the more heavily-Jewish population.

Ironically enough, Israel today is one of very few countries with a similar sort of strictly racially-based criteria for citizenship status and other privileges, with **the Jewish-only immigration policy now often enforced by DNA testing**, and marriages between Jews and non-Jews legally prohibited. A few years ago, the world media also carried **the remarkable story** of a Palestinian Arab sentenced to prison for rape because he had had consensual sexual relations with a Jewish woman by passing himself off as a fellow Jew.

Since Orthodox Judaism is strictly matrilineal and controls Israeli law, even Jews of other branches can experience unexpected difficulties due to conflicts between personal ethnic identity and official legal status. The vast majority of the wealthier and more influential Jewish families worldwide do not follow Orthodox religious traditions, and over the generations, they have often taken Gentile wives. However, even if the latter had converted to Judaism, their conversions are considered invalid by the Orthodox Rabbinate, and none of their resulting descendants are considered Jewish. So if some members of these families later develop a deep commitment to their Jewish heritage and immigrate to Israel, they are sometimes outraged to discover that they are officially classified as "goyim" under Orthodox law and legally prohibited from marrying Jews. These major political controversies periodically erupt and **sometimes reach the international media**.

Now it seems to me that any American official who proposed racial DNA tests to decide upon the admission or exclusion of prospective immigrants would have a very difficult time remaining in office, with the Jewish-activists of organizations like the ADL probably leading the attack. And the same would surely be true for any prosecutor or judge who sent non-whites to prison for the crime of "passing" as whites and thereby managing to seduce women from that latter group. A similar fate would befall advocates of such policies in Britain, France, or most other Western nations, with the local ADL-type organization certainly playing an important role. Yet in Israel, such existing laws merely occasion a little temporary embarrassment when they are covered in the international media, and then invariably remain in place after the commotion has died down and been forgotten. These sorts of issues are considered of little more importance than were the past wartime Nazi ties of the Israeli prime minister throughout most of the 1980s.

But perhaps the solution to this puzzling difference in public reaction lies in an old joke. A leftist wit once claimed that the reason America has never had a military coup is that it is the only country in the world that lacks an American embassy to organize such activities. And unlike the U.S., Britain, France, and many other predominately-white countries, Israel has no domestic Jewish-activist organization filling the powerful role of the ADL.

Over the last few years, many outside observers have noted a seemingly very odd political situation in Ukraine. That unfortunate country possesses powerful militant groups, whose public symbols, stated ideology, and political ancestry all unmistakably mark them as Neo-Nazis. Yet those **violent Neo-Nazi elements are all being bankrolled and controlled** by **a Jewish Oligarch** who holds dual Israeli citizenship. Furthermore, that peculiar alliance had been mid-wifed and blessed by some of America's leading Jewish Neocon figures, such as Victoria Nuland, who have successfully used their media influence to keep such explosive facts away from the American public.

At first glance, **a close relationship between Jewish Israelis and European Neo-Nazis** seems as grotesque and bizarre a misalliance as one could imagine, but after recently reading Brenner's fascinating book, my perspective substantially shifted. Indeed, the main difference between then and now is that during the 1930s, Zionist factions represented a very insignificant junior partner to a powerful Third Reich, while these days it is the Nazis who occupy the role of eager suppliants to the formidable power of International Zionism, which now so heavily dominates the American political system and through it, much of the world.

This article is available online at:
https://www.unz.com/runz/american-pravda-jews-and-nazis/

Holocaust Denial
Analyzing the History of a Controversial Movement
The Unz Review, August 27, 2018

Reason Magazine and Holocaust Denial

A few years ago I somehow heard about a ferocious online dispute involving a left-leaning journalist named Mark Ames and the editors of *Reason* magazine, the glossy flagship publication of America's burgeoning libertarian movement. Although I was deep in my difficult programming work, curiosity got the better of me, so I decided to take a look.

During the Immigration Wars of the 1990s, I'd become quite friendly with the *Reason* people, frequently visiting their offices, especially during my "English" campaign of 1998, when I'd located my own political headquarters in the same small Westside LA office building they used. As my content-archiving software project began absorbing more and more of my time during the early 2000s, I'd gradually lost touch with them, but even so, the 40-odd years of their magazine archives had become the first publication I'd incorporated into my system, and I was now pleased to discover that both sides in the ongoing feud had put my software to good use in exploring **those old *Reason* issues.**

Apparently, the libertarians grouped around *Reason* had successfully been making political inroads into Silicon Valley's enormously wealthy technology industry, and had now organized a major conference in San Francisco to gather together their supporters. Their left-leaning rivals decided to nip that project in the bud by highlighting some of the more unsavory ideological positions that mainstream libertarian leaders had once regularly espoused. Perhaps Ron Paul and other libertarians might oppose overseas wars and drug laws, and support cutting taxes and regulations, but they and their Republican Party allies were unspeakably vile on all sorts of other issues, and all "good thinkers" should therefore stay very far away.

The debate began in rather mundane fashion with an article by Ames entitled "**Homophobia, Racism, and the Kochs**" denouncing *Reason* for sharing a platform with a high-ranking Republican Congresswoman of Christian conservative views, as well as the magazine's reliance upon Koch funding and its alleged support for Apartheid South Africa during the 1970s and 1980s. The **response** by the *Reason* editor seemed quite persuasive, and he rightfully dismissed the guilt-by-association attacks. He also outlined the gross errors and omissions in the charges regarding South Africa, and ridiculed Ames as a notoriously error-prone "conspiracy theorist." Surely few outsiders would have paid any attention to such a typical exchange of mudslinging between rival ideological camps.

But then things took a very different turn, and a week later Ames returned with **a 5,000 word article** bearing a title sure to grab attention: "Holocaust Denial." He claimed that in 1976 *Reason* had published an entire special issue devoted to that explosive topic.

Surely everyone on the Internet has encountered numerous instances of Holocaust Denial over the years, but for a respectable magazine to have allotted a full issue to promoting that doctrine was something else entirely. For decades, Hollywood has sanctified the Holocaust, and in our deeply secular society accusations of Holocaust Denial are a bit like shouting "Witch!" in Old Salem or leveling accusations of Trotskyism in the Court of the Red Czar. Progressive Sam Seder's *Majority Report* radio show devoted **a full half-hour segment** to the charges against *Reason*, and Googling "Reason Magazine"+"Holocaust Denial" today yields thousands of hits. This substantial explosion of Internet controversy was what caught my own attention at the time.

My initial reaction was one of puzzlement. *Reason* had been the first periodical I had digitized in my system a dozen years earlier, and surely I would have noticed an entire issue promoting Holocaust Denial. However, I soon discovered that February 1976 had been excluded from the supposedly complete set the magazine had shipped me for processing, an omission that itself raises serious suspicions. But Ames had somehow located a copy in a research library and produced a full PDF, which **he conveniently placed on the Internet to support his accusations**.

Carefully reading his article and then glancing through the contents, I decided that his accusation was technically false but substantially true. Apparently the actual theme of the issue was "Historical Revisionism" and except for a couple of paragraphs buried here and there among the 76 pages, Holocaust Denial never came up, so characterizing it as a Holocaust Denial issue was obviously a grotesque exaggeration. But on the other hand, although few of the authors were familiar to me, it seemed undeniably true that they were numbered among America's more prominent Holocaust Deniers, and most of them were deeply associated with organizations situated in that same camp. Furthermore, there were strong indications that their positions on that topic must certainly have been known to the *Reason* editors who commissioned their pieces.

The clearest case comes when Ames quoted the explicit statements of Dr. Gary North, a prominent libertarian thinker who had served as one of Ron Paul's earliest Congressional aides and later became his longtime partner in politics and business:

> Probably the most far-out materials on World War II revisionism have been the seemingly endless scholarly studies of the supposed execution of 6 million Jews by Hitler. The anonymous author [Hoggan] of 'The Myth of the Six Million' has presented a solid case against the Establishment's favorite horror story—the supposed moral justification for our entry into the war…The untranslated books by the former Buchenwald inmate Prof. Paul Rassinier, have seriously challenged the story…A recent and very inexpensive book in magazine form, *Did Six Million Really Die?*, appeared in 1973, written by Richard Harwood.

A later issue carried a thousand word letter by Prof. Adam Reed of Rockefeller University, a past *Reason* contributor, strongly affirming the mainstream Holocaust narrative by quoting from standard works, and taking Dr. North to task for his citation of Holocaust Denial texts of doubtful quality. But North firmly stood his ground:

> "The second point, that about 6 million Jews really did die in the concentration camps, is one that will be open until the records of the period become fully available. I am not convinced yet, one way or the other. I am happy to have Dr.

Reed's interpretation of the data, but until the publishing companies and academic guild encourage the re-examination of the data, I shall continue to recommend that those interested in revisionist questions read *The Myth of the Six Million* and *Did Six Million Really Die?* as reasonable (though not necessarily irrefutable) pieces of historical revisionism. If a person can't make up his mind, he should do more reading."

Dr. James J. Martin was the lead contributor to the February Revisionism issue, and the preceding January issue had featured an extended Q&A by the editors, with one of the queries directly addressing the controversial topic:

REASON: Dr. Martin, do you believe (1) that the specific charge against the Nazis of having a mass extermination program of several million Jews is true, and (2) that the Allied atrocities were as great or greater than those of the Germans, from your study of the question?

MARTIN: Well, I never made a head count of all who lost their lives in the War-we've seen a wide variety of statistical materials, some of which have been pulled out of thin air. As a consequence, it's hard to make any kind of estimate of this sort, whether ten more were killed on the one side or the other is not a particularly entrancing subject as far as I'm concerned. Whether allegations can be proven it remains to be seen. I don't believe that the evidence of a planned extermination of the entire Jewish population of Europe is holding up. I have been influenced over the years by the works of Paul Rassinier, and he still has to be reckoned with. His works have been ignored for a long time, and sooner or later somebody's going to have to do a decent job of coping with what he has presented. I think Rassinier's general case is sound at the moment and I haven't seen any strong evidence to upset his allegations or his assertions that there was no planned program for the extermination of European Jews. His other main case is that there were no gas chamber extermination programs. The fact that a great many people lost their lives is incontrovertible—that the German concentration camps weren't health centers is well known-but they appear to have been far smaller and much less lethal than the Russian ones.

Another major contributor to the issue was Dr. Austin J. App, and just three years earlier he had published a short book bearing the lurid title *The Six Million Swindle: Blackmailing the German People for Hard Marks with Fabricated Corpses.*

In **a follow-up column** by Ames' own editor, the stunned reactions of various journalists are listed, with one of them Tweeting out "*I had no idea that Reason Magazine was once a haven for Holocaust Revisionism. Holy Moly.*" Despite the **angry obfuscations** of present-day *Reason* staffers, this description seems quite correct.

Indeed, there seems considerable circumstantial evidence that around that time "Holocaust Skepticism" extended rather broadly within the entire nascent libertarian movement. Aside from the sharp critique of the aforementioned Prof. Reed, the overwhelming majority of the reader responses seemed totally favorable, with Samuel Konkin III, editor of *New Libertarian Weekly* and various similar publications, suggesting that the February issue was one of the best they had ever published. David Nolan, founder of America's Libertarian Party, also praised the issue as "outstanding."

The two editors of the issue in question even today remain quite prominent figures at *Reason* and within American libertarianism, while **the masthead** then carried names such as David Brudnoy and Alan Reynolds, who both later became influential figures in conservative and libertarian politics. There seems no evidence of any resignations or angry recriminations following the issue's publication, which seems to have been digested with total equanimity, apparently arousing less rancor than might have been generated by a dispute over monetary policy.

I'd never paid much attention to Holocaust discussions over the years, but the name of Murray Rothbard on the 1976 *Reason* masthead prompted a memory. Rothbard is widely regarded as the founder of modern libertarianism, and I recalled in the 1990s reading somewhere that he had often ridiculed the Holocaust as being total nonsense, which had stuck in my mind as a typical example of libertarian eccentricity. A quick Google search seemed to **confirm my recollection** that Rothbard was an avowed Holocaust Denier.

Although the whole controversy regarding *Reason*'s editorial line of the mid-1970s soon died down, it remained a nagging puzzle in the back of my mind. I'd always been quite skeptical of libertarian ideology, but my *Reason* friends from the 1990s had certainly seemed like smart and rational people to me, hardly raving lunatics of any sort, and two of the ones I'd known best had been the co-editors of the controversial issue in question.

I could easily understand how zealous libertarian ideologues might be swept past the point of rationality on certain matters—perhaps arguing that the police and the army should be abolished as statist institutions—but the factual question of what had or had not happened to the Jews of Europe during World War II hardly fell into that sort of category. Furthermore, libertarianism had always attracted a very large Jewish contingent, especially in its upper ranks, and one of the issue editors came from that background, as did Rothbard and numerous others featured on the masthead. While deranged anti-Semitism is not impossible among Jews, I would think that it is somewhat less likely. Clearly something very odd must have been going on.

I was then too busy with my work to focus on the matter, but some months later I had more time, and began a detailed investigation. My first step was to carefully read the *Reason* articles produced by those controversial writers previously unknown to me. Although those pieces were not Holocaust-related, I thought they might give me a sense of their thinking.

To my surprise, the historiography seemed outstandingly good, and almost certainly accurate based on what I had picked up over the years from perfectly mainstream sources. Dr. Martin's **long article on the notorious framing of "Tokyo Rose"** was probably the best and most comprehensive treatment I had ever encountered on that topic, and Dr. App's analysis of **the tragedy of the Sudeten-Germans** was equally strong, raising several points I had previously not known. Percy Greaves effectively summarized many of **the very suspicious aspects of the Pearl Harbor attack**, and although his case for the prosecution against FDR was certainly not airtight, it accorded with the views presented by numerous scholars in other books on the subject. Moreover, his position was **seconded** by a young Bruce Bartlett, later a prominent Reagan and Bush official, and still later a strong Republican critic of George W. Bush, routinely feted by the *New York Times*. Most of the other writings also seemed of very high quality, including Dr. North's **summary of World War II Revisionism**. In general, the academic scholarship of those articles greatly surpassed anything found in opinion magazines of more recent decades, *Reason* itself included. Those so interested can click on the above links, read the articles in question, and decide for themselves.

Back then, *Reason* was a young and struggling magazine, with a shoestring staff and budget. Publishing articles of such obvious quality was surely a remarkable achievement for which the editors could feel justifiably proud, and the overwhelmingly positive letters they received seemed absolutely warranted. Meanwhile, the nasty attacks by Ames appeared to be those of a mere political hack who may not have even bothered actually reading the articles whose authors he vilified.

As a further sign of Ames' dishonesty, he flung the epithet "Nazi" some two dozen times in his hack-job, along with numerous uses of "anti-Semitic" as well, and Greaves was certainly the subject of many of those slurs. But although Greaves and Bartlett wrote back-to-back articles on exactly the same Pearl Harbor topic, and **according to Wikipedia**, the former was the academic advisor to the latter on that subject, Bartlett's name appears nowhere in Ames's hit-piece, presumably because denouncing a prominent policy expert much beloved by the *New York Times* as an "anti-Semitic Neo-Nazi" might prove self-defeating. Even leaving that aside, accusing the Jewish libertarians running *Reason* of being Nazi propagandists must surely be the sort of charge that would strain the credulity of even the most gullible.

Deborah Lipstadt and Holocaust Denial

With Ames' credibility totally shredded, I decided to carefully reread his article again, looking for what clues I could find to the whole bizarre situation. Academic scholars who publish very good history on certain subjects might still have totally irrational views on others, but normally one would assume otherwise.

It appeared that much of Ames' understanding of the issue had come from a certain Deborah Lipstadt, whom he characterized as a great Holocaust expert. Her name was very vaguely familiar to me as some sort of academic activist, who years before had won a major legal victory over a rightwing British historian named David Irving, and Irving himself received further denunciations in the Ames article.

However, one name did stick out. Apparently based on Lipstadt's information, Ames described Harry Elmer Barnes as "the godfather of American Holocaust denial literature" and Martin's "Holocaust denial guru."

A dozen years earlier, the name "Barnes" would have meant almost nothing to me. But as I produced my content-archiving system and digitized so many of America's most influential publications of the last 150 years, I had soon discovered that many of our most illustrious public intellectuals—Left, Right, and Center—**had been suddenly purged and "disappeared" around 1940** because of their stalwart opposition to FDR's extremely aggressive foreign policy, and Barnes, an eminent historian and sociologist, had been among the most prominent of those. He had been one of the earliest editors at *Foreign Affairs* and for many years afterward his important articles had graced the pages of *The New Republic* and *The Nation*, while even after his fall, he had edited ***Perpetual War for Perpetual Peace***, an important 1953 collection of essays by himself and other once-prominent figures. But to have a figure of such intellectual stature accused of being a Holocaust Denier, let alone the "godfather" of the entire movement, seemed rather bizarre to me.

Since Ames was merely an ignorant political hack transmitting the opinions of others, I focused on Lipstadt, his key source. Anyone who has spent much time on the comment-threads of relatively unfiltered websites has certainly encountered the controversial topic of Holocaust Denial, but I now decided to try to investigate the issue in much more serious fashion. A few clicks on the Amazon.com website, and her 1993 book ***Denying the Holocaust*** arrived in my mailbox a couple of days later, providing me an entrance into that mysterious world.

Reading the book was certainly a tremendous revelation to me. Lipstadt is a professor of Holocaust Studies with an appointment in Emory University's Department of Theology, and once I read the opening paragraph of her first chapter, I decided that her academic specialty might certainly be described as "Holocaust Theology."

> The producer was incredulous. She found it hard to believe that I was turning down an opportunity to appear on her nationally televised show. "But you are writing a book on this topic. It will be great publicity." I explained repeatedly that I would not participate in a debate with a Holocaust denier. The existence of the Holocaust was not a matter of debate. I would analyze and illustrate who they were and what they tried to do, but I would not appear with them...Unwilling to accept my no as final, she vigorously condemned Holocaust denial and all it represented. Then, in one last attempt to get me to change my mind, she asked me a question: "I certainly don't agree with them, but don't you think our viewers should hear the *other side*?"

Lipstadt's absolute horror at having someone actually dispute the tenets of her academic doctrine could not have been more blatant. Surely no zealous theologian of the European Dark Ages would have reacted any differently.

The second chapter of her book supported that impression. Since many of the individuals she castigates as Holocaust Deniers also supported the Revisionist perspective of the underlying causes of the First and Second World Wars, she harshly attacked those schools, but in rather strange fashion. In recent years, blogger Steve Sailer and **others** have ridiculed what they describe as the "point-and-sputter" style of debate, in which a "politically-incorrect" narrative is merely described and then automatically treated as self-evidently false without any accompanying need for actual refutation. This seemed to be the approach that Lipstadt took throughout her rather short book.

For example, she provided a very long list of leading academic scholars, prominent political figures, and influential journalists who had championed Revisionist history, noted that their views disagree with the more mainstream perspective she had presumably imbibed from her History 101 textbooks, and thereby regarded them as fully debunked. Certainly a Christian preacher attempting to refute the evolutionary theories of Harvard's E.O. Wilson by quoting a passage of Bible verse might take much the same approach. But few evangelical activists would be so foolish as to provide a very long list of eminent scientists who all took the same Darwinist position and then attempt to sweep them aside by citing a single verse from Genesis. Lipstadt seems to approach history much like a Bible-thumper, but a particularly dim-witted one. Moreover, many of the authors she attacked had already become familiar to me after a decade of my content-archiving work, and I had found their numerous books quite scholarly and persuasive.

Barnes, in particular, figured quite prominently in Lipstadt's chapter and throughout her book. The index listed his name on more than two dozen pages, and he is repeatedly described as the "godfather" of Holocaust Denial, and its seminal figure. Given such heavy coverage, I eagerly examined all those references and the accompanying footnotes to uncover the shocking statements he must have made during his very long scholarly career.

I was quite disappointed. There was not a single reference I could find to his supposed Holocaust Denial views until just the year before his death at age 79, and even that item is hardly what I had been led to believe. In a 9,300 word article on Revisionism for a libertarian publication, he ridicules a leading Holocaust source for claiming that Hitler had killed 25 million Jews, noting that total was nearly twice their entire worldwide population at the time. In addition, Barnes several times applied the word "allegedly" to the stories of the Nazi extermination scheme, a sacrilegious attitude that appears to have horrified a theologian such as Lipstadt. Finally, in a short, posthumously published review of a book by French scholar Paul Rassiner, Barnes found his estimate of just 1 million to 1.5 million Jewish deaths quite convincing, but his tone suggested that he had never previously investigated the matter himself.

So although that last item technically validated Lipstadt's accusation that Barnes was a Holocaust Denier, her evidence-free claims that he was the founder and leader of the field hardly enhanced her scholarly credibility. Meanwhile, all the many tens of thousands of words I had read by Barnes suggested that he was a careful and dispassionate historian.

A notorious incident that occurred soon after the Bolshevik Revolution came to my mind. Eminent philologist Timofei Florinsky, one of Russia's most internationally renowned academic scholars, was hauled before a revolutionary tribunal for a public interrogation about his views, and one of the judges, a drunken Jewish former prostitute, found his answers so irritating that she drew her revolver and shot him dead right there and then. Given Lipstadt's obvious emotional state, I had a strong suspicion that she might have wished she could deal in a similar fashion with Barnes and the numerous other scholars she denounced. Among other things, she noted with horror that more than two decades after his 1940 purge from public life, Barnes' books were still required reading at both Harvard and Columbia.

All of us reasonably extrapolate what we already know or can easily check against what is more difficult to verify, and the remaining chapters of Lipstadt's book left me very doubtful about the reliability of her work, all of which was written in a similar near-hysterical style. Since she had already been vaguely known to me from her well-publicized legal battle against historian David Irving more than a dozen years earlier, I was hardly surprised to discover that many pages were devoted to vilifying and insulting him in much the same manner as Barnes, so I decided to investigate that case.

I was only slightly surprised to discover that **Irving had been one of the world's most successful World War II historians**, whose remarkable documentary findings had completely upended our knowledge of that conflict and its origins, with his books selling in the many millions. His entire approach to controversial historical issues was to rely as much as possible upon hard documentary evidence, and his total inability to locate any such documents relating to the Holocaust drove Lipstadt and her fellow ethnic-activists into a frenzy of outrage, so after many years of effort they finally managed to wreck his career. Out of curiosity, I read a couple of his shorter books, which seemed absolutely outstanding historiography, written in a very measured tone, quite different from that of Lipstadt, whose own 2005 account of her legal triumph over Irving, *History on Trial*, merely confirmed my opinion of her incompetence.

Lipstadt's first book ***Beyond Belief***, published in 1986, tells an interesting story as well, with her descriptive subtitle being "The American Press and the Coming of the Holocaust, 1933-1945." Much of the volume consists of press clippings from the American print media of that era interspersed with her rather hysterical running commentary, but providing little analysis or judgment. Some of the journalists reported horrifying conditions for Jews in pre-war Germany while others claimed that such stories were wildly exaggerated, with Lipstadt automatically praising the former and denouncing the latter without providing any serious explanation.

Lenni Brenner's remarkable book ***Zionism in the Age of the Dictators*** had been published three years earlier. Although I only discovered it very recently, any half-competent specialist in her own topic would surely have noticed it, yet Lipstadt provided no hint of its existence. Perhaps the reality of the important Nazi-Zionist economic partnership of the 1930s, with Nazi officials traveling to Palestine as honored Zionist guests and leading Nazi newspapers praising the Zionist enterprise might have complicated her simple story of fanatic German Jew-hatred under Hitler steadily rising towards an exterminationist pitch. Her faculty appointment in a Department of Theology seemed very apt.

Lipstadt's wartime coverage was just as bad, perhaps worse. She cataloged perhaps a couple of hundred print news reports, each describing the massacre of hundreds of thousands or even millions of Jews by the Nazis. But she expressed her outrage that so many of these reports were buried deep within the inside pages of newspapers, a placement suggesting that they were regarded as hysterical wartime atrocity propaganda and probably fictional, with the editors sometimes explicitly stating that opinion. Indeed, among these under-emphasized stories was the claim that the Germans had recently killed 1.5 million Jews by individually injecting each one of them in the heart with a lethal drug. And although I don't see any mention of it, around that same time America's top Jewish leader Rabbi Stephen Wise was peddling the absurd report that the Nazis had slaughtered millions of Jews, turning their skins into lampshades and rendering their bodies into soap. Obviously, separating truth from falsehood during a blizzard of wartime propaganda was not nearly as easy as Lipstadt seemed to assume.

Ordinary Americans were apparently even more skeptical than newspaper editors. According to Lipstadt:

Writing in the Sunday *New York Times Magazine*, [Arthur] Koestler cited public opinion polls in the United States in which nine of ten average Americans dismissed the accusations against the Nazis as propaganda lies and flatly stated that they did not believe a word of them.

Lipstadt convincingly demonstrated that very few Americans seem to have believed in the reality of the Holocaust during the Second World War itself, despite considerable efforts by agitated Jewish activists to persuade them. Over the years, I have seen mention of numerous other books making this same basic point, and therefore harshly condemning the American political leaders of the time for having failed "to save the Jews."

Explicit and Implicit Holocaust Denial After World War II

Yet as I began further investigating the history of Holocaust Denial in the wake of the *Reason* contretemps, I was very surprised to discover that this same pattern of widespread disbelief in the Holocaust seems to have continued unabated *after* the end of the war and throughout the 1950s, being particularly strong among high-ranking American military figures, especially top generals and individuals with an Intelligence background, who seemingly would have had the best knowledge of the true events.

Some years ago, I came across a totally obscure 1951 book entitled ***Iron Curtain Over America*** by John Beaty, a well-regarded university professor. Beaty had spent his wartime years in Military Intelligence, being tasked with preparing the daily briefing reports distributed to all top American officials summarizing available intelligence information acquired during the previous 24 hours, which was obviously a position of considerable responsibility.

As a zealous anti-Communist, he regarded much of America's Jewish population as deeply implicated in subversive activity, therefore constituting a serious threat to traditional American freedoms. In particular, the growing Jewish stranglehold over publishing and the media was making it increasingly difficult for discordant views to reach the American people, with this regime of censorship constituting the "Iron Curtain" described in his title. He blamed Jewish interests for the totally unnecessary war with Hitler's Germany, which had long sought good relations with America, but instead had suffered total destruction for its strong opposition to Europe's Jewish-backed Communist menace.

Beaty also sharply denounced American support for the new state of Israel, which was potentially costing us the goodwill of so many millions of Muslims and Arabs. And as a very minor aside, he also criticized the Israelis for continuing to claim that Hitler had killed six million Jews, a highly implausible accusation that had no apparent basis in reality and seemed to be just a fraud concocted by Jews and Communists, aimed at poisoning our relations with postwar Germany and extracting money for the Jewish State from the long-suffering German people.

Furthermore, he was scathing toward the Nuremberg Trials, which he described as a "major indelible blot" upon America and "a travesty of justice." According to him, the proceedings were dominated by vengeful German Jews, many of whom engaged in falsification of testimony or even had criminal backgrounds. As a result, this "foul fiasco" merely taught Germans that "our government had no sense of justice." Sen. Robert Taft, the Republican leader of the immediate postwar era took a very similar position, which later won him the praise of John F. Kennedy in *Profiles in Courage*. The fact that the chief Soviet prosecutor at Nuremberg had played the same role during the notorious Stalinist show trials of the late 1930s, during which numerous Old Bolsheviks confessed to all sorts of absurd and ridiculous things, hardly enhanced the credibility of the proceedings to many outside observers.

Then as now, a book taking such controversial positions stood little chance of finding a mainstream New York publisher, but it was soon released by a small Dallas firm, and then became enormously successful, going through some seventeen printings over the next few years. According to Scott McConnell, founding editor of *The American Conservative*, Beaty's book became the second most popular conservative text of the 1950s, ranking only behind Russell Kirk's iconic classic, *The Conservative Mind*.

Moreover, although Jewish groups including the ADL harshly condemned the book, especially in their private lobbying, those efforts provoked a backlash, and numerous top American generals, both serving and retired, wholeheartedly endorsed Beaty's work, denouncing the ADL efforts at censorship and urging all Americans to read the volume.

Although Beaty's quite explicit Holocaust Denial might shock tender modern sensibilities, at the time it seems to have caused barely a ripple of concern and was almost totally ignored even by the vocal Jewish critics of the work.

Much of this very interesting story is told by Joseph Bendersky, an expert in Holocaust Studies, who devoted ten years of archival research to his 2000 book *The "Jewish Threat."* His work chronicles the extremely widespread anti-Semitism found within the U.S. Army and Military Intelligence throughout the first half of the twentieth century, with Jews being widely regarded as posing a serious security risk. The book runs well over 500 pages, but when I consulted the index I found no mention of the Rosenbergs nor Harry Dexter White nor any of the other very numerous Jewish spies revealed by the Venona Decrypts, and the term "Venona" itself is also missing from the index. Reports of the overwhelmingly Jewish leadership of the Russian Bolsheviks are mostly treated as bigotry and paranoia, as are descriptions of the similar ethnic skew of America's own Communist Party, let alone the heavy financial support of the Bolsheviks by Jewish international bankers. At one point, he dismisses the link between Jews and Communism in Germany by noting that "less than half" of the Communist Party leadership was Jewish; but since fewer than one in a hundred Germans came from that ethnic background, Jews were obviously over-represented among Communist leaders by as much as 5,000%. This seems to typify the sort of dishonesty and innumeracy I have regularly encountered among Jewish Holocaust experts.

Meanwhile, with the copyright having long lapsed, I'm pleased to add Beaty's work to my Controversial HTML Books selection, so individuals interested can read it and decide for themselves:

- **The Iron Curtain Over America**
  John Beaty • 1951 • 82,000 Words

Beaty's very brief 1951 discussion has been the earliest instance of explicit Holocaust Denial I have managed to locate, but the immediate postwar years seem absolutely rife with what might be described as "implicit Holocaust Denial," especially within the highest political circles.

Over the years, Holocaust scholars and activists have very rightfully emphasized the absolutely unprecedented nature of the historical events they have studied. They describe how some six million innocent Jewish civilians were deliberately exterminated, mostly in gas chambers, by one of Europe's most highly cultured nations, and emphasize that monstrous project was often accorded greater priority than Germany's own wartime military needs during the country's desperate struggle for survival. Furthermore, the Germans also undertook enormous efforts to totally eliminate all possible traces of their horrifying deed, with huge resources expended to cremate all those millions of bodies and scatter the ashes. This same disappearance technique was even sometimes applied to the contents of their mass graves, which were dug up long after initial burial, so that the rotting corpses could then be totally incinerated and all evidence eliminated. And although Germans are notorious for their extreme bureaucratic precision, this immense wartime project was apparently implemented without benefit of a single written document, or at least no such document has ever been located.

Lipstadt entitled her first book "Beyond Belief," and I think that all of us can agree that the historical event she and so many others in academia and Hollywood have made the centerpiece of their lives and careers is certainly one of the most extremely remarkable occurrences in all of human history. Indeed, perhaps only a Martian Invasion would have been more worthy of historical study, but Orson Welles's famous *War of the Worlds* radio-play which terrified so many millions of Americans in 1938 turned out to be a hoax rather than real.

The six million Jews who died in the Holocaust certainly constituted a very substantial fraction of all the wartime casualties in the European Theater, outnumbering by a factor of 100 all the British who died during the Blitz, and being dozens of times more numerous than all the Americans who fell there in battle. Furthermore, the sheer monstrosity of the crime against innocent civilians would surely have provided the best possible justification for the Allied war effort. Yet for many, many years after the war, a very strange sort of amnesia seems to have gripped most of the leading political protagonists in that regard.

Robert Faurisson, a French academic who became a prominent Holocaust Denier in the 1970s, once made an extremely interesting observation regarding the memoirs of Eisenhower, Churchill, and De Gaulle:

Three of the best known works on the Second World War are General Eisenhower's *Crusade in Europe* (New York: Doubleday [Country Life Press], 1948), Winston Churchill's *The Second World War* (London: Cassell, 6 vols., 1948-1954), and the *Mémoires de guerre* of General de Gaulle (Paris: Plon, 3 vols., 1954-1959). In these three works not the least mention of Nazi gas chambers is to be found.

Eisenhower's *Crusade in Europe* is a book of 559 pages; the six volumes of Churchill's *Second World War* total 4,448 pages; and de Gaulle's three-volume *Mémoires de guerre* is 2,054 pages. In this mass of writing, which altogether totals 7,061 pages (not including the introductory parts), published from 1948 to 1959, one will find no mention either of Nazi "gas chambers," a "genocide" of the Jews, or of "six million" Jewish victims of the war.

Given that the Holocaust would reasonably rank as the single most remarkable episode of the Second World War, such striking omissions must almost force us to place Eisenhower, Churchill, and De Gaulle among the ranks of "implicit Holocaust Deniers."

Many others seem to fall into that same category. In 1981, Lucy S. Dawidowicz, a leading Holocaust scholar, published a short book entitled ***The Holocaust and the Historians***, in which she denounced so many prominent historians for having totally ignored the reality of the Holocaust for many years following World War II. Indeed, discussion of that topic was almost entirely confined to the Jewish Studies programs which committed ethnic activists had newly established at numerous universities throughout the country. Although Lipstadt's poor scholarly habits and hysterical style hardly impressed me, she appears to have been among the most successful academics who began a career in those ethnic studies departments, which suggests that their average quality was far below her own.

Meanwhile, Dawidowicz emphasized that mainstream histories often entirely omitted the Holocaust from their presentations:

But it is plain from the most cursory review of textbooks and scholarly works by English and American historians that the awesome events of the Holocaust have not been given their historic due. For over two decades some secondary school and college texts never mentioned the subject at all, while others treated it so summarily or vaguely as to fail to convey sufficient information about the events themselves or their historical significance.

With regard to serious scholarship, she notes that when Friedrich Meinecke, universally acknowledged as Germany's most eminent historian, published *The German Catastrophe* in 1946, he harshly denounced Hitler as the leader of "a band of criminals" but made absolutely no mention of the Holocaust, which surely would have represented the height of such criminality. Major British accounts of Hitler and World War II by leading historians such as A.J.P. Taylor, H.R. Trevor-Roper, and Alan Bullock were almost as silent. A similar situation occurred in America as late as 1972 when the massive 1,237 page *Columbia History of the World*, having a Jewish co-editor, devoted a full chapter to World War II but confined its discussion of the Holocaust to just two short and somewhat ambiguous sentences. One almost gets a sense that many of these experienced professional historians regarded discussion of the Holocaust as a considerable embarrassment, a subject that they sought to avoid or at least completely minimize.

Dawidowicz even castigates *Slaughterhouse-Five*, the 1969 fictional masterpiece by Kurt Vonnegut, for its bald assertion that the firebombing of Dresden was "the greatest massacre in European history," a claim that seems to reduce the Holocaust to non-existence.

I myself had noticed something similar just a couple of years before Dawidowicz's book appeared. The English translation of German journalist Joachim Fest's widely praised *Hitler* had been published in 1974 and I had read it a few years later, finding it just as excellent as the critics had indicated. But I remember being a little puzzled that the 800 page book contained no more than a couple of pages discussing the Nazi death camps and the word "Jews" never even appeared in the index.

The vast majority of Hitler's Jewish victims came from Russia and the Eastern European nations included in the Soviet Bloc. That was also the location of all the extermination camps that are the central focus of Holocaust scholars, and therefore the Soviets were the source of most of the key evidence used at the Nuremberg Trials. Yet Dawidowicz notes that after Stalin grew increasingly suspicious of Jews and Israel a few years after the end of the war, virtually all mention of the Holocaust and German wartime atrocities against Jews vanished from the Soviet media and history books. A similar process occurred in the Warsaw Pact satellites, even while the top Communist Party leadership of many of those countries often remained very heavily Jewish for some years. Indeed, I recall reading quite a number of newspaper articles mentioning that after the Berlin Wall fell and the sundered halves of Europe were finally reunited, most Eastern Europeans had never even heard of the Holocaust.

These days, my morning newspapers seem to carry Holocaust-related stories with astonishing frequency, and probably no event of the twentieth century looms so large in our public consciousness. According to public survey data, even as far back as 1995, some 97% of Americans knew of the Holocaust, far more than were aware of the Pearl Harbor attack or America's use of the atomic bombs against Japan, while less than half our citizenry were aware that the Soviet Union had been our wartime ally. But I'd suspect that anyone who drew his knowledge from the mainstream newspapers and history books during the first couple of decades after the end of the Second World War might never have even been aware that any Holocaust had actually occurred.

In 1999 Peter Novick published a book on this general theme entitled ***The Holocaust in American Life***, citing that survey, and his introduction began by noting the very strange pattern the Holocaust exhibited in its cultural influence, which seems quite unique among all major historical events. In the case of almost all other searing historical occurrences such as the massive bloodshed of the Somme or the bitter Vietnam War, their greatest impact upon popular consciousness and media came soon afterward, with the major books and films often appearing within the first five or ten years when memories were fresh, and the influence peaking within a couple of decades, after which they were gradually forgotten.

Yet in the case of the Holocaust, this pattern was completely reversed. Hardly anyone discussed it for the first twenty years after the end of the World War II, while it gradually moved to the center of

American life in the 1970s, just as wartime memories were fading and many of the most prominent and knowledgeable figures from that era had departed the scene. Novick cites numerous studies and surveys demonstrating that this lack of interest and visibility certainly included the Jewish community itself, which had seemingly suffered so greatly under those events, yet apparently had almost completely forgotten about them during the 1950s and much of the 1960s.

I can certainly confirm that impression from my personal experience. Prior to the mid- or late-1970s, I had had only the vaguest impression that virtually all the Jews and Gypsies of Europe had been exterminated during the Second World War, and although the term "Holocaust" was in widespread use, it invariably referred to a "Nuclear Holocaust," a term long-since supplanted and scarcely used today. Then, after the Berlin Wall fell, I was quite surprised to discover that Eastern Europe was still filled with vast numbers of unexterminated Gypsies, who quickly flooded into the West and provoked all sorts of political controversies.

The Rediscovery of the Holocaust

The late scholar Raul Hilberg is universally acknowledged as the founder of modern Holocaust studies, which began with the 1961 publication of his massive volume *The Destruction of the European Jews*. In **his very interesting 2007 Hilberg obituary**, historian Norman Finkelstein emphasizes that prior to Hilberg's work, there had been virtually no writing on the Holocaust, and discussion of the topic was considered almost "taboo." For a recent event of such apparent enormity to have been so completely wiped away from public discussion and the consciousness of historians and political scientists can be explained in several different ways. But once I began to investigate the circumstances behind Hilberg's ground-breaking work, I encountered all sorts of strange ironies.

According to Wikipedia, Hilberg's family of Austrian Jews coincidentally arrived in the United States on the exact day in 1939 that war broke out, and in his early teens he was soon horrified to read all the news reports of the ongoing extermination of his fellow Jews in the continent his family had left behind, even telephoning Jewish leaders asking why they were doing so little to save their kinsmen from annihilation. He subsequently served in the U.S. military in Europe, then majored in Political Science at Brooklyn College after the end of the conflict. The inspiration for his future scholarly focus seems to have come when he was shocked by a remark made by one of his lecturers, Hans Rosenberg:

> The most wicked atrocities perpetrated on a civilian population in modern times occurred during the Napoleonic occupation of Spain.

When Hilberg asked how Rosenberg, himself a German-Jewish refugee, could have so totally ignored the murder of 6 million Jews, a monstrous crime committed just a couple of years earlier, Rosenberg sought to deflect the question, saying that "it was a complicated matter" and "history doesn't teach down into the present age." Since Rosenberg was a student of Meinecke, whom Lipstadt has bitterly denounced as an implicit Holocaust Denier, one wonders whether Rosenberg may have shared the beliefs of his mentor but was reluctant to admit that fact to his overwhelmingly Jewish students in emotionally-charged postwar Brooklyn.

Later, Hilberg conducted his doctoral research at Columbia under Franz Neumann, another German-Jewish refugee scholar. But when Hilberg indicated he wanted his research to focus on the extermination of Europe's Jews, Neumann strongly discouraged that topic, warning Hilberg that doing so would be professionally imprudent and might become "his academic funeral." When he attempted to publish his research in book form, it received numerous negative reviews, with Israel's Yad Vashem fearing it would encounter "hostile criticism," and over a six year period, it was rejected by several major publishing houses along with Princeton University, based on the advice of the influential Jewish intellectual Hannah Arendt. One naturally wonders whether all these established scholars may have quietly known something that a naive young doctoral candidate such as Hilberg did not. His book only appeared in print because a Jewish immigrant whose business had suffered under the Nazis funded the entire publication.

I'd never paid much attention to Holocaust issues, but the supporters of my local Palo Alto Library operate a monthly book sale, and with serious nonfiction hardcovers often priced at just a quarter each, my personal library has grown by hundreds of volumes over the years, now including several of the thickest and most influential Holocaust texts. Aside from Hilberg's classic volume, these include Nora Levin's *The Holocaust* (1968), Lucy Dawidowicz's *The War Against the Jews, 1933-1945* (1975), Martin Gilbert's *The Holocaust* (1985), and Daniel Goldhagen's *Hitler's Willing Executioners* (1996).

I claim absolutely no expertise in Holocaust issues, and analyzing the evidence and argumentation these voluminous works offer is entirely beyond my ability. But I decided to attempt to assess their overall credibility by exploring a few particular items, without actually bothering to read the thousands of pages of text they encompassed.

Consider the interesting case of Field Marshal Erhard Milch, Hermann Goering's very powerful number-two in the German Luftwaffe. His father was certainly a Jew, and according to researchers Robert Wistrich and Louis Snyder, there is archival evidence that his mother was Jewish as well. Now it is certainly not impossible that a Third Reich supposedly dedicated with grim fanaticism to the extermination of each and every Jew might have spent the entire war with a full- or half-Jew near the absolute top of its military hierarchy, but surely that puzzling anomaly would warrant careful explanation, and Milch's apparent Jewish background was certainly known during the Nuremberg Trials.

Yet when I carefully consulted the very comprehensive indexes of those five books, totaling over 3,500 pages, there is virtually no discussion of Milch, except a few very brief mentions of his name in connection with various military operations. Either the authors were unaware of Milch's Jewish background, or perhaps they hoped to keep that fact away from their readers lest it cause "confusion." Neither of these possibilities enhances the trust we should place in their research skills or their scholarly objectivity.

Indeed, the fascinating and widely-praised 2002 book *Hitler's Jewish Soldiers* by Bryan Mark Rigg notes that aside from Milch, Hitler's military contained over a dozen half-Jewish generals and admirals and another dozen quarter-Jews of that same high rank, plus a total of roughly 150,000 additional half- or quarter-Jewish soldiers, with a large fraction of these being officers. All of these individuals would have had some fully-Jewish parents or grand-parents, which seems decidedly odd behavior for a regime supposedly so focused on the total eradication of the Jewish race.

Another obvious matter casts further doubt upon the historical quality of those five immensely thick volumes of standard Holocaust narrative, which together occupy nearly a linear foot on my bookshelves. For prosecutors of any crime, establishing a plausible motive is certainly an important goal, and in the case of the Jewish Holocaust, these authors would seem to have an easy task at hand. Hitler and his German colleagues had always claimed that the Jews overwhelmingly dominated Bolshevik Communism, and much of their struggle against the former was in order to prevent further bloody deeds of the latter. So surely devoting an early chapter or so to describing this central Nazi doctrine would provide an airtight explanation of what drove the Nazis to their fiendish slaughters, rendering fully explicable the horrifying events that would occupy the remainder of their text.

Yet oddly enough, an examination of their indexes for "Bolsheviks," "Communism," and all variants reveals almost no discussion of this important issue. Goldhagen's 1996 book provides just a couple of short sentences spread across his 600 pages, and the other works seem to contain virtually nothing at all. Since all of these Holocaust books almost totally avoid Hitler's self-declared motive for his anti-Jewish actions, they are forced to desperately search for alternative explanations, seeking clues buried deep within the German past or turning to psychoanalytical speculations or perhaps deciding that what they describe as the greatest massacre in all human history was undertaken out of sheer Nazi wickedness.

The obvious reason for this glaring omission is that the authors are constructing a morality-play in which the Jews must be portrayed as absolutely blameless victims, and even hinting at their role in the numerous Communist atrocities that long preceded the rise of the Third Reich might cause readers to consider both sides of the issue. When purported historians go to absurd lengths to hide such glaring facts, they unmask themselves as propagandists, and we must be very cautious about trusting their reliability and candor in all other matters, whether great or small.

Indeed, the topic of Communism raises a far larger issue, one having rather touchy implications. Sometimes two simple compounds are separately inert, but when combined together may possess tremendous explosive force. From my introductory history classes and readings in high school, certain things had always seemed glaringly obvious to me even if the conclusions remained unmentionable, and I once assumed they were just as apparent to most others as well. But over the years I have begun to wonder whether perhaps this might not be correct.

Back in those late Cold War days, the death toll of innocent civilians from the Bolshevik Revolution and the first two decades of the Soviet Regime was generally reckoned at running well into the tens of millions when we include the casualties of the Russian Civil War, the government-induced famines, the Gulag, and the executions. I've heard that these numbers have been substantially revised downwards to perhaps as little as twenty million or so, but no matter. Although determined Soviet apologists may dispute such very large figures, they have always been part of the standard narrative history taught within the West.

Meanwhile, all historians know perfectly well that the Bolshevik leaders were overwhelmingly Jewish, with three of the five revolutionaries Lenin named as his plausible successors coming from that background. Although only around 4% of Russia's population was Jewish, a few years ago Vladimir Putin stated that **Jews constituted perhaps 80-85% of the early Soviet government**, an estimate fully consistent with the contemporaneous claims of **Winston Churchill**, *Times of London* correspondent **Robert Wilton**, and the officers of **American Military Intelligence**. Recent books by **Alexander Solzhenitsyn**, **Yuri Slezkine**, and **others** have all painted a very similar picture. And prior to World War II, Jews remained enormously over-represented in the Communist leadership, especially dominating the Gulag administration and the top ranks of the dreaded NKVD.

Both of these simple facts have been widely accepted in America throughout my entire lifetime. But combine them together with the relatively tiny size of worldwide Jewry, around 16 million prior to World War II, and the inescapable conclusion is that in per capita terms Jews were the greatest mass-murderers of the twentieth century, holding that unfortunate distinction by an enormous margin and with no other nationality coming even remotely close. And yet, by the astonishing alchemy of Hollywood, the greatest killers of the last one hundred years have somehow been transmuted into being seen as the greatest victims, a transformation so seemingly implausible that future generations will surely be left gasping in awe.

Today's American Neocons are just as heavily Jewish as were the Bolsheviks of a hundred years ago, and they have greatly benefited from the political immunity provided by this totally bizarre inversion of historical reality. Partly as a consequence of their media-fabricated victimhood status, they have managed to seize control over much of our political system, especially our foreign policy, and have spent the last few years doing their utmost to foment an absolutely insane war with nuclear-armed Russia. If they do manage to achieve that unfortunate goal, they will surely outdo the very impressive human body-count racked up by their ethnic ancestors, perhaps even by an order-of-magnitude or more.

Holocaust Frauds and Confusions

Since the Holocaust only became a major public topic after wartime memories had grown dim, the story has always seemed to suffer from the problems traditionally associated with "recovered memory syndrome." Truths and falsehoods were often mixed together in strange ways, and the door was opened wide to an astonishing number of outright frauds and liars.

For example, in the late 1970s I remember many of my high school classmates devouring *The Painted Bird* by Jerzy Kosinski, perhaps the first widely popular Holocaust memoir. But then a few years later, the media revealed that Kosinski's national best-seller was simply fraudulent, and the plagiarizing author eventually committed suicide. Indeed, there have been **so many fake Holocaust memoirs over the years** that they nearly constitute a literary genre of their own.

Probably the most world's most famous Holocaust survivor was Elie Wiesel, who parlayed the stories of his wartime suffering into becoming an enormous political celebrity. His career was capped with a Nobel Peace Prize in 1986, and the announcement declared him "a messenger to mankind." Yet journalist **Alexander Cockburn has per-**

suasively argued that Wiesel was simply a fraud, and his famous autobiographical work *Night* just another literary hoax.

Although the iconic figure of "the Six Million" has been endlessly repeated by our media, the estimated numbers of the dead have actually been shockingly variable over the years. Although I never paid much attention to Holocaust issues, I have closely read my major newspapers and magazines for decades, and had regularly seen the statement that the Nazi death machine had brutally exterminated five million Gentiles along with the six million Jews. But just last year, I was stunned to discover that former total was simply a whole-cloth invention by prominent Holocaust-activist Simon Wiesenthal, **who simply made the figure up one day** with the intent of giving non-Jews more of a stake in the Holocaust story. And despite being based on absolutely no evidence or research, his casual claim was never effectively refuted by actual Holocaust scholars, who knew it to be total nonsense, and therefore it was so regularly repeated in the media that I probably read it hundreds of times over the years, always assuming it had some firm grounding in proven reality.

Similarly, for decades I had always read the undeniable fact that the Nazis had exterminated 4 million inmates at Auschwitz, with most of the victims being Jews, and Lipstadt certainly treated that number as absolutely rock-solid historical reality. But in the early 1990s after the fall of Communism, **the official total was quietly revised downwards to as little as 1.1 million**. The fact that a sudden reduction in the official Holocaust body-count by 3 million has had so little impact upon our public Holocaust media narrative hardly seems to inspire great confidence in either the total figures or the media reporting of them.

Over the last couple of generations, our media has engraved that figure of Six Million so deeply onto the minds of every Western citizen that the meaning of the iconic number is universally understood, and those who question it risk a prison sentence in many European countries. Yet its actual origin is somewhat obscure. According to some accounts, Jewish groups lobbied President Truman into casually inserting it into one of his speeches, and thereafter it has endlessly echoed in the media down to the present day. Some angry Internet activist has put together a graphic displaying extracts from dozens of *New York Times* stories between 1869 and 1941 all citing the figure of 6 million Eastern European Jews as being threatened with death, suggesting that our official Holocaust body-count actually predated World War II by as much as three generations. I really wouldn't be surprised if that might be the original source of the number.

The New York Times
Expect the World®

"Holocaust" and "6 million Jews" stories brought to you ever since 1869 by Jew-owned "Newspaper of Record"

Oct 31, 1869	RELIGIOUS INTELLIGENCE.
Feb 10, 1889	
Sep 12, 1891	AN INDICTMENT OF RUSSIA
Mar 15, 1896	
Jun 11, 1900	ZIONISTS' MASS MEETING
Nov 27, 1902	
May 16th, 1903	MORE DETAILS OF THE KISHINEFF MASSACRE
Sept 16th, 1903	THE MACEDONIAN MASSACRES.
Oct 20, 1904	ZANGWILL HERE TO AID JEWISH COLONY SCHEME
Jan 29, 1905	END OF ZIONISM, MAYBE.
Nov 1, 1905	
Mar 25, 1906	Dr. Paul Nathan's View of Russian Massacre
Mar 13, 1910	MANY JEWS FLEE FROM RUSSIA
Apr 11, 1910	RUSSIAN JEWS IN SAD PLIGHT.
Oct 31, 1911	CHURCHES IN PLEA TO CZAR FOR JUSTICE
Dec 10, 1911	CONDITION OF JEWS IN RUSSIA WORST IN ITS HISTORY
Dec 2, 1914	APPEAL FOR AID FOR JEWS.
Jan 14, 1915	JEWS' INDIFFERENCE TO WAR AID REBUKED / MILLIONS IN DIRE DISTRESS
Oct 18, 1918	$1,000,000,000 FUND TO REBUILD JEWRY
Sep 8, 1919	UKRAINIAN JEWS AIM TO STOP POGROMS
Nov 12, 1919	TELLS SAD PLIGHT OF JEWS.
Apr 12, 1920	HOOVER PLEA NETS $1,600,000 FOR JEWS
May 3, 1920	ASK $1,500,000 HERE FOR EUROPE'S NEEDY
May 9, 1920	JEWISH CAMPAIGN EXTENDED A WEEK
May 16, 1920	NEW YORK CITY LAGS IN JEWISH CAMPAIGN
Jul 20, 1921	BEGS AMERICA SAVE 6,000,000 IN RUSSIA
Mar 29, 1933	ALDERMEN VOTE HITLER PROTEST
June 1st, 1933	GERMAN POET IS SAFE.
Sep 8, 1935	
May 31st, 1936	AMERICANS APPEAL FOR JEWISH REFUGEE
Aug 8, 1936	
Feb 23, 1938	"Jewish Tragedy" Pictured
May 2, 1938	NATION IS WARNED OF ANTI-SEMITISM
Jan 15, 1939	MASARYK TO WORK FOR ZIONIST CAUSE
Jan, 1939	3 JEWISH GROUPS UNITE FOR REFUGEES
Oct 2nd, 1941	YOM KIPPUR ENDS IN PLEA FOR PEACE
Jan 8, 1945	
Feb 11, 1945	WORSE PLIGHT SEEN FOR EUROPE'S JEWS; Palestine Agency Official Says Most of 1,200,000 Survivors Seek Havens in Zion
Feb 17, 1945	Schwartz Says Only 1,500,000 Jews Are Left In Europe as Result of German Murders

Sometimes the creation of a new Holocaust hoax was only narrowly averted. Throughout most of the twentieth century, Jews and blacks had been close political allies in America, with the top leadership of the NAACP almost invariably being Jewish, as were nearly all of Martin Luther King, Jr.'s top white advisors and a very large fraction of the key white activists involved in the black Civil Rights movement of the 1950s and 1960s. But by the late 1960s, a schism had erupted, with many younger black activists becoming deeply hostile to what they perceived as overwhelming Jewish influence, while more militant blacks, whether Muslim or otherwise, began siding with the Palestinians against Zionist Israel. This growing conflict became especially bitter during Jesse Jackson's presidential campaign of 1988 and reached a flash-point in the New York City of the early 1990s.

A couple of film-makers sought to help heal this rift by producing a major 1992 PBS documentary entitled *The Liberators*, recounting how black American troops had been among the first units that captured the Buchenwald and Dachau concentration camps, thereby freeing the tens of thousands of Jewish inmates from Nazi captivity. A historical narrative of such deep symbolic resonance quickly attracted overwhelming support from both black leaders and Jewish ones, with Jesse Jackson sharing the stage with Holocaust survivors and numerous Jewish luminaries at the Harlem premiere, and the film received an Oscar nomination. However, in early Febuary 1993 Jeffrey Goldberg took to the pages of *The New Republic* **to reveal that the story was merely a hoax**, based on falsified history. Although the film's Jewish co-producer angrily denounced her critics as racists and Holocaust Deniers, those charges stuck, and were eventually reported in the **New York Times** and other major media outlets. The leading Jewish organizations and Holocaust centers that had been heavily promoting the film soon distanced themselves, and in 2013 *The Times of Israel* **even marked the twenty-year anniversary** of what it described as a notorious hoax. But I suspect that if matters had gone a little differently, the story might soon have become so deeply embedded in the canonical Holocaust narrative that anyone questioning the facts would have been vilified as a racist.

A few years earlier, *The New Republic* had actually been in the forefront of promoting a different hoax also relating to Jewish issues, one with potentially enormous international political significance. In 1984 Joan Peters, an obscure Jewish writer, published a major historical work claiming that her extensive archival research revealed that the bulk of the present-day Palestinians were actually not native to Palestine, but instead were recently-arrived immigrants, drawn there by the heavy economic development produced by the Zionist settlers who had actually preceded them.

Her shocking findings received hundreds of glowing reviews and academic endorsements across the entire spectrum of the mainstream and elite American media, and her book quickly became a huge bestseller. Leading Jewish Holocaust luminaries such as Dawidowicz and Wiesel took center stage in praising her remarkable scholarship, which seemed likely to completely demolish the claims of the expelled Palestinians, thereby reshaping the nature of the Middle East conflict to Israel's great advantage.

However, a young graduate student in History at Princeton named Norman Finkelstein had considerable interest in the history of Zionism, and being very much surprised by her findings, decided to investigate those claims. Once he began carefully checking her footnotes and her alleged sources, he discovered they were entirely fraudulent, and her groundbreaking research merely amounted to a hoax, which some later suggested had been concocted by an intelligence organization and merely published under her name.

Although Finkelstein widely distributed **his important findings**, they were totally ignored by all the American journalists, scholars, and media organizations he contacted, **with the sole exception of Noam Chomsky**, and the growing Joan Peters Hoax might have destroyed the legal basis of the international Palestinian claims to their own Palestine homeland. But some independent-minded British publications eventually picked up his information, and the resulting wave of media embarrassment caused the Peters claims to fade into oblivion. Meanwhile, Finkelstein himself suffered severe retaliation as a consequence, and according to Chomsky was completely blacklisted by his Princeton department and the wider academic community.

More than a dozen years later, Finkelstein's work became the focus of a second major controversy. In the late 1990s, international Jewish organizations launched a major effort to extract many billions of dollars from the largest Swiss banks, arguing that such funds were the rightful property of European Jews who had died in the Holocaust. When the banks initially resisted, arguing that no solid evidence was being presented for such enormous claims, they were harshly denounced by America's Jewish-dominated media, and Jewish lobbying led the American government to threaten them with severe financial sanctions that could have destroyed their businesses. Faced with such serious extortionate pressure, the banks finally gave way and paid out the bulk of the funds being demanded, with those billions mostly retained by the Jewish organizations leading the campaign and spent on their own projects since the purported Jewish heirs were impossible to locate.

This situation led historian Finkelstein to publish a short book in 2000 entitled ***The Holocaust Industry***, in which he harshly critiqued what he characterized as a global Jewish money-making enterprise aimed at unfairly extracting wealth on behalf of the supposed Holocaust victims, often with little regard for truth or fairness. Although almost entirely ignored by the American media, it became a major bestseller in Europe, which eventually forced American publications to give it some attention. Among other things, Finkelstein noted that more than a half-century after the end of the Holocaust, the number of officially designated Holocaust survivors had grown so large that simple mortality considerations seemed to imply that huge numbers of European Jews must have survived the war. This obviously raised serious questions about how many might have actually died during that conflict and its accompanying Holocaust.

Over the years, I had noticed the same sorts of media reports claiming enormous totals of Holocaust survivors still alive now six or seven decades after the event. For example, even as late as 2009 an official at Israel's Jewish Agency justified laws criminalizing Holocaust Denial by **explaining** that almost 65 years after the end of the war "there are still hundreds of thousands of living Holocaust survivors," a statement which itself seemed to constitute rather explicit Holocaust Denial. Indeed, a very noticeable number of all the *New York Times* obituaries I read these days in my morning newspaper seem to include Holocaust survivors still expiring in their eighties and nineties.

Anyone who reads **serious history books** knows that Jews have generally enjoyed a reputation for producing many of the world's greatest swindlers and frauds, hardly surprising given **their notorious tendency to lie and dissemble**. Meanwhile, the Jewish community also seems to contain far more than its fair share of the emotionally disturbed and the mentally ill, and perhaps as a consequence has served as a launching-pad for many of the world's religious cults and fanatic ideological movements. Any exploration of the Holocaust certainly tends to support this rather negative appraisal.

The Holocaust and Hollywood

Although the Holocaust began to enter American consciousness during the 1960s and 1970s with the publication of major books by Hilberg, Levin, Dawidowicz, and others, together with the resulting articles and reviews that these generated, the initial social impact was probably not substantial, at least outside the Jewish community. Even highly successful books selling in the many tens of thousands of copies would have had little impact in a population of more than 200 million.

Our media completely shapes our perceived reality of the world, and although intellectuals and many of the highly educated are greatly influenced by books and other forms of printed content, the vast majority of the population understands the world through electronic media, especially that of popular entertainment.

Consider, for example, the 1974 publication of *Time on the Cross: The Economics of American Negro Slavery*, a magisterial two volume analysis by economists Robert William Fogel and Stanley L. Engerman. By applying quantitative methods, the study overturned generations of assumptions about that American social institution, demonstrating that black slaves in the South were encouraged to marry and maintain their households, while having diets and medical care comparable to that of the free white population and often superior to that of Northern industrial wage-earners. Moreover, following emancipation the life expectancy of freedmen declined by ten percent and their illnesses increased by twenty per cent. All of this is summarized in the extensive **Wikipedia entry**.

Although their results were controversial, the authors had the strongest possible academic credentials, with Fogel, an eminent scholar, being a leading figure in a school of economics who went on to win a Nobel Prize. And Fogel's ideological credentials were even more robust, given that he had had a lifelong commitment to black Civil Rights starting with the eight years he had spent as a young Communist Party organizer, while his 1949 marriage to a black woman had often subjected the couple to the indignities of the anti-miscegenation laws of that era. Consequently, their findings received unprecedented coverage in the mainstream media for an academic study and surely influenced numerous historians and journalists. Yet I think the long-term impact upon popular perceptions about slavery has been almost nil.

By contrast, in 1976 the *ABC* television network ran the prime-time miniseries *Roots*, a multi-generational account of a slave family. The story closely adhered to the traditionally harsh slavery narrative, while supposedly being based upon the recorded family history of Alex Haley, the author of the best-selling book of that same title. But although his work was later found to be fraudulent and apparently plagiarized, the ratings were stellar and the social impact enormous due to the audience of 100 million Americans who watched those episodes. Thus, even the most impressive written scholarship had absolutely no chance of competing with fictionalized television drama.

All three of America's television networks were under Jewish ownership or control, so it was hardly surprising that two years later *ABC* decided to repeat this process with the 1978 television miniseries *Holocaust*, which also achieved an audience of 100 million and generated enormous profits. It seems quite possible this may have been the first time many American families discovered that colossal but almost entirely invisible event of World War II.

The following year, William Styron published *Sophie's Choice*, a heart-rending tale involving deeply buried memories of the extermination of Christian Polish children in the Auschwitz gas chambers. Although such an occurrence was absolutely contrary to the doctrines of all Jewish Holocaust scholars, the novel became a huge national best-seller anyway, and a 1982 film of the same name soon followed, with Meryl Streep winning an Oscar for Best Actress. A decade later, Steven Spielberg's 1993 *Schindler's List* won a remarkable seven Oscars, while grossing nearly $100 million.

With **Hollywood so overwhelmingly Jewish**, the consequences were hardly surprising, and a huge cinematic genre soon developed. According to Finkelstein, Hollywood produced some 180 Holocaust films just during the years 1989-2004. Even the very partial subset of **Holocaust films listed on Wikipedia** has grown enormously long, but fortunately the Movie Database has winnowed down the catalog by providing a list of **the 50 Most Moving Holocaust Films.**

Many billions of dollars have surely been invested over the years on the total production costs of this ongoing business enterprise. For most ordinary people, "seeing is believing," and how could anyone seriously doubt the reality of the Holocaust after having seen all the gas chambers and mounds of murdered Jewish corpses constructed by highly-paid Hollywood set designers? Doubting the existence of Spiderman and the Incredible Hulk would be almost as absurd.

Some 2% of Americans have a Jewish background, while perhaps 95% possess Christian roots, but **the Wikipedia list of Christian films** seems rather scanty and rudimentary by comparison. Very few of those films were ever widely released, and the selection is stretched to even include *The Chronicles of Narnia*, which contains no mention of Christianity whatsoever. One of the very few prominent exceptions on the list is Mel Gibson's 2004 *The Passion of the Christ,* which he was forced to personally self-fund. And despite the enormous financial success of that movie, one of the most highly profitable domestic releases of all time, the project rendered Gibson a hugely vilified pariah in the industry over which he had once reigned as its biggest star, especially after word got around that **his own father was a Holocaust Denier.**

In many respects, Hollywood and the broader entertainment media today provide the unifying spiritual basis of our deeply secular society, and the overwhelming predominance of Holocaust-themed films over Christian ones has obvious implications. Meanwhile, in our globalized world, the American entertainment-media complex totally dominates Europe and the rest of the West, so that the ideas generated here effectively shape the minds of many hundreds of millions of people living elsewhere, whether or not they fully recognize that fact.

In 2009, Pope Benedict XVI sought to heal the long-standing Vatican II rift within the Catholic Church and reconcile with the breakaway Society of St. Pius X faction. But this became a major media controversy when it was discovered that Bishop Richard Williamson, one of the leading members of that latter organization, had long been **a Holocaust Denier and also believed that Jews should convert to**

Christianity. Although the many other differences in Catholic doctrinal faith were fully negotiable, apparently refusing to accept the reality of the Holocaust was not, and Williamson remained estranged from the Catholic Church. Soon afterward **he was even prosecuted for heresy** by the German government.

Internet critics have suggested that over the last couple of generations, energetic Jewish activists have successfully lobbied Western nations into replacing their traditional religion of Christianity with the new religion of Holocaustianity, and the Williamson Affair certainly seems to support that conclusion.

Consider the French satirical magazine *Charlie Hebdo*. Funded by Jewish interests, it spent years launching vicious attacks against Christianity, sometimes in crudely pornographic fashion, and also periodically vilified Islam. Such activities were hailed by French politicians as proof of the total freedom of thought allowed in the land of Voltaire. But the moment that one of its leading cartoonists made a very mild joke related to Jews, he was immediately fired, and if the publication had ever ridiculed the Holocaust, it surely would have been immediately shut down, and its entire staff possibly thrown into prison.

Western journalists and human rights advocates have often expressed support for the boldly transgressive activities of the **Jewish-funded Femen activists** when they desecrate Christian churches all around the world. But such pundits would certainly be in an uproar if anyone were to act in similar fashion toward the growing international network of Holocaust Museums, most of them built at public expense.

Indeed, one of the underlying sources of bitter Western conflict with Vladimir Putin's Russia seems to be that he has restored Christianity to a favored place in a society where the early Bolsheviks had once dynamited churches and massacred many thousands of priests. Western intellectual elites held far more positive feelings toward the USSR while its leaders retained a stridently anti-Christian attitude.

The Rise and Suppression of Holocaust Denial

Since the Holocaust had been almost unknown in America until the mid-1960s, explicit Holocaust Denial was equally non-existent, but as the former grew in visibility following the publication of Hilberg's 1961 book, the latter soon began to awaken as well.

Lipstadt's vilification of Barnes as the "godfather" of Holocaust Denial does contain a nugget of truth. His posthumously-published 1968 review endorsing Rassinier's denialist analysis seems to be the first such substantial statement published anywhere in America, at least if we exclude Beaty's very casual 1951 dismissal of the Jewish claims, which seems to have attracted negligible public attention.

Near the end of the 1960s, a right-wing publisher named Willis Carto came across a short and unpolished Holocaust Denial manuscript, apparently produced some years earlier, and then ignored legal niceties by simply putting it into print. The purported author soon sued for plagiarism, and although the case was ultimately settled, his identity eventually leaked out as being that of David L. Hoggan, a Barnes protege with a Harvard Ph.D. in history, serving as a junior faculty member at Stanford. His desire for anonymity was aimed at preventing the destruction of his career, but he failed in that effort, and further academic appointments quickly dried up.

Meanwhile, Murray Rothbard, the founding father of modern libertarianism, had always been a strong supporter of historical Revisionism, and greatly admired Barnes, who for decades had been the leading figure in that field. Barnes had also briefly hinted at his general skepticism about the Holocaust in **a lengthy 1967 article** appearing in the *Rampart Journal*, a short-lived libertarian publication, and this may have been noticed within those ideological circles. It appears that by the early 1970s, Holocaust Denial had become a topic of some discussion within America's heavily Jewish but fiercely free-thinking libertarian community, and this was to have an important consequence.

A professor of Electrical Engineering at Northwestern named Arthur R. Butz was casually visiting some libertarian gathering during this period when he happened to notice a pamphlet denouncing the Holocaust as a fraud. He had never previously given any thought to the issue, but such a shocking claim captured his attention, and he began looking into the matter early in 1972. He soon decided that the accusation was probably correct, but found the supporting evidence, including that presented in the unfinished and anonymous Hoggan book, far too sketchy, and decided it needed to be fleshed out in much more detailed and comprehensive fashion. He proceeded to undertake this project over the next few years, working with the methodical diligence of a trained academic engineer.

His major work, ***The Hoax of the Twentieth Century***, first appeared in print late in 1976, and immediately became the central text of the Holocaust Denial community, a position it still seems to retain down to this present day, while with all the updates and appendices, the length has grown to well over 200,000 words. Although no mention of this forthcoming book appeared in the February 1976 issue of *Reason*, it is possible that word of the pending publication had gotten around within libertarian circles, prompting the sudden new focus upon historical Revisionism.

Butz was a respectable tenured professor at Northwestern, and the release of his book laying out the Holocaust Denial case soon became a minor sensation, covered by the *New York Times* and other media outlets in January 1977. In one of her books, Lipstadt devotes a full chapter entitled "Entering the Mainstream" to Butz's work. According to a December 1980 *Commentary* article by Dawidowicz, Jewish donors and Jewish activists quickly mobilized, attempting to have Butz fired for his heretical views, but back then academic tenure still held firm and Butz survived, an outcome that seems to have greatly irritated Dawidowicz.

Such a detailed and comprehensive book laying out the Holocaust Denial case naturally had a considerable impact on the national debate, especially since the author was a mainstream and apparently apolitical academic, and an American edition of Butz's book soon appeared in 1977. I'm very pleased to have made arrangements to include the volume in my collection of Controversial HTML Books, so those interested can easily read it and decide for themselves.

- **The Hoax of the Twentieth Century**
  The Case Against the Presumed Extermination of European Jewry
  Arthur R. Butz • 1976/2015 • 225,000 Words

The following year, these Holocaust Denial trends seemed to gain further momentum as Carto opened a small new publishing enterprise in California called the Institute for Historical Review (IHR), which launched a quarterly periodical entitled *The Journal of Historical Review* in 1980. Both the IHR and its *JHR* publication centered their efforts around Revisionism in general, but with Holocaust Denial being their major focus. Lipstadt devotes an entire chapter to the IHR, later noting that most of the main authors of the February 1976 *Reason* issue soon became affiliated with that project or with other Carto enterprises, as did Butz, while the editorial board of the *JHR* was soon well-stocked with numerous Ph.D.'s, often earned at highly-reputable universities. For the next quarter century or so, the IHR would hold small conferences every year or two, with David Irving eventually becoming a regular presenter, and even fully mainstream figures such as

Pulitzer Prize-winning historian John Toland occasionally appearing as speakers.

As an important example of IHR efforts, in 1983 the organization published ***The Dissolution of Eastern Europe Jewry***, a very detailed quantitative analysis of the underlying demographics and population movements around the period encompassed by World War II, apparently the first such study undertaken. The author, writing under the pen-name Walter N. Sanning, sought to revise the extremely simplistic population analysis casually assumed by Holocaust historians.

Before the war, millions of Jews had lived in Eastern Europe, and after the war, those communities had mostly vanished. This undeniable fact has long stood as an implicit central pillar of the traditional Holocaust narrative. But drawing upon entirely mainstream sources, Sanning persuasively demonstrates that the situation was actually far more complicated than it might seem. For example, it was widely reported at the time that vast numbers of Polish Jews had been transported by the Soviets to locations deep within their territory, on both voluntary and involuntary terms, with future Israeli Prime Minister Menachem Begin being including in those transfers. In addition, huge numbers of heavily urbanized Soviet Jews were similarly evacuated ahead of the advancing German forces in 1941. The exact size of these population movements has long been uncertain and disputed, but Sanning's careful analysis of postwar Soviet census data and other sources suggests that the totals were likely towards the upper end of most estimates. Sanning makes no claim that his findings are definitive, but even if they are only partially correct, such results would certainly preclude the reality of traditional Holocaust numbers.

Another regular IHR participant was **Robert Faurisson**. As a professor of literature at the University of Lyons-2, **he began expressing his public skepticism about the Holocaust** during the 1970s, and the resulting media uproar led to efforts to remove him from his position, while a petition was signed on his behalf by 200 international scholars, including famed MIT professor Noam Chomsky. Faurisson stuck to his opinions, but attacks persisted, including a brutal beating by Jewish militants that hospitalized him, while a French political candidate espousing similar views was assassinated. Jewish activist organizations began lobbying for laws to broadly outlaw the activities of Faurisson and others, and in 1990, soon after the Berlin Wall fell and research at Auschwitz and other Holocaust sites suddenly became far easier, France passed a statute criminalizing Holocaust Denial, apparently the first nation after defeated Germany to do so. During the years that followed, large numbers of other Western countries did the same, setting the disturbing precedent of resolving scholarly disputes via prison sentences, a softer form of the same policy followed in Stalinist Russia.

Since Faurisson was a literary scholar, it is not entirely surprising that one of his major interests was *The Diary of Anne Frank*, generally regarded as the Holocaust's iconic literary classic, telling the story of a young Jewish girl who died after being deported from Holland to Auschwitz. He argued that the text was substantially fraudulent, written by someone else after the end of the war, and for decades various determined individuals have argued the case back and forth. I cannot properly evaluate any of their complex arguments, which apparently involve questions of ballpoint pen technology and textual emendations, nor have I ever read the book itself.

But for me, the most striking aspect of the story is the girl's actual fate under the official narrative, as recounted in the thoroughly establishmentarian **Wikipedia entry**. Apparently disease was raging in her camp despite the best efforts of the Germans to control it, and she soon became quite ill, mostly remaining bedridden in the infirmary, before eventually dying from typhus in Spring 1945 at a different camp about six months after her initial arrival. It seems rather odd to me that a young Jewish girl who fell severely ill at Auschwitz would have spent so much time in camp hospitals and eventually died there, given that we are told the primary purpose of Auschwitz and other such camps was the efficient extermination of its Jewish inmates.

By the mid-1990s the Holocaust Denial movement seemed to be gaining in public visibility, presumably aided by the doubts raised after the official 1992 announcement that **the estimated deaths at Auschwitz had been reduced by around 3 million**.

For example, the February 1995 issue of *Marco Polo*, a glossy Japanese magazine with a circulation of 250,000, carried a long article declaring that the gas chambers of the Holocaust were a propaganda hoax. Israel and Jewish-activist groups quickly responded, organizing a widespread advertising boycott of all the publications of the parent company, one of Japan's most respected publishers, which quickly folded in the face of that serious threat. All copies of the issue were recalled from the newspapers, the staffers were dismissed, and the entire magazine was soon shut down, while the president of the parent company was forced to resign.

In exploring the history of Holocaust Denial, I have noticed this same sort of recurrent pattern, most typically involving individuals rather than institutions. Someone highly-regarded and fully mainstream decides to investigate the controversial topic, and soon comes to conclusions that sharply deviate from the official narrative of the last two generations. For various reasons, those views become public, and he is immediately demonized by the Jewish-dominated media as a horrible extremist, perhaps mentally-deranged, while being relentlessly hounded by a ravenous pack of fanatic Jewish-activists. This usually brings about the destruction of his career.

In the early 1960s Stanford historian David Hoggan produced his anonymous manuscript *The Myth of the Six Million*, but once it got into circulation and his identity became known, his academic career was destroyed. A dozen years later, something along the same lines happened with Northwestern Electrical Engineering professor Arthur Butz, and only his academic tenure saved him from a similar fate.

Fred Leuchter was widely regarded as one of America's leading expert specialists on the technology of executions, and **a long article** in *The Atlantic* treated him as such. During the 1980s, Ernst Zundel, a prominent Canadian Holocaust Denier, was facing trial for his disbelief in the Auschwitz gas chambers, and one of his expert witnesses was an American prison warden with some experience in such systems, who recommended involving Leuchter, one of the foremost figures in the field. Leuchter soon took a trip to Poland and closely inspected the purported Auschwitz gas chambers, then published **the *Leuchter Report***, concluding that they were obviously a fraud and could not possibly have worked in the manner Holocaust scholars had always claimed. The ferocious attacks which followed soon cost him his entire business career and destroyed his marriage.

David Irving had ranked as the world's most successful World War II historian, with his books selling in the millions amid glowing coverage in the top British newspapers when he agreed to appear as an expert witness at the Zundel trial. He had always previously accepted the conventional Holocaust narrative, but reading the *Leuchter Report* changed his mind, and he concluded that the Auschwitz gas chambers were just a myth. He was quickly subjected to unrelenting media attacks, which first severely damaged and then ultimately **destroyed his very illustrious publishing career**, and he later even served time in an Austrian prison for his unacceptable views.

Dr. Germar Rudolf was a successful young German chemist working at the prestigious Max Planck Institute when he heard of the controversy regarding the *Leuchter Report,* which he found reasonably persuasive but containing some weaknesses. Therefore, he repeated the analysis on a more thorough basis, and published the results as **the *Chemistry of Auschwitz***, which came to the same conclusions as Leuchter. And just like Leuchter before him, Rudolf suffered the destruction of his career and his marriage, and since Germany treats these matters in harsher fashion, he eventually served five years in prison for his scientific impudence.

Most recently, Dr. Nicholas Kollerstrom, who had spent eleven years as a historian of science on the staff of University College, London, suffered this same fate in 2008. His scientific interests in the Holocaust provoked a media firestorm of vilification, and he was fired with a single day's notice, becoming the first member of his research institution ever expelled for ideological reasons. He had previously provided the Isaac Newton entry for a massive biographical encyclopedia of astronomers, and America's most prestigious science journal demanded that the entire work be pulped, destroying the work of over 100 writers, because it had been fatally tainted by having such a villainous contributor. He recounted this unfortunate personal history as an introduction to his 2014 book ***Breaking the Spell***, which I highly recommend.

Kollerstrom's text effectively summarizes much of the more recent Holocaust Denial evidence, including the official Auschwitz death books returned by Gorbachev after the end of the Cold War, which indicate that Jewish fatalities were some 99% lower than the widely-believed total. Furthermore, Jewish deaths actually showed a sharp decline once plentiful supplies of Zyklon B arrived, exactly contrary to what might have been expected under the conventional account. He also discusses the interesting new evidence contained in the British wartime decrypts of all German communications between the various concentration camps and the Berlin headquarters. Much of this material is presented in an interesting two hour interview on *Red Ice Radio*, conveniently available on YouTube:

- ***Breaking the Spell, The Holocaust Myth and Reality* • 2:12:59**
  https://www.bitchute.com/video/yqjW4EghPeO8/

The lives and careers of a very sizable number of other individuals have followed this same unfortunate sequence, which in much of Europe often ends in criminal prosecution and imprisonment. Most notably, a German lawyer who became a bit too bold in her legal arguments soon joined her client behind bars, and as a consequence, it has become increasingly difficult for accused Holocaust Deniers to secure effective legal representation. By Kollerstrom's estimates, many thousands of individuals are currently serving time across Europe for Holocaust Denial.

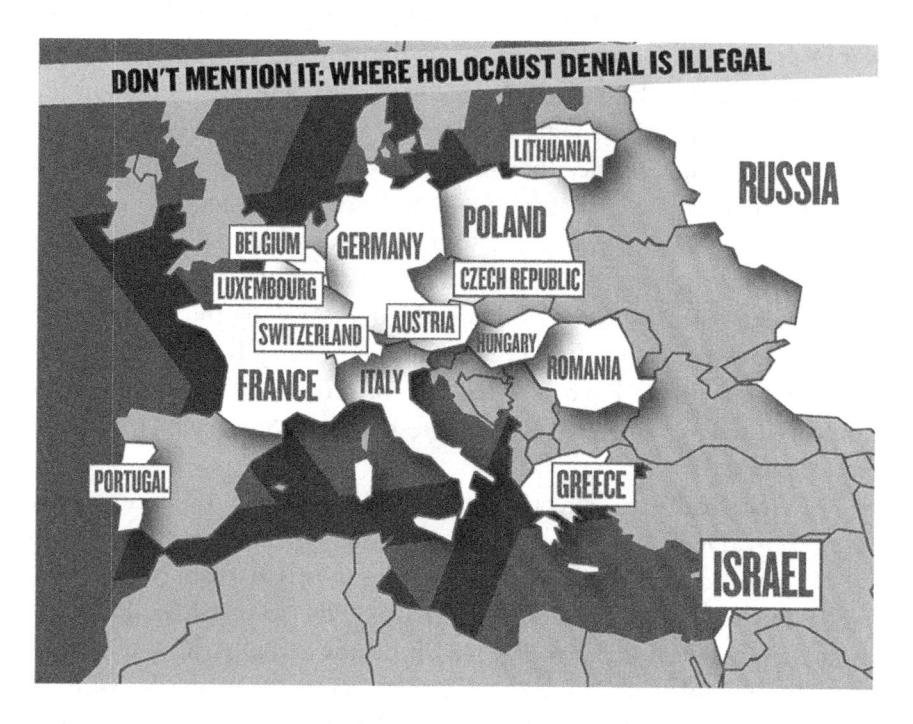

My impression is that by the late 1960s, the old Soviet Bloc countries had mostly stopped imprisoning people merely for questioning Marxist-Leninist dogma, and reserved their political prisons only for those actively organizing against the regime, while Holocaust Denial is treated today in far harsher fashion. One clear difference is that actual belief in Communist doctrine had entirely faded away to almost nothing even among the Communist leadership itself, while these days Holocaustianity is still a young and deeply held faith, at least within a small slice of the population that exerts enormously disproportionate leverage over our public institutions.

Another obvious factor is the many billions of dollars currently at stake in what Finkelstein has aptly characterized as "the Holocaust Industry." For example, potentially enormous new claims are now **being reopened against Poland** for Jewish property that was lost or confiscated during the World War II era.

In America, the situation is somewhat different, and our First Amendment still protects Holocaust Deniers against imprisonment, though the efforts of the ADL and various other groups to criminalize "hate speech" are clearly aimed at eventually removing that obstacle. But in the meantime, crippling social and economic sanctions are often used to pursue the same objectives.

Furthermore, various Internet monopolies have been gradually persuaded or co-opted into preventing the easy distribution of dissenting information. There have been stories in the media over the last few years that Google has been censoring or redirecting its Holocaust search results away from those disputing the official narrative. Even more ominously, Amazon, our current near-monopolistic retailer of books, last year took the unprecedented step of **banning thousands of Holocaust Denial works**, presumably lest they "confuse" curious readers, so it is fortunate that I had purchased mine a couple of years earlier. These parallels with George Orwell's *1984* are really quite striking, and the "Iron Curtain Over America" that Beaty had warned about in his 1951 book of that title seems much closer to becoming a full reality.

Various figures in the Holocaust Denial community have attempted to mitigate this informational blacklist, and Dr. Rudolf some time ago established a website **HolocaustHandbooks.com**, which allows a large number of the key volumes to be purchased or easily read online in a variety of different formats. But the growing censorship by Amazon, Google, and other Internet monopolies greatly reduces the likelihood that anyone will readily encounter the information.

Obviously, most supporters of the conventional Holocaust narrative would prefer to win their battles on the level playing fields of analysis rather than by utilizing economic or administrative means to incapacitate their opponents. But I have seen little evidence that they have enjoyed any serious success in this regard.

Aside from the various books by Lipstadt, which I found to be of poor quality and quite unpersuasive, one of the most energetic Holocaust supporters of the last couple of decades seems to have been Michael Shermer, the editor of *Skeptic* magazine, who had earned his degrees in psychology and the history of science.

In 1997, he published **Why People Believe Weird Things**, seeking to debunk all sorts of irrational beliefs popular in certain circles, with the book's subtitle describing these as "pseudo-science" and "superstition." His cover text focused on ESP, alien abductions, and witchcraft, but rebutting Holocaust Denial was the single largest portion of that book, encompassing three full chapters. His discussion of this latter subject was rather superficial, and he probably undercut his credibility by grouping it together with his debunking of the scientific reality of "race" as a similar right-wing fallacy, one also long since disproved by mainstream scientists. Regarding the latter issue, he went on to argue that the alleged black-white differences claimed in works such as *The Bell Curve* by Richard Herrnstein and Charles Murray was entirely pseudo-scientific nonsense, and he emphasized that book and similar ones had been promoted by the same pro-Nazi groups who advocated Holocaust Denial, with those two pernicious doctrines being closely linked together. Shermer had recruited Harvard professor Stephen Jay Gould to write the Foreword for his book and that raises serious questions about his knowledge or his judgment since Gould is widely regarded as one of the most notorious scientific frauds of the late twentieth century.

In 2000, Shermer returned to the battle, publishing **Denying History**, entirely focused on refuting Holocaust Denial. This time he recruited Holocaust scholar Alex Grobman as his co-author and acknowledged the generous financial support he had received from various Jewish organizations. A large portion of the text seemed to focus on the psychology and sociology of Holocaust Deniers, trying to explain why people could believe in such patently absurd nonsense. Indeed, so much space was devoted to those issues that he was forced to entirely skip over the official reduction of the Auschwitz body-count by 3 million just a few years earlier, thus avoiding any need to explain why this large shift had had no impact on the canonical Holocaust figure of Six Million.

Although various writers such as Shermer may have been encouraged by generous financial subsidies to make fools of themselves, their more violent allies on the extreme fringe have probably had a greater impact on the Holocaust debate. Although judicial and economic sanctions may deter the vast majority of Holocaust Deniers from showing their face, extra-legal violence has also often been deployed against those hardy souls who remain stubbornly unbowed.

For example, during the 1980s the offices and warehouse storage facilities of the IHR in Southern California were fire-bombed and totally destroyed by Jewish militants. And although Canada has traditionally had little political violence, in 1995 the large, ramshackle house that served as the residence and business office of Canada's Ernst Zundel, one of the world's leading publishers and distributers of Holocaust Denial literature, was similarly fire-bombed and burned to the ground. Zundel had already faced several criminal prosecutions on charges of spreading "false news," and eventually served years in prison, before being deported back to his native Germany, where he served additional imprisonment. Various other prominent Holocaust Deniers have even faced threats of assassination.

Most historians and other academic scholars are quiet souls, and surely the looming threat of such serious terroristic violence must have dissuaded many of them from involving themselves in such obviously controversial issues. Meanwhile, relentless financial and social pressure may gradually wear down both individuals and organizations, causing them to eventually either abandon the field or become far less active, with their places sometimes taken by newcomers.

The year after the 9/11 attacks, the *JHR* ceased print publication. The growth of the Internet was probably an important contributing factor, and with the national focus shifting so sharply toward foreign policy and the Middle East, its IHR parent organization became far less active, while much of the ongoing debate in Revisionism and

Holocaust Denial shifted to various other online venues. But at some point over the years, the *JHR* digitized many hundreds of its articles and posted them on its website, providing over three million words of generally very high-quality historical content.

Over the last couple of months, I have been repeatedly surprised to discover that the historians associated with the IHR had long ago published articles on topics quite parallel to some of my own. For example, after I published **an article on the Suvorov Hypothesis** that Germany's Barbarossa attack had preempted Stalin's planned attack and conquest of Europe, someone informed me that a reviewer had **extensively discussed** the same Suvorov book twenty years earlier in an issue of *JHR*. I also discovered **several pieces by CIA defector Victor Marchetti**, a important figure for JFK assassination researchers, who had received little attention in the mainstream media. There were also articles on the fate of **the Israeli attack on the *USS Liberty***, a topic almost entirely excluded from the mainstream media.

Casually browsing some of the archives, I was quite impressed with their quality, and since the archives were freely available for anyone to republish, I went ahead and incorporated them, making the millions of words of their Revisionist and Holocaust Denial content much more conveniently available to interested readers. The material is fully searchable, and also organized by Author, Topic, and Time Period, with a few sample links included below:

The Journal of Historical Review, 1980-2002 Issues

Author Archives:
- **David Irving – 11 Articles**
- **Arthur R. Butz – 15 Articles**
- **Robert Faurisson – 47 Articles**
- **James J. Martin – 13 Articles**
- **Percy L. Greaves, Jr. – 8 Articles**

Topic Archives:
- **Holocaust – 306 Articles**
- **World War II – 201 Articles**
- **Pearl Harbor – 15 Articles**
- **USS Liberty – 3 Articles**

So for those particularly interested in Holocaust Denial, well over a million words of such discussion may now be conveniently available, including works by many of the authors once so highly regarded by the early editors of *Reason* magazine.

Secretive Holocaust Denial

The steadily growing economic and political power of organized Jewish groups, backed by Hollywood image-making, eventually won the visible war and crushed the Holocaust Denial movement in the public arena, enforcing a particular historical narrative by criminal prosecutions across most of Europe and severe social and economic sanctions in America. But a stubborn underground resistance still exists, with its size being difficult to estimate.

Although my interest in the Holocaust had always been rather minimal, once the Internet came into being and my circle of friends and acquaintances greatly expanded, the topic would very occasionally come up. Over the years, a considerable number of seemingly rational people at one time or another privately let slip their extreme skepticism about various elements of the canonical Holocaust narrative, and such doubts seemed to represent merely the tip of the iceberg.

Every now and then someone in that category spoke a little too freely or became a target for retaliation on a different matter, and our media went into a feeding frenzy of Holocaust Denial accusations and counter-accusations.

For example, during the impeachment battles of the late 1990s, Clinton partisans believed that prominent liberal pundit Christopher Hitchens had betrayed the personal confidences of presidential aide Sidney Blumenthal, and journalist Edward Jay Epstein decided to retaliate in kind, widely circulating a memo to the media accusing Hitchens of secretly being a Holocaust Denier. He alleged that at a 1995 dinner gathering following a *New Yorker* anniversary celebration, Hitchens had drunk a little too much wine and began expounding to his table-mates that the Holocaust was simply a hoax. Epstein backed his claim by saying he had been so shocked at such statements that he had entered them into his personal diary. That telling detail and the fact that most of the other witnesses seemed suspiciously vague in their recollections persuaded me that Epstein was probably being truthful. A bitter feud between Hitchens and Epstein soon erupted.

In 2005 Hitchens denounced various opponents of Bush's Iraq War as anti-Semites, and in retaliation Alexander Cockburn published **a couple** of *Counterpunch* **columns** resurrecting that 1999 controversy, which is when I first discovered it. As a regular reader of *Counterpunch*, I was intrigued and Googling around a bit, quickly located media accounts of Epstein's explicit accusations. Numerous reports of the the incident still survive on the web, including **one from the *NY Daily News*** as well as a portion of **an *MSNBC* piece**, and although some of the more extensive ones have disappeared over the last dozen years, the media text I remember reading in 2005 has been preserved on the static HTML pages of **several websites**:

> Epstein told MSNBC that Hitchens had misspoken himself on the Holocaust on Feb. 12, 1995 – in fact, practically four years ago – as the two of them, along with some other friends, were dining in New York.
>
> Epstein was so shocked, he says, and considered Hitchens doubts so grave, that he went home and noted them in his diary!
>
> According to the Epstein diary: "Once seated in a booth, and freely sipping his free red wine, Hitchens advanced a theory more revealing than anything going on at the Hudson theater. His thesis, to the shock of everyone at the table, was that the Holocaust was a fiction developed by a conspiracy of interests bent on 'criminalizing the German Nation'"
>
> "He explained that no evidence of German mass murder had ever been found – and what gruesome artifacts had been found had been fabricated after the event," Epstein confided to his diary.
>
> "What of the testimony of Nazi generals at Nuremberg about the death camps," he asked.
>
> Hitchens, according to the Epstein diary notation, explained ". . . without missing a beat, that such admissions were obtained under Anglo-American torture." Epstein then asked, as noted in his diary: "'But what happened to the Jews in Europe?' Hitch shrugged and said, 'Many were killed by

local villagers when they ran away, others died natural deaths, and the remainder made it to Israel."

After reading these interesting columns, I began noticing that Cockburn himself sometimes provided hints suggesting that his own personal opinion on the Holocaust might be somewhat heretical, including his cryptical remarks that huge hoaxes were actually much easier to create and maintain than most people realized.

Just a few months after his attack on Hitchens, Cockburn published a two-part article strongly arguing that Nobel Peace Prize Winner Elie Wiesel, the most famous of all Holocaust survivors, **was simply a fraud**. I had always been taught that Zyklon B was the deadly agent used by the Nazis to exterminate the Jews of Auschwitz and I had vaguely become aware that Holocaust Deniers absurdly claimed the compound had instead been employed as a delousing agent in the camps, aimed at preventing the spread of Typhus; but then the following year, I was shocked to discover in **one of Cockburn's columns** that for decades the U.S. government had itself used Zyklon B as the primary delousing agent for immigrants entering at its Mexican border. I recall several other columns from the mid-2000s dancing around Holocaust issues, but I now seem unable to locate them within the *Counterpunch* archives.

My growing realization 15-odd years ago that substantial numbers of knowledgeable people appeared to be secret adherents of Holocaust Denial certainly reshaped my own unquestioning assumptions on that subject. The occasional newspaper account of a Holocaust Denier being discovered and then flayed and destroyed by the media easily explained why the public positions on that subject remained so unanimous. Being busy with other things, I don't think I ever had a conversation with anyone on that controversial subject or even so much as an email exchange, but I did keep my eyes and ears open, and huge doubts had certainly entered my mind many years before I ever bothered reading my first book on the subject.

Meanwhile, the concurrent collapse of my belief in our official ***American Pravda* narrative** on so many other controversial topics played a major role as well. Once I realized to my dismay that I couldn't believe a word of what our media and political leaders said about major events in the here and now, their credibility on controversial happenings so long ago and far away entirely disappeared. For these reasons, I had grown quite suspicious and held a very open mind on Holocaust matters as I eventually began reading books on both sides of the issue in the wake of the *Reason* controversy.

The Future of Holocaust Denial

For many years following the end of World War II very little seems to have been written about the momentous topic now known as the Holocaust. But from the 1960s onward, interest surged so enormously that many thousands or even tens of thousands of volumes on that once-ignored event have been produced. Therefore, the fifteen or twenty books that I have personally read is merely a sliver of that total.

I have invested only a few weeks of reading and research in studying this large and complex subject, and my knowledge is obviously dwarfed by that of the considerable number of individuals who have devoted many years or decades of their lives to such activity. For these reasons, the analysis I have presented above must surely contain numerous gaping errors that others could easily correct. But sometimes a newcomer may notice things that deeply-involved professionals might normally miss, and may also better understand the perspectives of those who have likewise never paid much attention to the subject.

Any conclusions I have drawn are obviously preliminary ones, and the weight others should attach to these must absolutely reflect my strictly amateur status. However, as an outsider exploring this contentious topic I think it far more likely than not that the standard Holocaust narrative is at least substantially false, and quite possibly, almost entirely so.

Despite this situation, the powerful media focus in support of the Holocaust over the last few decades has elevated it to a central position in Western culture. I wouldn't be surprised if it currently occupies a larger place in the minds of most ordinary folk than does the Second World War that encompassed it, and therefore possesses greater apparent reality.

However, some forms of shared beliefs may be a mile wide but an inch deep, and the casual assumptions of individuals who have never actually investigated a given subject may rapidly change. Also, the popular strength of doctrines that have long been maintained in place by severe social and economic sanctions, often backed by criminal penalties, may possibly be much weaker than anyone realizes.

Until thirty years ago, Communist rule over the USSR and its Warsaw Pact allies seemed absolutely permanent and unshakeable, but the roots of that belief had totally rotted away, leaving behind nothing more than a hollow facade. Then one day, a gust of wind came along, and the entire gigantic structure collapsed. I wouldn't be surprised if our current Holocaust narrative eventually suffers that same fate, perhaps with unfortunate consequences for those too closely associated with having maintained it.

This article is available online at:
https://www.unz.com/runz/american-pravda-holocaust-denial/

The ADL in American Society
From the Leo Frank Case to the Present Day
The Unz Review, October 15, 2018

The Fearsome Power of the ADL

In our modern era, there are surely few organizations that so terrify powerful Americans as the Anti-Defamation League (ADL) of B'nai B'rith, a central organ of the organized Jewish community.

Mel Gibson had long been one of the most popular stars in Hollywood and his 2004 film *The Passion of the Christ* became among the most profitable in world history, yet the ADL and its allies destroyed his career, and he eventually donated **millions of dollars to Jewish groups** in desperate hopes of regaining some of his public standing. When the ADL criticized a cartoon that had appeared in one of his newspapers, media titan Rupert Murdoch provided his **personal apology** to that organization, and the editors of *The Economist* **quickly retracted** a different cartoon once it came under ADL fire. Billionaire Tom Perkins, a famed Silicon Valley venture capitalist, was forced to issue **a heartfelt apology** after coming under ADL criticism for his choice of words in a *Wall Street Journal* column. These were all proud, powerful individuals, and they must have deeply resented being forced to seek such abject public forgiveness, but they did so nonetheless. The total list of ADL supplicants over the years is a very long one.

Given the fearsome reputation of the ADL and its notorious hair-trigger activists, there was a widespread belief that my small webzine would be completely annihilated when I first launched my recent series of controversial articles in early June by **praising the works of historian David Irving**, a figure long demonized by the ADL. Yet absolutely nothing happened.

During the next three months my subsequent articles directly challenged nearly every hot-button issue normally so fiercely defended by the ADL and its lackeys, so much so that a friendly journalist soon described me as the "**Kamikaze from California.**" Yet despite my 90,000 words of text and the 13,000 comments I had attracted, the continuing silence of the ADL was absolutely deafening. Meanwhile, my articles were read more than half a million times, with the following being a list of the most provocative pieces:

- **The Remarkable Historiography of David Irving**
  June 4, 2018 • 1,700 Words • 570 Comments

- **American Pravda: The JFK Assassination, Part II – Who Did It?**
  June 25, 2018 • 8,000 Words • 985 Comments

- **American Pravda: Oddities of the Jewish Religion**
  July 16, 2018 • 7,800 Words • 1,637 Comments

- **American Pravda: The Bolshevik Revolution and Its Aftermath**
  July 23, 2018 • 6,900 Words • 913 Comments

- **American Pravda: The Nature of Anti-Semitism**
  July 30, 2018 • 5,500 Words • 666 Comments

- **American Pravda: Jews and Nazis**
  August 6, 2018 • 6,800 Words • 554 Comments

- **American Pravda: Holocaust Denial**
  August 27, 2018 • 17,600 Words • 2,323 Comments

- **American Pravda: 9/11 Conspiracy Theories**
  September 10, 2018 • 11,000 Words • 2,355 Comments

When divine wrath fails to smite the heretic and terrifying enforcers of official dogma seem to have suddenly lost their taste for battle, others gradually begin to take notice and may grow emboldened. Eventually leading pro-Russian and Libertarian websites such as ***Russia Insider*** and ***LewRockwell*** began republishing some of my most controversial American Pravda articles, thus bringing my factual claims to the attention of broader audiences. After the conclusion of my series, I began directly ridiculing my strangely timorous ADL opponents, publishing a short column entitled "**Has the ADL Gone Into**

Hiding?" which led the redoubtable Paul Craig Roberts to describe me as "**the bravest man I know.**"

Apparently the combination of all these factors at long last grew too worrisome for the ADL, and stirring from their secret hiding place, its activists have now finally released **a short and rather milquetoast response** to my material, one which hardly much impresses me. A few days ago, they Tweeted out their column, together with a photo of their new nemesis.

Under Attack by the ADL

The ADL may boast an annual budget of $60 million and have many hundreds of full-time employees, but its research skills seem sorely lacking. I discovered that they opened their rebuke by denouncing me as a notorious "anti-immigrant activist." This seems an extremely odd claim given that I have published perhaps a quarter-million words on that contentious topic over the last twenty-five years, nearly all of it online and fully searchable, and my views have never been characterized in that fashion. To cite just one example, my article "**California and the End of White America**" appeared as a 1999 cover-story in *Commentary*, the flagship publication of The American Jewish Committee, and surely anyone reading it would be greatly puzzled by the ADL's description. Indeed, just a few years earlier, I had been **a top featured speaker at the October 1994 pro-immigrant protest** in downtown Los Angeles, a 70,000 strong political rally that was the largest such gathering in American history to that date.

Over the years, my political activities have been the subject of **many thousands of articles** in the mainstream media, including a half-dozen front-page stories in the *New York Times*, and these would provide a similar picture, as did the ***New Republic* cover story** chronicling my California successes. Moreover, my views on immigrants haven't changed all that much over the years as demonstrated by my more recent articles such as "**The Myth of Hispanic Crime,**" "**Immigration, Republicans, and the End of White America**" and "**A Grand Bargain on Immigration?**" Perhaps the intrepid ADL investigators should acquaint themselves with a powerful new technological tool called "Google."

I was equally unimpressed that they so hotly denounced me for substantially relying upon **the writings of Israel Shahak**, whom they characterized as viciously "anti-Semitic." As I had repeatedly emphasized, my own total lack of Aramaic and Hebrew necessarily forces me to rely upon the research of others, and the late Prof. Shahak, an award-winning Israeli academic, certainly seemed a fine source to use. After all, famed linguist Noam Chomsky had lauded Shahak's works for their "outstanding scholarship," and several of our other most prominent public intellectuals such as Christopher Hitchens, Edward Said, and Gore Vidal had been similarly lavish in their praise. Furthermore, one of Shahak's co-authors was **Norton Mezvinsky**, a prominent American academic specializing in Middle Eastern history, himself hardly an obscure figure given that both his brother and sister-in-law served in Congress and his nephew later married Chelsea Clinton. And as far as I'm aware almost none of Shahak's explicit claims about the Talmud or traditional Judaism have ever been directly challenged, while the **online availability** of his first book allows those so interested to conveniently read it and decide for themselves.

The ADL similarly denounced me for taking seriously the theories of Ariel Toaff, another Israeli academic. But Prof. Toaff, son of the Chief Rabbi of Rome, certainly ranks as one of the world's leading scholarly authorities on Medieval Jewry, and working together with his graduate students and other colleagues, he had devoted many years of effort to the research study in question, drawing upon extensive primary and secondary sources produced in eight different languages. I found **his 500 page book** quite persuasive, **as did Israeli journalist Israel Shamir**, and I have seen no credible rebuttals.

Now the work of all these prominent academics and intellectuals may not necessarily be correct, and perhaps I am mistaken in accepting their factual claims. But I would need to see something far more weighty than a casual dismissal in a few paragraphs contained within an anonymous ADL column, whose author for all I know might have been some ignorant young intern.

Those glaring flaws aside, most of the ADL's remaining catalogue of my numerous heretical positions seemed reasonably accurate, though obviously presented in a somewhat hostile and derogatory fashion and sorely lacking any links to my original pieces. But even this desultory listing of my mortal transgressions was woefully incomplete, with the ADL strangely failing to include mention of some of my most controversial claims.

For example, the authors excluded all reference to my discussion of the thoroughly documented **Nazi-Zionist economic partnership of the 1930s**, which played such a crucial role in laying the basis for the State of Israel. And the ADL similarly avoided mentioning the nearly 20,000 words I had allocated to discussing the very considerable evidence that the Israeli Mossad had played a central role in both **the JFK Assassination** and **the 9/11 Attacks**. Surely this must be one of the few times that the ADL has deliberately avoided leveling the charge of "conspiracy theorist" against an opponent whom they might have so easily slurred in that fashion. Perhaps they felt the evidence I provided was simply too strong for them to effectively challenge.

The ADL Censors the Internet and Hides Its Sordid Past

The worrisome incompetence of ADL researchers becomes particularly alarming when we consider that over the last couple of years that organization has been elevated into a content gatekeeping role at America's largest Internet companies, helping to determine what may or may not be said on the most important Social Media platforms such as Facebook, YouTube, and Twitter.

My local paper is the *San Jose Mercury News* and a couple of weeks ago it published **a major profile interview with Brittan Heller**, the ADL Director tasked with policing "hate speech" across the America-dominated portions of the Internet. She seemed like a perfectly pleasant young woman in her mid-thirties, a Stanford English major and a graduate of Yale Law, now living in Silicon Valley with her husband and her two cats, Luna and Stella. She emphasizes her own experience as a victim of cyber-harassment from a fellow college student whose romantic overtures she rejected and the later expertise she had gained as a Nazi-hunter for the U.S. government. But does that resume really provide her with the god-like knowledge suitable for overriding our traditional First Amendment rights and determining which views and which individuals should be allowed access to some two billion readers worldwide?

There is also a far more serious aspect to the situation. The choice of the ADL as the primary ideological overseer of America's Internet may seem natural and appropriate to politically-ignorant Americans, a category that unfortunately includes the technology executives leading the companies involved. But this reflects the remarkable cowardice and dishonesty of the American media from which all these individuals derive their knowledge of our world. The true recent history of the ADL is a remarkably sordid and disreputable tale.

In January 1993, the San Francisco Police Department reported that it had recently raided the Northern California headquarters of the ADL based upon information provided by the FBI. The SFPD discovered that the organization had been keeping **intelligence files on more than 600 civic organizations and 10,000 individuals**, overwhelmingly of a liberal orientation, with the SFPD inspector estimating that 75% of the material had been illegally obtained, much of it by secret payments to police officials. This was merely the tip of the iceberg in what clearly amounted to the largest domestic spying operation by any private organization in American history, and according to some sources, ADL agents across the country had targeted over 1,000 political, religious, labor, and civil rights organizations, with the New York headquarters of the ADL maintaining active dossiers on more than a million Americans.

Not long afterward, an ACLU official who had previously held a high-ranking position with the ADL revealed in an interview that his organization had been the actual source of the highly controversial 1960s surveillance on Martin Luther King, Jr., which it had then provided to FBI Director J. Edgar Hoover. For many years Hoover had been furiously denounced in the national media headlines for his use of tapes and other secret information on King's activities, but when a local San Francisco newspaper revealed that an ADL spying operation had actually been the source of all that sordid material, the bombshell revelation was totally ignored in the national media and **only reported by fringe organizations**, so that today almost no Americans are aware of that fact.

I know of no other private organization in American history that has been involved in even a sliver of such illegal domestic espionage activity, which appears to have been directed against almost all groups and prominent individuals—left, right, and center—suspected of being insufficiently aligned with Jewish and Israeli interests. Some of the illegal material found in the ADL's possession even raised dark suspicions that it had played a role in domestic terrorist attacks and political assassinations directed against foreign leaders. I am no legal expert, but given the massive scale of such illegal ADL activities, I wonder whether a plausible case might have been made to prosecute the entire organization under RICO statutes and sentence all of its leaders to long prison terms.

Instead, **the resulting government charges were quickly settled** with merely a trivial fine and a legal slap on the wrist, demonstrating the near-total impunity provided by massive Jewish political power in modern American society.

In effect, the ADL seems to have long operated as a privatized version of our country's secret political police, monitoring and enforcing its ideological doctrines on behalf of Jewish groups much as the Stasi did for the Communist rulers of East Germany. Given such a long history of criminal activity, allowing the ADL to extend its oversight to our largest Social Media platforms amounts to appointing the Mafia to supervise the FBI and the NSA, or taking a very large step towards implementing George Orwell's " Ministry of Truth" on behalf of Jewish interests.

In **his 1981 memoirs**, the far right Classics scholar Revilo P. Oliver characterized the ADL as "the formidable organization of Jewish cowboys who ride herd on their American cattle" and this seems a reasonably apt description to me.

The Leo Frank Case and the Creation of the ADL

Although I had long recognized the power and influence of the ADL, a leading Jewish-activist organization whose officials were so regularly quoted in my newspapers, until rather recently I had only the vaguest notions of its origins. I'm sure I'd heard the story mentioned at some point, but the account had never stuck in my mind.

Then perhaps a year or two ago, I happened to come across some discussion of the ADL's 2013 centenary celebration, in which the leadership reaffirmed the principles of its 1913 founding. The **initial impetus** had been the vain national effort to save the life of Leo Frank, a young Southern Jew unjustly accused of murder and eventually lynched. In the past, Frank's name and story would have been equally vague in my mind, only half-remembered from my introductory history textbooks as one of the most notable early KKK victims in the fiercely anti-Semitic Deep South of the early twentieth century. However, not long before seeing that piece on the ADL I'd read Albert Lindemann's highly-regarded study ***The Jew Accused***, and his short chapter on the notorious Frank case had completely exploded all my preconceptions.

First, Lindemann demonstrated that there was no evidence of any anti-Semitism behind Frank's arrest and conviction, with Jews constituting a highly-valued element of the affluent Atlanta society of the day, and no references to Frank's Jewish background, negative or otherwise, appearing in the media prior to the trial. Indeed, five of the Grand Jurors who voted to indict Frank for murder were themselves Jewish, and none of them ever voiced regret over their decision. In general, support for Frank seems to have been strongest among Jews from New York and other distant parts of the country and weakest among the Atlanta Jews with best knowledge of the local situation.

Furthermore, although Lindemann followed the secondary sources he relied upon in declaring that Frank was clearly innocent of the charges of rape and murder, the facts he recounted led me to the opposite conclusion, seeming to suggest strong evidence of Frank's guilt. When I much more recently read Lindemann's longer and more comprehensive historical study of anti-Semitism, *Esau's Tears*, I noticed that his abbreviated treatment of the Frank case no longer made any such claim of innocence, perhaps indicating that the author himself might have also had second thoughts about the weight of the evidence.

Based on this material, I voiced that opinion in **my recent article** on historical anti-Semitism, but my conclusions were necessarily quite tentative since they relied upon Lindemann's summary of the information provided in the secondary sources he had used, and I had the impression that virtually all those who had closely investigated the Frank case had concluded that Frank was innocent. But after my piece appeared, someone pointed me to a 2016 book from an unexpected source arguing for Frank's guilt. Now that I have ordered and read that volume, my understanding of the Frank case and its historical significance has been entirely transformed.

Mainstream publishers may often reject books that too sharply conflict with reigning dogma and sales of such works are unlikely to justify the extensive research required to produce the manuscript. Furthermore, both authors and publishers may face widespread vilification from a hostile media for taking such positions. For these reasons, those who publish such controversial material will often be acting from deep ideological motives rather than merely seeking professional advancement or monetary gain. As an example, it took a zealous Trotskyite leftist such as Lenni Brenner to brave the risk of ferocious attacks and invest the time and effort to produce his remarkable study of the crucial **Nazi-Zionist partnership of the 1930s**. And for similar reasons, we should not be totally surprised that the leading book arguing for the guilt of Leo Frank appeared as a volume in the series on the pernicious aspects of Jewish-Black historical relations produced by Louis Farrakhan's Nation of Islam (NOI), nor that the text lacked any identified author.

Anonymous works published by heavily-demonized religious-political movements naturally engender considerable caution, but once I began reading the 500 pages of *The Leo Frank Case: The Lynching of a Guilty Man* I was tremendously impressed by the quality of the historical analysis. I think I have only very rarely encountered a research monograph on a controversial historical event that provided such an enormous wealth of carefully-argued analysis backed by such copious evidence. The authors seemed to display complete mastery of the major secondary literature of the last one hundred years while drawing very heavily upon the various primary sources, including court records, personal correspondence, and contemporaneous publications, with the overwhelming majority of the 1200 footnotes referencing newspaper and magazine articles of that era. The case they made for Frank's guilt seemed absolutely overwhelming.

The basic outline of events is not disputed. In 1913 Georgia, a 13-year-old pencil company worker named Mary Phagan was last seen alive visiting the office of factory manager Leo Frank on a Saturday morning to collect her weekly paycheck, while her raped and murdered body was found in the basement early the next morning and Frank eventually arrested for the crime. As the wealthy young president of the

Atlanta chapter of B'nai B'rith, Frank ranked as one of the most prominent Jewish men in the South, and great resources were deployed in his legal defense, but after the longest and most expensive trial in state history, he was quickly convicted and sentenced to death.

The facts of the case against Frank eventually became a remarkable tangle of complex and often conflicting evidence and eyewitness testimony, with sworn statements regularly being retracted and then counter-retracted. But the crucial point that the NOI authors emphasize for properly deciphering this confusing situation is the enormous scale of the financial resources that were deployed on Frank's behalf, both prior to the trial and afterward, with virtually all of the funds coming from Jewish sources. Currency conversions are hardly precise, but relative to the American family incomes of the time, the total expenditures by Frank supporters may have been as high as $25 million in present-day dollars, quite possibly more than any other homicide defense in American history before or after, and an almost unimaginable sum for the impoverished Deep South of that period. Years later, a leading donor privately admitted that much of this money was spent on perjury and similar falsifications, something which is very readily apparent to anyone who closely studies the case. When we consider this vast ocean of pro-Frank funding and the sordid means for which it was often deployed, the details of the case become far less mysterious. There exists a mountain of demonstrably fabricated evidence and false testimony in favor of Frank, and no sign of anything similar on the other side.

The police initially suspected the black night watchman who found the girl's body, and he was quickly arrested and harshly interrogated. Soon afterward, a bloody shirt was found at his home, and Frank made several statements that seemed to implicate his employee in the crime. At one point, this black suspect may have come close to being summarily lynched by a mob, which would have closed the case. But he stuck to his story of innocence with remarkable composure, in sharp contrast to Frank's extremely nervous and suspicious behavior, and the police soon shifted their scrutiny toward the latter, culminating in his arrest. All researchers now recognize that the night watchman was entirely innocent, and the evidence against him planted.

The case against Frank steadily mounted. He was the last man known to have seen the young victim and he repeatedly changed important aspects of his story. Numerous former female employees reported his long history of sexually aggressive behavior toward them, especially directed towards the murdered girl herself. At the time of the murder, Frank claimed to have been working alone in his office, but a witness who went there reported he had been nowhere to be found. A vast amount of circumstantial evidence implicated Frank.

A black Frank family servant soon came forward with sworn testimony that Frank had confessed the murder to his wife on the morning after the killing, and this claim seemed supported by the latter's strange refusal to visit her husband in jail for the first two weeks after the day of his arrest.

Two separate firms of experienced private detectives were hired by Frank's lavishly-funded partisans, and the agents of both eventually came to the reluctant conclusion that Frank was guilty as charged.

As the investigation moved forward, a major break occurred as a certain Jim Conley, Frank's black janitor, came forward and confessed to having been Frank's accomplice in concealing the crime. At the trial he testified that Frank had regularly enlisted him as a lookout during his numerous sexual liaisons with his female employees, and after murdering Phagan, Frank had then offered him a huge sum of money to help remove and hide the body in the basement so that the crime could be pinned upon someone else. But with the legal noose tightening around Frank, Conley had begun to fear that he might be made the new scapegoat, and went to the authorities in order to save his own neck. Despite Conley's damning accusations, Frank repeatedly refused to confront him in the presence of the police, which was widely seen as further proof of Frank's guilt.

By the time of the trial itself, all sides were agreed that the murderer was either Frank, the wealthy Jewish businessman, or Conley, the semi-literate black janitor with a first-grade education and a long history of public drunkenness and petty crime. Frank's lawyers exploited this comparison to the fullest, emphasizing Frank's Jewish background as evidence for his innocence and indulging in the crudest sort of racial invective against his black accuser, whom they claimed was obviously the true rapist and murderer due to his bestial nature.

Those attorneys were the best that money could buy and the lead counsel was known as the one of the most skilled courtroom interrogators in the South. But although he subjected Conley to a grueling sixteen hours of intense cross-examination over three days, the latter never wavered in the major details of his extremely vivid story, which deeply impressed the local media and the jury. Meanwhile, Frank refused to take the stand at his own trial, thereby avoiding any public cross-examination of his often changing account.

Two notes written in crude black English had been discovered alongside Phagan's body, and everyone soon agreed that these were written by the murderer in hopes of misdirecting suspicion. So they were either written by a semi-literate black such as Conley or by an educated white attempting to imitate that style, and to my mind, the spelling and choice of words strongly suggests the latter, thereby implicating Frank.

Taking a broader overview, the theory advanced by Frank's legion of posthumous advocates seems to defy rationality. These journalists and scholars uniformly argue that Conley, a semi-literate black menial, had brutally raped and murdered a young white girl, and the legal authorities soon became aware of this fact, but conspired to set him free by supporting a complex and risky scheme to instead frame an innocent white businessman. Can we really believe that the police officials and prosecutors of a city in the Old South would have violated their oath of office in order to knowingly protect a black rapist and killer from legal punishment and thereby turn him loose upon their city streets, presumably to prey on future young white girls? This implausible reconstruction is particularly bizarre in that nearly all its advocates across the decades have been the staunchest of Jewish liberals, who have endlessly condemned the horrific racism of the Southern authorities of that era, but then unaccountably chose to make a special exception in this one particular case.

In many respects, the more important part of the Frank case began after his conviction and death sentence when many of America's wealthiest and most influential Jewish leaders began mobilizing to save him from the hangman. They soon established the ADL as a new vehicle for that purpose and succeeded in making the Frank murder case one of the most famous in American history to that date.

Although his role was largely concealed at the time, the most important new backer whom Frank attracted was Albert Lasker of

Chicago, the unchallenged monarch of American consumer advertising, which constituted the life's blood of all of our mainstream newspapers and magazines. Not only did he ultimately provide the lion's share of the funds for Frank's defense, but he focused his energies upon shaping the media coverage surrounding the case. Given his dominant business influence in that sector, we should not be surprised that a huge wave of unremitting pro-Frank propaganda soon began appearing across the country in both local and national publications, extending to most of America's most popular and highly-regarded media outlets, with scarcely a single word told on the other side of the story. This even included all of Atlanta's own leading newspapers, which suddenly reversed their previous positions and became convinced of Frank's innocence.

Lasker also enlisted other powerful Jewish figures in the Frank cause, including *New York Times* owner Adolph Ochs, *American Jewish Committee* president Louis Marshall, and leading Wall Street financier Jacob Schiff. The *Times*, in particular, began devoting enormous coverage to this previously-obscure Georgia murder case, and many of its articles were widely republished elsewhere. The NOI authors highlight this extraordinary national media attention: "The Black janitor whose testimony became central to Leo Frank's conviction became the most quoted Black person in American history up to that time. More of his words appeared in print in the *New York Times* than those of W.E.B. Du Bois, Marcus Garvey, and Booker T. Washington—*combined*."

Back a century ago just as today, our media creates our reality, and with Frank's innocence being proclaimed nationwide in near-unanimous fashion, a long list of prominent public figures were soon persuaded to demand a new trial for the convicted murderer, including Thomas Edison, Henry Ford, and Jane Addams.

Ironically enough, Lasker himself plunged into this crusade despite apparently having very mixed personal feelings about the man whose cause he was championing. His later biography reveals that upon his first personal meeting with Frank, he perceived him as "a pervert" and a "disgusting" individual, so much so that he even hoped that after he managed to free Frank, the latter would quickly perish in some accident. Furthermore, in his private correspondence he freely admitted that a large fraction of the massive funding that he and numerous other wealthy Jews from across the country were providing had been spent on perjured testimony and there are also strong hints that he explored bribing various judges. Given these facts, Lasker and Frank's other major backers were clearly guilty of serious felonies, and could have received lengthy prison terms for their illegal conduct.

With the *New York Times* and the rest of the liberal Northern media now providing such heavy coverage of the case, Frank's defense team was forced to abandon the racially-inflammatory rhetoric aimed at his black accuser which had previously been the centerpiece of their trial strategy. Instead, they began concocting a tale of rampant local anti-Semitism, previously unnoticed by all observers, and adopted it as a major grounds for their appeal of the verdict.

The unprincipled legal methods pursued by Frank's backers is illustrated by a single example. Georgia law normally required that a defendant be present in court to hear the reading of the verdict, but given the popular emotions in the case, the judge suggested that this provision be waived, and the prosecution assented only if the defense lawyers promised not to use this small irregularity as grounds for appeal. But after Frank was convicted, AJC President Marshall and his other backers orchestrated numerous unsuccessful state and federal appeals on exactly this minor technicality, merely hiring other lawyers to file the motions.

For almost two years, the nearly limitless funds deployed by Frank's supporters covered the costs of thirteen separate appeals on the state and federal levels, including to the U.S. Supreme Court, while the national media was used to endlessly vilify Georgia's system of justice in the harshest possible terms. Naturally, this soon generated a local reaction, and during this period outraged Georgians began denouncing the wealthy Jews who were spending such enormous sums to subvert the local criminal justice system.

One of the very few journalists willing to oppose Frank's position was Georgia publisher Tom Watson, a populist firebrand, and in an editorial he reasonably declared "We cannot have…one law for the Jew, and another for the Gentile" while he also later lamented that "It is a bad state of affairs when the idea gets abroad that the law is too weak to punish a man who has plenty of money." A former Georgia governor indignantly inquired "Are we to understand that anybody except a Jew can be punished for a crime." The clear facts indicate that there was indeed a massive miscarriage of justice in Frank's case, but virtually all of it occurred in Frank's favor.

All appeals were ultimately rejected and Frank's execution date for the rape and murder of the young girl finally drew near. But just days before he was scheduled to leave office, Georgia's outgoing governor commuted Frank's sentence, provoking an enormous storm of popular protest, especially since he was the business partner of Frank's chief defense lawyer, an obvious conflict of interest. Given the enormous funds that Frank's national supporters had been deploying on his behalf and the widespread past admissions of bribery in the case, there are obviously dark suspicions about what had prompted such a remarkably unpopular decision, which soon forced the former governor to exile himself from the state. A few weeks later, a group of Georgia citizens stormed Frank's prison farm, abducting and hanging him, with Frank becoming the first and only Jew lynched in American history.

Naturally, Frank's killing was roundly denounced in the national media that had long promoted his cause. But even in those quarters, there may have been a significant difference between public and private sentiments. No newspaper in the country had more strongly championed Frank's innocence than the *New York Times* of Adolph Ochs. Yet according to the personal diary of one of the *Times* editors, Ochs privately despised Frank, and perhaps even greeted his lynching with a sense of relief. No effort was ever made by Frank's wealthy supporters to bring any of the lynching party to justice.

The Accounts of Leonard Dinnerstein and Steve Oney

Although I have now come to regard the NOI volume as the most persuasive and definitive text on the Frank case, I naturally considered conflicting works before reaching this conclusion.

For nearly a half-century, the leading scholarly account of the incident had probably been Leonard Dinnerstein's book **The Leo Frank Case**, first published in 1966, and Dinnerstein, a University of Arizona professor specializing in Jewish history, entirely supported Frank's innocence. But although the work won a national award, carries glowing blurbs from several prestigious publications, and has surely graced the reading lists of endless college courses, I was not at all impressed. Among other things, the book appears to be the original source of some of the most lurid examples of alleged anti-Semitic public outbursts that apparently have no basis in reality and seem to have been simply fabricated by the author given his lack of any citations; the NOI authors note these stories have been quietly abandoned by all recent researchers. Even leaving aside such likely falsifications, which were widely cited by later writers and heavily contaminated the historical record, I found the short Dinnerstein work rather paltry and even pitiful when compared to that of its NOI counterpart.

A far longer and more substantial recent work was Steve Oney's 2003 ***And the Dead Shall Rise***, which runs nearly 750 pages and won the National Jewish Book Award, the Southern Book Critics Circle Prize, and the American Bar Association's Silver Gavel, probably establishing itself as today's canonical text on the historical incident. Oney had been a longtime Atlanta journalist and I was favorably impressed by his narrative skill, along with the numerous fascinating vignettes he provided to illustrate the Southern history of that general era. He also seemed a cautious researcher, drawing heavily upon the primary sources and avoiding much of the falsified history of the last century, while not entirely suppressing the massive evidence of bribery and perjury employed by the Frank forces.

But although Oney does mention much of this information, he strangely fails to connect the dots. For example, although he occasionally mentions some of the funds spent on Frank's behalf, he never attempts to convert them into present-day equivalents, leaving a naive reader to assume that such trivial amounts could not possibly have been used to pervert the course of justice. Furthermore, his entire book is written in chronological narrative form, with no footnotes provided in the text, and a large portion of the content being entirely extraneous to any attempt to determine Frank's guilt or innocence, contrasting very sharply with the more scholarly style of the NOI authors.

To my mind, a central element of the Frank case was the massive financial temptations being offered by Frank's Jewish backers, and the huge number of Atlanta citizens, both high and low, who apparently shifted their positions on Frank's guilt in eager hopes of capturing some of that largess. But although this important theme was heavily emphasized in the NOI book, Oney seems to mostly avoid this obvious factor, perhaps even for personal reasons. Print publications have suffered massive cutbacks in recent years and I noticed on the book flap that although Oney is described as a longtime Atlanta journalist, he had subsequently relocated to Los Angeles. Once I checked, I immediately discovered that Oney's book had became the basis for an independent film entitled ***The People v. Leo Frank***, and I wonder whether his hopes of capturing a sliver of Hollywood's vast lucre may not have encouraged him to so strongly suggest Frank's innocence. Would an account of Leo Frank as rapist and murderer ever be likely to reach the silver screen? The quiet influence of financial considerations is no different today than it was a century ago, and this factor must be taken into account when evaluating historical events.

The Historical Significance of the Frank Case

The NOI authors devote nearly all of their lengthy book to a careful analysis of the Frank case provided in suitably dispassionate form, but a sense of their justifiable outrage does occasionally poke through. In the years prior to Frank's killing, many thousands of black men throughout the South had been lynched, often based on a slender thread of suspicion, with few of these incidents receiving more than a few sentences of coverage in a local newspaper, and large numbers of whites had also perished under similar circumstances. Meanwhile, Frank had received benefit of the longest trial in modern Southern history, backed by the finest trial lawyers that money could buy, and based on overwhelming evidence had been sentenced to death for the rape and murder of a young girl. But when Frank's legal verdict was carried out by extra-judicial means, he immediately became the most famous lynching victim in American history, perhaps even attracting more media attention than all those thousands of other cases combined. Jewish money and Jewish media established him as a Jewish martyr who thereby effectively usurped the victimhood of the enormous number of innocent blacks who were killed both before and after him, none of whom were ever even recognized as individuals.

As Prof. Shahak has effectively demonstrated, traditional Talmudic Judaism regarded all non-Jews as being sub-human, with their lives possessing no value. Given that Frank's backers were followers of Reform Judaism, it seems quite unlikely that they accepted this doctrine or were even aware of its existence. But religious traditions of a thousand years standing can easily become embedded within a culture, and such unrecognized cultural sentiments may have easily shaped their reaction to Frank's legal predicament.

Influential historical accounts of the Frank case and its aftermath have contained lurid tales of the rampant public anti-Semitism visited upon Atlanta's Jewish community in the wake of the trial, even claiming that a substantial portion of the population was forced to flee as a consequence. However, a careful examination of the primary source evidence, including the contemporaneous newspaper coverage, provides absolutely no evidence of this, and it appears to be entirely fictional.

The NOI authors note that prior to Frank's trial American history had been virtually devoid of any evidence of significant anti-Semitism, with the previous most notable incident being the case of an extremely wealthy Jewish financier who was refused service at a fancy resort hotel. But by totally distorting the Frank case and focusing such massive national media coverage on his plight, Jewish leaders around the country succeeded in fabricating a powerful ideological narrative despite its lack of reality, perhaps intending the story to serve as a bonding experience to foster Jewish community cohesion.

As a further example of the widely promoted but apparently fraudulent history, the Jewish writers who have overwhelmingly dominated accounts of the Frank case have frequently claimed that it sparked the revival of the Ku Klux Klan soon afterward, with the group of citizens responsible for Frank's 1915 lynching supposedly serving as the inspiration for William Simmons' reestablishment of that organization a couple of years later. But there seems no evidence for this. Indeed, Simmons strongly emphasized the philo-Semitic nature of his new organization, which attracted considerable Jewish membership.

The primary factor behind the rebirth of the KKK was almost certainly the 1917 release of D.W. Griffith's overwhelmingly popular landmark film *Birth of a Nation*, which glorified the Klan of the Reconstruction Era. Given that the American film industry was so overwhelmingly Jewish at the time and the film's financial backers and leading Southern distributors came from that same background, it could be plausibly argued that the Jewish contribution to the creation of the 1920s Klan was a very crucial one, while the revenue from the film's distribution throughout the South actually financed Samuel Goldwyn's creation of MGM, Hollywood's leading studio.

In their introduction, the NOI authors make the fascinating point that the larger historical meaning of the Frank case in American racial history has been entirely lost. Prior to that trial, it was unprecedented for Southern courts to allow black testimony against a white man, let alone against a wealthy man being tried on serious charges; but the horrific nature of the crime and Conley's role as the sole witness required a break from that longstanding tradition. Thus, the authors not unreasonably argued that the Frank case may have been as important to the history of black progress in America as such landmark legal verdicts as *Plessy v. Ferguson* or *Brown v. Board*. But since almost the entire historical narrative has been produced by fervent Jewish advocates, these facts have been completely obscured and the case entirely misrepresented as an example of anti-Semitic persecution and public murder.

Let us summarize what seems to be the solidly established factual history of the Frank case, quite different than the traditional narrative. There is not the slightest evidence that Frank's Jewish background was a factor behind his arrest and conviction, nor the death sentence he received. The case set a remarkable precedent in Southern courtroom history with the testimony of a black man playing a central role in a white man's conviction. From the earliest stages of the murder investigation, Frank and his allies continually attempted to implicate a series of different innocent blacks by planting false evidence and using bribes to solicit perjured testimony, while the exceptionally harsh racial rhetoric that Frank and his attorneys directed towards those blacks was presumably intended to provoke their public lynching. Yet despite all these attempts by the Frank forces to play upon the notorious racial sentiments of the white Southerners of that era, the latter saw through these schemes and Frank was the one sentenced to hang for his rape and murder of that young girl.

Now suppose that all the facts of this famous case were exactly unchanged except that Frank had been a white Gentile. Surely the trial would be ranked as one of the greatest racial turning points in American history, perhaps even overshadowing *Brown v. Board* because of the extent of popular sentiment, and it would have been given a central place in all our modern textbooks. Meanwhile, Frank, his lawyers, and his heavy financial backers would probably be cast as among the vilest racial villains in all of American history for their repeated attempts to foment the lynching of various innocent blacks so that a wealthy white rapist and murderer could walk free. But because Frank was Jewish rather than Christian, this remarkable history has been completely inverted for over one hundred years by our Jewish-dominated media and historiography.

These are the important consequences that derive from control of the narrative and the flow of information, which allows murderers to be transmuted into martyrs and villains into heroes. The ADL was founded just over a century ago with the central goal of preventing a Jewish rapist and killer from being held legally accountable for his crimes, and over the decades, it eventually metastasized into a secret political police force not entirely dissimilar from the widely despised East German Stasi, but with its central goal seeming to be the maintenance of overwhelming Jewish control in a society that is 98% non-Jewish.

We should ask ourselves whether it is appropriate for an organization with such origins and such recent history to be granted enormous influence over the distribution of information across our Internet.

This article is available online at:
https://www.unz.com/runz/american-pravda-the-adl-in-american-society/

Amazon Book Censorship
Banning Black Historiography During Black History Month
The Unz Review, March 11, 2019

As most are surely aware, the last year or two has seen a growing crackdown on free speech and free thought across the Internet, with our constitutionally-protected First Amendment rights being circumvented through the agency of monopolistic private sector corporations such as Facebook, Twitter, and Google. Although as yet our government has not gained the power to ban discordant views nor punish their advocates, anonymous tech company censors regularly take these steps, seemingly based upon entirely opaque and arbitrary standards which lack any power of appeal. No one really knows why some individuals are banned or "de-platformed" and others are not, and surely this looming uncertainty has imposed self-censorship upon hundreds of individuals for every publicized victim who receives an exemplary punishment.

Some critics have attacked this policy as a new form of "McCarthyism," but this characterization seems based upon historical ignorance. Although the notorious junior senator from Wisconsin was an alcoholic prone to making reckless, unsubstantiated charges and therefore served as an extremely poor vessel for the movement he eventually came to symbolize, his accusations of massive Communist political subversion were absolutely correct and indeed somewhat understated. Over the last quarter-century, the public release of the Venona Decrypts has demonstrated that throughout most of the Franklin Roosevelt Administration and even afterward, the top levels of our national government were honeycombed with numerous spies and traitors deeply loyal to the Soviet Union rather than the United States. Today's ritualistic denunciations of McCarthyism are made by ignorant journalists who derive their understanding of the past from misleading Hollywood dramas rather than the meticulously researched volumes produced by leading academic scholars **such as John Earl Haynes and Harvey Klehr.**

In fact, just a few years before Sen. McCarthy burst upon the national scene, control of our federal government was nearly seized by agents of Stalin. From 1941 to 1944 FDR's Vice President was Henry

Wallace, who would have succeeded to the presidency if Roosevelt had renominated him in that latter year or had died prior to early 1945. And although Wallace himself was not disloyal, his top advisors were mostly Communist agents. Indeed, he later stated that **a Wallace Administration** would have included Laurence Duggan as Secretary of State and Harry Dexter White as Secretary of the Treasury, thereby installing Stalinist henchmen at the top of the Cabinet, presumably supported by numerous lower-level officials of a similar political ilk. One might jokingly speculate whether the Rosenbergs—later executed for treason—would have been placed in charge of our nuclear weapons development program.

That America's national government of the early 1940s actually came within a hair's breadth—or rather a heart-beat—of falling under Communist control is a very uncomfortable truth. And our history books and popular media have maintained such total silence about this remarkable episode that even among today's well-educated Americans I suspect that fewer than five in one hundred are aware of this grim reality. Surely this should cause all sensible people to become quite cautious about blithely accepting the standard narrative of other important historical events promoted by those same sources of obfuscation.

Even leaving aside this total whitewash of Communist infiltration during the 1930s and 1940s, the measures imposed upon the supposed martyrs of that era utterly differ in degree from those visited upon today's ideological dissenters. In the best-known cases, a few of Hollywood's most highly-paid screenwriters saw their income dry up due to their Communist affiliations and were forced to cut back on their lavish lifestyles, a personal suffering treated with utmost sympathy **in recent mainstream films** produced by their spiritual descendants. Meanwhile, today's targets of social wrath are almost always just working-stiffs, powerless nobodies fearfully voicing their controversial online opinions under a pseudonym before having their identities "doxxed" and then sometimes getting fired from their merely humdrum jobs.

And even that gross disparity drastically understates the difference between then and now. During the 1950s, any proposal to ban suspected Communists from making telephone calls, watching television, renting cars, or having bank accounts surely would have been universally ridiculed as utter lunacy. But in today's America, entirely equivalent measures are steadily growing more frequent and more severe, with very little public opposition.

Social media platforms have become the new electronic town square, and just a few weeks ago our own Israel Shamir's recounted how he was "**Banned by Facebook for Telling the Truth.**" He described the absurd levels of censorship that he and so many others have suffered on that platform, sometimes even being punished with a lengthy ban merely for posting a link to his own writings.

I don't much use Social Media myself since my long-form writings are hardly suitable for Facebook let alone the tiny character budget of Twitter. And although the latter seems effective as a means of promoting articles or distributing images or videos, the strict limits of a few dozen words surely render it much more appropriate for slogans or insults than anything more thoughtful or substantive. I find it difficult to believe that too many intelligent people have ever had their minds changed on anything significant by a few Tweets.

Amazon, however, is something else entirely. Its unmatched collection of available books comes close to fulfilling one of the original utopian goals of the very early days of the Computer Age. Over the last twenty years I've surely ordered many hundreds of volumes from that source, and reading them has played a huge role in transforming my beliefs on numerous important issues. For this reason, the growing wave of Amazon book-bannings carries very ominous overtones.

On February 19th, an article in *Quartz* **denounced Amazon** for continuing to carry "neo-Nazi and White Supremacist" books, and the following week most of the books in question were suddenly "disappeared" after many years of availability, in some cases apparently even vanishing from personal Kindle devices. An **article** published in *American Renaissance* provided one of the earliest accounts, and *Counter-Currents* has attempted to put together **a comprehensive list** of the dozens of vanished volumes.

The overwhelming majority of the banned works appear to be rightwing texts of a hortatory nature, generally falling under the rubric of White Nationalism or the Alt-Right. Glancing over the list, I found that I was only very slightly familiar with most of them, the most notable exception being *The Turner Diaries* by William Pierce, which became something of a national best-seller in 1995 when the media claimed that it had served as the inspiration for the Oklahoma City

Bombing. My own suspicion is that essays and articles of similar ideological sentiments exist in enormous quantities all across the Internet, and these possess vastly greater aggregate readership. It is not entirely clear what those pressuring Amazon had hoped to achieve by making those same ideas of white advocacy less available in concentrated book form. However, the almost unnoticed purge of various other Amazon books, of an entirely different nature, may have far greater negative ramifications.

The ADL ranks as one of our most formidable Jewish activist organizations, and according to **media accounts** it has been playing a central role in efforts to censor "hate speech" on leading Internet platforms such as Facebook, Twitter, and Google's YouTube. So it seems very likely to have also been behind Amazon's recent purge, especially once we discover the nature of some of the more significant books now banned.

Such a role for the ADL is extremely unfortunate, given that organization's long and very sordid history, which includes massive amounts of outright criminal activity, as I had discussed in **a long article** a few months ago. In fact, if not for the very widespread cowardice and dishonesty of our establishment media, the ADL would have long since lost all shreds of public credibility, and indeed most of its top leadership might well be serving long sentences in federal prison.

In recent years, almost no media mention of the late FBI Director J. Edgar Hoover fails to include condemnation of his sordid role in illegally recording Martin Luther King's personal activities, and then using that secret evidence in attempts at blackmail or intimidation, a devastating charge given King's subsequent elevation to secular sainthood. However, none of these accounts ever reveal that it was actually ADL operatives who were spying on King and bugging his hotel rooms, then passing their tapes on to Hoover, who merely listened to them.

And that telling example of illegal 1960s ADL surveillance represents merely the smallest tip of the organization's enormous domestic espionage activities, which have been directed against all individuals or organizations—left, right, or center—suspected of being insufficiently favorable toward Israel or Jews. By the time the FBI and local police departments broke a massive ADL spying operation in the early 1990s, the ADL was reported to be maintaining intelligence files on over one million Americans, a level of private domestic surveillance surely unequaled in our entire national history, with even some suggestions of possible involvement in political assassinations and terrorist attacks. But since the media quickly suppressed news of the scandal and the organization was punished with merely a slight slap on the wrist, there seems every likelihood that ADL spying activities on ordinary Americans have actually metastasized since that point in time.

In effect, the ADL seems to function as a privatized version of our secret political police, seeking to maintain the power of the interlocking Jewish groups that dominate our society, much like the Stasi did on behalf of East Germany's ruling Communist regime.

But for me, the most remarkable ADL revelation came in a book I purchased last year on Amazon, a book Amazon has now banned from sale. It seems that the ADL's very origin story of one hundred years ago, frequently mentioned in my introductory history textbooks and which I had never previously questioned, actually represented an absolute inversion of historical reality. As **I wrote**:

> Then perhaps a year or two ago, I happened to come across some discussion of the ADL's 2013 centenary celebration, in which the leadership reaffirmed the principles of its 1913 founding. The **initial impetus** had been the vain national effort to save the life of Leo Frank, a young Southern Jew unjustly accused of murder and eventually lynched. Not long before, Frank's name and story would have been equally vague in my mind, with the man half-remembered from my introductory history textbooks as one of the most notable early KKK victims in the fiercely anti-Semitic Deep South of the early twentieth century. However, not long before seeing that piece on the ADL I'd read Albert Lindemann's highly-regarded study *The Jew Accused*, and his short chapter on the notorious Frank case had completely exploded all my preconceptions.
>
> First, Lindemann demonstrated that there was no evidence of any anti-Semitism behind Frank's arrest and conviction, with Jews constituting a highly-valued element of the affluent Atlanta society of the day, and no references to Frank's Jewish background, negative or otherwise, appear-

ing in the media prior to the trial. Indeed, five of the Grand Jurors who voted to indict Frank for murder were themselves Jewish, and none of them ever voiced regret over their decision. In general, support for Frank seems to have been strongest among Jews from New York and other distant parts of the country and weakest among the Atlanta Jews with best knowledge of the local situation.

Furthermore, although Lindemann followed the secondary sources he relied upon in declaring that Frank was clearly innocent of the charges of rape and murder, the facts he recounted led me to the opposite conclusion, seeming to suggest strong evidence of Frank's guilt. When I much more recently read Lindemann's longer and more comprehensive historical study of anti-Semitism, *Esau's Tears*, I noticed that his abbreviated treatment of the Frank case no longer made any claim of innocence, perhaps indicating that the author himself might have also had second thoughts about the weight of the evidence.

Since I had had the impression that virtually all researchers who had investigated the Frank case had concluded that he was innocent of the rape and murder of 13-year-old Mary Phagan, I regarded my own contrary opinion as very tentative. But then someone pointed me to a 2016 book from an unexpected source that argued for Frank's guilt. With some doubts, I clicked a couple of Amazon buttons and ordered the volume, written by the unnamed researchers of Louis Farrakhan's Nation of Islam (NOI). As I explained at considerable length:

> Anonymous works published by heavily-demonized religious-political movements naturally engender considerable caution, but once I began reading the 500 pages of *The Leo Frank Case: The Lynching of a Guilty Man* I was tremendously impressed by the quality of the historical analysis. I think I have only very rarely encountered a research monograph on a controversial historical event that provided such an enormous wealth of carefully-argued analysis backed by such copious evidence. The authors seemed to display complete mastery of the major secondary literature of the last one hundred

years while drawing very heavily upon the various primary sources, including court records, personal correspondence, and contemporaneous publications, with the overwhelming majority of the 1200 footnotes referencing newspaper and magazine articles of that era. The case they made for Frank's guilt seemed absolutely overwhelming...

The facts of the case against Frank eventually became a remarkable tangle of complex and often conflicting evidence and eyewitness testimony, with sworn statements regularly being retracted and then counter-retracted. But the crucial point that the NOI authors emphasize for properly deciphering this confusing situation is the enormous scale of the financial resources that were deployed on Frank's behalf, both prior to the trial and afterward, with virtually all of the funds coming from Jewish sources. Currency conversions are hardly precise, but relative to the American family incomes of the time, the total expenditures by Frank supporters may have been as high as $25 million in present-day dollars, quite possibly more than any other homicide defense in American history before or after, and an almost unimaginable sum for the impoverished Deep South of that period. Years later, a leading donor privately admitted that much of this money was spent on perjury and similar falsifications, something which is very readily apparent to anyone who closely studies the case. When we consider this vast ocean of pro-Frank funding and the sordid means for which it was often deployed, the details of the case become far less mysterious. There exists a mountain of demonstrably fabricated evidence and false testimony in favor of Frank, and no sign of anything similar on the other side.

The police initially suspected the black night watchman who found the girl's body, and he was quickly arrested and harshly interrogated. Soon afterward, a bloody shirt was found at his home, and Frank made several statements that seemed to implicate his employee in the crime. At one point, this black suspect may have come close to being summarily lynched by a mob, which would have closed the case. But he stuck to his story of innocence with remarkable composure, in sharp contrast to Frank's extremely nervous and suspicious behavior, and the police soon shifted their scrutiny toward the latter, culminating in his arrest. All researchers now recognize that the night watchman was entirely innocent, and the material against him planted...

As the investigation moved forward, a major break occurred as a certain Jim Conley, Frank's black janitor, came forward and confessed to having been Frank's accomplice in concealing the crime. At the trial he testified that Frank had regularly enlisted him as a lookout during his numerous sexual liaisons with his female employees, and after murdering Phagan, had then offered him a huge sum of money to help remove and hide the body in the basement so that the crime could be pinned upon someone else. But with the legal noose tightening around Frank, Conley had begun to fear that he might be made the new scapegoat, and went to the authorities in order to save his own neck. Despite Conley's damning accusations, Frank repeatedly refused to confront him in the presence of the police, which was widely seen as further proof of Frank's guilt.

By the time of the trial itself, all sides were agreed that the murderer was either Frank, the wealthy Jewish businessman, or Conley, the semi-literate black janitor with a first-grade education and a long history of public drunkenness and petty crime. Frank's lawyers exploited this comparison to the fullest, emphasizing Frank's Jewish background as evidence for his innocence and indulging in the crudest sort of racial invective against his black accuser, whom they claimed was obviously the true rapist and murderer due to his bestial nature...

Taking a broader overview, the theory advanced by Frank's legion of posthumous advocates seems to defy rationality. These journalists and scholars uniformly argue that Conley, a semi-literate black menial, had brutally raped and murdered a young white girl, and the legal authorities soon became aware of this fact, but conspired to set him free by supporting a complex and risky scheme to instead frame an innocent white businessman. Can we really believe that the police officials and prosecutors of a city in the Old South would have violated their oath of office in order to knowingly protect a black rapist and killer from legal punishment and thereby turn him loose upon their city streets, presumably to prey on future young white girls? This implausible reconstruction is particularly bizarre in that nearly all its advocates across the decades have been the staunchest of Jewish liberals, who endlessly condemned the horrific racism of the Southern authorities of that era, but then unaccountably chose to make a special exception in this one particular case...

The NOI authors devote nearly all of their lengthy book to a careful analysis of the Frank case provided in suitably dispassionate form, but a sense of their justifiable outrage does occasionally poke through. In the years prior to Frank's killing, many thousands of black men throughout the South had been lynched, often based on a slender thread of suspicion, with few of these incidents receiving more than a few sentences of coverage in a local newspaper, and large numbers of whites had also perished in similar circumstances. Meanwhile, Frank had received benefit of the longest trial in modern Southern history, backed by the finest trial lawyers that money could buy, and based on overwhelming evidence had been sentenced to death for the rape and murder of a young girl. But when Frank's legal verdict was carried out by extra-judicial means, he immediately became the most famous lynching victim in American history, perhaps even attracting more media attention than all those thousands of other cases combined. Jewish money and Jewish media established him as a Jewish martyr who thereby effectively usurped the victimhood of the enormous number of innocent blacks who were killed both before and after him, none of whom were ever even recognized as individuals...

The NOI authors note that prior to Frank's trial American history had been virtually devoid of any evidence of significant anti-Semitism, with the previous most notable incident being the case of an extremely wealthy Jewish financier who was refused service at a fancy resort hotel. But by totally distorting the Frank case and focusing such massive national media coverage on his plight, Jewish leaders around the country succeeded in fabricating a powerful ideological narrative despite its lack of reality, perhaps intending the story to serve as a bonding experience to foster Jewish community cohesion...

Let us summarize what seems to be the solidly established factual history of the Frank case, quite different than the traditional narrative. There is not the slightest evidence that Frank's Jewish background was a factor behind his arrest and conviction, nor the death sentence he received. The case set a remarkable precedent in Southern courtroom history with the testimony of a black man playing a central role in a white man's conviction. From the earliest stages of the murder investigation, Frank and his allies continually attempted to implicate a series of different innocent blacks by planting false evidence and using bribes to solicit perjured testimony, while the exceptionally harsh racial rhetoric that Frank and his attorneys directed towards those blacks was presumably intended to provoke their public lynching. Yet despite all these attempts by the Frank forces to play upon the notorious racial sentiments of the white Southerners of that era, the latter saw through these schemes and Frank was the one sentenced to hang for his rape and murder of that young girl.

Now suppose that all the facts of this famous case were exactly unchanged except that Frank had been a white Gentile. Surely the trial would be ranked as one of the greatest racial turning points in American history, perhaps even overshadowing *Brown v. Board* because of the extent of popular sentiment, and it would have been given a central place in all our modern textbooks. Meanwhile, Frank, his lawyers, and his heavy financial backers would probably be cast as among the vilest racial villains in all of American history for their repeated attempts to foment the lynching of various innocent blacks so that a wealthy white rapist and murderer could walk free. But because Frank was Jewish rather than Christian, this remarkable history has been completely inverted for over one hundred years by our Jewish-dominated media and historiography.

Prior to the creation of the Internet and the establishment of Amazon's book-selling operation, this fascinating history would have remained completely unknown to me. Given its influential political role in our society, the ADL would certainly be concerned if it became widely known that the organization was founded with the central mission of ensuring that no wealthy and powerful Jew ever suffered punishment for the rape and murder of a young Christian girl, nor for trying to orchestrate the lynching of innocent black men in order to cover his own guilt.

When I published my original article in October, I naturally encouraged readers to order the remarkable book in question and decide for themselves. But Amazon has now chosen to ban that book of outstanding black historical scholarship at the height of Black History Month, a step taken just a few days after the ADL President made **his annual glowing tribute** to that national celebration of black pride. Those interested can still read my lengthy analysis of that book and the important historical event it describes.

- **American Pravda: The ADL in American Society**
  Ron Unz • October 15, 2018 • 7,300 Words

The true circumstances surrounding the establishment of the ADL is not the only work of serious historical scholarship to have suddenly been removed from Amazon's shelves, and most of the others seem to follow a very consistent pattern, certainly suggesting the hand of that organization and its kindred spirits.

For more than a half-century, Jewish political activists and engaged academics have pilloried white American society for its longstanding mistreatment of blacks, especially focusing upon the "original sin" of black slavery, and almost every morning my *New York Times* carries one or more articles filled with such denunciations. Americans of Anglo-Saxon founding stock are invariably portrayed as the villains of the story, with American Jews frequently cited as among the heroic supporters of the Civil Rights Movement that eventually rectified some of those injustices.

Yet just as in the case of Leo Frank, the true facts may be somewhat more complex. Over a quarter-century ago, the same group of provocative NOI researchers published a fascinating volume gathering together a huge quantity of historical evidence suggesting that prior to the Civil War, America's tiny Jewish population had actually played an enormously disproportionate role in establishing and promoting black slavery, with their co-ethnics sometimes even dominating that institution in the vast and exceptionally cruel slave plantations of Latin America, which were frequently operated like death-camps. These claims are hardly so implausible given that slave-trading had been a very traditional Jewish occupation in much of Europe and the Middle East for the last thousand years, and it is probably more than coincidence that the largest centers of Jewish settlement in Colonial America tended to be those cities focused on the slave trade.

I am hardly a specialist in pre-Civil War history, and weighing the strength of the evidence presented is beyond my expertise. But I did also order and read an angry rebuttal book published a couple of years later by a Dr. Harold Brackman, a Jewish historian working under the auspices of the Simon Wiesenthal Center, and found his arguments quite thin and unpersuasive.

Under normal circumstances, scholars of varied opinions would debate this controversial thesis back and forth and eventually come to some conclusion. But when Tony Martin, a prominent black scholar at Wellesley, merely put the provocative book on the reading list of one of his black history courses, he was ferociously vilified in the media and saw his career ruined, with concerted efforts made to fire him despite his tenured position. He later recounted the situation he faced in a short book.

I briefly mentioned the study and its thesis in **a July article** and suggested those intrigued by the dispute order it from Amazon and evaluate the evidence for themselves. Alas, that is no longer possible since Amazon has now banned the work, although all the subsequent books rebutting the thesis or discussing the huge controversy it aroused are still freely available. This strongly suggests that the evidence presented of a massive Jewish role in black slavery was simply too compelling to be easily refuted.

These anonymous black research studies prepared under the auspices of the Nation of Islam are hardly alone among serious historical texts now banned by Amazon. Indeed, groundbreaking works by eminent Jewish scholars may now also suffer a similar fate if they stray into forbidden territory. As **I wrote** at length last year:

> I do not doubt that much of the candid analysis provided above will be quite distressing to many individuals. Indeed, some may believe that such material far exceeds the boundaries of mere "anti-Semitism" and easily crosses the threshold into constituting an actual "blood libel" against the Jewish people. That extremely harsh accusation, widely used by stalwart defenders of Israeli behavior, refers to the notorious Christian superstition, prevalent throughout most of the Middle Ages and even into more modern times, that Jews sometimes kidnapped small Christian children in order to drain their blood for use in various magic rituals, especially in connection with the Purim religious holiday. One of my more shocking discoveries of the last dozen years is that there is a fairly strong likelihood that these seemingly impossible beliefs were actually true.
>
> I personally have no professional expertise whatsoever in Jewish ritual traditions, nor the practices of Medieval Jewry. But one of the world's foremost scholars in that field is Ariel Toaff, professor of Jewish Renaissance and Medieval Studies at Bar-Ilan University near Tel Aviv, and himself the son of the Chief Rabbi of Rome.
>
> In 2007, he published the Italian edition of his academic study *Blood Passovers*, based on many years of diligent research, assisted by his graduate students and guided by the suggestions of his various academic colleagues, with the initial print run of 1,000 copies selling out on the first day. Given Toaff's international eminence and such enormous interest, further international distribution, including an English edition by a prestigious American academic press would normally have followed. But the ADL and various other Jewish-activist groups regarded such a possibility with extreme disfavor, and although these activists lacked any scholarly credentials, they apparently applied sufficient pressure to cancel all additional publication. Although Prof. Toaff initially attempted to stand

his ground in stubborn fashion, he soon took the same course as Galileo, and his apologies naturally became the basis of the always-unreliable Wikipedia entry on the topic...

It appears that a considerable number of Ashkenazi Jews traditionally regarded Christian blood as having powerful magical properties and considered it a very valuable component of certain important ritual observances at particular religious holidays. Obviously, obtaining such blood in large amounts was fraught with considerable risk, which greatly enhanced its monetary value, and the trade in the vials of this commodity seems to have been widely practiced...

Obviously, the ritual murder of Christian children for their blood was viewed with enormous disfavor by the local Gentile population, and the widespread belief in its existence remained a source of bitter tension between the two communities, flaring up occasionally when a Christian child mysteriously disappeared at a particular time of year, or when a body was found that exhibited suspicious types of wounds or showed a strange loss of blood. Every now and then, a particular case would reach public prominence, often leading to a political test of strength between Jewish and anti-Jewish groups. During the mid-19th century, there was one such famous case in French-dominated Syria, and just before the outbreak of the First World War, Russia was wracked by a similar political conflict in the 1913 Beilis Affair in the Ukraine.

I first encountered these very surprising ideas almost a dozen years ago in a long article by Israel Shamir that was referenced in *Counterpunch*, and this would definitely be worth reading as **an overall summary**, together with **a couple** of his **follow-up columns**, while writer Andrew Hamilton offers **the most recent 2012 overview** of the controversy. Shamir also helpfully provides **a free copy of the book in PDF form**, an updated version with the footnotes properly noted in the text. Anyway, I lack the expertise to effectively judge the likelihood of the Toaff Hypothesis, so I would invite those interested to read Toaff's book or better yet the related articles and decide for themselves.

Amazon has now banned the English translation of Prof. Toaff's astonishing book, though it is still available on the Internet in PDF form at the link provided above.

All of these almost unprecedented Amazon book bannings occurred just in the last couple of weeks, and unless they are soon reversed, they may become just the first of many. The 1990s volumes on Judaism written by the late Israel Shahak, an award-winning professor at Hebrew University in Israel, might also be headed for oblivion. As **I wrote** last year:

> Although Shahak's books are quite short, they contain such a density of astonishing material, it would take many, many thousands of words to begin to summarize them. Essentially almost everything I had known—or thought I had known—about the religion of Judaism, at least in its zealously Orthodox traditional form, was utterly wrong...
>
> On the most basic level, the religion of most traditional Jews is actually not at all monotheistic, but instead contains a wide variety of different male and female gods, having quite complex relations to each other, with these entities and their properties varying enormously among the numerous different Jewish sub-sects, depending upon which portions of the Talmud and the Kabala they place uppermost. For example, the traditional Jewish religious cry "The Lord Is One" has always been interpreted by most people to be an monotheistic affirmation, and indeed, many Jews take exactly this same view. But large numbers of other Jews believe this declaration instead refers to achievement of sexual union between the primary male and female divine entities. And most bizarrely, Jews having such radically different views see absolutely no difficulty in praying side by side, and merely interpreting their identical chants in very different fashion.
>
> Furthermore, religious Jews apparently pray to Satan almost as readily as they pray to God, and depending upon the various rabbinical schools, the particular rituals and sacrifices they practice may be aimed at enlisting the support of the one

or the other. Once again, so long as the rituals are properly followed, the Satan-worshippers and the God-worshippers get along perfectly well and consider each other equally pious Jews, merely of a slightly different tradition. One point that Shahak repeatedly emphasizes is that in traditional Judaism the nature of the ritual itself is absolutely uppermost, while the interpretation of the ritual is rather secondary. So perhaps a Jew who washes his hands three times clockwise might be horrified by another who follows a counter-clockwise direction, but whether the hand-washing were meant to honor God or to honor Satan would be hardly be a matter of much consequence...

If these ritualistic issues constituted the central features of traditional religious Judaism, we might regard it as a rather colorful and eccentric survival of ancient times. But unfortunately, there is also a far darker side, primarily involving the relationship between Jews and non-Jews, with the highly derogatory term *goyim* frequently used to describe the latter. To put it bluntly, Jews have divine souls and *goyim* do not, being merely beasts in the shape of men. Indeed, the primary reason for the existence of non-Jews is to serve as the slaves of Jews, with some very high-ranking rabbis occasionally stating this well-known fact. In 2010, Israel's top Sephardic rabbi **used his weekly sermon to declare** that the only reason for the existence of non-Jews is to serve Jews and do work for them. The enslavement or extermination of all non-Jews seems an ultimate implied goal of the religion.

Jewish lives have infinite value, and non-Jewish ones none at all, which has obvious policy implications. For example, in a published article a prominent Israeli rabbi explained that if a Jew needed a liver, it would be perfectly fine, and indeed obligatory, to kill an innocent Gentile and take his. Perhaps we should not be too surprised that today Israel is widely regarded as **one of the world centers of organ-trafficking.**

As a further illustration of the seething hatred traditional Judaism radiates towards all those of a different background, saving the life of a non-Jew is generally considered improper or even prohibited, and taking any such action on the Sabbath would be an absolute violation of religious edict. Such dogmas are certainly ironic given the widespread presence of Jews in the medical profession during recent centuries, but they came to the fore in Israel when a religiously-minded military doctor took them to heart and his position was supported by the country's highest religious authorities.

And while religious Judaism has a decidedly negative view towards all non-Jews, Christianity in particular is regarded as a total abomination, which must be wiped from the face of the earth.

Whereas pious Muslims consider Jesus as the holy prophet of God and Muhammed's immediate predecessor, according to the Jewish Talmud, Jesus is perhaps the vilest being who ever lived, condemned to spend eternity in the bottommost pit of Hell, immersed in a boiling vat of excrement. Religious Jews regard the Muslim Quran as just another book, though a totally mistaken one, but the Christian Bible represents purest evil, and if circumstances permit, burning Bibles is a very praiseworthy act. Pious Jews are also enjoined to always spit three times at any cross or church they encounter, and direct a curse at all Christian cemeteries. Indeed, many deeply religious Jews utter a prayer each and every day for the immediate extermination of all Christians.

Over the years prominent Israeli rabbis have sometimes publicly debated whether Jewish power has now become sufficiently great that all the Christian churches of Jerusalem, Bethleham, and other nearby areas can finally be destroyed, and the entire Holy Land completely cleansed of all traces of its Christian contamination. Some have taken this position, but most have urged prudence, arguing that Jews needed to gain some additional strength before they should take such a risky step. These days, many tens of millions of zealous Christians and especially Christian Zionists are enthusiastic advocates for Jews, Judaism, and Israel, and I strongly suspect that at least some of that enthusiasm is based upon ignorance.

Shahak's scholarly research received glowing praise from some of America's most prominent public intellectuals, including Christopher

Hitchens, Gore Vidal, Noam Chomsky, and Edward Said, as well as prestigious publications such as *The London Review of Books* and *Middle East International*. But given the political implications of his revelations, I suspect they will soon only be available **on scattered websites** across the Internet.

A more detailed discussion of the works of Profs. Toaff and Shahak on these lesser-known aspects of the Jewish religion can be found in my long article from last July:

- **American Pravda: Oddities of the Jewish Religion**
  Ron Unz • July 16, 2018 • 7,800 Words

Other Amazon books seem to have recently fallen into limbo, still being sold by that website, but hidden away so that most readers would never discover them.

More than thirty-five years ago, Lenni Brenner, a Jewish leftist of anti-Zionist sympathies, published his ground-breaking research revealing the extensive Nazi-Zionist economic partnership of the 1930s, which laid the basis for the creation of the State of Israel. Although our media has almost entirely ignored that fascinating history, subsequent studies have fully confirmed Brenner's central framework.

I myself only became aware of Brenner's book last year and immediately purchased it on Amazon, then published an article in which **I discussed** his important findings:

> Although the Germans paid little attention to the entreaties of that minor organization, the far larger and more influential mainstream Zionist movement of Chaim Weizmann and David Ben-Gurion was something else entirely. And during most of the 1930s, these other Zionists had formed an important economic partnership with Nazi Germany, based upon an obvious commonality of interests. After all, Hitler regarded Germany's one percent Jewish population as a disruptive and potentially dangerous element which he wanted gone, and the Middle East seemed as good a destination for them as any other. Meanwhile, the Zionists had very similar objectives, and the creation of their new national homeland

in Palestine obviously required both Jewish immigrants and Jewish financial investment...

The importance of the Nazi-Zionist pact for Israel's establishment is difficult to overstate. According to a 1974 analysis in *Jewish Frontier* cited by Brenner, between 1933 and 1939 over 60% of all the investment in Jewish Palestine came from Nazi Germany. The worldwide impoverishment of the Great Depression had drastically reduced ongoing Jewish financial support from all other sources, and Brenner reasonably suggests that without Hitler's financial backing, the nascent Jewish colony, so tiny and fragile, might easily have shriveled up and died during that difficult period.

Such a conclusion leads to fascinating hypotheticals. When I first stumbled across references to the *Ha'avara* Agreement on websites here and there, one of the commenters mentioning the issue half-jokingly suggested that if Hitler had won the war, statues would surely have been built to him throughout Israel and he would today be recognized by Jews everywhere as the heroic Gentile leader who had played the central role in reestablishing a national homeland for the Jewish people in Palestine after almost 2000 years of bitter exile.

This sort of astonishing counter-factual possibility is not nearly as totally absurd as it might sound to our present-day ears. We must recognize that our historical understanding of reality is shaped by the media, and media organs are controlled by the winners of major wars and their allies, with inconvenient details often excluded to avoid confusing the public...

Once Hitler consolidated power in Germany, he quickly outlawed all other political organizations for the German people, with only the Nazi Party and Nazi political symbols being legally permitted. But a special exception was made for German Jews, and Germany's local Zionist Party was accorded complete legal status, with Zionist marches, Zionist uniforms, and Zionist flags all fully permitted. Under Hitler, there was strict censorship of all German publications, but the weekly Zionist newspaper was freely sold at all newsstands and street corners. The clear notion seemed to be that a German National Socialist Party was the proper political home for the country's 99% German majority, while Zionist National Socialism would fill the same role for the tiny Jewish minority.

In 1934, Zionist leaders invited an important SS official to spend six months visiting the Jewish settlement in Palestine, and upon his return, his very favorable impressions of the growing Zionist enterprise were published as a massive 12-part-series in Joseph Goebbel's *Der Angriff*, the flagship media organ of the Nazi Party, bearing the descriptive title "A Nazi Goes to Palestine."

Just last year, the Brenner books I purchased immediately popped up on the Amazon website, but these days they are hidden away, not even appearing on his **nearly empty author page**. One suspects that the ADL or similar organizations are very reluctant to have readers discover Brenner's extensive collection of primary source documents or the paperback edition of his historical narrative, whose cover shows the commemorative medal struck by Nazi Germany to mark its Zionist alliance, displaying the Swastika on one side and the Jewish Star-of-David on the other. Those interested in the entire complex and rather surprising historical relationship between Jews and the Third Reich during its dozen years of existence should consider reading my article on the subject.

- **American Pravda: Jews and Nazis**
  Ron Unz • August 6, 2018 • 6,800 Words

Jews today constitute less than 1% of the combined population of North America and the European Union, yet any honest observer would have to admit that organized Jewish groups totally dominate the politics and public life of those once-proud nations, which during past centuries had ruled most of the world.

The primary factor behind this astonishing control now exercised over populations that are 99% non-Jewish is probably the powerful leverage Jews today hold over money and media. But an important secondary factor has been the gradual elevation of the Jewish Holocaust of

World War II into the status of a near-sacred doctrine, largely replacing traditional Christianity as an official state religion, with dissenters generally treated as heretics and frequently subjected to government prosecution or imprisonment. Indeed, it seems that virtually every morning my newspapers are filled with Holocaust articles, most of them written with the same sort of sacred reverence that Catholic newspapers a century ago might have given to discussions of the Virgin Birth. However, because this so-called "Holocaustianity" purports to be a secular faith, it remains vulnerable to dispute on factual grounds, and many have suggested that its collapse would strike a mortal blow against reigning Jewish power.

The ADL and other Jewish activist organizations certainly seem extremely reluctant to take that risk. We should hardly be surprised that the first great large wave of Amazon book-bannings was **the early 2017 purge** of many dozens of scholarly texts by revisionist historians who had argued at great length and in considerable detail that the Holocaust was largely a hoax, concocted by Jewish activists and Hollywood filmmakers as a powerful shield against any criticism of Jewish or Israeli misbehavior. Although many of these books are still available for sale by **their publisher**, their complete disappearance from Amazon has greatly reduced their potential distribution.

Fortunately, I had purchased copies of several such books while Amazon still stocked them, and last year I published a long article summarizing my own conclusions about that complex and highly contentious topic. Although I am hardly an expert, it seemed to me that there was an enormous amount of persuasive evidence that the Holocaust is indeed substantially fraudulent, and quite possibly, almost entirely so. Those interested in considering my reasoning are welcome to do so and decide for themselves.

- **American Pravda: Holocaust Denial**
  Ron Unz • August 27, 2018 • 17,600 Words

Probably the most famous dystopian novel of the last one hundred years is George Orwell's 1984, and perhaps its most memorable observation is that those who control the past control the future and those who control the present control the past. We should recognize that serious books constitute the congealed nature of that past.

Our electronic media and its new social offshoot may dominate the thoughts of our population, and perhaps a single Tweet by a third-tier political celebrity might attract more readers in an hour than all the books discussed in this article have drawn in a year. But while effervescent, such electronic media emanations are transitory and fleeting, and quite likely to be forgotten an hour later. Meanwhile, serious books of ideas and scholarship have the potential to permanently reshape the contours of the reality accepted by the sort of individuals who may eventually alter our society. During a heated national election campaign, billions of dollars may be expended to temporarily shift public opinion on some issue or candidate, but a few weeks later, the effect has usually dissipated. Books may cost just a few dollars, but their potential impact is of a different order of weight and permanency.

Amazon today possesses a near-total monopoly over Internet book sales, and if American society continues to allow it to ban serious works of scholarship on political or ideological grounds, our future intellectual freedom has already been lost.

This article is available online at:

https://www.unz.com/runz/american-pravda-amazon-book-censorship/

Secrets of Military Intelligence
The Unz Review, June 10, 2019

Scoring a Game-Ending Own-Goal

Some may remember that in 2005 a major media controversy engulfed Harvard President Larry Summers over his remarks at an academic conference. Casually speaking off-the-record at the private gathering, Summers had **gingerly raised the hypothetical possibility** that on average men might be a bit better at mathematics than women, perhaps partially explaining the far larger number of males holding faculty positions in the math, science, and engineering departments.

These controversial speculations were soon leaked to the press, and an enormous firestorm of protest erupted, with MIT professor Nancy Hopkins claiming that merely hearing Summers' words at the event had left her physically ill, forcing her to quickly exit the room **lest she suffer a blackout and collapse**.

Harvard students and faculty members soon launched an organized campaign to have Summers removed from the summit of our academic world, with noted evolutionary-psychologist Steven Pinker being **one of the very few professors** willing to publicly defend him. Eventually, an unprecedented "no confidence" vote by the entire faculty and growing loss of confidence by the Board of Trustees **forced Summers to resign**, becoming the first Harvard President to suffer that fate in the university's 350 year history, thus apparently demonstrating the astonishing power of feminist "political correctness" on college campuses.

The true story for those who followed it was actually quite a bit more complex. Summers, a former Clinton Administration Treasury Secretary, had a long record of very doubtful behavior, which had outraged many faculty members for entirely different reasons. As I **wrote** a few years ago:

> Now I am hardly someone willing to defend Summers from a whole host of very serious and legitimate charges. He seems to have played a major role in **transmuting Harvard from a**

renowned university to an aggressive hedge fund, policies that subsequently brought my beloved alma mater to the very brink of bankruptcy during the 2008 financial crisis. Under his presidency, **Harvard paid out $26 million dollars to help settle international insider-trading charges** against Andrei Shleifer, one of his closest personal friends, who avoided prison as a consequence. And after such stellar financial and ethical achievements, he was naturally appointed as one of President Obama's top economic advisors, a position from which he strongly supported the massive bailout of Wall Street and the rest of our elite financial services sector, while ignoring Main Street suffering. Perhaps coincidentally, wealthy hedge funds had **paid him many millions of dollars** for providing a few hours a week of part-time consulting advice during the twelve months prior to his appointment.

Moreover, Summers had previously **denounced** anti-Israel activism by Harvard students and faculty members as "anti-Semitic," an accusation that **provoked fierce opposition**. A few years later, it also came out that Summers may have played a crucial role in favoring Mark Zuckerberg over the Winkelvoss brothers in their early battle for ownership of Facebook, while Summers' former assistant Sheryl Sandberg later became Facebook president, making her a multi-billionaire.

Although Summers' impolitic remarks regarding female math ability had certainly sparked his ouster, the underlying cause was probably his many years of extremely unbecoming behavior. Indeed, I think a reasonable case can be made that Summers was the worst and most disreputable president in all of Harvard's long history.

Still, even a broken or crooked clock is right twice a day, and I doubt that Larry Summers is the only person in the world who suspects that men might be a bit better at math than women. But some strongly disagree with this assessment, and in the wake of the Summers controversy one of his fiercest academic critics was a certain Janet Mertz, who specialized in cancer research at the University of Wisconsin.

In order to effectively refute Summers' odious speculations, she and her co-authors decided to carefully examine the total roster of participants in the International Math Olympiads for the years 1988-

2007. These 3200-odd individuals represent the world's highest-performing math students drawn from the secondary schools of dozens of countries, and the gender distribution across so many different cultures and years would surely constitute powerful quantitative evidence of whether males and females significantly differed in their average aptitudes. Since most of these thousands of international Math Olympians are drawn from countries having non-Western first names, determining the genders of each and every one is hardly a trivial undertaking, and we should greatly commend the diligent research that Mertz and her colleagues undertook to accomplish this task.

They published their important results in a 10,000 word academic journal article, whose "first and foremost" conclusion, provided in bold-italics, was that "***the myth that females cannot excel in mathematics must be put to rest.***" And in her subsequent **press interviews**, she proclaimed that her research had demonstrated that men and women had equal innate ability in mathematics, and that any current differences in performance were due to culture or bias, a result which our media gleefully promoted far and wide.

But strangely enough, when I actually bothered to read the text and tables of her eye-glazingly long and dull academic study, I noticed something quite intriguing, especially in the quantitative results conveniently summarized in Tables 6 and 7 (pp. 1252-53), and **mentioned** it in a column of my own:

> The first of these shows the gender-distribution of the 3200-odd Math Olympians of the leading 34 countries for the years 1988-2007, and a few minutes with a spreadsheet reveals that the skew is 95% male and 5% female. Furthermore, almost every single country, whether in Europe, Asia, or elsewhere, seems to follow this same pattern, with the female share ranging between 0% and 12% but mostly close to 5%; Serbia/Montenegro is the only major outlier at 20% female. Similarly, Table 7 provides a gender distribution of results for just the United States, and we find that just 5 of our 126 Math Olympians—or 4%—have been female. Various other prestigious math competitions seem to follow a roughly similar gender skew.

These remarkable findings are even more easily grasped when **we summarize the male percentages** of top math students aggregated across 1988-2008 for each individual country:

ASIA:
China, 96% male
India, 97% male
Iran, 98% male
Israel, 98% male
Japan, 98% male
Kazakhstan, 99% male
South Korea, 93% male
Taiwan, 95% male
Turkey, 96% male
Vietnam, 97% male

EUROPE:
Belarus, 94% male
Bulgaria, 91% male
Czech Republic, 96% male
Slovakia, 88% male
France 97% male
Germany, 94% male
Hungary, 94% male
Poland, 99% male
Romania, 94% male
Russia/USSR, 88% male
Serbia and Montenegro, 80% male
Ukraine, 93% male
United Kingdom, 93% male

OTHER:
Australia, 94% male
Brazil, 96% male
Canada, 90% male
USA, 96% male

INTERNATIONAL AVERAGE, 94.4% male

These are the empirical results that Mertz and her co-authors touted as conclusively demonstrating that males and females have equal mathematical ability. As near as I can tell, no previous journalist or researcher had noticed the considerable divergence between Mertz's empirical data and her stated conclusions, or perhaps any such individuals were just too intimidated to focus public attention on that discrepancy.

The "Jewish Threat" of American Military Intelligence

This striking disconnect between a study's purported findings and its actual results should alert us to similar possibilities elsewhere. Perhaps it is not so totally rare that diligent researchers whose ideological zeal sufficiently exceeds their mental ability may spend enormous time and effort gathering information but then interpreting it in a manner exactly contrary to its obvious meaning.

These thoughts recently came to my mind when I decided to read a remarkable analysis of the American military by Joseph W. Bendersky of Virginia Commonwealth University, a Jewish historian specializing in Holocaust Studies and the history of Nazi Germany. Last year, I had glanced at a few pages of his text for my long article on **Holocaust Denial**, but I now decided to carefully read the entire work, published in 2000.

Bendersky devoted ten full years of research to his book, exhaustively mining the archives of American Military Intelligence as well as the personal papers and correspondence of more than 100 senior military figures and intelligence officers. *The "Jewish Threat"* runs over 500 pages, including some 1350 footnotes, with the listed archival sources alone occupying seven full pages. His subtitle is "Anti-Semitic Politics of the U.S. Army" and he makes an extremely compelling case that during the first half of the twentieth century and even afterward, the top ranks of the U.S. military and especially Military Intelligence heavily subscribed to notions that today would be universally dismissed as "anti-Semitic conspiracy theories."

Put simply, U.S. military leaders in those decades widely believed that the world faced a direct threat from organized Jewry, which had seized control of Russia and similarly sought to subvert and gain mastery over America and the rest of Western civilization.

In these military circles, there was an overwhelming belief that powerful Jewish elements had financed and led Russia's Bolshevik Revolution, and were organizing similar Communist movements elsewhere aimed at destroying all existing Gentile elites and imposing Jewish supremacy throughout America and the rest of the Western world. While some of these Communist leaders were "idealists," many of the Jewish participants were cynical opportunists, seeking to use their gullible followers to destroy their ethnic rivals and thereby gain wealth and supreme power. Although Intelligence officers gradually came to doubt that the *Protocols of the Elders of Zion* was an authentic document, most believed that the notorious work provided a reasonably accurate description of the strategic plans of the Jewish leadership for subverting America and the rest of the world and establishing Jewish rule.

Although Bendersky's claims are certainly extraordinary ones, he provides an enormous wealth of compelling evidence to support them, quoting or summarizing thousands of declassified Intelligence files, and further supporting his case by drawing from the personal correspondence of many of the officers involved. He conclusively demonstrates that during the very same years that Henry Ford was publishing his controversial series *The International Jew*, similar ideas, but with a much sharper edge, were ubiquitous within our own Intelligence community. Indeed, whereas Ford mostly focused upon Jewish dishonesty, malfeasance, and corruption, our Military Intelligence professionals viewed organized Jewry as a deadly threat to American society and Western civilization in general. Hence the title of Bendersky's book.

- **The International Jew**
  The World's Foremost Problem
  Henry Ford • 1920 • 323,000 Words

These widespread beliefs had important political consequences. In recent decades, our leading immigration restrictionists have regularly argued that anti-Semitism played absolutely no role in the 1924 Immigration Act drastically curtailing European immigration; and the debates and speeches found in the Congressional Record have tended to support their claims. However, last year, I **speculated** that the widespread awareness of the Jewish leadership of the Bolshevik Revolution may have been a large factor behind the legislation, but one that was kept away from the public record. Bendersky's research fully confirms my suspicions, and he reveals that one of the former military officers most fearful of Jewish immigrant subversion actually played a crucial role in orchestrating passage of the legislation, whose central unstated goal was eliminating any further influx of Eastern European Jews.

The bulk of the fascinating material that Bendersky cites comes from Intelligence reports and official letters contained in permanent military archives. Therefore, we must keep in mind that the officers producing such documents would surely have chosen their words carefully and avoided putting all their controversial thoughts down on paper, raising the possibility that their actual beliefs may have been far more extreme. A particular late 1930s case involving one top general provides insight into the likely opinions and private conversations of some of those individuals.

Although his name would mean nothing today, Deputy Chief of Staff George Van Horn Moseley spent most of the 1930s as one of America's most highly-regarded generals, having been considered for the top command of our armed forces and also serving as a personal mentor to Dwight D. Eisenhower, future Secretary of State George C. Marshall, and numerous other leading military figures. He seems to have been well-liked within our military establishment, and had an excellent personal reputation.

Moseley also had very strong opinions on the major public issues of the day, and after his retirement in 1938 freed him from military discipline, he began to aggressively promote these views, going on a nationwide speaking tour. He repeatedly denounced Roosevelt's military buildup and in an early 1939 speech, he declared that "The war now being proposed is for the purpose of establishing Jewish hegemony throughout the world." He stated that only Jews would profit from the war, claimed that leading Wall Street Jews had financed the Russian Revolution, and warned Americans not to let history repeat itself. Although Moseley's outspokenness soon earned him a reprimand from the Roosevelt Administration, he also received private letters of support from other top generals and former president Herbert Hoover.

In his Congressional testimony just before the outbreak of World War II, Moseley became even more outspoken. He declared that the "murder squads" of Jewish Communists had killed "millions of Christians," but that "fortunately, the character of the German people was aroused" against these traitors within their midst and that therefore "We should not blame the Germans for settling the problem of the Jew within their borders for all time." He even urged our national leaders to "benefit" from the German example in addressing America's own festering domestic Jewish problem.

As might be expected, Moseley's 1939 praise of Germany's Jewish policy in front of Congress provoked a powerful media backlash, with a lead story in *The New Republic* denouncing him as a Nazi "fifth columnist" and *The Nation* attacking him in similar fashion; and after war broke out, most public figures gradually distanced themselves. But both Eisenhower and Marshall continued to privately regard him with great admiration and remained in friendly correspondence for many years, strongly suggesting that his harsh appraisal of Jews had hardly been a deep secret within his personal circle.

Bendersky claims that Moseley's fifty boxes of memoirs, private papers, and correspondence "embody every kind of anti-Semitic argument ever manifested in the history of Western civilization," and based on the various extreme examples he provides, few would dispute that verdict. But he also notes that Moseley's statements differed little from the depictions of Jews expressed by General George S. Patton immediately after World War II, and even maintained by some retired generals well into the 1970s.

Although I would not question the accuracy of Bendersky's exhaustive archival research, he seems considerably less sure-footed regarding American intellectual history and sometimes allows his personal sentiments to lead him into serious error. For example, his first chapter devotes a couple of pages to E.A. Ross, citing some of his unflattering descriptions of Jews and Jewish behavior, and suggesting he was a fanatic anti-Semite, who dreaded "the coming catastrophe of an America overrun by racially inferior people."

But Ross was actually one of our greatest early sociologists, and his 26 page discussion of Jewish immigrants published in 1913 was scrupulously fair-minded and even-handed, describing both positive and negative characteristics, following similar chapters on Irish, German, Scandinavian, Italian, and Slavic newcomers. And although Bendersky routinely denounces his own ideological villains as "Social Darwinists," the source he actually cites regarding Ross correctly identified the scholar as one of America's leading *critics* of Social Darwinism. Indeed, Ross's stature in left-wing circles was so great that he was selected as a member of the Dewey Commission, organized to independently adjudicate the angry conflicting accusations of Stalinists and Trotskyites. And in 1936, a Jewish leftist **fulsomely praised** Ross's long and distinguished scholarly career in the pages of *The New Masses*, the weekly periodical of the American Communist Party, only regretting that Ross had never been willing to embrace Marxism.

- **The Old World in the New**
  The Eastern European Hebrews
  E.A. Ross • 1914 • 5,000 Words

Similarly, Bendersky is completely out of his depth in discussing scientific issues, especially those involving anthropology and human behavior. He ridicules the "scientific racism" that he noted was widely found among the military officers he studied, claiming that such theories had already been conclusively debunked by Franz Boas and his fellow cultural anthropologists. But modern science has firmly established that the notions he so cavalierly dismisses were substantially if not entirely correct while those of Boas and his disciples were largely fallacious, and the Boasian conquest of the academic world actually imposed a half-century Dark Age upon the anthropological sciences, much like Lysenko had done in Soviet biology. Indeed, the views of Boas, an immigrant Jew, may have been primarily motivated by ideological considerations, and his most famous early work seemed to involve outright fraud: he claimed to have proven that the shape of human heads was determined by diet, and rapidly changed among immigrant groups in America.

But far more serious than Bendersky's lapses in areas outside of his professional expertise are the massive, glaring omissions found at the very heart of his thesis. His hundreds of pages of text certainly demonstrate that for decades our top military professionals were extremely concerned about the subversive activities of Jewish Communists, but he seems to casually dismiss those fears as nonsensical, almost delusional. Yet the actual facts are quite different. As I **briefly noted** last year after my cursory examination of his book:

> The book runs well over 500 pages, but when I consulted the index I found no mention of the Rosenbergs nor Harry Dexter White nor any of the other very numerous Jewish spies revealed by the Venona Decrypts, and the term "Venona" itself is also missing from the index. Reports of the overwhelmingly Jewish leadership of the Russian Bolsheviks are mostly treated as bigotry and paranoia, as are descriptions of the similar ethnic skew of America's own Communist Party, let alone the heavy financial support of the Bolsheviks by Jewish international bankers. At one point, he dismisses the link between Jews and Communism in Germany by noting that "less than half" of the Communist Party leadership was Jewish; but since fewer than one in a hundred Germans came from that ethnic background, Jews were obviously over-represented among Communist leaders by as much as 5,000%. This seems to typify the sort of dishonesty and innumeracy I have regularly encountered among Jewish Holocaust experts.

Admittedly, Bendersky's book was published just 18 months after the seminal first ***Venona*** volume of John Earl Haynes and Harvey Klehr appeared in early 1999. But the Venona Decrypts themselves had been declassified in 1995 and soon begun circulating within the academic community. For Bendersky to stubbornly ignore the undeniable reality that a large and overwhelmingly Jewish network of Stalinist agents was situated near the top of the Roosevelt Administration, while ridiculing the military officers who made such claims at the time, raises severe doubts about his credibility as an objective historian.

As I **pointed out** earlier this year:

> From 1941 to 1944 FDR's Vice President was Henry Wallace, who would have succeeded to the presidency if Roosevelt had renominated him in that latter year or had died prior to early 1945. And although Wallace himself was not disloyal, his top advisors were mostly Communist agents. Indeed, he later

stated that **a Wallace Administration** would have included Laurence Duggan as Secretary of State and Harry Dexter White as Secretary of the Treasury, thereby installing Stalinist henchmen at the top of the Cabinet, presumably supported by numerous lower-level officials of a similar political ilk. One might jokingly speculate whether the Rosenbergs—later executed for treason—would have been placed in charge of our nuclear weapons development program.

That America's national government of the early 1940s actually came within a hair's breadth—or rather a heartbeat—of falling under Communist control is a very uncomfortable truth. And our history books and popular media have maintained such total silence about this remarkable episode that even among today's well-educated Americans I suspect that fewer than five in one hundred are aware of this grim reality.

The Venona Project constituted the definitive proof of the massive extent of Soviet espionage activities in America, which for many decades had been routinely denied by many mainstream journalists and historians, and its findings also played a crucial secret role in dismantling that hostile spy network during the late 1940s and early 1950s. But Venona was nearly snuffed out just a year after its birth. In 1944 Soviet agents became aware of the crucial code-breaking effort, and soon afterwards arranged for the Roosevelt White House to issue a directive ordering the project shut down and all efforts to uncover Soviet spying abandoned. The only reason that Venona survived, allowing us to later reconstruct the fateful politics of that era, was that the determined Military Intelligence officer in charge of the project risked a court-martial by directly disobeying that explicit Presidential order and continuing his work.

That officer was Col. Carter W. Clarke, but his place in Bendersky's book is a much less favorable one, being described as a prominent member of the anti-Semitic "clique" who constitute the villains of the narrative. Indeed, Bendersky particularly condemns Clarke for still seeming to believe in the essential reality of the *Protocols* as late as the 1970s, quoting from a letter he wrote to a brother officer in 1977:

If, and a big—damned big IF, as the Jews claim the Protocols of the Elders of Zion were f—- cooked up by Russian Secret Police, why is it that so much they contain has already come to pass, and the rest so strongly advocated by the *Washington Post* and the *New York Times*.

Our historians must surely have a difficult time digesting the remarkable fact that the officer in charge of the vital Venona Project, whose selfless determination saved it from destruction by the Roosevelt Administration, actually remained a lifelong believer in the importance of the *Protocols of the Elders of Zion*.

The "Iron Curtain" of John Beaty

Let us take a step back and place Bendersky's findings in their proper context. We must recognize that during much of the era covered by his research, U.S. Military Intelligence constituted nearly the entirety of America's national security apparatus—being the equivalent of a combined CIA, NSA, and FBI—and was responsible for both international and domestic security, although the latter portfolio had gradually been assumed by J. Edgar Hoover's own expanding organization by the end of the 1920s.

Bendersky's years of diligent research demonstrate that for decades these experienced professionals—and many of their top commanding generals—were firmly convinced that major elements of the organized Jewish community were ruthlessly plotting to seize power in America, destroy all our traditional Constitutional liberties, and ultimately gain mastery over the entire world.

I have never believed in the existence of UFOs as alien spacecraft, always dismissing such notions as ridiculous nonsense. But suppose declassified government documents revealed that for decades nearly all of our top Air Force officers had been absolutely convinced of the reality of UFOs. Could I continue my insouciant refusal to even consider such possibilities? At the very least, those revelations would force me to sharply reassess the likely credibility of other individuals who had made similar claims during that same period.

As I **wrote** in 2018:

Some years ago, I came across a totally obscure 1951 book entitled *The Iron Curtain Over America* by John Beaty, a well-regarded university professor. Beaty had spent his wartime years in Military Intelligence, being tasked with preparing the daily briefing reports distributed to all top American officials summarizing available intelligence information acquired during the previous 24 hours, which was obviously a position of considerable responsibility.

As a zealous anti-Communist, he regarded much of America's Jewish population as deeply implicated in subversive activity, therefore constituting a serious threat to traditional American freedoms. In particular, the growing Jewish stranglehold over publishing and the media was making it increasingly difficult for discordant views to reach the American people, with this regime of censorship constituting the "Iron Curtain" described in his title. He blamed Jewish interests for the totally unnecessary war with Hitler's Germany, which had long sought good relations with America, but instead had suffered total destruction for its strong opposition to Europe's Jewish-backed Communist menace.

Beaty also sharply denounced American support for the new state of Israel, which was potentially costing us the goodwill of so many millions of Muslims and Arabs. And as a very minor aside, he also criticized the Israelis for continuing to claim that Hitler had killed six million Jews, a highly implausible accusation that had no apparent basis in reality and seemed to be just a fraud concocted by Jews and Communists, aimed at poisoning our relations with postwar Germany and extracting money for the Jewish State from the long-suffering German people.

He was scathing toward the Nuremberg Trials, which he described as a "major indelible blot" upon America and "a travesty of justice." According to him, the proceedings were dominated by vengeful German Jews, many of whom engaged in falsification of testimony or even had criminal backgrounds. As a result, this "foul fiasco" merely taught Germans that "our government had no sense of justice." Sen. Robert Taft, the Republican leader of the immediate postwar era took a very similar position, which later won him the praise of John F. Kennedy in *Profiles in Courage*. The fact that the chief Soviet prosecutor at Nuremberg had played the same role during the notorious Stalinist show trials of the late 1930s, during which numerous Old Bolsheviks confessed to all sorts of absurd and ridiculous things, hardly enhanced the credibility of the proceedings to many outside observers.

Then as now, a book taking such controversial positions stood little chance of finding a mainstream New York publisher, but it was soon released by a small Dallas firm, and then became enormously successful, going through some seventeen printings over the next few years. According to Scott McConnell, founding editor of *The American Conservative*, Beaty's book became the second most popular conservative text of the 1950s, ranking only behind Russell Kirk's iconic classic, *The Conservative Mind*.

Bendersky devotes several pages to a discussion of Beaty's book, which he claims "ranks among the most vicious anti-Semitic diatribes of the postwar era." He also describes the story of its tremendous national success, which followed an unusual trajectory.

Books by unknown authors that are released by tiny publishers rarely sell many copies, but the work came to the attention of George E. Stratemeyer, a retired general who had been one of Douglas MacArthur's commanders, and he wrote Beaty a letter of endorsement. Beaty began including that letter in his promotional materials, drawing the ire of the ADL, whose national chairman contacted Stratemeyer, demanding that he repudiate the book, which was described as a "primer for lunatic fringe groups" all across America. Instead, Stratemeyer delivered a blistering reply to the ADL, denouncing it for making "veiled threats" against "free expression and thoughts" and trying to establish Soviet-style repression in the United States. He declared that every "loyal citizen" should read *The Iron Curtain Over America*, whose pages finally revealed the truth about our national predicament, and he began actively promoting the book around the country while attacking the Jewish attempt to silence him. Numerous other top American generals and admirals soon joined Stratemeyer in publicly endorsing the work, as did a couple of influential members of the U.S. Senate, leading to its enormous national sales.

Having now discovered that Beaty's views were so totally consistent with those of nearly all our Military Intelligence professionals, I decided to reread his short book, and found myself deeply impressed. His erudition and level-headedness were exactly what one would expect from an accomplished academic with a Columbia Ph.D. who had risen to the rank of colonel during his five years of service in Military Intelligence and on the General Staff. Although strongly anti-Communist, by all indications Beaty was very much a moderate conservative, quite judicious in his claims and proposals. Bendersky's hysterical denunciation reflects rather badly upon the issuer of that *fatwa*.

Beaty's book was written nearly 70 years ago, at the very beginning of our long Cold War, and is hardly free from various widely-held errors of that time, nor from deep concerns about various calamities that did not come to pass, such as a Third World War. Moreover, it was published just a couple of years after Mao's victory in China and in the midst of our own involvement in the Korean War, so its discussion of those large contemporary events is far more lengthy and detailed than would probably be of interest to present-day readers. But leaving aside those minor blemishes, I think the account he provides of the true circumstances behind America's involvement in both the First and Second World Wars and their immediate aftermath is greatly superior to the heavily slanted and expurgated accounts we find in our standard history books. And Beaty's wartime responsibility for collating and summarizing all incoming intelligence information and then producing a daily digest for distribution to the White House and our other top officials surely provided him a far more accurate picture of the reality than that of the typical third-hand scribe.

At the very least, we should acknowledge that Beaty's volume provides an excellent summary of the beliefs of American Military Intelligence officers and many of our top generals during the first half of the twentieth century. With copyright having long lapsed, I'm pleased to make it available in convenient HTML format, allowing those so interested to read it and judge for themselves:

- **The Iron Curtain Over America**
  John Beaty • 1951 • 82,000 Words

Revilo P. Oliver and World War II

Despite Bendersky's fulminations, Beaty seems to have been someone of quite moderate sentiments, who viewed extremism of any type with great disfavor. After describing the ongoing seizure of power in American society by Jewish immigrants, mostly aligned with international Zionism or international Communism, his suggested responses were strikingly inoffensive. He urged American citizens to demonstrate their disapproval by writing letters to their newspapers and elected officials, signing petitions, and providing their political support to the patriotic elements of both the Democratic and Republican parties. He also argued that the most dangerous aspect of the current situation was the enfolding "Iron Curtain" of Jewish censorship that was preventing ordinary Americans from recognizing the great looming threat to their freedoms, and claimed that combating such media censorship was a task of the highest importance.

Others of similar background and views sometimes moved in far more extreme directions. About a dozen years ago I began noticing scattered references on fringe websites to a certain Revilo P. Oliver, an oddly-named political activist of the mid-twentieth century, apparently of enormous stature in Far Right circles. According to these accounts, after important World War II service at the War Department, he began a long and distinguished career as a Classics professor at the University of Illinois. Then, beginning in the mid-1950s, he became active in politics, establishing himself as a leading figure in the early days of both *National Review* and the John Birch Society, though he eventually broke with both those organizations when he came to regard them as too politically-compromised and ineffective. Thereafter, he gradually became more angry and extreme in his views, and by 1974 had become friendly with William Pierce of the National Alliance, suggesting the theme for his novel *The Turner Diaries,* which sold hundreds of thousands of copies as a huge underground bestseller and according to federal prosecutors later served as the inspiration for the 1995 Oklahoma City bombings.

Although I had never heard of Oliver nor his unusual career, most of the facts I could verify seemed correct. The early years of *National Review* had carried **more than 100 of his articles and reviews** and **a major feature** in *The Saturday Evening Post* discussed his rancorous break with The John Birch Society. A few years later, I became sufficiently curious that I ordered his 1981 book ***America's Decline: The Education of a Conservative***, which contained his political memoir and many of his writings. So few were available, that by chance the one I received was the author's own personal copy, with his address label glued to the cover and including a few pages of his personal correspondence and errata notes sent to his publisher. These days, the numerous copies available for sale on Amazon start at an outrageous price of almost $150, but fortunately the book is **also freely available for reading or downloading at Archive.org**.

When I first read Oliver's book seven or eight years ago, it constituted one of my earliest exposures to the literature of the Far Right, and I was not at all sure what to make of it. His enormous classical erudition was quite apparent, but his political rhetoric seemed totally outrageous, with the word "conspiracy" used with wild abandon, seemingly on almost every other page. Given his bitter political feuds with so many other right-wingers and the total lack of any mainstream endorsements, I viewed his claims with a great deal of skepticism, though a number of them stuck in my mind. However, after having very recently absorbed the remarkable material presented by Bendersky and then reread Beaty, I decided to revisit Oliver's volume, and see what I thought of it the second time round.

Bendersky makes no mention of Oliver, which is unfortunate since all the spurious accusations he had leveled against Ross and Beaty would have been entirely correct if made against Oliver. Unlike most right-wingers, then or now, Oliver was a militant atheist, holding scathing views towards Christianity, and he instead placed racial conflict at the absolute center of his world-view, making him exactly the sort of outspoken Social Darwinist not uncommon in the early years of the twentieth century, but long since driven into hiding. A good indication of the explicit harshness of Oliver's sentiments appears on the very first page of his preface, when he ridicules the total ineffectiveness of conservatives in combating "the existing situation, which has resulted from the invasion of their country by hordes of aliens who are, by a biological necessity, their racial enemies." This sort of statement would have been unimaginable in Beaty, who emphasized Christian charity and goodwill.

More than half of the fairly long text consists of pieces that appeared during 1955-1966 in *National Review, American Opinion* (the Birch magazine), and *Modern Age*, generally book reviews. Most of the topics are hardly of great current interest, and instead discuss the internal conflicts of Ancient Rome, or perhaps provide Oliver's views on Spengler, Toynbee, John Dewey, or Haitian history; but the material certainly establishes the impressive intellectual breadth of the author. According to the book's introduction, Oliver was conversant in eleven languages, including Sanskrit, and I can well credit that claim.

As mentioned, Oliver particularly despised Christianity and Christian preachers, and he devoted a substantial portion of the remainder of the book to ridiculing them and their doctrines, often deploying his great scholarship laced with crude invective, and generally writing in an arch, rather droll style. Although not of much interest to me, I'd think that those who share Oliver's religious disinclinations might find his remarks rather amusing.

However, the remaining one-third or so of the volume is focused on factual and political matters, much of the material being quite significant. According to the back cover, Oliver had spent World War II as director of a secret research group at the War Department, leading a staff that eventually grew to 175, and afterward was cited for his outstanding government service. His statements certainly present himself as extremely knowledgeable about the "hidden history" of that war, and he minced absolutely no words about his views. The combination of his strong academic background, his personal vantage point, and his extreme outspokenness would make him a uniquely valuable source on all those matters.

But that value is tempered by his credibility, cast into serious doubt by his often wild rhetoric. Whereas I would consider Beaty's book quite reliable, at least relative to the best information available at the time, and might place Henry Ford's *The International Jew* in much the same category, I would tend to be far more cautious in accepting Oliver's claims, especially given the strong emotions he expressed. Aside from his many reprinted articles, the rest of the book was written when he was in his seventies, and he repeatedly expressed his political despair concerning his many years of total failure in various right-wing projects. He declared that he had lost any hope of ever restoring the Aryan-controlled America of 1939, and instead foresaw our country's inevitable decline, alongside that of the rest of Western civilization. Moreover, many of the events he recounts had occurred three or four decades earlier, and even under the best of circumstances his recollections might have become a little garbled.

That being said, in rereading Oliver I was struck by how much of his description of America's involvement in the two world wars seemed so entirely consistent with Beaty's account, or that of numerous other highly-regarded journalists and historians of that era, such as the contributors to ***Perpetual War for Perpetual Peace.*** I had encountered this material some years after reading Oliver's book, and it greatly buttressed his credibility.

But unlike those other writers, Oliver often framed the same basic facts in extremely dramatic fashion. For example, he denounced Churchill's 1940 aerial bombing strategy as the most monstrous sort of war crime:

> Great Britain, in violation of all the ethics of civilized warfare that had theretofore been respected by our race, and in treacherous violation of solemnly assumed diplomatic covenants about "open cities", had secretly carried out intensive bombing of such open cities in Germany for the express purpose of killing enough unarmed and defenceless men and women to force the German government reluctantly to retaliate and bomb British cities and thus kill enough helpless British men, women, and children to generate among Englishmen enthusiasm for the insane war to which their government had committed them.
>
> It is impossible to imagine a governmental act more vile and more depraved than contriving death and suffering for its own people — for the very citizens whom it was exhorting to "loyalty" — and I suspect that an act of such infamous and savage treason would have nauseated even Genghis Khan or Hulagu or Tamerlane, Oriental barbarians universally reprobated for their insane blood-lust. History, so far as I recall, does not record that they ever butchered their own women and children to facilitate lying propaganda....In 1944 members of British Military Intelligence took it for granted that

after the war Marshal Sir Arthur Harris would be hanged or shot for high treason against the British people...

At the time I originally read those words, my knowledge of World War II was mostly limited to half-remembered portions of my old History 101 textbooks, and I was naturally quite skeptical at Oliver's astonishing charges. But during subsequent years, I discovered that the circumstances were exactly as Oliver claimed, with so notable a historian as David Irving having fully documented the evidence. So although we may question Oliver's exceptionally harsh characterization or his heated rhetoric, the factual case he makes seems not to be under serious dispute.

His discussion of America's own entrance in the war is equally strident. He emphasizes that his colleagues in the War Department had completely broken the most secure Japanese codes, giving our government complete knowledge of all Japanese plans:

> Perhaps the most exhilarating message ever read by American Military Intelligence was one sent by the Japanese government to their Ambassador in Berlin (as I recall), urging him not to hesitate to communicate certain information by telegrams and assuring him that "no human mind" could decipher messages that had been enciphered on the Purple Machine. That assurance justified the merriment it provoked...

However, just as many others have alleged, Oliver claims that Roosevelt then deliberately allowed the attack on Pearl Harbor to proceed and failed to warn the local military commanders, whom he then ordered court-martialed for their negligence:

> Everyone *now* knows, of course, that the message to the Japanese Ambassador in Washington, warning him that Japan was about to attack the United States, was read by Military Intelligence not long after the Ambassador himself received it, and that the frantic cover-up, involving some successful lying about details, was intended, not to preserve that secret, but to protect the traitors in Washington who made certain

that the Japanese attack, which they had labored so long to provoke, would be successful and produce the maximum loss of American lives and destruction of American ships.

Numerous historians seem to have thoroughly established that Roosevelt did everything he could to provoke a war with Japan. But Oliver adds a fascinating detail that I have never seen mentioned elsewhere:

> In January 1941, almost eleven months before Pearl Harbor, preparation for it began in Washington when Franklin D Roosevelt summoned the Portuguese Ambassador to the United States and, enjoining him to the utmost secrecy, asked him to inform Premier Salazar that Portugal need have no concern for the safety of Timor and her other possessions in Southeast Asia; the United States, he said, had decided to crush Japan forever by waiting until her military forces and lines of communication were stretched to the utmost and then suddenly launching an all-out war with massive attacks that Japan was not, and could not be, prepared to resist. As expected, the Portuguese Ambassador communicated the glad tidings to the head of his government, using his most secure method of communication, an enciphered code which the Portuguese doubtless imagined to be "unbreakable," but which Roosevelt well knew had been compromised by the Japanese, who were currently reading all messages sent in it by wireless. The statement, ostensibly entrusted in "strict secrecy" to the Portuguese Ambassador, was, of course, intended for the Japanese government, and, as a matter of fact, it became certain that the trick had succeeded when the contents of the Portuguese Ambassador's message to Salazar promptly appeared in a Japanese message enciphered by the Purple Machine. Roosevelt had only to wait for Japan to act on the "secret" information about American plans thus given her, and to order naval movements and diplomatic negotiations that would appear to the Japanese to confirm American intentions.

The fact that I have just mentioned is really the ultimate secret of Pearl Harbor, and seems to have been unknown to Admiral Theobald when he wrote his well-known book on the subject.

Oliver notes that Roosevelt had long sought to have America participate in the great European war **whose outbreak he had previously orchestrated**, but had been blocked by overwhelming domestic anti-war sentiment. His decision to provoke a Japanese attack as a "back door" to war only came after all his military provocations against Germany had failed to accomplish a similar result:

> His first plan was defeated by the prudence of the German government. While he yammered about the evils of aggression to the white Americans whom he despised and hated, Roosevelt used the United States Navy to commit innumerable acts of stealthy and treacherous aggression against Germany in a secret and undeclared war, hidden from the American people, hoping that such massive piracy would eventually so exasperate the Germans that they would declare war on the United States, whose men and resources could then be squandered to punish the Germans for trying to have a country of their own. These foul acts of the War Criminal were known, of course, to the officers and men of the Navy that carried out the orders of their Commander-in-Chief, and were commonly discussed in informed circles, but, so far as I know, were first and much belatedly chronicled by Patrick Abbazia in *Mr. Roosevelt's Navy: the Private War of the U.S. Atlantic Fleet, 1939-1942*, published by the Naval Institute Press in Annapolis in 1975.
>
> ...Although the U.S. Navy's acts of outrageous piracy on the high seas were successfully concealed from the majority of the American people before Pearl Harbor, they were, of course, well known to the Japanese, and partly account for Roosevelt's success in deceiving them with his "confidences" to the Portuguese Ambassador...they assumed that when Roosevelt was ready to attack them, his power over the American press and communications would enable him to

simulate an attack they had not in fact made. That the deception was successful was, of course, shown in December 1941, when they made a desperate effort to avert the treacherous blow they feared.

Once America thus entered the war, Oliver then focuses on the horrific way the Allies waged it, using aerial bombardment to deliberately slaughter the civilian population of Germany:

> Both British and Americans have always claimed to be humane and have loudly condemned unnecessary bloodshed, mass massacres, and sadistic delight in the infliction of pain...in 1945 their professions could still be credited without doubt, and that meant they would be stricken with remorse for a ferocious act of unmitigated savagery unparalleled in the history of our race and unsurpassed in the record of any race. The bombing of the unfortified city of Dresden, nicely timed to insure an agonizing death to the maximum number of white women and children, has been accurately described by David Irving in *The Destruction of Dresden* (London, 1963), but the essentials of that sickening atrocity were known soon after it was perpetrated. To be sure, it is true that such an act might have been ordered by Hulagu, the celebrated Mongol who found pleasure in ordering the extermination of the population of all cities that did not open their gates to him — and of some that did — so that the severed heads of the inhabitants could be piled up into pyramids as perishable but impressive monuments to his glory. The Americans and British, however, deem themselves more civilized than Hulagu and less sadistic.

He also harshly condemns the very brutal nature of the American occupation of Germany that followed the end of the war:

> ...with the American invasion of German territory began the innumerable atrocities against her civilian population — the atrocities against prisoners began even earlier — that have

brought on our people the reputation of Attila's hordes. The outrages were innumerable and no one, so far as I know, has even tried to compile a list of typical incidents of rape and torture and mayhem and murder. Most of the unspeakable atrocities, it is true, were committed by savages and Jews in American uniforms, but many, it must be confessed, were perpetrated by Americans, louts from the dregs of our own society or normal men crazed with hatred. All victorious armies, it is true, contain elements that want to outrage the vanquished, and few commanders in "democratic" wars can maintain the tight discipline that made Wellington's armies the marvels of Europe or the discipline that generally characterized the German armies in both World Wars; what so brands us with shame is that the atrocities were encouraged by our supreme commander in Europe, whose orders, presumably issued when he was not drunk or occupied with his doxies, made it difficult or hazardous for responsible American generals to observe what had been the rules of civilized warfare. Almost every American soldier in Germany had witnessed the barbarous treatment of the vanquished, the citizens of one of the greatest nations of Western civilization and our own kinsmen, and — despite the efforts to incite them to inhuman hate with Jewish propaganda — many of our soldiers witnessed such outrages with pity and shame. The cumulative effect of their reports when they returned to their own country should have been great. It is needless to multiply examples, some of which may be found in F.J.P. Veale's *Advance to Barbarism* (London, 1953).

And he suggests that the Nuremberg Tribunals brought everlasting shame upon his own country:

I was, of course, profoundly shocked by the foul murders at Nuremberg that brought on the American people an indelible shame. Savages and Oriental barbarians normally kill, with or without torture, the enemies whom they have overcome, but even they do not sink so low in the scale of humanity as to perform the obscene farce of holding quasi-judicial trials before they kill, and had the Americans — for, given their absolute power, the responsibility must fall on them, and their guilt cannot be shifted to their supposed allies — had the Americans, I say, merely slaughtered the German generals, they could claim to be morally no worse than Apaches, Balubas, and other primitives. Civilized peoples spare the lives of the vanquished, showing to their leaders a respectful consideration, and the deepest instincts of our race demand a chivalrous courtesy to brave opponents whom the fortunes of war have put in our power.

To punish warriors who, against overwhelming odds, fought for their country with a courage and determination that excited the wonder of the world, and deliberately to kill them because they were not cowards and traitors, because they did not betray their nation — that was an act of vileness of which we long believed our race incapable. And to augment the infamy of our act, we stigmatized them as "War Criminals" which they most certainly were not, for if that phrase has meaning, it applies to traitors who knowingly involve their nations in a war contrived to inflict loss, suffering, and death on their own people, who are thus made to fight for their own effective defeat — traitors such as Churchill, Roosevelt, and their white accomplices. And to add an ultimate obscenity to the sadistic crime, "trials" were held to convict the vanquished according to "laws" invented for the purpose, and on the basis of perjured testimony extorted from prisoners of war by torture…

…The moral responsibility for those fiendish crimes, therefore, falls on our own War Criminals, and, as a practical matter, nations always bear the responsibility for the acts of the individuals whom they, however mistakenly, placed in power. We cannot reasonably blame Dzhugashvili, alias Stalin: he was not a War Criminal, for he acted, logically and ruthlessly, to augment the power and the territory of the Soviet Empire, and he (whatever his personal motives may have been) was the architect of the regime that transformed a degraded and barbarous rabble into what is now the greatest military power on earth.

Oliver's memoirs were published by a tiny London press in a cheap paper binding, lacked even an index, and were hardly likely to ever reach a substantial audience. That, together with the internal evidence of his text, leads me to believe that he was quite sincere in his statements, at least with regard to all these sorts of historical and political matters. And given those beliefs, we should hardly be surprised at the heated rhetoric he directs against the targets of his wrath, especially Roosevelt, whom he repeatedly references as "the great War Criminal."

Sincerity is obviously no guarantee of accuracy. But Bendersky's extensive review of private letters and personal memoirs reveals that a large portion of our Military Intelligence officers and top generals seemed to closely share Oliver's appraisal of Roosevelt, whose eventual death provoked widespread "exultation" and "fierce delight" in their social circle. Finally, one of them wrote, "The evil man was dead!"

Moreover, although Oliver's words are as heated as those of Beaty are measured, the factual claims of the two authors are quite similar with regard to World War II, so that all the high-ranking generals who enthusiastically endorsed Beaty's bestselling 1951 book may be regarded as providing some implicit backing for Oliver.

Consider also the personal diaries and reported conversations of Gen. George S. Patton, one of our most renowned field commanders. These reveal that shortly after the end of fighting he became outraged over how he had been totally deceived regarding the circumstances of the conflict, and he planned to return to the U.S., resign his military commission, and begin a national speaking-tour to provide the American people with the true facts about the war. Instead, he died in a highly-suspicious car accident the day before his scheduled departure, and there is **very considerable evidence** that he was actually assassinated by the American OSS.

The Creation of *National Review* and the John Birch Society

Oliver's discussion of the Second World War provides remarkably vivid rhetorical flourishes and some intriguing details, but his basic analysis is not so different from that of Beaty or numerous other writers. Moreover, Beaty had a far superior vantage point during the conflict, while his book was published just a few years after the end of fighting and was also far more widely endorsed and distributed. So although Oliver's extreme candor may add much color to our historical picture, I think his memoirs are probably more useful for their other elements, such as his unique insights into the origins of both *National Review* and the John Birch Society, two of the leading right-wing organizations established during the 1950s.

Oliver opens his book by describing his departure from DC and wartime government service in the fall of 1945, fully confident that the horrific national treachery he had witnessed at the top of the American government would soon inspire "a reaction of national indignation that would become sheer fury." As he puts it:

> That reaction, I thought, would occur automatically, and my only concern was for the welfare of a few friends who had innocently and ignorantly agitated for war before the unspeakable monster in the White House successfully tricked the Japanese into destroying the American fleet at Pearl Harbor. I wondered whether a plea of ignorance would save them from the reprisals I foresaw!

He spent the next decade entirely engaged in his Classical scholarship and establishing an academic career, while noting some of the hopeful early signs of the political uprising that he fully expected to see:

> In 1949 Congressman Rankin introduced a bill that would recognize as subversive and outlaw the "Anti-"Defamation League of B'nai B'rith, the formidable organization of Jewish cowboys who ride herd on their American cattle…In both the Houses of Representatives and the Senate committees were beginning investigations of covert treason and alien subversion…Then Senator McCarthy undertook a somewhat more thorough investigation, which seemed to open a visible leak in the vast dike of deceit erected by our enemies, and it was easy to assume that the little jet of water that spurted through that leak would grow hydraulically until the dam broke and released an irresistible flood.

However, by 1954 he recognized that McCarthy's political destruction was at hand, and the opposing forces he so despised had gained the upper hand. He faced the crucial decision of whether to involve himself in politics, and if so, what form that might take.

One of his friends, a right-wing Yale professor named Wilmoore Kendall, argued that a crucial factor in the Jewish domination of American public life was their control over influential opinion journals such as *The Nation* and *The New Republic*, and that launching a competing publication might be the most effective remedy. For this purpose, he had recruited a prize student of his named William F. Buckley, Jr., who could draw upon the financial resources of his wealthy father, long known in certain circles for his discreet sponsorship of various anti-Jewish publications and "his drastic private opinion about the aliens' perversion of our national life."

A few years earlier, H.L. Mencken's famous literary monthly *The American Mercury* had fallen on hard times and been purchased by one of America's wealthiest men, Russell Maguire, who hoped to use it partly as a vehicle for his extremely strong anti-Jewish sentiments. Indeed, one of Maguire's senior staffers for a couple of years was George Lincoln Rockwell, best known for later founding the American Nazi Party. But according to Oliver, enormous concerted pressure by Jewish interests upon both newsstands and printers had caused great difficulties for that publication, which were to eventually force Maguire to abandon the effort and sell the magazine.

Kendall and Oliver hoped that Buckley's new effort might succeed where Maguire's was failing, perhaps by avoiding any direct mention of Jewish issues and instead focusing upon threats from Communists, socialists, and liberals, who were far less risky targets to attack. Buckley had previously gained some journalistic experience by working at the *Mercury* for a couple of years, so he was probably well aware of the challenging political environment he might face.

Although L. Brent Bozell, another one of his young Yale proteges, would also be working with Buckley on the new venture, Kendall told Oliver that he had failed to locate a single university professor willing to risk his name as a contributor. This prompted Oliver to take up the challenge with such determination that more of his pieces appeared in *National Review* during the 1950s than almost any other writer, even ahead of Kendall himself. Apparently Oliver had already become friendly with Buckley, **having been a member of the latter's 1950 wedding party**.

But from Oliver's perspective, the project proved a dismal failure. Against all advice, Buckley founded his magazine as a profit-making enterprise, circulating a prospectus, selling stock and debentures, and promising his early backers an excellent financial return. Instead, like every other political magazine, it always lost money and was soon forced to plead for donations, greatly irritating his initial investors.

Another concern was that just before launch, a couple of Jewish former Communists then running an existing conservative magazine caught wind of the new publication and offered to betray their employer and bring over all their existing subscribers if they were given senior roles. Although they were duly brought on board, their planned coup at *The Freeman* failed, and no promised bounty of subscribers appeared. In later hindsight, Oliver became deeply suspicious of these developments and how the publication had been so quickly diverted from its intended mission, writing:

> …it was only long after Professor Kendall had been shouldered out of the organization and I had severed my connections with it that I perceived that whenever a potentially influential journal is founded, it receives the assistance of talented "conservative" Jews, who are charged with the duty of supervising the Aryan children and making certain that they play only approved games.

Oliver also emphasized the severe dilemma faced by the magazine and all other organizations intended to combat the influence of Jews and Communists. For obvious reasons, these almost invariably centered themselves around strong support for Christianity. But Oliver was a militant atheist who detested religious faith and therefore believed that such an approach inevitably alienated "the very large number of educated men who…were repelled by the hypocrisy, obscurantism, and rabid ambitions of the clergy." Thus, Christian anti-Communist movements often tended to produce a large backlash of sympathy for Communism in elite circles.

Small ideological publications are notorious for their bitter intrigues and angry disputes, and I have made no effort to compare

Oliver's brief sketch of the creation of *National Review* with other accounts, which would surely provide very different perspectives. But I think his basic facts ring true to me.

By 1958 Oliver had established himself as one of *National Review*'s leading contributors, and he was contacted by a wealthy Massachusetts businessman named Robert Welch, who had been an early investor in the magazine but was greatly disappointed by its political ineffectiveness, so the two men corresponded and gradually became quite friendly. Welch said he was concerned that the publication focused largely on frivolity and pseudo-literary endeavors, while it increasingly minimized or ignored the conspiratorial role of the Jewish aliens who had gained such a degree of control over the country. The two men eventually met, and according to Oliver seemed to be entirely in agreement about America's plight, which they discussed in complete candor.

Late that same year, Welch described his plans for regaining control of the country by the creation of a semi-secret national organization of patriotic individuals, primarily drawn from the upper middle classes and prosperous businessmen, which eventually became known as the John Birch Society. With its structure and strategy inspired by the Communist Party, it was to be tightly organized into individual local cells, whose members would then establish a network of front organizations for particular political projects, all seemingly unconnected but actually under their dominant influence. Secret directives would be passed along to each local chapter by the word of mouth via coordinators dispatched from Welch's central headquarters, a system also modeled after the strict hierarchical discipline of Communist movements.

Welch privately unveiled his proposal to a small group of prospective co-founders, all of whom with the exception of Oliver were wealthy businessmen. He candidly admitted his own atheism and explained that Christianity would have no role in the project, which cost him a couple of potential supporters; but about a dozen committed themselves, notably including Fred Koch, founding father of Koch Industries. Minimal emphasis was to be placed upon Jewish matters, partly to avoid drawing media fire and partly in hopes that a growing schism between Zionist and non-Zionist Jews might weaken their powerful adversary, or if the former gained the upper hand, perhaps help ensure the removal of all Jews to the Middle East.

As the project moved forward, a monthly magazine called *American Opinion* was launched and Oliver took responsibility for a large portion of each issue. Given his academic and political prominence, he also became one of the leading speakers for the organization in public venues and also an influential visitor to many of its local chapters.

Although Oliver remained a top figure in the organization until 1966, in later years he concluded that Welch's serious mistakes had doomed the project to failure within just a couple of years after its establishment. Very early on, a Jewish journalist had obtained a copy of some of Welch's secret, controversial writings and their public disclosure had panicked one of the most prominent Birch leaders, soon producing a major media scandal. Welch repeatedly vacillated between defending and denying his secret manuscript, forcing his associates to take contradictory positions, and making the entire leadership seem both dishonest and ridiculous, a pattern that was to be repeated in future years.

According to Oliver, nearly eighty thousand men and women enlisted in the organization during the first decade, but he feared that their energetic efforts and commitment were entirely wasted, producing nothing of any value. As the years went by, the organization's ineffectiveness became more apparent, while Welch's autocratic control blocked any necessary changes from within since his executive council functioned merely as a powerless fig-leaf. Although Oliver remained convinced that Welch had been sincere when he began the effort, the accumulation of so many unnecessary missteps eventually led him to suspect deliberate sabotage. He claimed that his careful investigation revealed that the organization's financial problems had forced Welch to turn in desperation to outside Jewish donors, who then became his secret overlords, eventually leading Oliver to rancorously break with the organization in 1966 and denounce it as a fraud. Although I have no easy means of verifying most of Oliver's claims, his story hardly seems implausible.

Oliver also makes an important point about the severe dilemma produced by Welch's strategy. One of the central goals of the organization had been to combat organized Jewish influence in America, but any mention of Jews was forbidden, so the officially designed term for their subversive foes was the "International Communist Conspiracy." Oliver admitted that the usage of that ubiquitous phrase became "forced" and "monotonous," and indeed it or its variants appear with remarkable regularity in his articles reprinted from the Birch magazine.

According to Oliver, the intent was to allow members to draw their own logical conclusions about who was really behind the "conspiracy" they opposed while allowing the organization itself to maintain plausible deniability. But the result was total failure, with Jewish organizations fully understanding the game being played, while intelligent individuals quickly concluded that the Birch organization was either dishonest or delusional, hardly an unreasonable inference. As an example of this situation, the late investigative journalist Michael Collins Piper in 2005 told the story of how at the age of sixteen he had embraced a **'One-Minute' Membership in the John Birch Society**. Indeed, by the late 1960s, any public expressions of anti-Semitism by Birch members became grounds for immediate expulsion, a rather ironic situation for an organization originally founded just a decade earlier with avowedly anti-Semitic goals.

Secrets of the Jewish Holocaust

Following his 1966 rupture with Welch, Oliver greatly reduced his political writing, which henceforth only appeared in much smaller and more extreme venues than the Birch magazine. His book contains just a couple of such later pieces, but the second of these, published in a right-wing British magazine during 1980, is of some interest.

Just as we might expect, Oliver had always been particularly scathing towards the supposed Jewish Holocaust, and near the very beginning of his book, he states his own views in typically forceful fashion:

> The Americans...were howling with indignation over the supposed extermination by the Germans of some millions of Jews, many of whom had taken the opportunity to crawl into the United States, and...one could have supposed in 1945 that when the hoax, devised to pep up the cattle that were being stampeded into Europe, was exposed, even Americans would feel some indignation at having been so completely bamboozled.

The prompt exposure of the bloody swindle seemed inevitable, particularly since the agents of the O.S.S., commonly known in military circles as the Office of Soviet Stooges, who had been dispatched to conquered Germany to set up gas chambers to lend some verisimilitude to the hoax, had been so lazy and feckless that they merely sent back pictures of shower baths, which were so absurd that they had to be suppressed to avoid ridicule. No one could have believed in 1945 that the lie would be used to extort thirty billion dollars from the helpless Germans and would be rammed into the minds of German children by uncouth American "educators" — or that civilized men would have to wait until 1950 for Paul Rassinier, who had been himself a prisoner in a German concentration camp, to challenge the infamous lie, or until 1976 for Professor Arthur Butz's detailed and exhaustive refutation of the venomous imposture on Aryan credulity.

- **The Hoax of the Twentieth Century**
  The Case Against the Presumed Extermination of European Jewry
  Arthur R. Butz • 1976/2015 • 225,000 Words

In his republished article, Oliver discussed this same topic at far greater length and in the context of its broader theoretical implications. After recounting various examples of historical frauds and cover-ups, starting with the possibly forged letter of the younger Pliny, he expressed his amazement at the continuing widespread acceptance of the Holocaust story, despite the existence of hundreds of thousands of direct eyewitnesses to the contrary. He suggested that such an astonishing scholarly situation must force us to reassess our assumptions about the nature of evidentiary methods in historiography.

Oliver's peremptory dismissal of the standard Holocaust narrative led me to take a closer look at the treatment of the same topic in Bendersky's book, and I noticed something quite odd. As discussed above, his exhaustive research in official files and personal archives conclusively established that during World War II a very considerable fraction of all our Military Intelligence officers and top generals were vehemently hostile to Jewish organizations and also held beliefs that today would be regarded as utterly delusional. The author's academic specialty is Holocaust studies, so it is hardly surprising that his longest chapter focused on that particular subject, bearing the title "Officers and the Holocaust, 1940-1945." But a close examination of the contents raises some troubling questions.

Across more than sixty pages, Bendersky provides hundreds of direct quotes, mostly from the same officers who are the subject of the rest of his book. But after carefully reading the chapter twice, I was unable to find a single one of those statements referring to the massive slaughter of Jews that constitutes what we commonly call the Holocaust, nor to any of its central elements, such as the existence of death camps or gas chambers.

The forty page chapter that follows focuses on the plight of the Jewish "survivors" in post-war Europe, and the same utter silence applies. Bendersky is disgusted by the cruel sentiments expressed by these American military men towards the Jewish former camp inmates, and he frequently quotes them characterizing the latter as thieves, liars, and criminals; but the officers seem strangely unaware that those unfortunate souls had only just barely escaped an organized mass extermination campaign that had so recently claimed the lives of the vast majority of their fellows. Numerous statements and quotes regarding Jewish extermination are provided, but all of these come from various Jewish activists and organizations, while there is nothing but silence from all of the military officers themselves.

Bendersky's ten years of archival research brought to light personal letters and memoirs of military officers written decades after the end of the war, and in both those chapters he freely quotes from these invaluable materials, sometimes including private remarks from the late 1970s, long after the Holocaust had become a major topic in American public life. Yet not a single statement of sadness, regret, or horror is provided. Thus, a prominent Holocaust historian spends a decade researching a book about the private views of our military officers towards Jews and Jewish topics, but the one hundred pages he devotes to the Holocaust and its immediate aftermath contains not a single directly-relevant quote from those individuals, which is simply astonishing. A yawning chasm seems to exist at the center of his lengthy historical volume, or put another way, a particular barking dog is quite deafening in its silence.

I am not an archival researcher and have no interest in reviewing the many tens of thousands of pages of source material located at dozens of repositories across the country that Bendersky so diligently examined while producing his important book. Perhaps during their entire wartime activity and also the decades of their later lives, not a single one of the hundred-odd important military officers who were the focus of his investigation ever once broached the subject of the Holocaust or the slaughter of Jews during World War II. But I think there is another distinct possibility.

As mentioned earlier, Beaty spent his war years carefully reviewing the sum-total of all incoming intelligence information each day and then producing an official digest for distribution to the White House and our other top leaders. And in his 1951 book, published just a few years after the end of fighting, he dismissed the supposed Holocaust as a ridiculous wartime concoction by dishonest Jewish and Communist propagandists that had no basis in reality. Soon afterward, Beaty's book was fully endorsed and promoted by many of our leading World War II generals, including those who were subjects of Bendersky's archival research. And although the ADL and various other Jewish organizations fiercely denounced Beaty, there is no sign that they ever challenged his absolutely explicit "Holocaust denial."

I suspect that Bendersky gradually discovered that such "Holocaust denial" was remarkably common in the private papers of many of his Military Intelligence officers and top generals, which presented him with a serious dilemma. If only one or two of those individuals had expressed such sentiments, their shocking statements could be cited as further evidence of their delusional anti-Semitism. But what if a substantial majority of those officers—who certainly had possessed the best knowledge of the reality of World War II—held private beliefs that were very similar to those publicly expressed by their former colleagues Beaty and Oliver? In such a situation, Bendersky may have decided that certain closed doors should remain in that state, and entirely skirted the topic.

At the age of 89, Richard Lynn surely ranks as the "grand old man" of IQ research, and in 2002 he and his co-author Tatu Vanhanen published their seminal work *IQ and the Wealth of Nations*. Their volume strongly argued that mental ability as measured by standardized tests was overwhelmingly determined by hereditary genetic factors, and for nearly two decades their research findings have constituted a central pillar of the IQ movement that they have long inspired. But as I argued in **a major article** several years ago, the massive quantity of evidence they presented actually demonstrates the exact opposite conclusion:

> We are now faced with a mystery arguably greater than that of IQ itself. Given the powerful ammunition that Lynn and Vanhanen have provided to those opposing their own "Strong IQ Hypothesis," we must wonder why this has never attracted the attention of either of the warring camps in the endless, bitter IQ dispute, despite their alleged familiarity with the work of these two prominent scholars. In effect, I would suggest that the heralded 300-page work by Lynn and Vanhanen constituted a game-ending own-goal against their IQ-determinist side, but that neither of the competing ideological teams ever noticed.

For ideologically-blinkered scholars to sometimes produce research that constitutes "a game-ending own-goal" may be much more common than most of us would expect. Janet Mertz and her zealously feminist co-authors expended enormous time and effort to conclusively establish that across nearly all nations of the world, regardless of culture, region, or language, the group of highest-performing math students has almost always been roughly 95% male and just 5% female, a result that would seem to deeply undercut their hypothesis that men and women have equal mathematical ability.

Similarly, ten years of exhaustive archival research by Joseph Bendersky produced a volume that seems to utterly demolish our conventional narrative of Jewish political activism in both Europe and America between the two world wars. Moreover, when carefully considered I think his text constitutes a dagger aimed with deadly accuracy straight at the heart of our conventional Holocaust narrative, his own lifelong area of study and a central pillar of the West's current ideological framework.

Over the last year or two, pressure from the ADL and other Jewish activist organizations has induced **Amazon to ban all books** that challenge the Holocaust or other beliefs deeply held by organized Jewry. Most of these purged works are quite obscure, and many are of indifferent quality. Moreover, their public impact has been severely diminished by the real or perceived ideological associations of their authors.

Meanwhile, for nearly twenty years a book of absolutely devastating historical importance has sat on the Amazon shelves, freely available for sale and bearing glowing cover-blurbs by mainstream, reputable scholars, but by its Amazon sales-rank, selling almost no copies, a massive, unexploded shell whom nearly no one seems to have properly recognized. I suggest that interested readers purchase their copies of Bendersky's outstanding opus before steps are taken to permanently flush it down the memory hole.

This article is available online at:
https://www.unz.com/runz/american-pravda-secrets-of-military-intelligence/

The Power of Organized Crime
How a Young Syndicate Lawyer from Chicago Earned a Fortune Looting the Property of the Japanese-Americans, then Lived Happily Ever After as America's Most Respected Civil Libertarian Federal Appellate Court Judge
The Unz Review, July 15, 2019

The Presence of Organized Crime in Our Society

As I was growing up in the suburban San Fernando Valley of Los Angeles during the 1960s and 1970s, organized crime seemed like a very distant thing, confined to the densely-populated cities of the East Coast or to America's past, much like the corrupt political machines with which it was usually associated.

I never heard any stories of ballot-box stuffing or political precinct captains controlling a swath of no-show city jobs or traffic tickets being "fixed" by a friend at City Hall. The notion of local grocery stores paying protection money or taking numbers bets from their clientele on behalf of bookies would have seemed quite outlandish to me.

All these personal impressions were strongly reinforced by the electronic media that so heavily shapes our perceptions of reality. A couple of the popular shows I sometimes watched in reruns were the police procedural dramas *Dragnet* and *Adam-12*, both set in Southern California, and although each episode focused on one or more serious crimes, these were almost never of the "organized" variety. The same was true for *Perry Mason* episodes, although those longer courtroom dramas would have been naturally suited to the plotting of Syndicate members. The popular *Rockford Files* of the late 1970s did sometimes feature mobsters, but these individuals were almost always temporary visitors to LA from New York or Chicago or Las Vegas, with the plotlines sometimes humorously treating these gangsters as struggling fish out of water in the very different world of sunny Southern California. By contrast, a contemporaneous detective show set in New York like *Kojak* seemed to feature mafioso characters in every third or fourth episode.

The offerings of the Silver Screen generally followed the same pattern. Gangster films, ranging from the crudest B-flicks to the Academy Award-winning *Godfather* masterpieces, were almost never set on the West Coast. And although a film like Roman Polanski's *Chinatown* might be focused on the deadly criminal intrigues of the 1930s Los Angeles financial elites, the villain was just a ruthless businessman, employing a couple of murderous hired thugs.

Children soon become aware that the dramatic concoctions of Hollywood are not necessarily accurate, but when everything we see on screens big and small so closely matches our direct personal experience, that amalgamation of images and daily life produces a very firm sense of reality.

Even the occasional exception seemed to support the general rule. In the 1970s, I remember once watching a local television news crew interview an elderly Jewish man named Mickey Cohen on a local park bench, breathlessly describing him as having once been the reigning mobster king of Los Angeles. While I didn't doubt that in bygone days the crotchety little fellow had once been a hardened criminal, I remained somewhat skeptical that LA had ever contained enough mobsters to warrant having a king, let alone that such a figure would have been drawn from our notoriously law-abiding Jewish community.

Throughout the 1960s and 1970s crime became a steadily rising problem in the once-quiet suburbs of Los Angeles, but virtually none of those incidents seemed much like a Francis Ford Coppola epic. The Crips and Bloods of South-Central regularly killed each other and innocent bystanders, while burglaries and robberies—as well as occasional rapes and murders—sometimes spilled over the Hollywood Hills into the Valley. Terrifying serial killers like the Hillside Strangler provoked widespread fear as did the horrible deeds of the Manson Family, while the fiery final shootout of the Symbionese Liberation Army near Inglewood drew national headlines; but none of this seemed much like the activities of the Gambinos or Columbos of NYC. Indeed, I and my friends would sometimes joke that since the Mafia was supposedly so effective at keeping street crime away from its own New York City neighborhoods, perhaps LA would have been better off if it had had a sizeable Sicilian population.

When I sometimes gave the matter a little thought, the utter lack of any organized crime in California seemed fairly easy to explain. East

Coast cities had been settled by waves of foreign immigrants, impoverished newcomers who spoke no English, and their total ignorance of American ways left them quite vulnerable to criminal exploitation. Such situations were an ideal breeding ground for corruption, political machines, and crime syndicates, with the centuries-old secret societies of Sicily and Southern Italy providing the obvious seeds for the last of those. Meanwhile, most of California had been settled by longstanding American citizens, often relocating from the placid Midwest, and Iowans who spoke perfect English and whose families had been voting in U.S. elections for six generations were far less vulnerable to political intimidation or criminal exploitation.

Since organized crime obviously did not exist in California, I was never quite sure how much to believe about its supposed size and power elsewhere in the country. Al Capone had been imprisoned and died decades before I was born and with the end of Roaring Twenties, violent gangsterism seemed to have mostly disappeared as well. Every now and then the newspapers might carry the story of an Eastern Mafia chieftain killed by his rivals, but those occasional events provided little indication about the actual power those individuals had wielded while alive. In 1977, teenage members of an obscure Chinese immigrant street gang in San Francisco used automatic weapons to attack their rivals at a local restaurant, leaving sixteen dead or wounded, a bodycount that seemed comparable to the total number of traditional Mafia killings nationwide over a period of several years.

During the 1970s I also starting hearing lurid tales that the Mafia had stolen the 1960 election for President John F. Kennedy and might even have been involved in his subsequent assassination, but the respectable media seemed to treat those claims with enormous scorn, so I tended to regard them as *National Enquirer* type nonsense, not much different than ridiculous UFO stories. Growing up when I did, the Kennedys had seemed like America's own royal family, and I was very skeptical that control of the White House at the absolute height of the American Century had been swung by Mafia bosses. There were stories that Old Joe Kennedy, the family patriarch, had dabbled in bootlegging during the 1920s, but that had been during Prohibition, a very different era than the aftermath of the quiet and prosperous Eisenhower years of the 1950s.

Twentieth century American history had never been of much interest to me, so I am not entirely sure at what point my understanding of these issues began to change. I think it may have been just a few years ago, when I was absolutely shocked to discover that there was overwhelming evidence that the JFK Assassination had indeed been part of a large conspiracy, a revelation absolutely contrary to what I had always been led to believe by the media throughout my life. But when a highly-regarded national journalist such as David Talbot gathered together the copious evidence in his book **Brothers**, and his conclusions were endorsed by an eminent presidential historian such as Alan Brinkley writing **in the pages** of the august *New York Times*, such a shift became unavoidable. And it seemed clear that elements of organized crime had been heavily involved in that presidential assassination.

My awakening to the reality of the JFK Assassination took some time to digest, but a year or so later I began investigating that era more carefully, and decided to finally read ***The Dark Side of Camelot***, a huge 1997 bestseller by Seymour Hersh, perhaps our most renowned investigative journalist. Although it focused primarily on the long-suppressed misdeeds of the Kennedy Administration and only lightly touched upon the assassination that ended it, nearly all of the material seemed very consistent with what I had recently read in the other books centered entirely upon the 1963 events in Dallas. And the long-time relationship between the Kennedys and organized crime, sometimes hostile and sometimes friendly, was absolutely eye-opening for what it revealed about the immense hidden power of that latter social institution.

When several highly-regarded journalists come to identical conclusions and back their shocking claims with copious credible evidence, we must accept the reality of what they have presented.

For example, it seems absolutely undeniable that the Chicago Syndicate helped steal the 1960 election for Kennedy, using their control over the election machinery of that extremely corrupt city to carry Illinois's crucial 27 electoral votes and place JFK in the White House instead of his opponent Vice President Richard Nixon.

That outcome had been accomplished through the intense personal lobbying of top mob bosses by Joseph Kennedy, Sr. His efforts were greatly assisted by the advocacy of singer Frank Sinatra, an entertainer with strong personal ties both to the Kennedys and the underworld, and the Syndicate believed they had an understanding that a victorious Kennedy Administration would go easy on them. But instead, newly appointed Attorney-General Robert Kennedy redoubled the government's war on organized crime, leading outraged mob boss Sam Giancana to nearly order the killing of Sinatra in retaliation. Certainly the perceived betrayal greatly facilitated the involvement of various gangster elements in the subsequent Dallas assassination.

Ironically enough, organized crime itself had been sharply divided in that 1960 election. Jimmy Hoffa, head of the very powerful and fully mobbed-up Teamsters Union, had become a bitter foe of Robert Kennedy during the latter's 1957 service as Chief Counsel of the Senate "Rackets Committee," and Hoffa therefore became one of Nixon's most important backers, secretly delivering his campaign committee a million dollars in cash and encouraging all the Teamster locals and the affiliated gangster groups he could influence to give the Republican candidate their enthusiastic support.

The actual relationship between crime lords and the new American president was a complex and contradictory one, with brother Robert fiercely prosecuting the mob even as the CIA enlisted the support of the same groups—and sometimes even the same individuals—in their unsuccessful efforts to assassinate Cuba's Communist dictator, Fidel Castro.

Although I was quite surprised when I discovered that all these gossipy rumors were actually based upon solid evidence, even more shocking were the less sanguinary facts that finally came to my attention. Although scrupulously ignored by respectable journalists and historians, there was strong evidence that elements of organized crime had already deeply penetrated the commanding heights of corporate America, and sometimes secured important government decisions on their behalf.

Consider, for example, the General Dynamics corporation, which already ranked as one of America's leading defense contractors by the 1950s, and whose name had always held a vague place in my mind not too different from that of Lockheed or Boeing. Years earlier I had read with considerable shock **an offhand paragraph** by the late journalist Alexander Cockburn, a fearless muckraker:

Talking of continuity, a notorious scandal of the Kennedy years was JFK's defense secretary, Robert McNamara, overruling all expert review and procurement recommendations and insisting that General Dynamics rather than Boeing make the disastrous F-111, at that time one of the largest procurement contracts in the Pentagon's history...Crown, of Chicago Sand and Gravel, had $300 million of the mob's money in General Dynamics' debentures, and after the disaster of the Convair, General Dynamics needed the F-111 to avoid going belly-up, taking the mob's $300 million with it.

Although I later became quite friendly with Cockburn and respected his opinion, at the time I treated his casual claims with considerable skepticism. However, Hersh's far more detailed coverage fully confirmed that story, and reported some of its even more amazing details. Apparently agents of the aerospace corporation were observed burglarizing the home of JFK's favorite mistress, and Hersh suggested that the incriminating blackmail evidence they presumably obtained was the reason why Defense Secretary Robert McNamara overruled all of his Pentagon brass and awarded the largest military government contract in world history to the Syndicate-backed firm. Moreover, even by government procurement standards, the resulting F-111 was a remarkable disaster, never achieving any of its intended performance goals despite suffering nearly 700% in cost-overruns. So a financial investment of organized crime was salvaged at great cost both to our military effectiveness and to the American taxpayer.

The World of the Chicago Syndicate

Given that organized crime had apparently played a far greater national role in twentieth century American history than I had realized from my readings of mainstream newspapers and magazines, I recently decided to expand my knowledge in that area. Someone brought to my attention the work of investigative journalist Gus Russo, a prominent author on that topic. Russo had worked as a lead reporter for the award-winning PBS *Frontline* series and filled similar roles at other television networks, while being nominated for a 1998 Pulitzer Prize for his book on the JFK-Mafia alliance against Castro.

Over a dozen years ago, Russo published a pair of massive volumes on the history of organized crime focused on two particular regions, with *The Outfit* in 2001 discussing Chicago and *Supermob* in 2006 dealing with California. Taken together these two works of deep investigative research run more than 1100 pages and over a half million words, apparently dwarfing almost anything else in that subject area. By the 1990s declassification of a vast quantity of government documents, including FBI wiretaps and Congressional files, allowed Russo access to this previously unavailable material. He supplemented this crucial archival research with the secondary source material contained in hundreds of books and articles, as well as more than 200 personal interviews, and his especially extensive second volume references this wealth of source material with more than 1500 footnotes. The numerous laudatory cover-blurbs by prominent prosecutors, former law enforcement agents, and experts on organized crime strongly attest to the credibility of his research, which certainly must have absorbed many years of concentrated effort.

As a newcomer to the subject of the Chicago Syndicate, my first surprise was the remarkable continuity and longevity of that criminal enterprise. I had always vaguely assumed that after Al Capone's imprisonment and the repeal of Prohibition, his gang had largely disintegrated or at least had lost most of its power, but this was entirely incorrect. Instead, over the next few decades, Capone's successors greatly reduced the public violence that had provoked a harsh federal crackdown, but simultaneously multiplied their wealth and power by gaining control of numerous other sources of revenue, many of them legitimate unions and businesses, and also expanded their geographical reach across various other states. Chicago's gangland leadership also seemed remarkably stable throughout most of the next half-century, so that even as late as the 1970s, the paramount Syndicate authority was exercised by an individual who had originally enlisted with Capone in the 1920s as a violent young hoodlum, soon winning widespread renown for allegedly beating to death two of Big Al's treacherous henchmen with a baseball bat.

Authors have a natural tendency to emphasize the importance of their particular subjects, but I think Russo makes a persuasive case that the unity and stability of the Chicago underworld gave it a considerable advantage over its New York City counterparts, whose permanent division into five separate Mafia families led to an uneasy local peace occasionally punctuated by violent conflict. As a result, the disunited New York gangsters were never able to exercise much control over their local city government let alone the rival criminal power-centers of other East Coast cities, while the Chicago Syndicate seems to have always been a very powerful force in city politics, and successfully extended its suzerainty throughout much of the Midwest, the Rocky Mountain states, and into California.

Another surprise was the ethnic skew of the Chicago Outfit and its closest collaborators. Across the East Coast, full Mafia membership was traditionally restricted to Sicilians or other Italians, but none of those rules seemed to apply in the Windy City. During the 1920s there had been a series of bloody battles between Capone's Italian mob and the violent Irish gangsters who controlled the Northside, with Jews being substantially represented in both groups. But Capone had steadily eliminated his opponents, winning a final, crushing victory with the St. Valentine's Day Massacre of 1929, after which Irish names mostly disappear from the crime narrative, while the presence of Slavs or Germans had always been rare, despite their huge local populations.

But although the top Syndicate leadership remained almost entirely Italian—with a Welsh immigrant being the sole exception—roughly half of all the key figures found in Russo's detailed narrative turned out to be Jewish. From the 1930s onward, organized crime in Chicago was essentially an Italian-Jewish partnership, with the Italians concentrating on the violent muscle side of the business and the Jews more likely to be involved in money-laundering, political corruption, and legal manipulation.

The deep underworld links of individuals whom my mainstream histories had never characterized as "mobbed up" was eye-opening. For example, I'd always known of Walter Annenberg as the very wealthy publisher of TV Guide and a close friend of the Reagans, endowing the massive Annenberg Foundation to support various non-profit projects, including PBS. However, the family fortune had been established by his father Moe Annenberg, who created America's largest bookie wire service in close alliance with Capone and his Chicago successors. The elder Annenberg eventually served time in federal prison for evading taxes on his enormous illegal income and paid the largest tax fine in American history, while arranging that charges be dropped against his son Walter, who was his partner in the business. Russo actually defends Annenberg, arguing that he was unfairly targeted for prosecution by the Roosevelt Administration because of his political opposition to FDR.

As another example, my history textbooks had frequently mentioned that President Harry Truman had been a product of the Pendergast machine of Kansas City, Missouri, whose activities I'd always assumed were restricted to local politics and perhaps a bit of municipal graft. But according to Russo, the city was second only to Chicago in its municipal corruption, with the local police force run by an ex-Capone mobster and ten percent of the officers having criminal records, while Pendergast himself had been a prominent participant at the 1929 national gangster convention in Atlantic City as well as later mob summits. Truman's handwritten journal records the criminal actions he had regularly allowed in return for his elected judgeship.

According to Russo, Pendergast later decided to elevate Truman to the U.S. Senate mostly to gain protection from the backlash over the recent local murder of four federal agents, and Truman's victorious Senate campaign had involved several additional killings. Over the course of the Truman Administration, Attorney-General Tom Clark was apparently promoted to the Supreme Court in exchange for arranging the early release of a top Capone lieutenant who was then serving time in federal prison, a scandal that led the *Chicago Tribune* to demand Clark's impeachment.

Truman himself had reached the White House because he was placed on the 1944 ticket as FDR's Vice President, and his nomination had been pushed by garment union leader Sidney Hillman, president of the CIO and sometimes described as the second most powerful man in America. According to contemporaneous news accounts backed by declassified government files, the successful rise of Hillman's union had been facilitated by a close alliance with the gangsters of New York's Murder, Inc., whose leader Lepke Buchalter was eventually executed for one of Hillman's hits.

During this era, the huge growth in the power and influence of organized crime had not passed unnoticed by those outside its orbit, and they sometimes chose to focus upon it for their own reasons, but often suffered unexpected setbacks. In 1950 freshman Tennessee Senator Estes Kefauver decided to raise his public profile for a future presidential run by leading a national crusade against gangster power and holding public hearings to vilify their leaders. However, Kefauver was a notorious womanizer and during his preliminary visit to Chicago, compromising photos were taken of him in the arms of two mob-supplied women, after which the Senator changed his mind about requiring testimony from his top Syndicate target.

Sometimes real life gangsters impinged upon their Hollywood counterparts in ironic ways. In 1959 Desi Arnaz began producing *The Untouchables*, a popular television show presenting weekly Prohibition Era battles between G-Man Eliot Ness and mobsters Al Capone and Frank Nitti, with the TV drama playing a major role in shaping the public perceptions of organized crime. According to later mob memoirs, the top Chicago gangsters soon became outraged at what they regarded as a highly inaccurate portrayal of their own history and one that they considered slanderous toward Italian-Americans, so after Arnaz ignored the warnings they sent him via Frank Sinatra, they arranged to have him killed. But their California agents dragged their feet about assassinating the world-famous star of *I Love Lucy*, and Capone's widow soon vetoed the hit because her son had been Arnaz's best friend during their days as Florida high school classmates.

This very crude attempt of Chicago's Italian gangsters to protest their perceived ethnic portrayal in a simple television show raises a much broader point, which should be carefully considered. Aside from our personal experiences in real life, nearly everything we know about the world comes from the media, with electronic entertainment being especially dominant for most people. During the 1930s and 1940s gangster movies of varying quality had been quite popular, and to some extent *The Untouchables* helped revive that genre for the newly powerful medium of television. Meanwhile, with the exception of cartoon-focused Disney, all of Hollywood's major studios had almost always been owned or run by Jews, who also controlled all our radio and television networks. So for decades nearly everything ordinary Americans heard or saw arrived through that very specific ethnic filter.

The popular perceptions of the nature of organized crime demonstrated the impact of that situation. Throughout the middle decades of the twentieth century, gangsters were sometimes presented without any clear ethnic tinge, frequently as Italians or perhaps Irish, but only very rarely identified as Jewish, thus establishing an implicit framework of reality that was considerably misleading.

As I gradually came to recognize this distortion of history a couple of decades ago, I once decided to conduct a simple thought-experiment by mentally listing the dozen most prominent figures that casually came to my mind from the Gangster Era. Al Capone was obviously the most infamous, followed by Lucky Luciano, Meyer Lansky, and Bugsy Siegel. After that came a number of somewhat lesser figures: Frank Costello, Legs Diamond, Lepke Buchalter, Dutch Schultz, Bugsy Moran, Johnny Torrio, Hymie Weiss, and Arnold Rothstein. I had never studied American crime history so my list was vague and impressionistic, but I was surprised to realize that a milieu I'd always regarded as overwhelmingly Italian was actually mostly Jewish, suggesting that I had accepted the misleading headlines of a historical narrative without focusing upon its actual contents. Indeed, **Brooklyn's notorious Murder Inc.** was originally established by Lansky and Siegel and seems to have been overwhelmingly Jewish, while living up to its name by its many hundreds of killings, with one of its leading members supposedly having a personal body-count of 100 or more victims. But since I'd never heard of a single Jewish gangster in Chicago, I was still very surprised that such individuals comprised nearly half of the leading figures in Russo's comprehensive history.

The Political Conquest of California

Russo's 2001 volume may well rank as the definitive history of Chicago organized crime, and after years of additional research he published ***Supermob***, a 2006 sequel focused upon my own state of California, which I found even more interesting and deeply disturbing. While his first book was primarily an account of a city's underworld and its evolution under the heirs of Al Capone, this one told the story of how individuals who had gotten their start among those Syndicate gangsters went on to achieve far greater wealth and power in the "upperworld" of business respectability. And the ethnic dimensions of organized crime, which had been an important subtext of that first work became absolutely central to this second one.

His sweeping narrative explains that during the years immediately following World War II, a group of interconnected individuals who were alumni of the Chicago Syndicate relocated to California and largely took over the politics of the Golden State, even while the local and national media averted their eyes from these important developments, rendering them invisible to the general public. He makes a strong case for the reality of these extraordinary claims.

An important point emphasized by the author is that this transformation was facilitated by the political reforms of former governor Hiram Johnson and other leading California progressives in the early decades of the twentieth century. Seeking to prevent the rise of the political "bossism" endemic to many Eastern states, they had drastically curtailed the power of political parties by allowing candidate cross-registration and other measures intended to greatly reduce the influence of the party infrastructure. But the state's population then skyrocketed by over 50% between 1940 and 1950 and by nearly another 50% in the decade that followed, largely due to new arrivals from elsewhere in the country. With parties having little power and most candidates being unknown to this vast influx of new California voters, advertising money became the crucial ingredient of political success in such a huge state with expensive media markets, so those able to raise the necessary funding might rise very rapidly in political circles. Furthermore, individuals who had been trained in the ruthless political jungle of Chicago found naive California a far easier environment in which to operate.

Art White, a leading Los Angeles political reporter of that era, later explained these unusual political circumstances:

> California was to become a state full of strangers, political waifs and mavericks who registered in their party of preference only to find that they had come to a place where political ideology was of no importance. Republicans ran as Democrats and Democrats ran as Republicans. With disconcerting regularity, Republicans, having won both party nominations, were elected in the primaries.
>
> Since party designations had no meaning to the electorate, elections were won by the candidate with the most money, the greatest number of billboards, direct mail pieces, and the most radio time.
>
> Any individual who could devise a system to furnish these campaign necessities on a sustained basis was on his

way to becoming a political boss, California style. The boss... could have a say, perhaps the final word, in the appointment of judges from the municipal courts to the state supreme court. Other appointive jobs included inheritance tax appraisers, deputy attorney generals, state department heads and commissioners of departments. With a handful of such appointments in his pocket, the boss could protect his economic interests.

One of the most striking examples of such rapid success was the career of former Chicago attorney Paul Ziffren, whose meteoric rise in the backroom world of California politics was fueled by his ability to raise enormous sums of money for his favored candidates. Soon after arriving in Los Angeles during the mid-1940s, his strong relationship with the Truman White House allowed him to quickly supplant the leading local Democrats in national influence. By 1953 he had been named the Democratic National Committeeman for California, and was hailed for "reinvigorating" the state party, which had successfully captured both houses of the state legislature for the first time in 75 years. He won the fulsome praise of the party's National Chairman, who described him as the most important individual Democrat behind that success.

Ziffren's lifelong mob associations pervade some one hundred pages of Russo's book, but in 1954 he successfully elected Pat Brown as California's Attorney-General, who then repaid that crucial backing by naming Ziffren's brother as the Assistant Attorney-General for Southern California, thereby providing the Syndicate's ongoing activities with a great deal of legal protection despite the continuing hostility of local law enforcement departments.

This new kingmaker of California Democratic politics saw his legal risks further diminish the following year when Alex Greenberg, his longtime business partner, was shot to death gangland style on the streets of Chicago, taking to the grave his personal knowledge of Ziffren's enormous web of Syndicate-related real estate transactions. Ziffren's power and influence lasted for decades, and when he finally died in 1991 at the age of seventy-seven, his mourners included former California governors Pat and Jerry Brown, future governor Gray Davis, and numerous top Hollywood stars, while he received **uniform-**

ly **glowing tributes** in the *Los Angeles Times* and other newspapers, none of which provided a hint of his nefarious personal background.

The California Republican Party frequently pursued similar financial temptations. While Ziffren was successfully raising funds from mysterious sources for the 1950 U.S. Senate campaign of Helen Gahagun Douglas, longtime mob lawyer Murray Chotiner was performing the same task for her successful foe Richard Nixon, whose victory established Chotiner as a leading Republican strategist, both in California and nationwide. Ironically enough, while candidates regularly denounced the underworld ties of their opponents, all these rival Democratic and Republican "Supermob" lawyers had nearby homes and offices in Beverly Hills and generally remained good friends with each other and even occasional business partners, perhaps exchanging casual gossip about the strengths and weaknesses of the various candidates whose campaigns they regularly ran, much like jockeys might do about their different racetrack mounts.

Pat Brown reached the governorship in an upset against Chotiner's Republican candidate in 1958, and then won reelection against Nixon in 1962, but lost in 1966 to newcomer Ronald Reagan. Reagan's own political rise had been orchestrated by Hollywood mogul Lew Wasserman of MCA, yet another Chicago transplant. Wasserman together with his mentor Jules Stein also had decades of mob-ties stretching back to Al Capone himself, having regularly employed gangster muscle to strong-arm their business partners and suppress their competitors.

Russo provides the remarkable account of how Wasserman had propelled Reagan, then a washed-up B movie actor, into the presidency of the Screen Actors Guild in 1959 in order to obtain a special industry exemption for MCA, afterward rewarding the future president with an extremely lucrative TV contract. As a result of this successful regulatory maneuver, MCA's unique business opportunities established Wasserman as the reigning king of Hollywood for decades and he subsequently played a major role in elevating Reagan to the governorship.

Russo's own factual account of these events draws upon ***Dark Victory: Ronald Reagan, MCA, and the Mob***, a heavily-researched 1986 volume by veteran crime journalist Dan Moldea, which I had previously read and found quite persuasive. The enormous clout of MCA and its executives seem to have severely reduced distribution and media coverage of Moldea's book, while the author was forced to resign from The Institute of Policy Studies, a leftwing DC thinktank dependent upon financing from MCA-connected donors. A very similar fate had previously befallen popular author Henry Denker's 1972 novel *The Kingmaker*, a *roman a clef* portraying Wasserman and the political rise of Reagan, which also saw its distribution widely suppressed despite its excellent reviews.

Although Wasserman achieved great wealth and enormous social prominence, he never cast aside his long criminal associations, and for decades his closest personal friend was the Syndicate's California liaison.

That individual was attorney Sidney Korshak, who constitutes the central figure in Russo's long narrative, with one of his rare public photographs gracing the cover. Korshak had gotten his start working for the Capone gang in Chicago, and he soon gained a reputation for his deft ability to bridge the worlds of criminal gangs, racketeer-influenced unions, and legitimate businesses. This effectiveness and his near-total lack of a paper trail in public records or the media established him as the ideal representative of the Chicago Syndicate, and according to later Congressional testimony, they moved him out to Southern California in the early 1950s to oversee their rapidly-expanding West Coast operations.

In the years that followed, Korshak became one of the leading powerbrokers in Hollywood, while also having enormous influence over the unions of the Western states and the businesses dependent upon them, sometimes having the ability to start or stop strikes with merely a phone call. Although nominally still a lawyer, he had no office nor staff, and conducted most of his business activities from a private phone he had installed at his favorite table of a leading Beverly Hills bistro, sometimes walking outside for his more delicate conversations in order to avoid eavesdropping. All references to his overlords back in Chicago were given in code, so that upon returning from their honeymoon, Korshak's new wife noted the long list of opaque messages that had been left by George Washington, Thomas Jefferson, Abraham Lincoln, and Theodore Roosevelt. FBI wiretaps revealed that the Syndicate bosses warned California gangsters never to contact Korshak directly, but instead to always use his Chicago superiors as the conduit for all requests and communications.

Throughout his long career Korshak went to enormous lengths to maintain his near-total public invisibility, and although he regularly attended Hollywood events and elite dinner-parties, there was a horrified stir when an uninformed screenwriter once accidentally snapped his photograph. Despite a growing awareness of his tremendous power in Southern California and his very unsavory ties, he successfully deployed his connections and influence to ward off almost all newspaper coverage. In 1962 the top management of the *Los Angeles Times* suddenly dismantled that newspaper's star investigative unit in order to terminate a long series they had begun running on the Teamsters Union funding for suspicious real estate transactions, which would have inevitably led to Korshak and his inner circle of Syndicate associates. As the *Times'* managing editor later described the situation: "Once you get to the point where you can get a guy to talk, then either you or he or both are going to end up in a lime pit somewhere."

By 1969 widespread local awareness of Korshak's enormous hidden power and deep gangland ties finally prompted the national editor of the *Times* to commission his profile by a young reporter. Despite a great deal of lobbying pressure, this story finally ran, though in sufficiently tame form that Korshak later boasted that all this friends regarded it as a personal advertisement. Still, to avoid any such future coverage, he soon offered Buff Chandler, the newspaper's matriarch, an immediate donation of $25,000 to ensure that his name would never again appear in print, an agreement she accepted and honored. Over the years, several determined journalists across California would find their heavily-researched stories killed by their editorial superiors, sometimes causing them to quit their newspapers in disgust.

During Korshak's decades of power, one of the extremely rare major profiles of his activities appeared in *The New York Times*, written in 1976 by fellow-Chicagoan Seymour Hersh, who had already gained renown for breaking the My Lai massacre story a few years earlier, a triumph that earned him a Pulitzer Prize and numerous other accolades. As Hersh later explained, when he began his research, outraged police officials and previously muzzled journalists quickly provided him with troves of background material. But he also soon discovered that Korshak had obtained all his calling records and travel itinerary from a *Times* employee, and he later had a chilling phone conversation with the subject of his probe from a pay phone in West LA. Although Korshak was careful to never explicitly threaten him, his dialogue was very heavily laced with words like "murder…bodies…blood…death…killings," and Hersh still vividly recalled that conversation decades later. He later learned from others that Korshak regularly employed that style of intimidation in such situations.

Although powerful lobbying by Korshak's allies and threats of lawsuits led two top *Times* executives to try to stop the investigation, and the Teamsters eventually struck the newspaper on the very eve of the series' scheduled appearance, Hersh's stories ran, and they provoked a great deal of national attention, although they were studiously ignored by the *Los Angeles Times*. Afterward, Hersh was contacted by one of Korshak's nieces, who provided a personal anecdote that included a casual mention of how in his younger days at a family Passover seder Korshak had expressed satisfaction after receiving a phone call reporting the successful assassination of an Illinois political reformer. In a rare personal interview with Russo, Hersh tersely summarized his appraisal of Korshak: "He was the godfather. There's no question, he ordered people hit."

Aspects of Korshak's lifestyle certainly comported with such notions. His walled and gated home was patrolled by armed guards, reportedly former members of the Israeli military. A studio executive who visited him found the front door answered by a man with a gun, a situation that he had never previously encountered.

Such considerations of personal security may not have been unwarranted. According to FBI documents later released, Korshak had hardly been monogamous in his loyalties, and he had sought to maintain his legal immunity by providing a steady stream of confidential information to Las Vegas law enforcement and the Bureau, facts that surely would have put his life at serious risk if they had been discovered by his underworld confederates. Indeed, when Korshak was in his eighties, he was once suddenly approached by a Hollywood reporter on the street, and reacted as if he assumed that his number had finally come up, then was greatly relieved to discover that the fellow was just a journalist rather than the hitman whose arrival he had long anticipated.

Korshak's massive impact is described in enormous detail across the pages of Russo's thick volume. He played crucial roles in electing California governors, made Al Pacino available as the star of *The Godfather*, apparently helped ensure that Roman Polanski escaped punishment for raping and sodomizing a thirteen-year-old girl, and was involved in a vast number of legal and illegal business transactions whose dollar values seemingly total in the billions. But with his name almost never appearing in the media, the general public was surely unaware of his existence when he died of natural causes in 1996. At that point, the news media suddenly regained its courage, and his passing was announced in headlines that must have somewhat puzzled their previously ill-informed readers, with *The New York Times* running "Sidney Korshak, 88, Dies; Fabled Fixer for the Chicago Mob" and *The Los Angeles Times* "Sidney Korshak, Alleged Mafia Liaison to Hollywood, Dies at 88."

Looting the Property of the Japanese-American Nisei

Money was undoubtedly the mother's milk of postwar California politics. But the speed with which these recent Chicago arrivals transformed themselves into powerful financial figures in their new state was greatly assisted by their participation in a particularly lucrative windfall. They were leading beneficiaries of one of the worst governmental violations of constitutional rights in our national history, and Russo devotes an entire chapter to this dark tale.

Like all other Asians, California's ethnic Japanese population had long suffered under the harshest sort of racial discrimination, being denied naturalized citizenship and therefore prohibited from owning land, while nearly all additional immigration from their homeland had been banned in the 1920s. Yet although they had arrived as penniless farm laborers mostly around the turn of the century, their intense work-ethnic and diligent savings had established them as a small but reasonably prosperous community by the late 1930s. The Fourteenth Amendment granted citizenship to their American-born children, thus allowing their families to eventually acquire large amounts of farmland and other properties, with their visible success sometimes provoking considerable envy from their white neighbors and competitors.

As **I have discussed elsewhere**, FDR's desperate attempt to circumvent overwhelming public opposition to America's involvement in World War II eventually led to his endless 1941 provocations against

Japan, which successfully culminated in the attack on Pearl Harbor. Soon afterward, demagogic appeals by politicians and media pundits led much of the public to begin demanding the incarceration of all ethnic Japanese, U.S. citizens or not, and by early 1942 FDR signed an executive order shipping some 120,000 Japanese-Americans off to grim concentration camps, with those individuals sometimes being forced to leave their homes on very short notice. As a result, they lost nearly all the property they had steadily accumulated over two generations, most of which was either seized or otherwise ended up in government hands. Similar government edicts led to the confiscation of numerous German-owned businesses throughout America, many of which possessed enormously valuable assets.

Within a couple of years, these federal holdings had swelled to include half a million acres of the state's best farmland, some 1,265 small Japanese-owned hotels, and numerous urban parcels throughout Los Angeles, San Jose, and other cities. In 1942 the federal government estimated the value of these former Japanese-American properties at around $3 billion in present day dollars, but the huge postwar California economic and population boom would surely have greatly increased the worth of this real estate portfolio by the early 1950s. The business assets and patent holdings of the seized German companies were worth additional billions.

Following the end of the war, all this property needed to be sold off, and powerful Chicago interests recognized this tremendous opportunity. The 1946 elections had produced a crushing national defeat for the ruling Democrats, with the Republicans regaining control of both houses of Congress for the first time since 1932. President Truman thus faced a desperate battle for reelection, and Chicago's powerful political machine deployed its considerable political clout to place the sales process in the hands of David L. Bazelon, a young Chicago lawyer and leading Democratic fund-raiser with deep Syndicate ties. Bazelon had taken a pay cut of 80% to enter government service, but he soon boasted to the *Washington Post* that he had become "one of the largest businessmen in the country." His motive quickly became apparent as he arranged the sale of assets for a fraction of their real value to his circle of Chicago friends and associates, sometimes apparently receiving a secret slice of the lucrative ownership stakes in return.

As an extreme example, Bazelon almost immediately sold Chicago's Henry Crown a twenty-six thousand acre California mine site, containing tens of millions of dollars worth of coal, for a mere $150,000. A private $1 million sale of seized German property in 1948 to a group formed by his lifelong best friend and former law partner Paul Ziffren was worth $40 million by 1954, and Ziffren soon rewarded Bazelon with a 9.2% share of his multimillion-dollar real estate holding company. Another major beneficiary of Bazelon's unusual sales practices later told a Congressional investigating committee that he gave Bazelon a 25% share of his large hotel holding company because he "was just feeling good and generous and was grateful."

These particular hidden gifts to Bazelon only later came to light through chance references that were eventually uncovered by diligent researchers, so we may assume that such transactions probably represented just the tip of an enormous iceberg. It seems plausible that Bazelon received quiet kickbacks totaling many millions or perhaps even tens of millions in present-day dollars in exchange for his very favorable distribution of billions in government assets to the network of beneficiaries who shared his roots in the Chicago Syndicate.

This vast transfer of wealth in the early postwar years from the plundered *Nisei* gave all these mobbed-up Chicago newcomers the financial wherewithal to soon gain substantial control of California's money-based political system. As Art White, the veteran Los Angeles political journalist, later described the situation:

> During these years some hundreds of associates of Greenberg, Evans, and others of the Capone crime syndicate, and of Arvey and Ziffren, poured hundreds of millions of dollars into California. They bought real estate, including hotel chains through apparently unrelated corporations from San Diego to Sacramento. They invested in vast tracts of land, built or bought motels, giant office buildings, and other commercial properties. More importantly, they invaded the loan field, establishing banks and home loan institutions. By 1953, Ziffren and his associates had gained control of an enormous block of California's economy. They could finance political campaigns with the best of the native barons.

Russo notes that the FBI analysts subsequently endorsed White's conclusions:

> When the FBI reviewed White's research into the extent of the relationship between the Capones and Ziffren, it concluded with a rare declaration vindicating White's conclusions: "The extraordinary success of the adventurer [Ziffren]—and by the same token his backers, who can be traced right into the Midwest and East Coast hoodlum world—*has been proven and documented.* (Author's italics).

Russo's Appendix A provides a long but partial list of the major properties acquired by Chicago's Supermob associates.

The dispossession of California's Japanese-Americans certainly constituted a central factor in the enormous growth of Syndicate-connected wealth and power in that state, and Russo describes it as "an inadvertent boost for the fortunes of the Supermob." He may be entirely correct, but other possibilities come to mind.

During World War II, California was located many thousands of miles from the Pacific theater of operations, while Hawaii was obviously far closer and also served as America's most vital military base; yet the larger population of Japanese-Americans living on those islands **escaped any such mass incarceration**. America's top Republican leader, Sen. Robert Taft, was absolutely opposed to the wholesale imprisonment of the Japanese-Americans, as was FBI Director J. Edgar Hoover, hardly a man noted for his deep civil libertarian tendencies.

Meanwhile, the earliest and most prominent advocate of the internment policy was California Attorney-General Earl Warren, who used the political issue with great effectiveness to unseat the state's incumbent Democratic governor in the 1942 election. And we should note that Warren's successful gubernatorial campaign was masterminded by Chotiner, a Beverly Hills attorney with strong underworld connections, who later became a good friend and sometime business partner of Korshak and the other members of the local Chicago Syndicate network.

Perhaps Warren and his backers merely believed that demonizing a small and powerless racial minority and demanding that they be placed behind barbed wire would represent an excellent path to statewide political victory in the aftermath of Pearl Harbor. But they may also have considered that the concurrent seizure of billions in accumulated property might provide lucrative later opportunities for unscrupulous individuals, opportunities that were indeed fully realized just a few years later.

Bazelon's secret financial payoffs were not the only reward he received for his generous distribution of billions in government-controlled property to his circle of fellow Capone Syndicate alumni. According to the files of a Congressional committee, Bazelon in 1946 had supposedly told a confidant that he was very worried about an IRS investigation into the work he had earlier done for a large Syndicate-controlled brewing company, and that he "needed a federal judgeship to get him cleaned up." So after Truman's reelection, Bazelon, despite completely lacking any judicial or scholarly experience, was named to the Washington D.C. Court of Appeals, the most prestigious appellate circuit, becoming at age forty the youngest such federal judge in U.S. history. This elevation came through the maneuver of a recess appointment, thereby preventing any initial Congressional review of the disturbing rumors already circulating about the practices he had followed in his distribution of billions in seized government assets.

Former FDR cabinet secretary Harold Ickes, a principled and progressive New Dealer, reacted with total outrage, denouncing the Bazelon appointment as "deplorable" and an "all-time low" **in the pages** of *The New Republic*, and calling for a Senate investigation into his distribution of seized property. As a former Chicago newsman, Ickes had been a longtime opponent of the Capone Syndicate and its corruption, and he personally wrote Truman in an unsuccessful last-ditch attempt to sink the nomination: "I happen to know a good deal about Bazelon and I consider him to be thoroughly unfit for the job he holds, to say nothing of a United States judgeship, either on the Court of Appeals or on the District Court."

Until reading these books by Russo, I had never heard of Korshak, nor the vast majority of the other leading figures who seemed to have played such important roles in the criminal conquest of California, such as Ziffren, Greenberg, Fred Evans, Al Hart, and Jake Factor. But

Bazelon was a name well known to me from the nearly two decades he later spent as the Chief Judge of America's most important appellate court, where he probably established himself as the most influential jurist not found on the Supreme Court. Indeed, Supreme Court Justice William J. Brennan, Jr. later described him as "one of the most important judicial figures of the century."

In all the newspaper and magazine articles discussing Bazelon's long career, he was uniformly portrayed in extremely favorable terms by liberal or mainstream journalists, often characterized as one of our greatest civil libertarians for his passionate championship of the abused and the downtrodden. Meanwhile, conservatives often criticized him as a "bleeding-heart liberal" whose judicial activism overly favored the rights of criminals and the mentally ill.

But based upon the true history of his early decades, neither of these characterizations seems entirely plausible to me, and during all those years and contentious disputes, there never even once appeared a hint of his horrific past record of massive personal corruption and outright criminality in support of his fellow alumni of the Capone Syndicate. Perhaps none of those journalists nor their editors were aware of the facts or perhaps they did not dare raise such a dangerous topic in public. When he died in 1993 at the age of 83, his hugely glowing obituaries in *The New York Times* and *The Washington Post* gave no hint of his sordid past, and despite the massive documentation provided in Russo's thick 2006 volume, **his extensive personal Wikipedia page** still remains pristine pure of any such taint.

As Russo notes with considerable outrage, the histories of nearly all of Bazelon's fellow Supermob criminal confederates who gained political control of California have similarly been whitewashed and forgotten, with almost none of their sordid path to wealth and power ever appearing in the media, and their glowing obituaries instead hailing them as among America's greatest civil libertarians and most generous philanthropists. In an interview with Russo, Connie Carlson, the former chief white-collar crime investigator for California's Attorney-General, acidly noted: "Isn't it interesting how all these 'civil libertarians' ended up with the confiscated Japanese land?"

Reaching the Commanding Heights of Corporate America

So we see that a small network of organized crime alumni from Chicago seized great political power in California before I was even born and utilized it to protect their corrupt financial schemes. Indeed, in 1978 the head of the Chicago Syndicate reportedly reacted to the encroachments of New York Mafia boss Joe Bonnano by telling one of his enforcers: "Watch that fucking Bonanno…he wants what's ours—what's always been ours, California. He can't have Arizona, and he sure has hell can't have California." But as I grew up in the world substantially controlled by such individuals, I never once noticed nor suspected a thing.

The explanation of this paradox is obvious. The petty racketeers and municipal chiselers whose corrupt endeavors were generally run on a small scale either mostly stayed behind in the Windy City or never permanently established themselves among the sprawling and prosperous middle class suburbs that sprang up all across postwar California. And the notable absence of such highly-visible local corruption and organized crime manifestations in our ordinary daily lives led most of us to assume that such activities were almost entirely absent in our state. We never suspected that a small group of similar criminals were situated in the upper strata of our society, but with far greater financial goals and protected by a cowed or compromised local media. Presumably the large-scale mobsters were pleased that the absence of their small-fry counterparts helped them to maintain their invisibility.

Several years ago, I published an article **that included mention** of this important distinction between micro-corruption and macro-corruption:

> However, although American micro-corruption is rare, we seem to suffer from appalling levels of macro-corruption, situations in which our various ruling elites squander or misappropriate tens or even hundreds of billions of dollars of our national wealth, sometimes doing so just barely on one side of technical legality and sometimes on the other.
>
> Sweden is among the cleanest societies in Europe, while Sicily is perhaps the most corrupt. But suppose a large clan of ruthless Sicilian Mafiosi moved to Sweden and somehow managed to gain control of its government. On a day-to-day

basis, little would change, with Swedish traffic policemen and building inspectors performing their duties with the same sort of incorruptible efficiency as before, and I suspect that Sweden's Transparency International rankings would scarcely decline. But meanwhile, a large fraction of Sweden's accumulated national wealth might gradually be stolen and transferred to secret Cayman Islands bank accounts, or invested in Latin American drug cartels, and eventually the entire plundered economy would collapse.

Although many of the younger and hungrier individuals who had begun their careers in association with the Chicago Syndicate relocated to California, most of their richer and better-established counterparts remained behind in Chicago, though they seemed to have greatly shared in Bazelon's bounty. These families are now numbered among America's wealthiest, and strong evidence of macro-corruption seems to pervade their activities across the generations.

As mentioned, one of the first suggestions I encountered regarding the important business ties between the underworld and big business was Cockburn's casual mention of Henry Crown's large mob-financed stake in General Dynamics, and the subsequent Pentagon bail-out he arranged. The financial rise of the Chicago-based Crown family figures prominently in Russo's narrative, far beyond their 1947 acquisition of a huge California property from Bazelon for less than 1% of the value of the coal it contained. Crown had launched his supply business in 1919, regularly securing lucrative government contracts in Chicago's graft-ridden business environment, then later enlisting in the military during World War II as a procurement officer. During his service, he was responsible for some $1 billion in military purchases, with his company being sued by the government for price-gouging just a month before his 1945 discharge. Russo recounts some of the transactions by which the Crowns greatly increased their wealth in the postwar period, including their use of the financial backing of the Teamsters to merge their company with General Dynamics, thereby obtaining a substantial ownership share. The Crowns today are worth nearly $9 billion, with roughly half of their fortune due to their remaining 10% stake in that huge military contractor.

Russo also describes how the even richer Pritzkers of Chicago arranged for Jay A. Pritzker, the family scion, to serve as Bazelon's assistant in the disposition of seized assets, with that wealthy young man's DC hotel bill dwarfing his meager government salary during the year he was employed there. Congressional investigators later discovered that he had purchased a seized manufacturing company for just 7% of its value, but given the huge gift of stock that his father later bestowed upon Bazelon, numerous other such transactions may have remained hidden. Many dozens of the pages of Russo's book document the underworld associations of several generations of Pritzkers, which began not long after the founding father opened his Chicago law firm in 1902. The enormously diversified current assets of the Pritzker family are listed in Russo's Appendix B, which occupies nearly six full pages, and the Pritzkers today remain one of the wealthiest families in our country, with total assets of nearly $30 billion, and an enormous record of involvement in recent politics.

Russo came of age during the Watergate era of investigatory journalism and one of his reviewers suggests that his ideological leanings are those of the New Left, a plausible claim given his occasional scathing references to big business, Ronald Reagan, and American foreign policy. Since most of the Supermob members who seized political power in California were Democrats aligned with the liberal wing of that party, Russo often seems uncomfortable in reporting that their conservative Republican opponents sometimes unsuccessfully levied charges of underworld ties against them, but he grudgingly concedes that such accusations were substantially correct.

Bazelon was a major figure in Russo's narrative, and given the author's ideological leanings, he includes a paragraph or two on the former's long subsequent appellate career, noting with apparent approval his ground-breaking liberal rulings on behalf of the rights of the accused and of the mentally-ill. But although the author notes the obvious hypocrisy this involved, he never attempts to directly explore what seems like a very strange juxtaposition of naked criminal self-interest together with extreme social altruism, all bound together in a single individual.

A casual cynic might humorously suggest that Bazelon's tireless efforts to expand the rights of criminals were aimed at protecting himself and his circle of Syndicate friends, but this seems implausible. The sort of corrupt and highly-sophisticated financial dealings in which they specialized were heavily mediated by experienced lawyers and hardly gained much from the expanded protections afforded to simple street-robbers or to the criminally-insane. On the other hand, an idealist might speculate that Bazelon experienced enormous remorse over the vast fortunes that he and his associates had corruptly obtained through the broken lives of 120,000 innocent Japanese-Americans, and his legal rulings were attempts to expiate this guilt. I am skeptical of this analysis.

Another rather cynical possibility would be that his long national leadership role on human rights and civil liberties was intended to win the plaudits of liberal intellectuals and the media, thereby preempting any later attempt to resurrect the damning evidence provided by the five year FBI investigation of his corrupt sales practices, whose final report ran some 560 pages; and this may be the most plausible explanation. With so much of the modern edifice of liberal jurisprudence based upon Bazelon's rulings, its adherents might be extremely reluctant to allow discussion of the deep criminality of one of its leading architects.

But there is an even more disturbing possibility that comes to mind. Medical personnel and lab technicians usually wear spotless white coats so that even the slightest speck of potentially-dangerous foreign matter can easily be detected and removed. In a society having very low rates of ordinary street crime or social disorder, public attention would naturally focus upon the sort of business corruption and financial crime that constituted the regular activity of Bazelon and his Supermob circle, who would inevitably become the primary targets of law enforcement efforts. But suppose that same society became overwhelmed with the sorts of robberies, muggings, and rapes that evoke the most public fear, along with the chaos and disorder caused by the frightening public behavior of large numbers of the newly-released mentally-ill. Surely under such conditions, the citizenry would demand that the authorities concentrate their main efforts on those most immediate threats to public safety, necessarily drawing them away from the white collar crimes being committed in lawyers' offices.

I do not think that this analysis is nearly as implausible as it might seem upon first consideration. Over the last few decades, the bulk of the American population has become totally impoverished, with published reports by the Federal Reserve and other organizations indicating that **60% of the population have less than $1,000** in available savings, with **40% lacking even $400**. Only a generation or so ago, perfectly good college educations were so inexpensive that many students could cover most of their costs through a part-time job, yet today accumulated student loan debt is over $1.5 trillion dollars, and with any bankruptcy discharge legally prohibited, this gigantic looming burden has created an entire young generation of permanent debt-slaves, who find it financially impossible to get married or purchase their first home. American health care is the most expensive and least efficient in the developed world, and these costs impose a huge parasitic burden upon the rest of our economy, as well as raising the serious risk that a little bad luck might permanently damage the finances of an ordinary family. But while most ordinary Americans have become much poorer, a tiny financial elite has increased its own wealth beyond all comprehension.

During the 1950s and early 1960s, American candidates and campaigns regularly focused upon economic issues, and this sort of extreme economic divergence would certainly have been at the center of most political campaigns. But these days, our politics has instead become dominated by highly-divisive social issues of much less practical significance, with the latest example being the astonishing focus on "transgender rights," which impacts only the tiniest sliver of the population and would have been universally ridiculed as pure political satire just a few years ago. Is it so far-fetched to suggest that these issues have been deliberately promoted as popular distractions, lightning rods to divert attention from the simple reality that while most people have grown much poorer, our ruling elites have vastly multiplied their wealth?

And the personal background of these elites often is remarkably similar to that of Bazelon and his corrupt network of confederates. A ruling elite whose greed, incompetence, and parasitism has greatly damaged the interests of the general public is obviously quite vulnerable, especially if so many of its members derive from a small, distinct minority. But if they succeed in splitting the public into a whole range of mutually-hostile fractions, divided along ideological and ethnic lines, this vulnerability is considerably reduced.

Although versions of this highly-cynical but generally successful political strategy may well have been in operation for the last few decades, I doubt whether more than a tiny fraction of those involved are consciously aware of it. After all, most people—and even most elites—tend to believe whatever they hear and read in their personal selection of trusted media sources. According to biologists, nearly all the individual members of a given school of fish automatically cluster towards each other by instinct, so that if just one or two individuals happen to move in a particular willful direction, all the others will soon follow their lead.

For example, I would not be entirely surprised if Bazelon and a few of his close associates consciously began efforts to disrupt the orderliness of American society so that they would be free to pursue their corrupt or criminal activities undisturbed, much like rodents would prefer a litter-filled and decrepit house in which to build their hidden nests. But it seems quite plausible that most of their liberal epigones have subsequently followed those same ideas while remaining completely ignorant of the very cynical motives that may have originally inspired them.

Consider Bazelon's grand-daughters Emily and Lara, a journalist and an academic respectively, whose bylines I have regularly noticed over the years **in the pages** of *The New York Times* and various other elite publications, generally promoting all sorts of mainstream-liberal causes and policies. Given that they were raised under very different circumstances, I tend to doubt that either of them has anything like the long record of criminality which the elder Bazelon had accumulated as he clawed his way to the top of our society. Indeed, I wouldn't be surprised if they remain as completely unaware of his dark history as I had been until quite recently. Perhaps they had simply read all the same media stories on their illustrious grandfather that I did, and regarded him as a towering pillar of liberal moral rectitude, whose principled ideals they deeply committed themselves to follow. So as a consequence, it is quite possible that some of the policies they zealously advocate may have been explicitly designed to be destructive to our society, but they remain totally ignorant of that crucial fact.

The Jewish Aspects of Organized Crime

Discussions of ethnicity are extremely sensitive in contemporary American society, especially when they might reflect unfavorably upon Jews. For many decades, our educational and media systems have deeply conditioned us to avert our gaze from such matters, even when they are clearly visible; but some patterns become so overwhelmingly apparent that they cannot be avoided.

Throughout my lengthy discussion of the corrupt looting of the seized Japanese-American property by men with strong Syndicate ties, who subsequently achieved the political conquest of California, virtually every participant whom I mentioned came from a Jewish background, even including those bearing the most Anglo-Saxon of names.

And this remarkable skew merely reflects the actual contents of Russo's very deeply researched 300,000 word study. Although some of the heroic figures who did their utmost to expose and frustrate the growing power of organized crime were Jewish, notably journalists Seymour Hersh and *Colliers'* Lester Velie, that same ethnic background was found in nearly all of the dozens of Supermob members whose overwhelming success across the second half of the twentieth century becomes depressingly evident throughout the sweep of Russo's narrative arc. When examining the leading beneficiaries of the expropriated Japanese or the Syndicate alumni who seized control of California politics, it takes considerable effort to locate a single Gentile.

While I had been very surprised to discover from Russo's first book that nearly half of the prominent organized crime figures in Chicago were Jewish, I was absolutely astonished to discover from his sequel that nearly all their former colleagues who had moved on to acquire vastly greater wealth and political power in California fell into that same category. And whereas all the Chicago gangsters were always notorious as gangsters, most of their far more successful California counterparts had their backgrounds carefully airbrushed by the media, instead being portrayed as highly successful businessmen, political leaders, or philanthropists.

To his enormous credit, Russo does not flinch from this reality, candidly presenting the origins and backgrounds of the key figures he discusses, and indeed the definition of the "Supermob" which he places at the top of his preface highlights the "Russian Jewish heritage" of the "group of men from the Midwest…who made fortunes in the 20th century American West in collusion with notorious members of organized crime." He follows this by summarizing the central thesis of his fascinating text:

> Two types of power dominated the twentieth century: the visible, embodied in politicians, corporate moguls, crime bosses, and law enforcement; and the invisible, concentrated in the hands of a few power brokers generally of Eastern European and Jewish immigrant heritage. Operating safely in the shadows, these men often pulled the strings of the visible power brokers. Although they remained nameless to the public, they were notorious among a smattering of enterprising investigators who, over decades, followed their brilliant, amoral, and frequently criminal careers. The late Senate investigator and author Walter Sheridan dubbed them the Supermob.

Although I had merely glanced over this short passage at the beginning of his very long book, I returned to it afterward, and found it an extremely accurate summary of his massively-researched study.

Russo may or may not be aware of it, but for most of the last couple of centuries, Eastern European Jews have enjoyed a tremendous reputation for rampant criminality, especially involving crimes of corruption, vice, or financial gain. Since the end of World War II, overwhelming Jewish influence in the media and academic worlds has led to massive suppression of this historical reality, much like the criminal activities of the Supermob disappeared almost without a trace prior to Russo's ground-breaking research. But his story would hardly have surprised knowledgeable Americans a century or more ago. Before Jewish political and media had fully established itself, writers sometimes candidly discussed such criminal tendencies in ways that might seem extremely discordant to naive present-day Americans.

In 1908 former general Theodore Bingham was serving as Police Commissioner of New York City, and near the end of that year he published **a long article** on his city's foreign criminals in *The North*

American Review, then one of our leading intellectual magazines. His discussion seemed quite careful and even-handed, but he noted that Jews had three times the crime rate of the remaining population of his overwhelmingly immigrant city, a figure considerably higher than that of any other group, even including the Black Hand-plagued Italians. This factual assessment sparked a huge outcry by Jewish organizations, and although he immediately rendered a personal apology, he nevertheless was summarily removed from office a few months later.

In 1913, E.A. Ross, one of our greatest early sociologists, published a fascinating analysis of different immigrant groups. He noted the high incarceration rates of Italians, but emphasized that this was mostly due to acts of personal violence unrelated to criminal activity, the predations of the Mafia notwithstanding, while despite the long-standing Irish reputation for drunken brawling their crime rates had receded to being among the lowest of any group a couple of generations after their immigration peak. By contrast, although he emphasized the high ability of Jews, he could not avoid also mentioning their notorious tendency for swindling and dishonesty, with their predatory crime being the highest of any group, while they sought to avoid punishment by widespread use of perjury. These sorts of candid observations by Ross have apparently prompted many decades of his unfair vilification by subsequent Jewish historians.

- **The Old World in the New**
  The Eastern European Hebrews
  E.A. Ross • 1914 • 5,000 Words

By the 1920s, Jewish media influence had reached the point at which newspapers and magazines had become very reluctant to report on the misbehavior of that group, which led wealthy industrialist Henry Ford to begin publishing *The Dearborn Independent*, a weekly paper with enormous national circulation, willing to violate those growing taboos. He later collected together the series of articles dealing with Jewish misdeeds, and published them in four volumes as *The International Jew*. Despite its notorious reputation, the collection mostly consists of rather mundane accounts of corruption, criminality, and financial misbehavior that seem little different from what Russo was to document a few decades later.

- **The International Jew**
  The World's Foremost Problem
  Henry Ford • 1920 • 323,000 Words

Prior to the modern decline of belief in religion and other elements of the supernatural, swearing binding oaths to God constituted an important means of enforcing business contracts and determining guilt in legal proceedings, with present-day courtroom procedures still containing a vestigial element of those notions. So some years ago I was quite shocked to discover from **Prof. Israel Shahak** that traditionally-observant Jews annually undergo a religious ceremony that declares all their future oaths for the forthcoming year null and void in advance, thereby freeing them from any such restrictions. This religious loophole was obviously an important competitive advantage for those engaging in dishonest economic activity let alone outright criminality.

In 1997 Cambridge University Press published ***Esau's Tears*** by eminent scholar Albert Lindemann, a 500 page study of 19th century European anti-Semitism. His historical evidence demonstrated a very widespread pattern of Jewish criminality across Europe, with nineteenth century France having been rocked by huge financial scandals engineered by immigrant Jews, which impoverished large numbers of small investors. The situation in Russia was **even more serious**:

> As Lindemann candidly describes the tension between Russia's very rapidly growing Jewish population and its governing authorities, he cannot avoid mentioning the notorious Jewish reputation for bribery, corruption, and general dishonesty, with numerous figures of all political backgrounds noting that the remarkable Jewish propensity to commit perjury in the courtroom led to severe problems in the effective administration of justice.

Some historical tendencies remain remarkably consistent over time.

All of us have our own areas of special expertise, and naturally tend to accept the conventional narrative on most other matters. Prior to reading Russo's two lengthy works, much of my media-influenced understanding of American organized crime would have been entirely mistaken.

Towards the end of his second volume, Russo notes the tremendous hypocrisy surrounding Bazelon's ring of Jewish beneficiaries, who acquired the properties of the interned Japanese not long after their own German relatives had been similarly victimized by the Nazis. In the past, I would have casually nodded my head at this obvious analogy, but I now think he may be mistaken in his history.

Not long ago, I came across a very interesting book written by Sir Arthur Bryant, an influential historian whose **Wikipedia page** describes him as the personal favorite of Winston Churchill and two other British prime ministers. He had worked on *Unfinished Victory* during the late 1930s, then somewhat modified it for publication in early 1940, a few months after the outbreak of World War II had considerably altered the political landscape. But not long afterward, the war became much more bitter and there was a harsh crackdown on discordant voices in British society, so Bryant became alarmed over what he had written and attempted to remove all existing copies from circulation. Therefore the only ones available for sale on Amazon are **exorbitantly priced**, but fortunately the work is also freely available at **Archive.org**.

Writing before the "official version" of historical events had been rigidly determined, Bryant describes Germany's very difficult domestic situation between the two world wars, its problematic relationship with its tiny Jewish minority, and the circumstances behind the rise of Hitler, providing a very different perspective on these important events than what we usually read in our standard textbooks.

Among other surprising facts, he notes that although Jews were just 1% of the total population, even five years after Hitler had come to power and implemented various anti-Semitic policies, they still apparently owned "something like a third of the real property" in that country, with the great bulk of these vast holdings having been acquired from desperate, starving Germans in the terrible years of the early 1920s. Thus, much of Germany's 99% German population had recently been dispossessed of the assets they had built up over generations, sometimes due to the same sort of corrupt financial practices that Bazelon and his friends had used to enrich themselves in California at the expense of the Japanese.

So although Russo is correct in believing that there was a strong correspondence between the distressing events he covers in California and the somewhat earlier developments in Germany, the analogy may not be exactly what he believes it to be.

James Garner and *The Rockford Files*

During the late 1970s my favorite show on television was *The Rockford Files*, in which James Garner played a wise-cracking private-eye in Los Angeles, and I was quite disappointed when the series was cancelled at the end of 1979. A foreign friend of mine in college noted that Garner's very square jaw and bold demeanor made him look remarkably like a young Ronald Reagan, who had been lifted to enormous political heights by his usefulness to Lew Wasserman, whose MCA-Universal also happened to produce Garner's show. But just a couple of years ago I happened to discover the backstory to those events, and how the actor's willingness to stand up for his rights may have led him to a sharply different fate.

Garner had agreed to relatively low personal fees for each *Rockford* episode in exchange for a substantial share of the overall profits, which seemed likely to be enormous once it went into syndication. But near the end of the fifth season, he accidentally discovered that under studio accounting the extremely popular show had accrued cumulative total losses of $9.5 million, and was unlikely to ever turn much of a profit. Garner had suffered a great deal of damage during his very physically-demanding series, doing nearly all of his own stunt-work and typically involved in two fist-fights or beatings in each episode. Soon afterward, he stopped coming to the set based on his doctor's recommendation that he seek immediate treatment for a bleeding ulcer, although MCA accused him of malingering, and NBC soon canceled the series. Although it was extremely rare back then for actors to undertake the huge expense of pursuing litigation against a studio, Garner was wealthy enough to do so, and he decided to sue MCA for $20 million over what he claimed was its fraudulent accounting, which had deprived him of his contractual share of the profits. Such successful action by a leading television star might obviously inspire all sorts of other Hollywood figures to demand similar changes.

One week after the last *Rockford Files* episode aired on NBC, Garner was driving in slow, rush-hour traffic on Coldwater Canyon Drive when his car was bumped by another vehicle. After he stopped to get insurance information, he was immediately attacked and severely beaten by the driver, who turned out to be a young former Green Beret, resulting in three days of hospitalization for 51-year-old actor. By a rather strange coincidence, the personal chauffeur of MCA Chairman Lew Wasserman happened to be present as an observer at the scene. Despite his serious injuries, Garner eventually went ahead with his lawsuit, which was finally successfully settled after eight years of litigation. But perhaps the unusual incident led many other, less well-established actors to reflect upon the sudden misfortune that might enter their lives under the wrong circumstances.

Oddly enough, the brutal public beating of one of the biggest stars on television received much less attention than one would expect, or at least I never heard of it at the time, nor during the decades that followed, only learning of it from Moldea's book on MCA's dark history. Moreover, the attack seems to have been almost entirely scrubbed from the Internet, with my inadequate Google skills only locating the most obscure sources, such as a PDF copy of an AP wire story in **the Tuscaloosa News of Alabama**, though the details are provided in Garner's 2011 memoirs, ***The Garner Files***. It's quite possible that the incident was exactly what it purported to be, the sort of random, violent assault that can happen to any of us without cause or warning, even including leading television stars locked in bitter contract disputes with a major studio having deep Syndicate roots. But I do think the story would have fit perfectly well into Russo's narrative of the early Chicago days of MCA in the 1930s, when its top executives worked closely with the thugs of Al Capone.

This article is available online at:
https://www.unz.com/runz/american-pravda-the-power-of-organized-crime/

Mossad Assassinations
The JFK Assassination and the 9/11 Attacks?
The Unz Review, January 27, 2020

From the Peace of Westphalia to the Law of the Jungle

The January 2nd American assassination of Gen. Qassem Soleimani of Iran was an event of enormous moment.

Gen. Soleimani had been the highest-ranking military figure in his nation of 80 million, and with a storied career of 30 years, one of the most universally popular and highly regarded. Most analysts ranked him second in influence only to Ayatollah Ali Khamenei, Iran's elderly Supreme Leader, and there were widespread reports that he was being urged to run for the presidency in the 2021 elections.

The circumstances of his peacetime death were also quite remarkable. His vehicle was incinerated by the missile of an American Reaper drone near Iraq's Baghdad international airport just after he had arrived there on a regular commercial flight for peace negotiations originally suggested by the American government.

Our major media hardly ignored the gravity of this sudden, unexpected killing of so high-ranking a political and military figure, and gave it enormous attention. A day or so later, the front page of my morning *New York Times* was almost entirely filled with coverage of the event and its implications, along with several inside pages devoted to the same topic. Later that same week, America's national newspaper of record allocated more than one-third of all the pages of its front section to the same shocking story.

But even such copious coverage by teams of veteran journalists failed to provide the incident with its proper context and implications. Last year, the Trump Administration **had declared** the Iranian Revolutionary Guard "a terrorist organization," drawing widespread criticism and even ridicule from national security experts appalled at the notion of classifying a major branch of Iran's armed forces as "terrorists." Gen. Soleimani was a top commander in that body, and this apparently provided the legal fig-leaf for his assassination in broad daylight while on a diplomatic peace mission.

But note that Congress has been considering **legislation declaring Russia an official state sponsor of terrorism**, and Stephen Cohen, the eminent Russia scholar, has argued that no foreign leader since the end of World War II has been so massively demonized by the American media as Russian President Vladimir Putin. For years, numerous agitated **pundits have denounced Putin** as "the new Hitler," and some prominent figures have even called for **his overthrow** or death. So we are now only a step or two removed from undertaking a public campaign to assassinate the leader of a country whose nuclear arsenal could quickly annihilate the bulk of the American population. Cohen has repeatedly warned that the current danger of global nuclear war may exceed that which we faced during the days of the 1962 Cuban Missile Crisis, and can we entirely dismiss his concerns?

Even if we focus solely upon Gen. Solemaini's killing and entirely disregard its dangerous implications, there seem few modern precedents for the official public assassination of a top-ranking political figure by the forces of another major country. In groping for past examples, the only ones that come to mind occurred almost three generations ago during World War II, when Czech agents assisted by the Allies assassinated Reinhard Heydrich in Prague in 1941 and the US military later shot down the plane of Japanese admiral Isoroku Yamamoto in 1943. But these events occurred in the heat of a brutal global war, and the Allied leadership hardly portrayed them as official government assassinations. Historian David Irving reveals that when one of Adolf Hitler's aides suggested that an attempt be made to assassinate Soviet leaders in that same conflict, the German Fuhrer immediately forbade such practices as obvious violations of the laws of war.

The 1914 terrorist assassination of Archduke Franz Ferdinand, heir to the throne of Austria-Hungary, was certainly organized by fanatical elements of Serbian Intelligence, but the Serbian government fiercely denied its own complicity, and no major European power was ever directly implicated in the plot. The aftermath of the killing soon led to the outbreak of World War I, and although many millions died in the trenches over the next few years, it would have been completely unthinkable for one of the major belligerents to consider assassinating the leadership of another.

A century earlier, the Napoleonic Wars had raged across the entire continent of Europe for most of a generation, but I don't recall reading of any governmental assassination plots during that era, let alone in the quite gentlemanly wars of the preceding 18th century when Frederick the Great and Maria Theresa disputed ownership of the wealthy province of Silesia by military means. I am hardly a specialist in modern European history, but after the 1648 Peace of Westphalia ended the Thirty Years War and regularized the rules of warfare, no assassination as high-profile as that of Gen. Soleimani comes to mind.

The bloody Wars of Religion during previous centuries did see their share of assassination schemes. For example, I think that Philip II of Spain supposedly encouraged various plots to assassinate Queen Elizabeth I of England on grounds that she was a murderous heretic, and their repeated failure helped persuade him to launch the ill-fated Spanish Armada; but being a pious Catholic, he probably would have balked at using the ruse of peace-negotiations to lure Elizabeth to her doom. In any event, that was more than four centuries ago, so America has now placed itself in rather uncharted waters.

Different peoples possess different political traditions, and this may play a major role in influencing the behavior of the countries they establish. Bolivia and Paraguay were created in the early 18th century as shards from the decaying Spanish Empire, and according to Wikipedia they have experienced nearly three dozen successful coups in their history, the bulk of these prior to 1950, while Mexico has had a half-dozen. By contrast, the U.S. and Canada were founded as Anglo-Saxon settler colonies, and neither history records even a failed attempt.

During our Revolutionary War, George Washington, Thomas Jefferson, and our other Founding Fathers fully recognized that if their effort failed, they would all be hanged as rebels by the British. However, I have never heard that they feared falling to an assassin's blade, nor that King George III ever considered using such an underhanded means of attack. During the first century and more of our nation's history, nearly all our presidents and other top political leaders traced their ancestry back to the British Isles, and political assassinations were exceptionally rare, with Abraham Lincoln's death being one of the very few that comes to mind.

At the height of the Cold War, our CIA did involve itself in various secret assassination plots against Cuba's Communist dictator Fidel Castro and other foreign leaders considered hostile to US interests. But when these facts later came out in the 1970s, they evoked such enormous outrage from the public and the media, that three consecutive American presidents—**Gerald R. Ford**, **Jimmy Carter**, and **Ronald Reagan**—all issued successive Executive Orders absolutely prohibiting assassinations by the CIA or any other agent of the US government.

Although some cynics might claim that these public declarations represented mere window-dressing, **a March 2018 book review** in the *New York Times* strongly suggests otherwise. Kenneth M. Pollack spent years as a CIA analyst and National Security Council staffer, then went on to publish a number of influential books on foreign policy and military strategy over the last two decades. He had originally joined the CIA in 1988, and opens his review by declaring:

> One of the very first things I was taught when I joined the CIA was that we do not conduct assassinations. It was drilled into new recruits over and over again.

Yet Pollack notes with dismay that over the last quarter-century, these once solid prohibitions have been steadily eaten away, with the process rapidly accelerating after the 9/11 attacks of 2001. The laws on our books may not have changed, but

> Today, it seems that all that is left of this policy is a euphemism.
>
> We don't call them assassinations anymore. Now, they are "targeted killings," most often performed by drone strike, and they have become America's go-to weapon in the war on terror.

The Bush Administration had conducted 47 of these assassinations-by-another-name, while his successor Barack Obama, a constitutional scholar and Nobel Peace Prize winner, had raised his own total to 542. Not without justification, Pollack wonders whether assassination has become "a very effective drug, but [one that] treats only the symptom and so offers no cure."

Thus over the last couple of decades American policy has followed a disturbing trajectory in its use of assassination as a tool of foreign policy, first restricting its application only to the most extreme circumstances, next targeting small numbers of high-profile "terrorists" hiding in rough terrain, then escalating those same killings to the many hundreds. And now under President Trump, the fateful step has been taken of America claiming the right to assassinate any world leader not to our liking whom we unilaterally declare worthy of death.

Pollack had made his career as a Clinton Democrat, and is best known for his 2002 book *The Threatening Storm* that strongly endorsed President Bush's proposed invasion of Iraq and was **enormously influential** in producing bipartisan support for that ill-fated policy. I have no doubt that he is a committed supporter of Israel, and he probably falls into a category that I would loosely describe as "Left Neocon."

But while reviewing a history of Israel's own long use of assassination as a mainstay of its national security policy, he seems deeply disturbed that America might now be following along that same terrible path. Less than two years later, our sudden assassination of a top Iranian leader demonstrates that his fears may have been greatly understated.

"Rise and Kill First"

The book reviewed by Pollack was ***Rise and Kill First*** by *New York Times* reporter Ronen Bergman, a weighty study of the Mossad, Israel's foreign intelligence service, together with its sister agencies. The author devoted six years of research to the project, which was based upon a thousand personal interviews and access to an enormous number of official documents previously unavailable. As suggested by the title, his primary focus was Israel's long history of assassinations, and across his 750 pages and thousand-odd source references he recounts the details of an enormous number of such incidents.

That sort of topic is obviously fraught with controversy, but Bergman's volume carries glowing cover-blurbs from Pulitzer Prize-winning authors on espionage matters, and the official cooperation he received is indicated by similar endorsements from both a former

Mossad chief and Ehud Barak, a past Prime Minister of Israel who himself had once led assassination squads. Over the last couple of decades, former CIA officer Robert Baer has become one of our most prominent authors in this same field, and he praises the book as "hands down" the best he has ever read on intelligence, Israel, or the Middle East. The reviews across our elite media were equally laudatory.

Although I had seen some discussions of the book when it appeared, I only got around to reading it a few months ago. And while I was deeply impressed by the thorough and meticulous journalism, I found the pages rather grim and depressing reading, with their endless accounts of Israeli agents killing their real or perceived enemies in operations that sometimes involved kidnappings and brutal torture, or resulted in considerable loss of life to innocent bystanders. Although the overwhelming majority of the attacks described took place in the various countries of the Middle East or the occupied Palestinian territories of the West Bank and Gaza, others ranged across the world, including Europe. The narrative history began in the 1920s, decades before the actual creation of the Jewish state or its Mossad organization, and extended down to the present day.

The sheer quantity of such foreign assassinations was really quite remarkable, with the knowledgeable reviewer in the *New York Times* suggesting that the Israeli total over the last half-century or so seemed far greater than that of any other nation. I might even go farther: if we excluded domestic killings, I wouldn't be surprised if Israel's body-count greatly exceeded the combined total for that of all other major countries in the world. I think all the lurid revelations of lethal CIA or KGB Cold War assassination plots that I have seen discussed in newspaper articles might fit comfortably into just a chapter or two of Bergman's extremely long book.

National militaries have always been nervous about deploying biological weapons, knowing full well that once released, the deadly microbes might easily spread back across the border and inflict great suffering upon the civilians of the country that deployed them. Similarly, intelligence operatives who have spent their long careers so heavily focused upon planning, organizing, and implementing what amount to officially-sanctioned murders may develop ways of thinking that become a danger both to each other and to the larger society they serve, and some examples of this possibility leak out here and there in Bergman's comprehensive narrative.

In the so-called "Askelon Incident" of 1984, a couple of captured Palestinians were beaten to death in public by the notoriously ruthless head of the Shin Bet domestic security agency and his subordinates. Under normal circumstances, this deed would have carried no consequences, but the incident happened to be captured by the camera by a nearby Israeli photo-journalist, who managed to avoid confiscation of his film. His resulting scoop sparked an international media scandal, even reaching the pages of the *New York Times*, and this forced a governmental investigation aimed at criminal prosecution. To protect themselves, the Shin Bet leadership infiltrated the inquiry and organized an effort to fabricate evidence pinning the murders upon ordinary Israeli soldiers and a leading general, all of whom were completely innocent. A senior Shin Bet officer who expressed misgivings about this plot apparently came close to being murdered by his colleagues until he agreed to falsify his official testimony. Organizations that increasingly operate like mafia crime families may eventually adopt similar cultural norms.

Israeli operatives sometimes even contemplated the elimination of their own top-ranking leaders whose policies they viewed as sufficiently counter-productive. For decades, Gen. Ariel Sharon had been one of Israel's greatest military heroes and someone of extreme right-wing sentiments. As Defense Minister in 1982, he orchestrated the Israeli invasion of Lebanon, which soon turned into a major political debacle, seriously damaging Israel's international standing by inflicting great destruction upon that neighboring country and its capital city of Beirut. As Sharon stubbornly continued his military strategy and the problems grew more severe, a group of disgruntled officers decided that the best means of cutting Israel's losses was to assassinate Sharon, though that proposal was never carried out.

An even more striking example occurred a decade later. For many years, Palestinian leader Yasir Arafat had been the leading object of Israeli antipathy, so much so that at one point Israel made plans to shoot down an international civilian jetliner in order to assassinate him. But after the end of the Cold War, pressure from America and Europe led Prime Minister Yitzhak Rabin to sign the 1993 Oslo Peace Accords with his Palestinian foe. Although the Israeli leader received worldwide praise and shared a Nobel Peace Prize for his peacemaking efforts, powerful segments of the Israeli public and its political class regarded the act as a betrayal, with some extreme nationalists and religious zealots demanding that he be killed for his treason. A couple of years later, he was indeed shot dead by a lone gunman from those ideological circles, becoming the first Middle Eastern leader in decades to suffer that fate. Although his killer was mentally unbalanced and stubbornly insisted that he acted alone, he had had a long history of intelligence associations, and Bergman delicately notes that the gunman slipped past Rabin's numerous bodyguards "with astonishing ease" in order to fire his three fatal shots at close range.

Many observers drew parallels between Rabin's assassination and that of our own president in Dallas three decades earlier, and the latter's heir and namesake, John F. Kennedy, Jr., developed a strong personal interest in the tragic event. In March 1997, his glossy political magazine *George* published an article by the Israeli assassin's mother, implicating her own country's security services in the crime, a theory also promoted by the late Israeli-Canadian writer Barry Chamish. These accusations sparked a furious international debate, but after Kennedy himself died in an unusual plane crash a couple of years later and his magazine quickly folded, the controversy soon subsided. The *George* archives are not online nor easily available, so I cannot effectively judge the credibility of the charges.

Having himself narrowly avoided assassination by Israeli operatives, Sharon gradually regained his political influence, and did so without compromising his hard-line views, even boastfully describing himself as a "Judeo-Nazi" to an appalled journalist. A few years after Rabin's death, he provoked major Palestinian protests, then used the resulting violence to win election as Prime Minister, and once in office, his very harsh methods led to a widespread uprising in Occupied Palestine. But Sharon merely redoubled his repression, and after world attention was diverted by 9/11 attacks and the American invasion of Iraq, he began assassinating numerous top Palestinian political and religious leaders in attacks that sometimes inflicted heavy civilian casualties.

The central object of Sharon's anger was Palestine President Yasir Arafat, who suddenly took ill and died, thereby joining his erstwhile negotiating partner Rabin in permanent repose. Arafat's wife claimed that he had been poisoned and produced some medical evidence to support this charge, while longtime Israeli political figure Uri Avnery published **numerous** articles **substantiating** those **accusations**. Bergman simply reports the categorical Israeli denials while noting that "the timing of Arafat's death was quite peculiar," then emphasizes that even if he knew the truth, he couldn't publish it since his entire book was written under strict Israeli censorship.

This last point seems an extremely important one, and although it only appears just that one time in the body of the text, the disclaimer obviously applies to the entirety of the long volume and should always be kept in the back of our minds. Bergman's book runs some 350,000 words and even if every single sentence were written with the most scrupulous honesty, we must recognize the huge difference between "the Truth" and "the Whole Truth."

Another item also raised my suspicions. Thirty years ago, a disaffected Mossad officer named Victor Ostrovsky left that organization and wrote ***By Way of Deception***, a highly critical book recounting numerous alleged operations known to him, especially those contrary to American and Western interests. The Israeli government and its pro-Israel advocates launched an unprecedented legal campaign to block publication, but this produced a major backlash and media uproar, with the heavy publicity landing the book as #1 on the *New York Times* bestseller list. I finally got around to reading his book about a decade ago and was shocked by many of the remarkable claims, while being reliably informed that CIA personnel had judged his material as probably accurate when they reviewed it.

Although much of Ostrovsky's information was impossible to independently confirm, for more than a quarter-century his international bestseller and its 1994 sequel *The Other Side of Deception* have heavily shaped our understanding of Mossad and its activities, so I naturally expected to see a detailed discussion, whether supportive or critical, in Bergman's exhaustive parallel work. Instead, there was only a single reference to Ostrovsky buried in a footnote on p. 684. We are told of Mossad's utter horror at the numerous deep secrets that Ostrovsky was preparing to reveal, which led its top leadership to formulate a plan to assassinate him. Ostrovsky only survived because Prime Minister Yitzhak Shamir, who had formerly spent decades as the Mossad assassination chief, vetoed the proposal on the grounds that "We don't kill Jews." Although this reference is brief and almost hidden, I regard it as providing considerable support for Ostrovsky's general credibility.

Having thus acquired serious doubts about the completeness of Bergman's seemingly comprehensive narrative history, I noted a curious fact. I have no specialized expertise in intelligence operations in general nor those of Mossad in particular, so I found it quite remarkable that the overwhelming majority of all the higher-profile incidents recounted by Bergman were already familiar to me merely from the decades I had spent closely reading the *New York Times* every morning. Is it really plausible that six years of exhaustive research and so many personal interviews would have uncovered so few major operations that had not already been known and reported in the international media? Bergman obviously provides a wealth of detail previously limited to insiders, along with numerous unreported assassinations of relatively minor individuals, but it seems strange that he came up with so few major new revelations.

Indeed, some major gaps in his coverage are quite apparent to anyone who has even somewhat investigated the topic, and these begin in the early chapters of his volume, which include coverage of the Zionist prehistory in Palestine prior to the establishment of the Jewish state.

Bergman would have severely damaged his credibility if he had failed to include the infamous 1940s Zionist assassinations of Britain's Lord Moyne or U.N. Peace Negotiator Count Folke Bernadotte. But he unaccountably fails to mention that in 1937 the more right-wing Zionist faction whose political heirs have dominated Israel in recent decades assassinated Chaim Arlosoroff, the highest-ranking Zionist figure in Palestine. Moreover, he omits a number of similar incidents, including some of those targeting top Western leaders. As **I wrote last year:**

> Indeed, the inclination of the more right-wing Zionist factions toward assassination, terrorism, and other forms of essentially criminal behavior was really quite remarkable. For example, in 1943 Shamir **had arranged the assassination of his factional rival**, a year after the two men had escaped together from imprisonment for a bank robbery in which bystanders had been killed, and he claimed he had acted

to avert the planned assassination of David Ben-Gurion, the top Zionist leader and Israel's future founding-premier. Shamir and his faction certainly continued this sort of behavior into the 1940s, successfully assassinating Lord Moyne, the British Minister for the Middle East, and Count Folke Bernadotte, the UN Peace Negotiator, though they failed in their other attempts to kill **American President Harry Truman** and **British Foreign Minister Ernest Bevin**, and **their plans to assassinate Winston Churchill** apparently never moved past the discussion stage. His group also **pioneered the use of terrorist car-bombs and other explosive attacks against innocent civilian targets,** all long before any Arabs or Muslims had **ever thought of using similar tactics**; and Begin's larger and more "moderate" Zionist faction did much the same.

As far as I know, the early Zionists had a record of political terrorism almost unmatched in world history, and in 1974 Prime Minister Menachem Begin **once even boasted** to a television interviewer of having been the founding father of terrorism across the world.

In the aftermath of World War II, Zionists were bitterly hostile towards all Germans, and Bergman describes the campaign of kidnappings and murders they soon unleashed, both in parts of Europe and in Palestine, which claimed as many as two hundred lives. A small ethnic German community had lived peacefully in the Holy Land for many generations, but after some of its leading figures were killed, the rest permanently fled the country, and their abandoned property was seized by Zionist organizations, a pattern which would soon be replicated on a vastly larger scale with regard to the Palestinian Arabs.

These facts were new to me, and Bergman seemingly treats this wave of vengeance-killings with considerable sympathy, noting that many of the victims had actively supported the German war effort. But oddly enough, he fails to mention that throughout the 1930s, the main Zionist movement had itself maintained **a strong economic partnership with Hitler's Germany**, whose financial support was crucial to the establishment of the Jewish state. Moreover, after the war began a small right-wing Zionist faction led by a future prime minister of Israel **actually attempted to enlist in the Axis military alliance**, offering to undertake a campaign of espionage and terrorism against the British military in support of the Nazi war effort. These undeniable historical facts have obviously been a source of immense embarrassment to Zionist partisans, and over the last few decades they have done their utmost to expunge them from public awareness, so as a native-born Israeli now in his mid-40s, Bergman may simply be unaware of this reality.

"Who Killed Zia?"

Bergman's long book contains thirty-five chapters of which only the first two cover the period prior to the creation of Israel, and if his notable omissions were limited to those, they would constitute a mere blemish on an otherwise reliable historical narrative. But a considerable number of major lacunae seem evident across the decades that follow, though they may be less the fault of the author himself than the tight Israeli censorship he faced or the realities of the American publishing industry. By the year 2018, pro-Israeli influence over America and other Western countries had reached such enormous proportions that Israel would risk little international damage by admitting to numerous illegal assassinations of various prominent figures in the Arab world or the Middle East. But other sorts of past deeds might still be considered far too damaging to yet acknowledge.

In 1991 renowned investigative journalist Seymour Hersh published *The Samson Option*, describing Israel's secret nuclear weapons development program of the early 1960s, which was regarded as an absolute national priority by Prime Minister David Ben-Gurion, There are widespread claims that it was the threatened use of that arsenal that later blackmailed the Nixon Administration into its all-out effort to rescue Israel from the brink of military defeat during the 1973 war, a decision that provoked the Arab Oil Embargo and led to many years of economic hardship for the West.

The Islamic world quickly recognized the strategic imbalance produced by their lack of nuclear deterrent capability, and various efforts were made to redress that balance, which Tel Aviv did its utmost to frustrate. Bergman covers in great detail the widespread campaigns of espionage, sabotage, and assassination by which the Israelis successfully forestalled the Iraqi nuclear program of Saddam Hussein, finally culminating in the long-distance 1981 air raid that destroyed his Osirik reactor complex. The author also covers the destruction of a Syrian nuclear reactor in 2007 and Mossad's assassination campaign that claimed the lives of several leading Iranian physicists a few years later. But all these events were reported at the time in our major newspapers, so no new ground is being broken. Meanwhile, an important story not widely known is entirely missing.

About seven months ago, my morning *New York Times* carried **a glowing 1,500 word tribute** to former U.S. ambassador John Gunther Dean, dead at age 93, giving that eminent diplomat the sort of lengthy obituary usually reserved these days for a rap-star slain in a gun-battle with his drug-dealer. Dean's father had been a leader of his local Jewish community in Germany, and after the family left for America on the eve of World War II, Dean became a naturalized citizen in 1944. He went on to have a very distinguished diplomatic career, notably serving during the Fall of Cambodia, and under normal circumstances, the piece would have meant no more to me than it did to nearly all its other readers. But I had spent much of the first decade of the 2000s digitizing the complete archives of hundreds of our leading periodicals, and every now and then a particularly intriguing title led me to read the article in question. Such was the case with "Who Killed Zia?" which appeared in 2005.

Throughout the 1980s, Pakistan had been the lynchpin of America's opposition to the Soviet occupation of Afghanistan, with its military dictator Zia ul-Haq being one of our most important regional allies. Then in 1988, he and most of his top leadership died in a mysterious plane crash, which also claimed the lives of the U.S. ambassador and an American general.

Although the deaths might have been accidental, Zia's wide assortment of bitter enemies led most observers to assume foul play, and there was some evidence that a nerve gas agent, possibly released from a crate of mangos, had been used to incapacitate the crew and thereby cause the crash.

At the time, Dean had reached the pinnacle of his career, serving as our ambassador in neighboring India, while the U.S. ambassador killed in the crash, Arnold Raphel, had been his closest personal friend, also Jewish. By 2005, Dean was elderly and long-retired, and he finally decided to break his seventeen years of silence and reveal the strange circumstances surrounding the event, saying that he was convinced that the Israeli Mossad had been responsible.

A few years before his death, Zia had boldly declared that the production of an "Islamic atomic bomb" was a top Pakistani priority. Although his primary motive was the need to balance India's small nuclear arsenal, he promised to share such powerful weapons with other Muslim countries, including those in the Middle East. Dean describes the tremendous alarm Israel expressed at this possibility, and how pro-Israel members of Congress began a fierce lobbying campaign to stop Zia's efforts. According to journalist Eric Margolis, a leading expert on South Asia, Israel **repeatedly tried** to enlist India in launching a joint all-out attack against Pakistan's nuclear facilities, but after carefully considering the possibility, the Indian government declined.

This left Israel in a quandary. Zia was a proud and powerful military dictator and his very close ties with the U.S. greatly strengthened his diplomatic leverage. Moreover, Pakistan was 2,000 miles from Israel and possessed a strong military, so that any sort of long-distance bombing raid similar to the one used against the Iraqi nuclear program was impossible. That left assassination as the remaining option.

Given Dean's awareness of the diplomatic atmosphere prior to Zia's death, he immediately suspected an Israeli hand, and his past personal experiences supported that possibility. Eight years earlier, while posted in Lebanon, the Israelis had sought to enlist his personal support in their local projects, drawing upon his sympathy as a fellow Jew. But when he rejected those overtures and declared that his primary loyalty was to America, an attempt was made to assassinate him, with the munitions used being eventually traced back to Israel.

Although Dean was tempted to immediately disclose his strong suspicions regarding the annihilation of the Pakistani government to the international media, he decided instead to pursue proper diplomatic channels, and immediately departed for Washington to share his views with his State Department superiors and other top Administration officials. But upon reaching DC, he was quickly declared mentally incompetent, prevented from returning to his India posting, and soon forced to resign. His four decade long career in government service ended summarily at that point. Meanwhile, the US government refused to assist Pakistan's efforts to properly investigate the fatal crash and instead tried to convince a skeptical world that Pakistan's entire top leadership had died because of a simple mechanical failure in their American aircraft.

This remarkable account would surely seem like the plot of an implausible Hollywood movie, but the sources were extremely reputable. The author of the 5,000 word article was Barbara Crossette, the former *New York Times* bureau chief for South Asia, who had held that post at the time of Zia's death, while the piece appeared in *World Policy Journal*, the prestigious quarterly of The New School in New York City. The publisher was academic Stephen Schlesinger, son of famed historian Arthur J. Schlesinger, Jr.

One might naturally expect that such explosive charges from so solid a source might provoke considerable press attention, but Margolis noted that the story was instead totally ignored and boycotted by the entire North American media. Schlesinger had spent a decade at the helm of his periodical, but a couple of issues later he had vanished from the masthead and his employment at the New School had come to an end. The article is no longer available on the *World Policy Journal* website, but the text can still be accessed via **Archive.org**, allowing those so interested to read it and decide for themselves.

The complete historical blackout of that incident has continued down to the present day. Dean's detailed *Times* obituary portrayed his long and distinguished career in highly flattering terms, yet failed to devote even a single sentence to the bizarre circumstances under which it ended.

At the time I originally read that article a dozen or so years ago, I had mixed feelings about the likelihood of Dean's provocative hypothesis. Top national leaders in South Asia do die by assassination rather regularly, but the means employed are almost always quite crude, usually involving one or more gunman firing at close range or perhaps a suicide-bomber. By contrast, the highly sophisticated methods apparently used to eliminate the Pakistani government seemed to suggest a very different sort of state actor. Bergman's book catalogs the enormous number and variety of Mossad's assassination technologies.

Given the important nature of Dean's accusations and the highly reputable venue in which they had appeared, Bergman must certainly have been aware of the story, so I wondered what arguments his Mossad sources might provide to rebut or debunk them. Instead, I discovered that the incident appears nowhere in Bergman's exhaustive volume, perhaps reflecting the author's reluctance to assist in deceiving his readers.

I also noticed that Bergman made absolutely no mention of the earlier assassination attempt against Dean when he was serving as our ambassador in Lebanon, even though the serial numbers of the anti-tank rockets fired at his armored limousine were traced to a batch sold to Israel. However, **sharp-eyed journalist Philip Weiss did notice** that the shadowy organization which officially claimed credit for the attack was revealed by Bergman to have been a Israel-created front group used for numerous car-bombings and other terrorist attacks. This seems to confirm Israel's responsibility in the assassination plot.

Let us assume that this analysis is correct and that there is a good likelihood that Mossad was indeed behind Zia's death. The broader implications are considerable.

Pakistan was one of the world's largest countries in 1988, having a population that was already over 100 million and growing rapidly, while also possessing a powerful military. One of America's main Cold War projects had been to defeat the Soviets in Afghanistan, and Pakistan had played the central role in that effort, ranking its leadership as one of our most important global allies. The sudden assassination of President Zia and most of his pro-American government, along with our own ambassador, thus represented a huge potential blow to U.S. interests. Yet when one of our top diplomats reported Mossad as the likely culprit, the whistleblower was immediately purged and a major cover-up begun, with no whisper of the story ever reaching our media or our citizenry, even after he repeated the charges years later in a prestigious publication. Bergman's comprehensive book contains no hint of the story, and none of the knowledgeable reviewers seem to have noted this lapse.

If an event of such magnitude could be totally ignored by our entire media and omitted from Bergman's book, many other important incidents may also have escaped notice.

"By Way of Deception"

A good starting point for such investigation might be Ostrovsky's works, given the desperate concern of the Mossad leadership at the secrets he revealed in his manuscript and their hopes of shutting his mouth by killing him. So I decided to reread his work after a decade or so and with Bergman's material now reasonably fresh in my mind.

Ostrovsky's 1990 book runs just a fraction of the length of Bergman's volume and is written in a far more casual style while totally lacking any of the latter's copious source references. Much of the text is simply a personal narrative, and although both he and Bergman had Mossad as their subject, his overwhelming focus was on espionage issues and the techniques of spycraft rather than the details of particular assassinations, although a certain number of the latter were included. On an entirely impressionistic level, the style of the Mossad operations described seemed quite similar to those presented by Bergman, so much so that if various incidents were switched between the two books, I doubt that anyone could easily tell the difference.

In assessing Ostrovsky's credibility, a couple of minor items caught my eye. Early on, he states that at the age of 14 he placed second in Israel in target shooting and at 18 he was commissioned as the youngest officer in the Israeli military. These seem like significant, factual claims, which if true would help to explain the repeated efforts by Mossad to recruit him, while if false would surely have been used by Israel's partisans to discredit him as a liar. I have seen no indication that his statements were ever disputed.

Mossad assassinations were a relatively minor focus of Ostrovsky's 1990 book, but it is interesting to compare those handful of examples to the many hundreds of lethal incidents covered by Bergman. Some of the differences in detail and coverage seem to follow a pattern.

For example, Ostrovsky's opening chapter described the subtle means by which Israel pierced the security of Saddam Hussein's nuclear weapons project of the late 1970s, successfully sabotaging his equipment, assassinating his scientists, and eventually destroying the completed reactor in a daring 1981 bombing raid. As part of this effort, they lured one of his top physicists to Paris, and after failing to recruit the scientist, killed him instead. Bergman devotes a page or two to that same incident, but fails to mention that the French prostitute who had unwittingly been part of their scheme was also killed the following month after she became fearful at what had happened and contacted the police. One wonders if numerous other collateral killings of Europeans and Americans accidentally caught up in these deadly events may also have been carefully airbrushed out of Bergman's Mossad-sourced narrative.

An even more obvious example comes much later in Ostrovsky's book, when he describes how Mossad became alarmed upon discovering that Arafat was attempting to open peace negotiations with Israel in 1981, and soon assassinated the ranking PLO official assigned to that task. This incident is missing from Bergman's book, despite its comprehensive catalog of far less significant Mossad victims.

One of the most notorious assassinations on American soil occurred in 1976, when a car-bomb explosion in the heart of Washington D.C. took the lives of exiled former Chilean Foreign Minister Orlando Letelier and his young American assistant. The Chilean secret service were soon found responsible, and a major international scandal erupted, especially since the Chileans had already begun liquidating numerous other perceived opponents throughout Latin America. Ostrovsky explains how Mossad had trained the Chileans in such assassination techniques as part of a complex arms sale agreement, but Bergman makes no mention of this history.

One of the leading Mossad figures in Bergman's narrative is Mike Harari, who spent some fifteen years holding senior positions in its assassination division, and according to the index his name appears on more than 50 different pages. The author generally portrays Harari in a gauzy light, while admitting his central role in the infamous Lillehammer Affair, in which his agents killed a totally innocent Moroccan waiter living in a Norwegian town through a case of mistaken identity, a murder that resulted in the conviction and imprisonment of several Mossad agents and severe damage to Israel's international reputation. By contrast, Ostrovsky portrays Harari as a deeply corrupt individual, who after his retirement became heavily involved in international drug-dealing and served as a top henchman of notorious Panamanian dictator Manuel Noriega. After Noriega fell, the new American-backed government gleefully announced Harari's arrest, but the ex-Mossad officer somehow managed to escape back to Israel, while his former boss received a thirty year sentence in American federal prison.

Widespread financial and sexual impropriety within the Mossad hierarchy was a recurrent theme throughout Ostrovsky's narrative, and his stories seem fairly credible. Israel had been founded on strict socialistic principles and these still held sway during the 1980s, so that government employees were usually paid a mere pittance. For example, Mossad case officers earned between $500 and $1,500 per month depending upon their rank, while controlling vastly larger operational budgets and making decisions potentially worth millions to interested parties, a situation that obviously might lead to serious temptations. Ostrovsky notes that although one of his superiors had spent his whole career working for the government on that sort of meager salary, he had somehow managed to acquire a huge personal estate, complete with its own small forest. My own impression is that although intelligence operatives in America may often launch lucrative private careers after they retire, any agents who became conspicuously wealthy while still working for the CIA would be facing serious legal risk.

Ostrovsky was also disturbed by the other sorts of impropriety he claims to have encountered. He and his fellow trainees allegedly discovered that their top leadership sometimes staged late-night sexual orgies in the secure areas of the official training facilities, while adultery was rampant within Mossad, especially involving supervising officers and the wives of the agents they had in the field. Moderate former Prime Minister Yitzhak Rabin was widely disliked in the organization and one Mossad officer regularly bragged that he had personally brought down Rabin's government in 1976 by publicizing a minor violation of financial regulations. This foreshadows Bergman's far more serious suggestion of the very suspicious circumstances behind Rabin's assassination two decades later.

Ostrovsky emphasized the remarkable nature of Mossad as an organization, especially when compared to its late Cold War peers serving the two superpowers. The KGB had 250,000 worldwide employees and the CIA tens of thousands, but Mossad's entire staff barely numbered 1,200, including secretaries and cleaning personnel. While the KGB deployed an army of 15,000 case officers, Mossad operated with merely 30 to 35.

This astonishing efficiency was made possible by Mossad's heavy reliance on a huge network of loyal Jewish volunteer "helpers" or *sayanim* scattered all across the world, who could be called upon at a moment's notice to assist in an espionage or assassination operation, immediately lend large sums of money, or provide safe houses, offices, or equipment. London alone contained some 7,000 of these individuals, with the worldwide total surely numbering in the many tens or even hundreds of thousands. Only full-blooded Jews were considered eligible for this role, and Ostrovsky expresses considerable misgivings about a system that seemed so strongly to confirm every traditional accusation that Jews functioned as a "state within a state," with so many of them being disloyal to the country in which they held their citizenship. Meanwhile, the term *sayanim* appears nowhere in Bergman's 27 page index, and there is almost no mention of their use in his text, although Ostrovsky plausibly argues that the system was absolutely central to Mossad's operational efficiency.

Ostrovsky also starkly portrays the utter contempt that many Mossad officers expressed toward their purported allies in the other Western intelligence services, trying to cheat their supposed partners at every turn and taking as much as they could get while giving as little as possible in return. He describes what seems like a remarkable degree of outright hatred, almost xenophobia, towards all non-Jews and their leaders, however friendly. For example, Margaret Thatcher was widely regarded as one of the most pro-Jewish and pro-Israel prime ministers in British history, filling her cabinet with members of that tiny 0.5% minority and regularly praising plucky little Israel as a rare Middle Eastern democracy. Yet the Mossad members deeply hated her, usually referred to her as "the bitch," and were convinced that she was an anti-Semite.

If European Gentiles were regular objects of hatred, peoples from other, less developed parts of the world were often ridiculed in harshly racialist terms, with Israel's Third World allies sometimes casually described as "monkeylike" and "not long out of the trees."

Occasionally, such extreme arrogance risked diplomatic disaster as was suggested by an amusing vignette. During the 1980s, there was a bitter civil war in Sri Lanka between the Sinhalese and the Tamils, which also drew in a military contingent from neighboring India. At one point, Mossad was simultaneously training special forces contingents from all three of these mutually-hostile forces at the same time and in the same facility, so that they nearly encountered each other, which surely would have produced a huge diplomatic black eye for Israel.

The author describes his increasing disillusionment with an organization that he claimed was subject to rampant internal factionalism and dishonesty. He was also increasingly concerned about the extreme right-wing sentiments that seemed to pervade so much of Mossad, leading him to wonder if it wasn't becoming a serious threat to Israeli democracy and the very survival of the country. According to his account, he was unfairly made the scapegoat for a failed mission and believing his life at risk, he fled Israel with his wife and returned to his birthplace of Canada.

After deciding to write his book, Ostrovsky recruited as his co-author Claire Hoy, a prominent Canadian political journalist, and despite tremendous pressure from Israel and its partisans, their project succeeded, with the book becoming a huge international best-seller, spending nine weeks as #1 on the *New York Times* list and soon having over a million copies in print.

Although Hoy had spent 25 years as a highly successful writer and this book project was by far his greatest publishing triumph, not long afterwards **he was financially bankrupt** and the butt of widespread media ridicule, having suffered the sort of personal misfortune that so often seems to visit those who are critical of Israel or Jewish activities. Perhaps as a consequence, when Ostrovsky published his 1994 sequel, *The Other Side of Deception*, no co-author was listed.

"The Other Side of Deception"

The contents of Ostrovsky's first book had mostly been rather mundane, lacking any shocking revelations. He merely described the inner workings of Mossad and recounted some of its major operations, thereby piercing the veil of secrecy that had long shrouded one of the world's most effective intelligence services. But having established his reputation with an international bestseller, the author felt confident enough to include numerous bombshells in his 1994 sequel, so that individual readers must decide for themselves whether these were factual or merely a product of his wild imagination. Bergman's comprehensive bibliography lists some 350 titles, but although Ostrovsky's first book is included, his second is not.

Portions of Ostrovsky's original narrative had certainly struck me as rather vague and odd. Why had he supposedly been scapegoated for a failed mission and drummed out of the service? And since he had left Mossad in early 1986 but only began work on his book two years later, I wondered what he had been doing during the intervening period. I also found it difficult to understand how a rather junior officer had obtained such a wealth of detailed information about Mossad operations in which he himself had not been personally involved. There seemed many missing pieces to the story.

These explanations were all supplied in the opening portions of his sequel, though they are obviously impossible to verify. According to the author, his departure had occurred as a byproduct of an ongoing internal struggle at Mossad, in which a moderate dissident faction intended to use him to undermine the credibility of the organization and thereby weaken its dominant leadership, whose policies they opposed.

Reading **this second book** eight or nine years ago, one of the earliest claims seemed totally outlandish. Apparently, the director of Mossad had traditionally been an outsider appointed by the prime minister, and that policy had long rankled many of its senior figures, who preferred to see one of their own put in charge. In 1982, their furious lobbying for such an internal promotion had once again been ignored, and instead a celebrated Israeli general had been named, who soon made plans to clean house in support of different policies. But instead of accepting this situation, some disgruntled Mossad elements arranged his assassination in Lebanon just before he was scheduled to officially take office. Some evidence of the successful plot immediately came to light and was later confirmed, igniting a subterranean factional conflict involving both Mossad personnel and some members of the military, a struggle that ultimately drew in Ostrovsky.

This story came towards the beginning of the book, and struck me as so wildly implausible that I became deeply suspicious of everything that followed. But after reading Bergman's authoritative volume, I am now not so sure. After all, we know that around the same time, a different intelligence faction had seriously considered assassinating Israel's defense minister, and there are strong suspicions that security operatives orchestrated the later assassination of Prime Minister Rabin. So perhaps the elimination of a disfavored Mossad director-designate is not so totally absurd. And Wikipedia does indeed confirm that **Gen. Yekutiel Adam**, Israel's Deputy Chief of Staff, was named Mossad Director in mid-1982 but then killed in Lebanon just a couple of weeks before he was scheduled to take office, thereby becoming the highest-ranking Israeli ever to die on the battlefield.

According to Ostrovsky and his factional allies, powerful elements within Mossad were transforming it into a dangerous, rogue organization, which threatened Israeli democracy and blocked any possibility of peace with the Palestinians. These individuals might even act in direct opposition to the top Mossad leadership, whom they often regarded as overly weak and compromising.

Early in 1982, some of the more moderate Mossad elements backed by the outgoing director had tasked one of their officers in Paris to open diplomatic channels with the Palestinians, and he did so via an American attache whom he enlisted in the effort. But when the harder-line faction discovered this plan, they frustrated the project by assassinating both the Mossad agent and his unlucky American collaborator, while throwing the blame upon some extremist Palestinian group. I obviously can't verify the truth of this remarkable story, but the *New York Times* archive does confirm Ostrovsky's account of the mysterious 1982 killings of **Yakov Barsimantov** and **Charles Robert Ray**, puzzling incidents that left experts searching for a motive.

Ostrovsky claims to have been deeply shocked and disbelieving when he was initially informed of this history of hard-line Mossad elements assassinating both Israeli officials and their own colleagues over policy differences, but he was gradually persuaded of the reality. So as a private citizen now living in Canada, he agreed to undertake a campaign to disrupt Mossad's existing intelligence operations, hoping to sufficiently discredit the organization that the dominant faction would lose influence or at least have their dangerous activities curtailed by the Israeli government. Although he would receive some assistance by the moderate elements that had recruited him, the project was obviously an extremely dangerous one, with his life very much at risk if his actions were discovered.

Presenting himself as a disgruntled former Mossad officer who was seeking revenge against his past employer, he spent much of the next year or two approaching the intelligence services of Britain, France, Jordan, and Egypt, offering to assist them in uncovering the Israeli espionage networks in their countries in exchange for substantial financial payments. No similarly knowledgeable Mossad defector had ever previously come forward, and although some of these services were initially suspicious, he eventually won their trust, while the information he provided was quite valuable in breaking up various local Israeli spy-rings, most of which had previously been unsuspected. Meanwhile, his Mossad confederates kept him informed of any signs that his activities had been detected.

The detailed account of Ostrovsky's anti-Mossad counter-intelligence campaign occupies well over half the book, and I have no easy means of determining whether his stories are real or fantasy, or perhaps some mixture of the two. The author does provide copies of his 1986 plane tickets to Amman, Jordan and Cairo, Egypt, where supposedly he was debriefed at length by the local security services, and in 1988 a major international scandal did erupt when the British very publicly closed down a large number of Mossad safe-houses and expelled numerous Israeli agents. Personally, I found most of Ostrovsky's account reasonably credible, but perhaps individuals who possess actual professional expertise in intelligence operations might come to a different conclusion.

Although two years of these attacks against Mossad intelligence networks had inflicted serious damage, the overall political results were much less than desired. The existing leadership still held a firm grip on the organization and the Israeli government gave no sign of taking action. So Ostrovsky finally concluded that a different approach might be more effective, and he decided to write a book about Mossad and its inner workings.

His internal allies were initially quite skeptical, but he eventually won them over, and they fully participated in the writing project. Some of these individuals had spent many years at Mossad, even rising to a senior level, and they were the source of the extremely detailed material on particular operations in the 1990 book, which had seemed far beyond the knowledge of a very junior officer such as Ostrovsky.

Mossad's attempt to legally suppress the book was a terrible blunder and generated the massive publicity that made it an international bestseller. Outside observers were mystified that the Israelis had adopted such a counter-productive media strategy, but according to Ostrovsky, his internal allies had helped persuade the Mossad leadership to take that approach. They also tried to keep him abreast of any Mossad plans to abduct or assassinate him.

During the production of the 1990 book, Ostrovsky and his allies had discussed numerous past operations, but only a fraction of these were ultimately included in the text. So when the author decided to produce his sequel, he had a wealth of historical material to draw upon, which included several bombshells.

The first of these came with regard to Israel's major role in the illegal sales of American military equipment to Iran during the bitter Iran-Iraq war of the 1980s, a story that eventually exploded into the headlines as the notorious "Iran-Contra Scandal," although our media did its utmost to hide Israel's central involvement in the affair.

The arms trade with Iran was an extremely lucrative one for Israel, soon expanded to the training of military pilots. The deep ideological antipathy that the Islamic Republic held for the Jewish state required that this business be conducted via third parties, so a smuggling route was established through the small German state of Schleswig-Holstein. However, when an effort was later made to enlist the support of the state's top elected official, he rejected the proposal. The Mossad leaders were fearful that he might interfere in the business, so they successfully fabricated a scandal to unseat him and installed a more pliable German politician in his place. Unfortunately, the disgraced official raised a fuss and demanded public hearings to clear his name, so Mossad agents lured him to Geneva, and after he rejected a large bribe to keep quiet, killed him, disguising the death so that police ruled it a suicide.

During my original reading, this very lengthy and detailed incident, which ran over 4,000 words, seemed quite doubtful to me. I'd never previously heard of Uwe Barschel, but he was described as a close personal friend of German Chancellor Helmut Kohl, and I found it totally implausible that Mossad had so casually removed a popular and influential European elected official from office, then afterward murdered him. My deep suspicions regarding the rest of Ostrovsky's book were further magnified.

However, in recently revisiting the incident, I **discovered** that seven months after the book appeared, the *Washington Post* **reported** that the Barschel case had been reopened, with German, Spanish, and Swiss police investigations finding strong indications of a murder committed exactly along the lines previously suggested by Ostrovsky. Once again, the surprising claims of the Mossad defector had apparently checked out, and I now became much more willing to believe that at least most of his subsequent revelations were probably correct. And there were quite a long list of those.

(As an aside, Ostrovsky noted one of the crucial sources of Mossad's growing internal influence in Germany. The threat of domestic German terrorism led the German government to regularly send large numbers of its security and police officials to Israel for training, and these individuals became ideal targets for intelligence recruitment, continuing to collaborate with their Israeli handlers long after they had returned home and resumed their careers. Thus, although the topmost ranks of those organizations were generally loyal to their country, the mid-ranks gradually became honeycombed with Mossad assets, who could be used for various projects. This raises obvious concerns about America's post-9/11 policy of sending such large numbers of our own police officials to Israel for similar training, as well as the tendency for nearly all newly elected members of Congress to travel there as well.)

I vaguely recalled the early 1980s controversy surrounding UN Secretary-General Kurt Waldheim, who was discovered to have lied about his World War II military service, and left office under a dark cloud, with his name becoming synonymous with long-hidden Nazi war-crimes. Yet according to Ostrovsky, the entire scandal was fabricated by Mossad, which placed incriminating documents obtained from other files into that of Waldheim. The UN leader had become increasingly critical of Israel's military attacks on South Lebanon, so the falsified evidence was used to launch a smear campaign in the media that destroyed him.

And if Ostrovsky can be credited, for many decades Israel itself had engaged in activities that would have occupied center-stage at the Nuremberg Trials. According to his account, from the late 1960s onward, Mossad had maintained a small laboratory facility at Nes Ziyyona just south of Tel Aviv for the lethal testing of nuclear, chemical, and bacteriological compounds upon hapless Palestinians selected for elimination. This ongoing process of deadly testing allowed Israel to perfect its assassination technologies while also upgrading its powerful arsenal of unconventional weapons that would be available in the event of war. Although during the 1970s, the American media endlessly focused on the terrible depravity of the CIA, I don't ever recall hearing any accusations along these lines.

At one point, Ostrovsky had been surprised to discover that Mossad agents were accompanying Israeli doctors on their medical missions to South Africa, where they treated impoverished Africans at an outpatient clinic in Soweto. The explanation he received was a grim one, namely that private Israeli companies were using the unknowing blacks as human guinea-pigs for the testing of medical compounds in ways that could not legally have been done in Israel itself. I obviously have no means of verifying this claim, but I had sometimes wondered how Israel eventually came to dominate so much of world's generic drug industry, which naturally relies upon the cheapest and most efficient means of testing and production.

Also quite interesting was the story he told of the rise and fall of British press tycoon Robert Maxwell, a Czech immigrant of Jewish background. According to his account, Maxwell had closely collaborated with Mossad throughout his career, and the intelligence service had been crucial in facilitating his rise to power, lending him money early on and deploying their allies in labor unions and the banking industry to weakened his media acquisition targets. Once Maxwell's empire had been created, he repaid his benefactors in ways both legal and illegal, supporting Israel's policies in his newspapers while also providing Mossad with a slush fund, secretly financing their off-the-books European operations with cash from his corporate pension account. Those latter outlays were normally meant to serve as temporary loans, but in 1991 Mossad was slow in returning the funds and he grew financially desperate as his fragile empire tottered. When he hinted at the dangerous secrets he might be forced to reveal unless he were paid, Mossad killed him instead and disguised it as suicide.

Once again, Ostrovsky's claims cannot be verified, but the dead publisher was given a hero's funeral in Israel, with the serving Prime Minister deeply praising his important services to the Jewish state while three of his predecessors were also in attendance, and Maxwell was buried with full honors in the Mount of Olives. Most recently, his daughter Ghislaine reached the headlines as the closest associate of notorious blackmailer Jeffrey Epstein, and the woman is widely believed to have been a Mossad agent, now possibly hiding in Israel.

But Ostrovsky's most potentially dramatic story occurred in late 1991 and filled one of his last short chapters. In the aftermath of America's great military victory over Iraq in the Gulf War, President George H.W. Bush decided to invest some of his considerable political capital in finally forcing peace in the Middle East between Arabs and Israelis. Right-wing Prime Minister Yitzhak Shamir was bitterly opposed to any of the proposed concessions, so Bush began placing financial pressure upon the Jewish state, blocking loan guarantees despite the efforts of America's powerful Israel Lobby. Within certain circles, he was soon vilified as a diabolical enemy of the Jews.

Ostrovsky explains that when faced with strong opposition by an American president, pro-Israel groups have traditionally cultivated his Vice President as a backdoor means of regaining their influence. For example, when President Kennedy fiercely opposed Israel's nuclear weapons development program in the early 1960s, the Israel Lobby focused their efforts upon Vice President Lyndon Johnson, and this strategy was rewarded when the latter doubled aid to Israel soon after taking office. Similarly, in 1991 they emphasized their friendship with Vice President Dan Quayle, an easy task since his chief of staff and top advisor was William Kristol, a leading Jewish Neocon.

However, an extreme faction in Mossad settled upon a much more direct means of solving Israel's political problems and decided to assassinate President Bush at his international peace conference in Madrid while throwing the blame upon three Palestinian militants. On October 1, 1991, Ostrovsky received a frantic phone call from his leading Mossad collaborator informing him of the plan and desperately seeking his assistance in thwarting it. He initially reacted with total disbelief, finding it difficult to accept that even Mossad hard-liners would consider such a reckless act, but he soon agreed to do whatever he could to publicize the plot and somehow bring it to the attention of the Bush Administration without being dismissed as a mere "conspiracy theorist."

Since Ostrovsky was now a prominent author, he was frequently invited to speak on Middle East issues to elite groups, and at his next opportunity, he emphasized the intense hostility of Israeli right-wingers to Bush's proposals, and strongly suggested that the president's life was in danger. As it happened, a member of the small audience brought those concerns to the attention of former Congressman Pete McCloskey, an old friend of the president, who soon discussed the situation with Ostrovsky by phone, then flew to Ottawa for a lengthy personal meeting to assess the credibility of the threat. Concluding that the danger was serious and real, McCloskey immediately began using his DC connections to approach members of the Secret Service, finally persuading them to contact Ostrovsky, who explained his inside sources of information. The story was soon leaked to the media, generating extensive coverage by influential columnist Jack Anderson and others, and the resulting publicity caused the assassination plot to be abandoned.

Once again I was quite skeptical after reading this account, so I decided to contact a few people I knew, and they informed me that the Bush Administration had indeed taken Ostrovsky's warnings about the alleged Mossad assassination plot very seriously at the time, which seemingly confirmed much of the author's story.

Following his publishing triumph and his success in foiling the alleged plot against the life of President Bush in late 1991, Ostrovsky largely lost touch with his internal Mossad allies, and instead focused on his own private life and new writing career in Canada. Furthermore, the June 1992 Israeli elections brought to power the much more moderate government of Prime Minister Rabin, which seemed to greatly reduce the need for any further anti-Mossad efforts. But government shifts may sometimes have unexpected consequences, especially in the lethal world of intelligence operations, where personal relationships are often sacrificed to expediency.

After the publication of his 1990 book, Ostrovsky had become fearful of being abducted or killed, so as a consequence he had avoided crossing the Atlantic and visiting Europe. But in 1993, his former Mossad allies began urging him to travel to Holland and Belgium to promote the release of new translations of his international bestseller. They firmly assured him that the political changes in Israel meant that he would now be perfectly safe, and he finally agreed to take the trip despite considerable misgivings. But although he took some reasonable security precautions, an odd incident in Brussels convinced him that he had narrowly escaped a Mossad kidnapping. Growing alarmed, he called his senior Mossad contact at home, but instead of getting any reassurance, he received a strangely cold and unfriendly response, which included a reference to the notorious case of a individual who had once betrayed Mossad and then been killed together with his wife and three children.

Rightly or wrongly, Ostrovsky concluded that the fall of Israel's hard-line government had apparently given the more moderate Mossad faction a chance of gaining control of their organization. Tempted by such power, they now regarded him as a dangerous and expendable loose end, someone who might eventually reveal their own past involvement in anti-Mossad intelligence activities as well as the highly damaging book project.

Believing his former allies now wanted to eliminate him, he quickly began work on his sequel, which would put the full story into the public record, thereby greatly reducing any benefits of shutting his mouth. I also noticed that his new book repeatedly mentioned his secret possession of a comprehensive collection of the names and photos of Mossad's international operatives and whether true or not, that possibility might serve as a life-insurance policy by greatly increasing the risks if Israel took any action against him.

This short description of events closed Ostrovsky's second book, explaining why the volume had been written and contained so much sensitive material that had been excluded from the previous one.

"Final Judgment" on the JFK Assassination

Ostrovsky's sequel was released late in 1994 by HarperCollins, a leading publisher. But despite its explosive contents, this time Israel and its allies had learned their lesson, and they greeted the work with near-total silence rather than hysterical attacks, so it received relatively little attention and sold only a fraction of the previous number of copies. Among mainstream publications, I could only locate one short and rather negative **capsule review** in *Foreign Affairs*.

However, another book published at the beginning of that same year on related issues suffered from a far more complete public blackout that has now still endured for over a quarter-century, and this was not merely because of its obscure origins. Despite the severe handicap of such a near-total media boycott, the work went on to become an underground bestseller, eventually having over 40,000 copies in print, widely read and perhaps discussed in certain circles, but almost never publicly mentioned. *Final Judgment* by the late Michael Collins Piper set forth the explosive hypothesis that Mossad had played a central role in the most famous assassination of the twentieth century, the 1963 killing of President John F. Kennedy.

While Ostrovsky's books drew upon his personal knowledge of Israel's secret intelligence service, Piper was a journalist and researcher who had spent his entire career at Liberty Lobby, a small activist organization based in DC. Being sharply critical of Israeli policies and Zionist influence in America, the group was usually portrayed by the media as part of the far right anti-Semitic populist fringe, and almost entirely ignored by all mainstream outlets. Its weekly tabloid *Spotlight*, which usually focused on controversial topics, had once reached a remarkable circulation of well over 300,000 in the unsettled times of the late 1970s, but then declined substantially in readership during the more placid and optimistic Reagan Era that followed.

Liberty Lobby had never much delved into JFK assassination issues, but in 1978 it published an article on the subject by Victor Marchetti, a prominent former CIA official, and as a result was soon sued for defamation by E. Howard Hunt of Watergate fame, with the lawsuit threatening its survival. In 1982 this ongoing legal battle attracted the involvement of Mark Lane, an experienced attorney of a leftist Jewish background who had been the founding father of JFK conspiracy investigations. Lane **won the case at trial** in 1985 and thereafter remained a close ally of the organization.

Piper gradually became friendly with Lane and by the early 1990s he himself had grown interested in the JFK assassination. In January 1994, he published his major work, *Final Judgment*, which presented an enormous body of circumstantial evidence backing his theory that Mossad had been heavily involved in the JFK assassination. I summarized and discussed the Piper Hypothesis in **my own 2018 article**:

> For decades following the 1963 assassination, virtually no suspicions had ever been directed towards Israel, and as a consequence none of the hundreds or thousands of assassination conspiracy books that appeared during the 1960s, 1970s, and 1980s had hinted at any role for the Mossad, though nearly

every other possible culprit, ranging from the Vatican to the Illuminati, came under scrutiny. Kennedy had received over 80% of the Jewish vote in his 1960 election, American Jews featured very prominently in his White House, and he was greatly lionized by Jewish media figures, celebrities, and intellectuals ranging from New York City to Hollywood to the Ivy League. Moreover, individuals with a Jewish background such as Mark Lane and Edward Epstein had been among the leading early proponents of an assassination conspiracy, with their controversial theories championed by influential Jewish cultural celebrities such as Mort Sahl and Norman Mailer. Given that the Kennedy Administration was widely perceived as pro-Israel, there seemed no possible motive for any Mossad involvement, and bizarre, totally unsubstantiated accusations of such a monumental nature directed against the Jewish state were hardly likely to gain much traction in an overwhelmingly pro-Israel publishing industry.

However, in the early 1990s highly regarded journalists and researchers began exposing the circumstances surrounding the development of Israel's nuclear weapons arsenal. Seymour Hersh's 1991 book **The Samson Option: Israel's Nuclear Arsenal and American Foreign Policy** described the extreme efforts of the Kennedy Administration to force Israel to allow international inspections of its allegedly non-military nuclear reactor at Dimona, and thereby prevent its use in producing nuclear weapons. *Dangerous Liaisons: The Inside Story of the U.S.-Israeli Covert Relationship* by Andrew and Leslie Cockburn appeared in the same year, and covered similar ground.

Although entirely hidden from public awareness at the time, the early 1960s political conflict between the American and Israeli governments over nuclear weapons development had represented a top foreign policy priority of the Kennedy Administration, which had made nuclear non-proliferation one of its central international initiatives. It is notable that John McCone, Kennedy's choice as CIA Director, had previously served on the Atomic Energy Commission under

Eisenhower, being the individual who leaked the fact that Israel was building a nuclear reactor to produce plutonium.

The pressure and financial aid threats secretly applied to Israel by the Kennedy Administration eventually became so severe that they led to the resignation of Israel's founding Prime Minister David Ben-Gurion in June 1963. But all these efforts were almost entirely halted or reversed once Kennedy was replaced by Johnson in November of that same year. Piper notes that Stephen Green's 1984 book ***Taking Sides: America's Secret Relations With a Militant Israel*** had previously documented that U.S. Middle East Policy completely reversed itself following Kennedy's assassination, but this important finding had attracted little attention at the time.

Skeptics of a plausible institutional basis for a JFK assassination conspiracy have often noted the extreme continuity in both foreign and domestic policies between the Kennedy and Johnson Administrations, arguing that this casts severe doubt on any such possible motive. Although this analysis seems largely correct, America's behavior towards Israel and its nuclear weapons program stands as a very notable exception to this pattern.

An additional major area of concern for Israeli officials may have involved the efforts of the Kennedy Administration to sharply restrict the activities of pro-Israel political lobbies. During his 1960 presidential campaign, Kennedy had met in New York City with a group of wealthy Israel advocates, led by financier Abraham Feinberg, and they had offered enormous financial support in exchange for a controlling influence in Middle Eastern policy. Kennedy managed to fob them off with vague assurances, but he considered the incident so troubling that the next morning he sought out journalist Charles Bartlett, one of his closest friends, and expressed his outrage that American foreign policy might fall under the control of partisans of a foreign power, promising that if he became president, he would rectify that situation. And indeed, once he had installed his brother Robert as Attorney General, the latter initiated a major legal effort to force pro-Israel groups to register themselves as foreign agents, which would have drastically reduced their power and influence. But after JFK's death, this project was quickly abandoned, and as part of the settlement, the leading pro-Israel lobby merely agreed to reconstitute itself as AIPAC.

Final Judgment went through a number of reprintings following its original 1994 appearance, and by the sixth edition released in 2004, had grown to over 650 pages, including numerous long appendices and over 1100 footnotes, the overwhelming majority of these referencing fully mainstream sources. The body of the text was merely serviceable in organization and polish, reflecting the total boycott by all publishers, mainstream or alternative, but I found the contents themselves remarkable and generally quite compelling. Despite the most extreme blackout by all media outlets, the book sold more than 40,000 copies over the yers, making it something of an underground bestseller, and surely bringing it to the attention of everyone in the JFK assassination research community, though apparently almost none of them were willing to mention its existence. I suspect these other writers realized that even any mere acknowledgement of the existence of the book, if only to ridicule or dismiss it, might prove fatal to their media and publishing career. Piper himself died in 2015, aged 54, suffering from the health problems and heavy-drinking often associated with grim poverty, and other journalists may have been reluctant to risk that same dismal fate.

As an example of this strange situation, the bibliography of Talbot's 2005 book contains almost 140 entries, some rather obscure, but has no space for *Final Judgment*, nor does his very comprehensive index include any entry for "Jews" or "Israel." Indeed, at one point he very delicately characterizes Sen. Robert Kennedy's entirely Jewish senior staff by stating "There was not a Catholic among them." His 2015 sequel is equally circumspect, and although the index does contain numerous entries pertaining to Jews, all these references are in regards to World War II and the Nazis, including his discussion of the alleged Nazi ties of Allen Dulles, his principal *bête noire*. Stone's book, while fearlessly convicting President Lyndon Johnson of the JFK assassination, also strangely excludes "Jews" and "Israel" from the long index and *Final Judgment* from the bibliography, and Douglass's book follows this same pattern.

Furthermore, the extreme concerns that the Piper Hypothesis seems to have provoked among JFK assassination researchers may explain a strange anomaly. Although Mark Lane was himself of Jewish origins and left-wing roots, after his victory for Liberty Lobby in the Hunt libel trial, he spent many years associated with that organization in a legal capacity, and apparently became quite friendly with Piper, one of its leading writers. According to Piper, Lane told him that *Final Judgment* made "a solid case" for a major Mossad role in the assassination, and he viewed the theory as fully complementary to his own focus on CIA involvement. I suspect that concerns about these associations may explain why Lane was almost completely airbrushed out of the Douglass and 2007 Talbot books, and discussed in the second Talbot book only when his work was absolutely essential to Talbot's own analysis. By contrast, *New York Times* staff writers are hardly likely to be as versed in the lesser-known aspects of the JFK assassination research community, and being ignorant of this hidden controversy, they gave Lane **the long and glowing obituary** that his career fully warranted.

When weighing the possible suspects for a given crime, considering their past pattern of behavior is often a helpful approach. As discussed above, I can think of no historical example in which organized crime initiated a serious assassination attempt against any American political figure even moderately prominent on the national stage. And despite a few suspicions here and there, the same applies to the CIA.

By contrast, the Israeli Mossad and the Zionist groups that preceded the establishment of the Jewish state seem to have had a very long track record of assassinations, including those of high-ranking political figures who might normally be regarded as inviolate. Lord Moyne, the British Minister of State for the Middle East, was assassinated in 1944 and Count Folke Bernadotte, the UN Peace Negotiator sent to help resolve the first Arab-Israel war, suffered the same fate in September 1948. Not even an American president was entirely free of such risks, and Piper notes that the memoirs of Harry Truman's daughter Margaret reveal that Zionist militants had tried to assassinate her father using a letter laced with toxic chemicals in 1947 when they believed he was dragging his heels in supporting Israel, although that failed attempt was never made public. The Zionist faction responsible for all of these incidents was led by Yitzhak Shamir, who later became a leader of Mossad and director of its assassination program during the 1960s, before eventually becoming Prime Minister of Israel in 1986...

There are other notable elements that tend to support the Piper Hypothesis. Once we accept the existence of a JFK assassination conspiracy, the one individual who is virtually certain to have been a participant was Jack Ruby, and his organized crime ties were almost entirely to the huge but rarely-mentioned Jewish wing of that enterprise, presided over by Meyer Lansky, an extremely fervent supporter of Israel. Ruby himself had particularly strong connections with Lansky lieutenant Mickey Cohen, who dominated the Los Angeles underworld and had been personally involved in gun-running to Israel prior to the 1948 war. Indeed, **according to Dallas rabbi Hillel Silverman**, Ruby had privately explained his killing of Oswald by saying "I did it for the Jewish people."

An intriguing aspect to Oliver Stone's landmark *JFK* film should also be mentioned. Arnon Milchan, the wealthy Hollywood producer who backed the project, was not only an Israeli citizen, but had also reportedly **played a central role in the enormous espionage project** to divert American technology and materials to Israel's nuclear weapons project, the exact undertaking that the Kennedy Administration had made such efforts to block. Milchan has even sometimes been described as "**the Israeli James Bond.**" And although the film ran a full three hours in length, *JFK* scrupulously avoided presenting any of the details that Piper later regarded as initial clues to an Israeli dimension, instead seeming to finger America's fanatic home-grown anti-Communist movement and the Cold War leadership of the military-industrial complex as the guilty parties.

Summarizing over 300,000 words of Piper's history and analysis in just a few paragraphs is obviously an impossible undertaking, but the above discussion provides a reasonable taste of the enormous mass of circumstantial evidence mustered in favor of the Piper Hypothesis.

In many respects, JFK Assassination Studies has become its own academic discipline, and my credentials are quite limited. I have read perhaps a dozen books in the subject, and have also tried to approach the issues with the clean slate and fresh eyes of an outsider, but any serious expert would surely have digested scores or even hundreds of the volumes in the field. While the overall analysis of *Final Judgment* struck me as quite persuasive, a good fraction of the names and references were unfamiliar, and I simply do not have the background to assess their credibility, nor whether the description of the material presented is accurate.

Under normal circumstances, I would turn to the reviews or critiques produced by other authors, and comparing them against Piper's claims, then decide which argument seemed the stronger. But although *Final Judgment* was published a quarter-century ago, the near-absolute blanket of silence surrounding the Piper Hypothesis, especially from the more influential and credible researchers, renders this impossible.

However, Piper's inability to secure any regular publisher and the widespread efforts to smother his theory out of existence, have had an ironic consequence. Since the book went out of print years ago, I had a relatively easy time securing the rights to include it in my collection of controversial HTML Books, and I have now done so, thereby allowing everyone on the Internet to conveniently read the entire text and decide for themselves, while easily checking the multitude of references or searching for particular words or phrases.

- **Final Judgment**
  The Missing Link in the JFK Assassination Conspiracy
  Michael Collins Piper • 2005 • 310,000 Words

This edition actually incorporates several much shorter works, originally published separately. One of these, consisting of an extended Q&A, describes the genesis of the idea and answers numerous questions surrounding it, and for some readers might represent a better starting point.

- **Default Judgment**
  Questions, Answers & Reflections About the Crime of the Century
  Michael Collins Piper • 2005 • 48,000 Words

There are also numerous extended Piper interviews or presentations easily available on YouTube, and when I watched two or three of them a couple of years ago, I thought he effectively summarized many of his main arguments, but I cannot remember which ones they were.

Some additional evidence tends to support Piper's arguments for likely Mossad involvement in the death of our president.
David Talbot's influential 2007 book **Brothers** revealed that Robert F. Kennedy had been convinced almost from the first that his brother had been struck down in a conspiracy, but he held his tongue, telling his circle of friends that he stood little chance of tracking down and punishing the guilty parties until he himself reached the White House. By June 1968, he seemed on the threshold of achieving that goal, but was felled by an assassin's bullet just moments after winning the crucial California presidential primary. The logical assumption is that his death was engineered by the same elements as that of his elder

brother, who were now acting to protect themselves from the consequences of their earlier crime.

A young Palestinian named Sirhan Sirhan had fired a pistol at the scene and was quickly arrested and convicted for the murder. But Talbot emphasizes that the coroner's report revealed that the fatal bullet came from a completely different direction, while the acoustical record proves that far more shots were fired than the capacity of the alleged killer's gun. Such hard evidence seems to demonstrate a conspiracy.

Sirhan himself seemed dazed and confused, later claiming to have no memory of events, and Talbot mentions that various assassination researchers have long argued that he was merely a convenient patsy in the plot, perhaps acting under some form of hypnosis or conditioning. Nearly all these writers are usually reluctant to note that the selection of a Palestinian as scapegoat in the killing seems to point in a certain obvious direction, but Bergman's recent book also includes a major new revelation. At exactly the same moment that Sirhan was being wrestled to the floor of the Ambassador Hotel ballroom in Los Angeles, another young Palestinian **was undergoing** intensive rounds of hypnotic conditioning at the hands of Mossad in Israel, being programmed to assassinate PLO leader Yasir Arafat; and although that effort ultimately failed, such a coincidence seems to stretch the bounds of plausibility.

Three decades later, JFK's heir and namesake had developed a growing public profile as publisher of his popular political magazine *George*, which attracted considerable international controversy when he published a long article claiming that the assassination of Israeli Prime Minister Rabin had been orchestrated by hard-liners within Israel's own security services. There were also strong indications that JFK Jr. might soon enter politics, perhaps running for the US Senate as a stepping-stone to the White House.

Instead, he died in an unusual 1999 light plane crash, and a later edition of Piper's book outlined some of the suspicious circumstances, which the author believed suggested an Israeli hand. For years Piper had made efforts to bring his explosive book to the attention of JFK's son, and he thought that he might have finally succeeded. Israeli-Canadian author Barry Chamish also believed that it was JFK Jr.'s discovery of the Piper Hypothesis that had led the younger Kennedy to promote the Rabin assassination conspiracy theory in his magazine.

Last year, French researcher Laurent Guyénot published **an exhaustive analysis** of JFK Jr.'s death, arguing that he was probably killed by Israel. My own reading of the material he presents is rather different, and although there are a number of somewhat suspicious items, I think that the evidence of foul play—let alone Mossad involvement—is rather thin, leading me to conclude that the plane crash was probably just the tragic accident portrayed by the media. But the aftermath of the death did highlight an important ideological divide.

For six decades, members of the Kennedy family have been wildly popular among ordinary American Jews, probably attracting greater political enthusiasm than almost any other public figures. But this undeniable reality has masked an entirely different perspective found within a particular section of that same community.

John Podhoretz, a leading scion of the militantly pro-Israel Neocons, was opinion editor of *The New York Post* at the time of the fatal plane crash, and he immediately published an astonishing column entitled "**A Conversation in Hell**" in which he positively reveled at the death of the young Kennedy. He portrayed patriarch Joseph Kennedy as an unspeakable anti-Semite who had sold his soul to the Devil for his own worldly success and that of his family, then suggested that all the subsequent assassinations and other early deaths of Kennedys merely constituted the fine print of that Satanic bargain. So brutally harsh a piece surely indicates that those bitter sentiments were hardly uncommon within Podhoretz's small ultra-Zionist social circle, which probably overlapped with similar right-wing elements in Israel. So this reaction demonstrates that the exact same political figures who were most deeply beloved by the overwhelming majority of American Jews may have also been regarded as mortal enemies by an influential segment of the Jewish state and its corps of Mossad assassins.

When I published my original 2018 article on the JFK assassination, I naturally noted the widespread use of assassination by Zionist groups, a pattern that had long predated the creation of the Jewish state, and I cited some of the supportive evidence contained in the two Ostrovsky books. But at the time, I still had considerable doubts about Ostrovsky's credibility, especially regarding the shocking claims in his second book, and I had not yet read Bergman's volume, which had just been published a few months earlier. So although there seemed considerable evidence for the Piper Hypothesis, I regarded it as far from conclusive.

However, I have now digested Bergman's book, which documents the enormous volume of international Mossad assassinations, and I have also concluded that Ostrovsky's claims were far more solid than I had previously assumed. As a result my opinion has substantially shifted. Instead of merely being a solid possibility, I believe there is actually a strong likelihood that Mossad together with its American collaborators played a central role in the Kennedy assassinations of the 1960s, leading me to fully affirm the Piper Hypothesis. Guyénot has relied upon many of the same sources and has come to **roughly similar conclusions**.

The Strange Death of James Forrestal, and Other Fatalities

Once we recognize that Israel's Mossad was probably responsible for the assassination of President John F. Kennedy, our understanding of post-war American history may require substantial reevaluation.

The JFK assassination was possibly the most famous event of the second half of the twentieth century, and it inspired a vast outpouring of media coverage and journalistic investigation that seemingly explored every nook and crany of the story. Yet for the first three decades after the killing in Dallas, virtually no whisper of suspicion was ever directed at Israel, and during the quarter-century since Piper published his ground-breaking 1994 book, scarcely any of his analysis has leaked into the English-language media. If a story of such enormity has remained so well hidden for so long, perhaps it was neither the first nor the last.

If the Kennedy brothers did indeed perish due to a conflict over our Middle Eastern policy, they were certainly not the first prominent Western leaders to suffer that fate, especially when we consider the bitter political battles a generation earlier over the establishment of Israel. All our standard history books describe the mid-1940s Zionist assassinations of Lord Moyne of Britain and U.N. Peace Negotiator Count Folke Bernodotte, though they rarely mention the failed attempts on the lives of **President Harry S. Truman** and **Britain Foreign Secretary Ernest Bevin** around the same time.

But another leading American public figure also died during that period under rather strange circumstances, and although his demise is always mentioned, the crucial political context is excluded, as I discussed at length in **a 2018 article**:

> Sometimes our standard history textbooks provide two seemingly unrelated stories, which become far more important only once we discover that they are actually parts of a single connected whole. The strange death of James Forrestal certainly falls into this category.
>
> During the 1930s Forrestal had reached the pinnacle of Wall Street, serving as CEO of Dillon, Read, one of the most prestigious investment banks. With World War II looming, Roosevelt drew him into government service in 1940, partly because his strong Republican credentials helped emphasize the bipartisan nature of the war effort, and he soon became Undersecretary of the Navy. Upon the death of his elderly superior in 1944, Forrestal was elevated to the Cabinet as Navy Secretary, and after the contentious battle over the reorganization of our military departments, he became America's first Secretary of Defense in 1947, holding authority over the Army, Navy, Air Force, and Marines. Along with Secretary of State Gen. George Marshall, Forrestal probably ranked as the most influential member of Truman's Cabinet. However, just a few months after Truman's 1948 reelection, we are told that Forrestal became paranoid and depressed, resigned his powerful position, and weeks later committed suicide by jumping from an 18th story window at Bethesda Naval Hospital. Knowing almost nothing about Forrestal or his background, I always nodded my head over this odd historical event.
>
> Meanwhile, an entirely different page or chapter of my history textbooks usually carried the dramatic story of the bitter political conflict that wracked the Truman Administration over the recognition of the State of Israel, which had taken place the previous year. I read that George Marshall argued such a step would be totally disastrous for American interests by potentially alienating many hundreds of millions of Arabs and Muslims, who held the enormous oil wealth of the

Middle East, and felt so strongly about the matter that he threatened to resign. However, Truman, heavily influenced by the personal lobbying of his old Jewish haberdashery business partner Eddie Jacobson, ultimately decided upon recognition, and Marshall stayed in the government.

However, almost a decade ago, I somehow stumbled across an interesting book *Zionism* by Alan Hart, a journalist and author who had served as a longtime BBC Middle East Correspondent, in which I discovered that these two different stories were part of a seamless whole. By his account, although Marshall had indeed strongly opposed recognition of Israel, it had actually been Forrestal who spearheaded that effort in Truman's Cabinet and was most identified with that position, resulting in numerous harsh attacks in the media and his later departure from the Truman Cabinet. Hart also raised very considerable doubts about whether Forrestal's subsequent death had actually been suicide, citing an obscure website for a detailed analysis of that last issue.

It is a commonplace that the Internet has democratized the distribution of information, allowing those who create knowledge to connect with those who consume it without the need for a gate-keeping intermediary. I have encountered few better examples of the unleashed potential of this new system than "**Who Killed Forrestal?**", an exhaustive analysis by a certain David Martin, who describes himself as an economist and political blogger. Running many tens of thousands of words, his series of articles on the fate of America's first Secretary of Defense provides an exhaustive discussion of all the source materials, including the small handful of published books describing Forrestal's life and strange death, supplemented by contemporaneous newspaper articles and numerous relevant government documents obtained by personal FOIA requests. The verdict of murder followed by a massive governmental cover-up seems solidly established.

As mentioned, Forrestal's role as the Truman Administration's principal opponent of Israel's creation had made him the subject of an almost unprecedented campaign of personal media vilification in both print and radio, spearheaded by the country's two most powerful columnists of the right and the left, Walter Winchell and Drew Pearson, only the former being Jewish, but both heavily connected with the ADL and extremely pro-Zionist, with their attacks and accusations even continuing after his resignation and death.

Once we move past the wild exaggerations of Forrestal's alleged psychological problems promoted by these very hostile media pundits and their many allies, much of Forrestal's supposed paranoia apparently consisted of his belief that he was being followed around Washington, D.C., his phones may have been tapped, and his life might be in danger at the hands of Zionist agents. And perhaps such concerns were not so entirely unreasonable given certain contemporaneous events...

Indeed, State Department official Robert Lovett, a relatively minor and low-profile opponent of Zionist interests, reported receiving numerous threatening phone calls late at night around the same time, which greatly concerned him. Martin also cites subsequent books by Zionist partisans who boasted of the effective use their side had made of blackmail, apparently obtained by wire-tapping, to ensure sufficient political support for Israel's creation.

Meanwhile, behind the scenes, powerful financial forces may have been gathering to ensure that President Truman ignored the unified recommendations of all his diplomatic and national security advisors. Years later, both **Gore Vidal** and **Alexander Cockburn** would separately report that it eventually became common knowledge in DC political circles that during the desperate days of Truman's underdog 1948 reelection campaign, he had secretly accepted a cash payment of $2 million from wealthy Zionists in exchange for recognizing Israel, a sum perhaps comparable to $20 million or more in present-day dollars.

Republican Thomas Dewey had been heavily favored to win the 1948 presidential election, and after Truman's surprising upset, Forrestal's political position was certainly not helped when Pearson claimed in a newspaper column that Forrestal had secretly met with Dewey during the campaign, making arrangements to be kept on in a Dewey Administration.

Suffering political defeat regarding Middle East policy and facing ceaseless media attacks, Forrestal resigned his Cabinet post under pressure. Almost immediately afterwards, he was checked into the Bethesda Naval Hospital for observation, supposedly suffering from severe fatigue and exhaustion, and he remained there for seven weeks, with his access to visitors sharply restricted. He was finally scheduled to be released on May 22, 1949, but just hours before his brother Henry came to pick him up, his body was found below the window of his 18th floor room, with a knotted cord wound tightly around his neck. Based upon an official press release, the newspapers all reported his unfortunate suicide, suggesting that he had first tried to hang himself, but failing that approach, had leapt out his window instead. A half page of copied Greek verse was found in his room, and in the heydey of Freudian psychoanalyical thinking, this was regarded as the subconscious trigger for his sudden death impulse, being treated as almost the equivalent of an actual suicide note. My own history textbooks simplified this complex story to merely say "suicide," which is what I read and never questioned.

Martin raises numerous very serious doubts with this official verdict. Among other things, published interviews with Forrestal's surviving brother and friends reveal that none of them believed Forrestal had taken his own life, and that they had all been prevented from seeing him until near the very end of his entire period of confinement. Indeed, the brother recounted that just the day before, Forrestal had been in fine spirits, saying that upon his release, he planned to use some of his very considerable personal wealth to buy a newspaper and begin revealing to the American people many of the suppressed facts concerning America's entry into World War II, of which he had direct knowledge, supplemented by the extremely extensive personal diary that he had kept for many years. Upon Forrestal's confinement, that diary, running thousands of pages, had been seized by the government, and after his death was apparently published only in heavily edited and expurgated form, though it nonetheless still became a historical sensation.

The government documents unearthed by Martin raise additional doubts about the story presented in all the standard history books. Forrestal's medical files seem to lack any official autopsy report, there is visible evidence of broken glass in his room, suggesting a violent struggle, and most remarkably, the page of copied Greek verse—always cited as the main indication of Forrestal's final suicidal intent—was actually not written in Forrestal's own hand.

Aside from newspaper accounts and government documents, much of Martin's analysis, including the extensive personal interviews of Forrestal's friends and relatives, is based upon a short book entitled *The Death of James Forrestal*, published in 1966 by one Cornell Simpson, almost certainly a pseudonym. Simpson states that his investigative research had been conducted just a few years after Forrestal's death and although his book was originally scheduled for release his publisher grew concerned over the extremely controversial nature of the material included and cancelled the project. According to Simpson, years later he decided to take his unchanged manuscript off the shelf and have it published by Western Islands press, which turns out to have been an imprint of the John Birch Society, the notoriously conspiratorial rightwing organization then near the height of its national influence. For these reasons, certain aspects of the book are of considerable interest even beyond the contents directly relating to Forrestal.

The first part of the book consists of a detailed presentation of the actual evidence regarding Forrestal's highly suspicious death, including the numerous interviews with his friends and relatives, while the second portion focuses on the nefarious plots of the world-wide Communist movement, a Birch Society staple. Allegedly, Forrestal's staunch anti-Communism had been what targeted him for destruction by Communist agents, and there is virtually no reference to any controversy regarding his enormous public battle over Israel's establishment, although that was certainly the primary factor behind his political downfall. Martin notes these strange inconsistencies, and even wonders whether certain aspects of the book and its release may have been intended to deflect attention from this Zionist dimension towards some nefarious Communist plot.

Consider, for example, David Niles, whose name has lapsed into total obscurity, but who had been one of the very few senior FDR aides retained by his successor, and according to observers, Niles eventually became one of the most powerful figures behind the scenes of the Truman Administration. Various accounts suggest he played a leading role in Forrestal's removal, and Simpson's book supports this, suggesting that he was Communist agent of some sort. However, although the Venona Papers reveal that Niles had sometimes cooperated with Soviet agents in their espionage activities, he apparently did so either for money or for some other considerations, and was certainly not part of their own intelligence network. Instead, both Martin and Hart provide an enormous amount of evidence that Niles's loyalty was overwhelmingly to Zionism, and indeed by 1950 his espionage activities on behalf of Israel became so extremely blatant that Gen. Omar Bradley, Chairman of the Joint Chiefs of Staff, threatened to immediately resign unless Niles was fired, forcing Truman's hand.

Forrestal was a wealthy and pugnacious Irish Catholic, and I think there is very considerable evidence that his death was the result of factors quite similar to those that probably claimed the life of an even more prominent Irish Catholic in Dallas 14 years later.

There are some other possible fatalities that follow this pattern, though the evidence in those cases is far less strong. Piper's 1994 opus is focused primarily on the JFK assassination, but over half his 650 pages are given over to long series of appendices dealing with somewhat related topics. One of these discusses the strange deaths of a couple of former high-ranking CIA officials, suggesting they might have involved foul play.

Former CIA Director William Colby had apparently long been regarded as highly skeptical of the nature of America's relationship with Israel, and therefore was characterized by pro-Israel members of the media as a notorious "Arabist." Indeed, while serving as director in 1974, he had finally ended the career of longtime CIA counter-intelligence chief James Angleton, whose extreme affinity with Israel and its Mossad had sometimes raised serious doubts about his true loyalties. Piper says that by 1996 Colby had grown sufficiently concerned about Israel's infiltration and manipulation of the US government and its intelligence community that he arranged a meeting with high-level Arab officials in DC, suggesting that they all work together to counter this disturbing situation. A few weeks later, Colby disappeared and his drowned body was eventually found, with the official verdict being that he supposedly perished near his home in a canoeing accident, although his former Arab interlocutors alleged foul play.

Piper goes on to also describe the earlier death of John Paisley, the former longtime deputy director of the CIA's Office of Strategic Research, and also a strong critic of the influence of Israel and its close Neocon allies in American national security policy. In late 1978, Paisley's body was found floating in the Chesapeake Bay with a bullet in the head, and although the death was officially ruled a suicide, Piper claims that few believed the story. According to him, Richard Clement, who had headed the Interagency Committee on Counterterrorism during the Reagan Administration, explained in 1996:

> The Israelis had no compunction about "terminating" key American intelligence officials who threatened to blow the whistle on them. Those of us familiar with the case of Paisley know that he was killed by Mossad. But no one, not even in Congress, wants to stand up and say so publicly.

Piper notes the bitter political battles that other Washington national security experts, such as former CIA Deputy Director Adm. Bobby Ray Inman, had experienced over the years with elements of the Israel Lobby in Congress and the media. After Inman was nominated by President Clinton to lead the Defense Department, a firestorm of criticism by pro-Israel partisans forced his withdrawal.

I have made no effort to investigate the material cited by Piper in his short discussion. These examples were previously unknown to me, and all of the evidence he provides seems purely circumstantial, hardly making a case that rises above mere suspicion. But I do regard the author as a reasonably solid investigative journalist and researcher, whose views should be taken seriously. Therefore, those so interested can read his 5,000 word **Appendix Six** and decide for themselves.

The 9/11 Attacks – What Happened?

Although somewhat related, political assassinations and terrorist attacks are distinct topics, and Bergman's comprehensive volume explicitly focuses on the former, so we cannot fault him for providing only slight coverage of the latter. But the historical pattern of Israeli activity, especially with regard to false-flag attacks, is really quite remarkable, as I noted in **a 2018 article**:

> One of history's largest terrorist attacks prior to 9/11 was **the 1946 bombing of the King David Hotel in Jerusalem** by Zionist militants dressed as Arabs, which killed 91 people and largely destroyed the structure. In the famous **Lavon Affair of 1954**, Israeli agents launched a wave of terrorist attacks against Western targets in Egypt, intending to have those blamed on anti-Western Arab groups. There are **strong claims** that in 1950 Israeli Mossad agents began a series of false-flag terrorist bombings against Jewish targets in Baghdad, successfully using those violent methods to help persuade Iraq's thousand-year-old Jewish community to emigrate to the Jewish state. In 1967, Israel launched **a deliberate air and sea attack against the *U.S.S. Liberty***, intending to leave no survivors, killing or wounding over 200 American servicemen before word of the attack reached our Sixth Fleet and the Israelis withdrew.
>
> The enormous extent of pro-Israel influence in world political and media circles meant that none of these brutal attacks ever drew serious retaliation, and in nearly all cases, they were quickly thrown down the memory hole, so that today probably no more than one in a hundred Americans

is even aware of them. Furthermore, most of these incidents came to light due to chance circumstances, so we may easily suspect that many other attacks of a similar nature have never become part of the historical record.

Of these famous incidents, Bergman only includes mention of the King David Hotel bombing. But much later in his narrative, he describes the huge wave of false-flag terrorist attacks unleashed in 1981 by Israeli Defense Minister Ariel Sharon, who recruited a former high-ranking Mossad official to manage the project.

Under Israeli direction, large car bombs began exploding in the Palestinian neighborhoods of Beirut and other Lebanese cities, killing or injuring enormous numbers of civilians. A single attack in October inflicted nearly 400 casualties, and by December, there were eighteen bombings per month, with their effectiveness greatly enhanced by the use of innovative new Israeli drone technology. Official responsibility for all the attacks was claimed by a previously unknown Lebanese organization, but the intent was to provoke the PLO into military retaliation against Israel, thereby justifying Sharon's planned invasion of the neighboring country.

Since the PLO stubbornly refused to take the bait, plans were put into motion for the huge bombing of an entire Beirut sports stadium using tons of explosives during a January 1st political ceremony, with the death and destruction expected to be "of unprecedented proportions, even in terms of Lebanon." But Sharon's political enemies learned of the plot and emphasized that many foreign diplomats including the Soviet ambassador were expected to be present and probably would be killed, so after a bitter debate, Prime Minister Begin ordered the attack aborted. A future Mossad chief mentions the major headaches they then faced in removing the large quantity of explosives that they had already planted within the structure.

I think that this thoroughly documented history of major Israeli false-flag terrorist attacks, including those against American and other Western targets, should be carefully kept in mind when we consider the 9/11 attacks, whose aftermath has massively transformed our society and cost us so many trillions of dollars. I analyzed the strange circumstances of the attacks and their likely nature at considerable length in **my 2018 article**:

> Oddly enough, for many years after 9/11, I paid very little attention to the details of the attacks themselves. I was entirely preoccupied with building **my content-archiving software system**, and with the little time I could spare for public policy matters, I was totally focused on the ongoing Iraq War disaster, as well as my terrible fears that Bush might at any moment suddenly extend the conflict to Iran. Despite Neocon lies shamelessly echoed by our corrupt media, neither Iraq nor Iran had had anything whatsoever to do with the 9/11 attacks, so those events gradually faded in my consciousness, and I suspect the same was true for most other Americans. Al Qaeda had largely disappeared and Bin Laden was supposedly hiding in a cave somewhere. Despite endless Homeland Security "threat alerts," there had been no further Islamic terrorism on American soil, and relatively little anywhere else outside of the Iraq charnel house. So the precise details of the 9/11 plots had become almost irrelevant to me.
>
> Others I knew seemed to feel the same way. Virtually all the exchanges I had with my old friend Bill Odom, the three-star general who had run the NSA for Ronald Reagan, had concerned the Iraq War and risk it might spread to Iran, as well as the bitter anger he felt toward Bush's perversion of his beloved NSA into an extra-constitutional tool of domestic espionage. When the *New York Times* broke the story of the massive extent of domestic NSA spying, Gen. Odom declared that President Bush should be impeached and NSA Director Michael Hayden court-martialed. But in all the years prior to **his untimely passing in 2008**, I don't recall the 9/11 attacks themselves even once coming up as a topic in our discussions...
>
> Admittedly, I'd occasionally heard of some considerable oddities regarding the 9/11 attacks here and there, and these certainly raised some suspicions. Most days I would glance at the *Antiwar.com* front page, and it seemed that some Israeli Mossad agents had been caught while filming the plane at-

tacks in NYC, while **a much larger Mossad "art student" spy operation around the country** had also been broken up around the same time. Apparently, *FoxNews* had even broadcast **a multi-part series on the latter topic** before that expose was scuttled and "disappeared" under ADL pressure.

Although I wasn't entirely sure about the credibility of those claims, it did seem plausible that Mossad had known of the attacks in advance and allowed them to proceed, recognizing the huge benefits that Israel would derive from the anti-Arab backlash. I think I was vaguely aware that *Antiwar.com* editorial director Justin Raimondo had published *The Terror Enigma*, a short book about some of those strange facts, bearing the provocative subtitle "9/11 and the Israeli Connection," but I never considered reading it. In 2007, ***Counterpunch* itself** published **a fascinating follow-up story** about the arrest of that group of Israeli Mossad agents in NYC, who were caught filming and apparently celebrating the plane attacks on that fateful day, and the Mossad activity seemed to be far larger than I had previously realized. But all these details remained a little fuzzy in my mind next to my overriding concerns about wars in Iraq and Iran.

However, by the end of 2008 my focus had begun to change. Bush was leaving office without having started an Iranian war, and America had successfully dodged the bullet of an even more dangerous John McCain administration. I assumed that Barack Obama would be a terrible president and he proved worse than my expectations, but I still breathed a huge sigh of relief every day that he was in the White House.

Moreover, around that same time I'd stumbled across an astonishing detail of the 9/11 attacks that demonstrated the remarkable depths of my own ignorance. In a *Counterpunch* article, I'd discovered that immediately following the attacks, the supposed terrorist mastermind **Osama bin Laden had publicly denied any involvement**, even declaring that no good Muslim would have committed such deeds.

Once I checked around a little and **fully confirmed that fact**, I was flabbergasted. 9/11 was not only the most successful terrorist attack in the history of the world, but may have been greater in its physical magnitude than all past terrorist operations combined. The entire purpose of terrorism is to allow a small organization to show the world that it can inflict serious losses upon a powerful state, and I had never previously heard of any terrorist leader denying his role in a successful operation, let alone the greatest in history. Something seemed extremely wrong in the media-generated narrative that I had previously accepted. I began to wonder if I had been as deluded as the tens of millions of Americans in 2003 and 2004 who naively believed that Saddam had been the mastermind behind the September 11th attacks. We live in a world of illusions generated by our media, and I suddenly felt that I had noticed a tear in the paper-mache mountains displayed in the background of a Hollywood sound-stage. If Osama was probably not the author of 9/11, what other huge falsehoods had I blindly accepted?

A couple of years later, I came across a very interesting column by Eric Margolis, a prominent Canadian foreign policy journalist purged from the broadcast media for his strong opposition to the Iraq War. He had long published a weekly column in the *Toronto Sun* and when that tenure ended, he used his closing appearance to run a double-length piece expressing **his very strong doubts about the official 9/11 story**, even noting that the former director of Pakistani Intelligence insisted that Israel had been behind the attacks...

I eventually discovered that in 2003 former German Cabinet Minister Andreas von Bülow had published **a best-selling book strongly suggesting** that the CIA rather than Bin Laden was behind the attacks, while in 2007 former Italian President Francesco Cossiga had **similarly argued** that the CIA and the Israeli Mossad had been responsible, claiming that fact was well known among Western intelligence agencies.

Over the years, all these discordant claims had gradually raised my suspicions about the official 9/11 story to rather strong levels, but it was only very recently that I finally found the time to begin to seriously investigate the subject and read eight or ten of the main **9/11 Truther books**, mostly those by Prof. David Ray Griffin, the widely acknowledged leader in that field. And his books, together with the writings of his numerous colleagues and allies, revealed all sorts of very telling details, most of which had previously been unknown to me. I was also greatly impressed by the sheer number of seemingly reputable individuals of no apparent ideological bent who had become adherents of the 9/11 Truth movement over the years...

When utterly astonishing claims of an extremely controversial nature are made over a period of many years by **numerous seemingly reputable academics and other experts**, and they are entirely ignored or suppressed but never effectively rebutted, reasonable conclusions seem to point in an obvious direction. Based on my very recent readings in this topic, the total number of huge flaws in the official 9/11 story has now grown extremely long, probably numbering in the many dozens. Most of these individual items seem reasonably likely and if we decide that even just two or three of them are correct, we must totally reject the official narrative that so many of us have believed for so long...

Now I am merely just an amateur in the complex intelligence craft of extracting nuggets of truth from a mountain of manufactured falsehood. Although the arguments of the 9/11 Truth Movement seem quite persuasive to me, I would obviously have felt much more comfortable if they were seconded by an experienced professional, such as a top CIA analyst. A few years ago, I was shocked to discover that was indeed the case.

William Christison **had spent 29 years at the CIA**, rising to become one of its senior figures as Director of its Office of Regional and Political Analysis, with 200 research analysts serving under him. In August 2006, he published **a remarkable 2,700 word article** explaining why he no longer believed the official 9/11 story and felt sure that the 9/11 Commission Report constituted a cover-up, with the truth being quite different. The following year, he provided a forceful endorsement to **one of Griffin's books**, writing that "[There's] a strong body of evidence showing the official U.S. Government story of what happened on September 11, 2001 to be almost certainly a monstrous series of lies." And Christison's extreme 9/11 skepticism was seconded by that of **many other highly regarded former US intelligence professionals**.

We might expect that if a former CIA intelligence officer of Christison's rank were to denounce the official 9/11 report as a fraud and a cover-up, such a story would constitute front-page news. But it was never reported anywhere in our mainstream media, and I only stumbled upon it a decade later.

Even our supposed "alternative" media outlets were nearly as silent. Throughout the 2000s, Christison and his wife Kathleen, also a former CIA analyst, had been regular contributors to *Counterpunch*, publishing **many dozens of articles there** and certainly being its most highly credentialed writers on intelligence and national security matters. But editor Alexander Cockburn refused to publish any of their 9/11 skepticism, so it never came to my attention at the time. Indeed, when I mentioned Christison's views to current *Counterpunch* editor Jeffrey St. Clair a couple of years ago, he was stunned to discover that the friend he had regarded so very highly had actually become a "9/11 Truther." When media organs serve as ideological gatekeepers, a condition of widespread ignorance becomes unavoidable...

With so many gaping holes in the official story of the events of seventeen years ago, each of us is free to choose to focus on those we personally consider most persuasive, and I have several of my own. Danish Chemistry professor Niels Harrit was one of the scientists who analyzed the debris of the destroyed buildings and detected the residual presence of nano-thermite, a military-grade explosive compound, and I found him quite credible during **his hour-long interview** on *Red Ice Radio*. The notion that an undamaged hijacker passport was found on an NYC street after the massive, fiery destruction of the skyscrapers is totally absurd, as was the claim that the top hijacker conveniently lost his luggage at one of the airports and it was found to contain a large mass of incriminating information. The testimonies of the dozens of firefighters **who heard explosions** just before the collapse of the buildings seems totally inexplicable under the official account. The sudden total collapse of Building Seven, never hit by any jetliners is also extremely implausible.

The 9/11 Attacks – Who Did It?

Let us now suppose that the overwhelming weight of evidence is correct, and concur with high-ranking former CIA intelligence analysts, distinguished academics, and experienced professionals that the 9/11 attacks were not what they appeared to be. We recognize the extreme implausibility that three huge skyscrapers in New York City suddenly collapsed at free-fall velocity into their own footprints after just two of them were hit by airplanes, and also that a large civilian jetliner probably did not strike the Pentagon leaving behind absolutely no wreckage and only a small hole. What actually did happen, and more importantly, who was responsible?

The first question is obviously impossible to answer without an honest and thorough official investigation of the evidence. Until that occurs, we should not be surprised that numerous, somewhat conflicting hypotheses have been advanced and debated within the confines of the 9/11 Truth community. But the second question is probably the more important and relevant one, and I think it has always represented a source of extreme vulnerability to 9/11 Truthers.

The most typical approach, as generally followed in the numerous Griffin books, is to avoid the issue entirely and focus solely on the gaping flaws in the official narrative. This is a perfectly acceptable position but leaves all sorts of serious doubts. What organized group would have been sufficiently powerful and daring to carry off an attack of such vast scale against the central heart of the world's sole superpower? And how were they possibly able to orchestrate such a massively effective media and political cover-up, even enlisting the participation of the U.S. government itself?

The much smaller fraction of 9/11 Truthers who choose to address this "whodunit" question seem to be overwhelmingly concentrated among rank-and-file grassroots activists rather than the prestigious experts, and they usually answer "inside job!" Their widespread belief seems to be that the top political leadership of the Bush Administration, probably including Vice President Dick Cheney and Defense Secretary Donald Rumsfeld, had organized the terrorist attacks, either with or without the knowledge of their ignorant nominal superior, President George W. Bush. The suggested motives included justifying military attacks against various countries, supporting the financial interests of the powerful oil industry and military-industrial complex, and enabling the destruction of traditional American civil liberties. Since the vast majority of politically-active Truthers seem to come from the far left of the ideological spectrum, they regard these notions as logical and almost self-evident.

Although not explicitly endorsing those Truther conspiracies, filmmaker Michael Moore's leftist box office hit *Fahrenheit 9/11* seemed to raise such similar suspicions. His small budget documentary earned an astonishing $220 million by suggesting that the very close business ties between the Bush family, Cheney, the oil companies, and the Saudis were responsible for the Iraq War aftermath of the terrorist attacks, as well as the domestic crackdown on civil liberties, which was part-and-parcel of the right-wing Republican agenda.

Unfortunately, this apparently plausible picture seems to have almost no basis in reality. During the drive to the Iraq War, I read *Times* articles interviewing numerous top oil men in Texas who expressed total puzzlement at why America was planning to attack Saddam, saying that they could only assume that President Bush knew something that they themselves did not. Saudi Arabian leaders were adamantly opposed to an American attack on Iraq, and made every effort to prevent it. Prior to his joining the Bush Administration,

Cheney had served as CEO of Halliburton, an oil services giant, and his firm had heavily lobbied for the lifting of U.S. economic sanctions against Iraq. Prof. James Petras, a scholar of strong Marxist leanings, published an excellent 2008 book entitled ***Zionism, Militarism, and the Decline of US Power*** in which he conclusively demonstrated that Zionist interests rather than those of the oil industry had dominated the Bush Administration in the wake of the 9/11 attacks, and promoted the Iraq War.

As for the Michael Moore film, I remember at the time sharing a laugh with a (Jewish) friend of mine, both of us finding it ridiculous that a government so overwhelmingly permeated by fanatically pro-Israel Neocons was being portrayed as being in thrall to the Saudis. Not only did the plotline of Moore's film demonstrate the fearsome power of Jewish Hollywood, but its huge success suggested that most of the American public had apparently never heard of the Neocons.

Bush critics properly ridiculed the president for his tongue-tied statement that the 9/11 terrorists had attacked America "for its freedoms" and Truthers have reasonably branded as implausible the claims that the massive attacks were organized by a cave-dwelling Islamic preacher. But the suggestion that they were led and organized by the top figures of the Bush Administration seems even more preposterous.

Cheney and Rumsfeld had both spent decades as stalwarts of the moderate pro-business wing of the Republican Party, each serving in top government positions and also as CEOs of major corporations. The notion that they capped their careers by joining a new Republican administration in early 2001 and almost immediately set about organizing a gigantic false-flag terrorist attack upon the proudest towers of our largest city together with our own national military headquarters, intending to kill many thousands of Americans in the process, is too ridiculous to even be part of a leftist political satire.

Let's step back a bit. In the entire history of the world, I can think of no documented case in which the top political leadership of a country has launched a major false-flag attack upon its own centers of power and finance and tried to kill large numbers of its own people. The America of 2001 was a peaceful and prosperous country run by relatively bland political leaders focused upon the traditional Republican goals of enacting tax-cuts for the rich and reducing environmental regulations. Too many Truther activists have apparently drawn their understanding of the world from the caricatures of leftist comic-books in which corporate Republicans are all diabolical Dr. Evils, seeking to kill Americans out of sheer malevolence, and Alexander Cockburn was absolutely correct **to ridicule them** at least on that particular score.

Consider also the simple practicalities of the situation. The gigantic nature of the 9/11 attacks as postulated by the Truth movement would have clearly required enormous planning and probably involved the work of many dozens or even hundreds of skilled agents. Ordering CIA operatives or special military units to organize secret attacks against civilian targets in Venezuela or Yemen is one thing, but directing them to mount attacks against the Pentagon and the heart of New York City would be fraught with stupendous risk.

Bush had lost the popular vote in November 2000 and had only reached the White House because of a few dangling chads in Florida and the controversial decision of a deeply divided Supreme Court. As a consequence, most of the American media regarded his new administration with enormous hostility. If the first act of such a newly-sworn presidential team had been ordering the CIA or the military to prepare attacks against New York City and the Pentagon, surely those orders would have been regarded as issued by a group of lunatics, and immediately leaked to the hostile national press.

The whole scenario of top American leaders being the masterminds behind 9/11 is beyond ridiculous, and those 9/11 Truthers who make or imply such claims—doing so without a single shred of solid evidence—have unfortunately played a major role in discrediting their entire movement. In fact, the common meaning of the "inside job" scenario is so patently absurd and self-defeating that one might even suspect that the claim was encouraged by those seeking to discredit the entire 9/11 Truth movement as a consequence.

The focus on Cheney and Rumsfeld seems particularly ill-directed. Although I've never met nor had any dealings with either of those individuals, I was quite actively involved in DC politics during the 1990s, and can say with some assurance that prior to 9/11, neither of them were regarded as Neocons. Instead, they were the archetypical examples of moderate business-type mainstream Republicans, stretching all the way back to their years at the top of the Ford Administration during the mid-1970s.

Skeptics of this claim may note that they signed the **1997 declaration issued by the Project for the New American Century** (PNAC), a leading Neocon foreign policy manifesto organized by Bill Kristol, but I would regard that as something of a red herring. In DC circles, individuals are always recruiting their friends to sign various declarations, which may or may not be indicative of anything, and I remember Kristol trying to get me to sign the PNAC statement as well. Since my private views on that issue were absolutely 100% contrary to the Neocon position, which I regarded as foreign policy lunacy, I deflected his request and very politely turned him down. But I was quite friendly with him at the time, so if I had been someone without strong opinions in that area, I probably would have agreed.

This raises a larger point. By 2000, the Neocons had gained almost total control of all the major conservative/Republican media outlets and the foreign policy wings of nearly all the similarly aligned thinktanks in DC, successfully purging most of their traditional opponents. So although Cheney and Rumsfeld were not themselves Neocons, they were swimming in a Neocon sea, with a very large fraction of all the information they received coming from such sources and with their top aides such as "Scooter" Libby, Paul Wolfowitz, and Douglas Feith being Neocons. Rumsfeld was already somewhat elderly while Cheney had suffered several heart-attacks starting at age 37, so under those circumstances it may have been relatively easy for them to be shifted toward certain policy positions.

Indeed, the entire demonization of Cheney and Rumsfeld in anti-Iraq War circles has seemed somewhat suspicious to me. I always wondered whether the heavily Jewish liberal media had focused its wrath upon those two individuals in order to deflect culpability from the Jewish Neocons who were the obvious originators of that disastrous policy; and the same may be true of the 9/11 Truthers, who probably feared accusations of anti-Semitism. Regarding that former issue, a prominent Israeli columnist was characteristically blunt on the matter in 2003, strongly suggesting that **25 Neocon intellectuals**, nearly all of them Jewish, were primarily responsible for the war. Under normal circumstances, the president himself would have surely been portrayed as the evil mastermind behind the 9/11 plot, but "W" was too widely known for his ignorance for such accusations to be credible.

It does seem entirely plausible that Cheney, Rumsfeld, and other top Bush leaders may have been manipulated into taking certain actions that inadvertently fostered the 9/11 plot, while a few lower-level Bush appointees might have been more directly involved, perhaps even as outright conspirators. But I do not think this is the usual meaning of the "inside job" accusation.

So where do we now stand? It seems very likely that the 9/11 attacks were the work of an organization far more powerful and professionally-skilled than a rag-tag band of nineteen random Arabs armed with box-cutters, but also that the attacks were very unlikely to have been the work of the American government itself. So who actually attacked our country on that fateful day seventeen years ago, killing thousands of our fellow citizens?

Effective intelligence operations are concealed in a hall of mirrors, often extremely difficult for outsiders to penetrate, and false-flag terrorist attacks certainly fall into this category. But if we apply a different metaphor, the complexities of such events may be seen as a Gordian Knot, almost impossible to disentangle, but vulnerable to the sword-stroke of asking the simple question "Who benefited?"

America and most of the world certainly did not, and the disastrous legacies of that fateful day have transformed our own society and wrecked many other countries. The endless American wars soon unleashed have already cost us many trillions of dollars and set our nation on the road to bankruptcy while killing or displacing many millions of innocent Middle Easterners. Most recently, that resulting flood of desperate refugees has begun engulfing Europe, and the peace and prosperity of that ancient continent is now under severe threat.

Our traditional civil liberties and constitutional protections have been drastically eroded, with our society having taken long steps toward becoming an outright police state. American citizens now passively accept unimaginable infringements on their personal freedoms, all originally begun under the guise of preventing terrorism.

I find it difficult to think of any country in the world that clearly gained as a result of the 9/11 attacks and America's military reaction, with one single, solitary exception.

During 2000 and most of 2001, America was a peaceful prosperous country, but a certain small Middle Eastern nation had found itself in an increasingly desperate situation. Israel then seemed to be fighting for its life against the massive waves of domestic terrorism that constituted the Second Palestinian Intifada.

Ariel Sharon was widely believed to have deliberately provoked that uprising in September 2000 by marching to the Temple Mount backed by a thousand armed police, and the resulting violence and polarization of Israeli society had successfully installed him as Prime Minister in early 2001. But once in office, his brutal measures failed to end the wave of continuing attacks, which increasingly took the form of suicide-bombings against civilian targets. Many believed that the violence might soon trigger a huge outflow of Israeli citizens, perhaps producing a death-spiral for the Jewish state. Iraq, Iran, Libya, and other major Muslim powers were supporting the Palestinians with money, rhetoric, and sometimes weaponry, and Israeli society seemed close to crumbling. I remember hearing from some of my DC friends that numerous Israeli policy experts were suddenly seeking berths at Neocon thinktanks so that they could relocate to America.

Sharon was a notoriously bloody and reckless leader, with a long history of undertaking strategic gambles of astonishing boldness, sometimes betting everything on a single roll of the dice. He had spent decades seeking the Prime Ministership, but having finally obtained it, he now had his back to the wall, with no obvious source of rescue in sight.

The 9/11 attacks changed everything. Suddenly the world's sole superpower was fully mobilized against Arab and Muslim terrorist movements, especially those connected with the Middle East. Sharon's close Neocon political allies in America used the unexpected crisis as an opportunity to seize control of America's foreign policy and national security apparatus, with an NSA staffer later reporting that Israeli generals freely roamed the halls of the Pentagon without any security controls. Meanwhile, the excuse of preventing domestic terrorism was used to implement newly centralized American police controls that were soon employed to harass or even shut down various anti-Zionist political organizations. One of the Israeli Mossad agents arrested by the police in New York City as he and his fellows were celebrating the 9/11 attacks and producing a souvenir film of the burning World Trade Center towers told the officers that "We are Israelis... Your problems are our problems." And so they immediately became.

General Wesley Clark reported that soon after the 9/11 attacks he was informed that a secret military plan had somehow come into being under which **America would attack and destroy seven major Muslim countries over the next few years**, including Iraq, Iran, Syria, and Libya, which coincidentally were all of Israel's strongest regional adversaries and the leading supporters of the Palestinians. As America began to expend enormous oceans of blood and treasure attacking all of Israel's enemies after 9/11, Israel itself no longer needed to do so. Partly as a consequence, almost no other nation in the world has so enormously improved its strategic and economic situation during the last seventeen years, even while a large fraction of the American population has become completely impoverished during that same period and our national debt has grown to insurmountable levels. A parasite can often grow fat even as its host suffers and declines.

I have emphasized that for many years after the 9/11 attacks I paid little attention to the details and had only the vaguest notion that there even existed an organized 9/11 Truth movement. But if someone had ever convinced me that the terrorist attacks had been false-flag operations and someone other than Osama had been responsible, my immediate guess would have been Israel and its Mossad.

Certainly no other nation in the world can remotely match Israel's track-record of remarkably bold high-level assassinations and false-flag attacks, terrorist and otherwise, against other countries, even including America and its military. Furthermore, the enormous dominance of Jewish and pro-Israel elements in the American establishment media and increasingly that of many other major countries in the West has long ensured that even when the solid evidence of such attacks was discovered, very few ordinary Americans would ever hear those facts...

Once we accept that the 9/11 attacks were probably a false-flag operation, a central clue to the likely perpetrators has been their extraordinary success in ensuring that such a wealth of enormously suspicious evidence has been totally ignored by virtually the entire American media, whether liberal or conservative, left-wing or right-wing...

In the particular case at hand, the considerable number of zealously pro-Israel Neocons situated just beneath the public surface of the Bush Administration in 2001 could have greatly facilitated both the successful organization of the attacks and their effective cover-up and concealment, with Libby, Wolfowitz, Feith, and Richard Perle being merely the most obvious names. Whether such individuals were knowing conspirators or merely had personal ties allowing them to be exploited in furthering the plot is entirely unclear.

Most of this information must surely have long been apparent to knowledgeable observers, and I strongly suspect that many individuals who had paid much greater attention than myself to the details of the 9/11 attacks may have quickly formed a tentative conclusion along these same lines. But for obvious social and political reasons, there is a great reluctance to publicly point the finger of blame towards Israel on a matter of such enormous magnitude. Hence, except for a few fringe activists here and there, such dark suspicions remained private.

Meanwhile, the leaders of the 9/11 Truth movement probably feared they would be destroyed by media accusations of deranged anti-Semitism if they had ever expressed even a hint of such ideas. This political strategy may have been necessary, but by failing to name any plausible culprit, they created a vacuum that was soon filled by "useful idiots" who shouted "inside job!" while pointing an accusing finger toward Cheney and Rumsfeld, and thereby did so much to discredit the entire 9/11 Truth movement.

This unfortunate conspiracy of silence finally ended in 2009 when Dr. Alan Sabrosky, former Director of Studies at the US Army War College, stepped forward and **publicly declared** that the Israeli Mossad had very likely been responsible for the 9/11 attacks, writing a series of columns on the subject, and eventually presenting his views in a number of media interviews, along with **additional analyses**.

Obviously, such explosive charges never reached the pages of my morning *Times*, but they did receive considerable if transitory coverage in portions of the alternative media, and I remember seeing the links very prominently featured at *Antiwar.com* and widely discussed elsewhere. I had never previously heard of Sabrosky, so I consulted my archiving system and immediately discovered that **he had a perfectly respectable record** of publication on military affairs in mainstream foreign policy periodicals and had also held a series of academic appointments at prestigious institutions. Reading one or two of his articles on 9/11, I felt he made a rather persuasive case for Mossad involvement, with some of his information already known to me but much of it not.

Since I was very busy with my software work and had never spent any time investigating 9/11 or reading any of the books on the topic, my belief in his claims back then was obviously quite tentative. But now that I have finally looked into the subject in much greater detail and done a great deal of reading, I think it seems quite likely that his 2009 analysis was entirely correct.

I would particularly recommend his long 2011 interview on Iranian Press TV, which I first watched just a couple of days ago. He came across as highly credible and forthright in his claims:

- ***Dr. Alan Sabrosky Blows the Lid Off Zionist Involvement in 9/11 Terror Attacks* • 24:11**
  https://www.bitchute.com/video/tpYjyFbJzPZh/

He also provided a pugnacious conclusion in **a much longer 2010 radio interview:**

- ***"They Did It" - Alan Sabrosky* • 2:58**
  https://www.bitchute.com/video/BigWEQyw6Cb7/

Sabrosky focused much of his attention upon a particular segment of a Dutch documentary film on the 9/11 attacks produced several years earlier. In that fascinating interview, a professional demolition expert named Danny Jowenko who was largely ignorant of the 9/11 attacks immediately identified the filmed collapse of WTC Building 7 as a controlled-demolition, and the remarkable clip was broadcast worldwide on *Press TV* and widely discussed across the Internet.

- *911 - Danny Jowenko on WTC7 Controlled Demolition* • 2:36
  https://www.youtube.com/watch?v=Sl2RIqT-4bk

And by a very strange coincidence, just three days after Jowenko's broadcast video interview had received such heavy attention, **he had the misfortune to die in a frontal collision with a tree in Holland.** I'd suspect that the community of professional demolition experts is a small one, and Jowenko's surviving industry colleagues may have quickly concluded that serious misfortune might visit those who rendered controversial expert opinions on the collapse of the three World Trade Center towers.

Meanwhile, **the ADL soon mounted a huge and largely successful** effort to have *Press TV* banned in the West for promoting "anti-Semitic conspiracy theories," even persuading YouTube to entirely eliminate the huge video archive of those past shows, notably including Sabrosky's long interview.

Most recently, Sabrosky provided an hour-long presentation at this June's **Deep Truth video panel conference**, during which he expressed considerable pessimism about America's political predicament, and suggested that the Zionist control over our politics and media had grown even stronger over the last decade.

His discussion was **soon rebroadcast by *Guns & Butter***, a prominent progressive radio program, which as a consequence **was soon purged from its home station** after seventeen years of great national popularity and strong listener support.

The **late Alan Hart**, a very distinguished British broadcast journalist and foreign correspondent, also **broke his silence in 2010** and similarly pointed to the Israelis as the likely culprits behind the 9/11 attacks. Those interested may wish to listen to **his extended interview**.

Journalist Christopher Bollyn was one of the first writers to explore the possible Israeli links to the 9/11 attacks, and the details contained in his long series of newspaper articles are often quoted by other researchers. In 2012, he gathered together this material and published it in the form of a book entitled *Solving 9-11*, thereby making his information on the possible role of the Israeli Mossad available to a much wider audience, with **a version being available online**. Unfortunately his printed volume severely suffers from the typical lack of resources available to the writers on the political fringe, with poor organization and frequent repetition of the same points due to its origins in a set of individual articles, and this may diminish its credibility among some readers. So those who purchase it should be forewarned about these serious stylistic weaknesses.

Probably a much better compendium of the very extensive evidence pointing to the Israeli hand behind the 9/11 attacks has been more recently provided by French writer Laurent Guyénot, both in his 2017 book *JFK-9/11: 50 Years of the Deep State* and also his 8,500 word article "**9/11 was an Israeli Job**", published concurrently with this one and providing a far greater wealth of detail than is contained here. While I would not necessarily endorse all of his claims and arguments, his overall analysis seems fully consistent with my own.

These writers have provided a great deal of material in support of the Israeli Mossad Hypothesis, but I would focus attention on just one important point. We would normally expect that terrorist attacks resulting in the complete destruction of three gigantic office buildings in New York City and an aerial assault on the Pentagon would be an operation of enormous size and scale, involving very considerable organizational infrastructure and manpower. In the aftermath of the attacks, the US government undertook great efforts to locate and arrest the surviving Islamic conspirators, but scarcely managed to find a single one. Apparently, they had all died in the attacks themselves or otherwise simply vanished into thin air.

But without making much effort at all, the American government did quickly round up and arrest **some 200 Israeli Mossad agents**, many of whom had been based in exactly the same geographical locations as the purported 19 Arab hijackers. Furthermore, **NYC police arrested some of these agents while they were publicly celebrating the 9/11 attacks**, and others were caught driving vans in the New York area containing explosives or their residual traces. Most of these Mossad agents refused to answer any questions, and many of those who did failed polygraph tests, but under massive political pressure all were eventually released and deported back to Israel. A couple of years ago, much of this information was very effectively presented in a short video available on YouTube.

There is another fascinating tidbit that I have very rarely seen mentioned. Just a month after the 9/11 attacks, two Israelis were caught sneaking weapons and explosives into the Mexican Parliament building, a story that naturally produced several banner-headlines in leading Mexican newspapers at the time but which was greeted by total silence in the American media. Eventually, under massive political pressure, all charges were dropped and the Israeli agents were deported back home. This remarkable incident was only reported on **a small Hispanic-activist website**, and discussed in **a few other places**. Some years ago I easily found the scanned front pages of the Mexican newspapers reporting those dramatic events on the Internet, but I can no longer easily locate them. The details are obviously somewhat fragmentary and possibly garbled, but certainly quite intriguing.

One might speculate that if supposed Islamic terrorists had followed up their 9/11 attacks by attacking and destroying the Mexican parliament building a month later, Latin American support for America's military invasions in the Middle East would have been greatly magnified. Furthermore, any scenes of such massive destruction in the Mexican capital by Arab terrorists would surely have been broadcast non-stop on *Univision*, America's dominant Spanish-language network, fully solidifying Hispanic support for President Bush's military endeavors.

Although my growing suspicions about the 9/11 attacks stretch back a decade or more, my serious investigation of the topic is quite recent, so I am certainly a newcomer to the field. But sometimes an outsider can notice things that may escape the attention of those who have spent so many years deeply immersed in a given topic.

From my perspective, a huge fraction of the 9/11 Truth community spends far too much of its time absorbed in the particular details of the attacks, debating the precise method by which the World Trade Center towers in New York were brought down or what actually struck the Pentagon. But these sorts of issues seem of little ultimate significance.

I would argue that the only important aspect of such technical issues is whether the overall evidence is sufficiently strong to establish the falsehood of the official 9/11 narrative and also demonstrate that the attacks must have been the work of a highly sophisticated organization with access to advanced military technology rather than a rag-tag band of 19 Arabs armed with box-cutters. Beyond that, none of those details matter.

In that regard, I believe that the volume of factual material collected by determined researchers over the last seventeen years has easily met that requirement, perhaps even ten or twenty times over. For example, even agreeing upon a single particular item such as the clear presence of nano-thermite, a military-grade explosive compound, would immediately satisfy those two criteria. So I see little point in endless debates over whether nano-thermite was used, or nano-thermite plus something else, or just something else entirely. And such complex technical debates may serve to obscure the larger picture, while confusing and intimidating any casually-interested onlookers, thereby being quite counter-productive to the overall goals of the 9/11 Truth movement.

Once we have concluded that the culprits were part of a highly sophisticated organization, we can then focus on the *Who* and the *Why*, which surely would be of greater importance than the particular details of the *How*. Yet currently all the endless debate over the *How* tends to crowd out the *Who* and the *Why*, and I wonder whether this unfortunate situation might even be intentional.

Perhaps one reason is that once sincere 9/11 Truthers do focus on those more important questions, the vast weight of the evidence clearly points in a single direction, implicating Israel and its Mossad intelligence service, with the case being overwhelmingly strong in motive, means, and opportunity. And leveling accusations of blame at Israel and its domestic collaborators for the greatest attack ever launched against America on our own soil entails enormous social and political risks.

But such difficulties must be weighed against the reality of three thousand American civilian lives and the subsequent seventeen years of our multi-trillion-dollar wars, which have produced tens of thousands of dead or wounded American servicemen and the death or displacement of many millions of innocent Middle Easterners.

The members of the 9/11 Truth movement must therefore ask themselves whether or not "Truth" is indeed the central goal of their efforts.

Important Historical Realities, Long Hidden in Plain Sight

Many of the events discussed above were among the most important in modern American history, and the evidence supporting the controversial analysis provided seems quite substantial. Numerous contemporary observers would certainly have been aware of at least some of the key information, so serious media investigations should have been launched that would have soon unearthed much of the remaining material. Yet nothing like that happened at the time, and even today the vast majority of Americans remain totally ignorant of these long-established facts.

This paradox is explained by the overwhelming political and media influence of the ethnic and ideological partisans of Israel, which ensured that certain questions were not asked nor crucial points raised. Throughout the second half of the twentieth century, our understanding of the world was overwhelmingly shaped by our centralized electronic media, which was almost entirely in Jewish hands during this period, with all three television networks and eight of nine major Hollywood studios being owned or controlled by such individuals, along with most of our leading newspapers and publishing houses. As **I wrote** a couple of years ago:

> We naively tend to assume that our media accurately reflects the events of our world and its history, but instead what we all too often see are only the tremendously distorted images of a circus fun-house mirror, with small items sometimes transformed into large ones, and large ones into small. The contours of historical reality may be warped into almost unrecognizable shapes, with some important elements completely disappearing from the record and others appearing out of nowhere. I've often suggested that the media creates our reality, but given such glaring omissions and distortions, the reality produced is often largely fictional.

Only the rise of the decentralized Internet over the last couple of decades has allowed the widespread and unfiltered distribution of the information needed for serious investigation of these important incidents. Without the Internet virtually none of the material I have discussed at such length would ever have become known to me. Ostrovsky may have ranked as a #1 *New York Times* bestselling author with a million copies of his books in print, but before the Internet I never would have heard of him.

Once we pierce the concealing veil of media obfuscation and distortion, some realities of the post-war era become clear. The extent to which the agents of the Jewish state and its Zionist predecessor organizations have engaged in the most rampant international crime and violations of the accepted rules of warfare is really quite extraordinary, perhaps having few parallels in modern world history. Their use of political assassination as a central tool of their statecraft even recalls the notorious activities of the Old Man of the Mountains of the 13th century Middle East, whose deadly techniques gave us the very word "assassin."

To some extent, the steadily rising trajectory of Israel's international misbehavior may be a natural result of the total impunity its leaders have long enjoyed, almost never suffering any adverse consequences from their actions. A petty thief may graduate into burglary and then armed-robbery and murder if he comes to believe that he is entirely immune from any judicial sanction.

During the 1940s, Zionist leaders organized massive terrorist attacks against Western targets and assassinated high-ranking British and United Nations officials, but never paid any serious political price. Their likely killing of America's first defense secretary and their earlier attempt upon the life of our president were entirely covered up by our complicit media. In the mid-1950s, the leadership of newly-established Israel embarked upon a series of false-flag terrorist attacks against American targets during the Lavon Affair, and even when their agents were caught and their plot revealed, they received no punishment. Given such a track-record, perhaps we should not be surprised that they then became sufficiently emboldened to probably orchestrate the assassination of President John F. Kennedy, whose successful elimination gave them unprecedented influence over the world's leading superpower.

During the notorious Tonkin Gulf Incident of 1964, a U.S. ship involved in hostile activities off the coast of Vietnam was attacked by North Vietnamese torpedo boats. Our vessel suffered little damage and no casualties, but the American military retaliation unleashed a decade of warfare, eventually resulting in the destruction of most of that country and perhaps two million Vietnamese deaths.

By contrast, when the U.S.S. Liberty was deliberately attacked in international waters by Israeli forces in 1967, an attack that killed or wounded more than 200 American servicemen, the only response of that same American government was massive suppression of the facts, followed by an increase in financial support to the Jewish state. The decades that followed saw numerous major attacks by Israel and its Mossad against American officials and our intelligence service, eventually crowned in 1991 by yet another assassination plot against an insufficiently pliable American president. But our only reaction during this period was steadily-increasing political subservience. Given such a pattern of response, the huge 2001 gamble that the Israeli government finally may have taken by organizing the massive 9/11 false-flag terrorist attacks against our country becomes much more understandable.

Although more than seven decades of almost complete impunity has certainly been a necessary factor behind Israel's remarkable willingness to rely so heavily upon assassination and terrorism in achieving its geopolitical objectives, religious and ideological factors may also play a significant role. In 1943, future Israeli Prime Minister Yitzhak Shamir made **a rather telling assertion** in his official Zionist publication:

> "Neither Jewish ethics nor Jewish tradition can disqualify terrorism as a means of combat. We are very far from having any moral qualms as far as our national war goes. We have before us the command of the Torah, whose morality surpasses that of any other body of laws in the world: 'Ye shall blot them out to the last man.'"

Neither Shamir nor any other early Zionist leader adhered to traditional Judaism, but anyone who investigates the true tenets of that particular religious faith would have to admit that his claims were correct. As **I wrote** in 2018:

> If these ritualistic issues constituted the central features of traditional religious Judaism, we might regard it as a rather colorful and eccentric survival of ancient times. But unfortunately, there is also a far darker side, primarily involving the relationship between Jews and non-Jews, with the highly derogatory term *goyim* frequently used to describe the latter. To put it bluntly, Jews have divine souls and *goyim* do not, being merely beasts in the shape of men. Indeed, the primary reason for the existence of non-Jews is to serve as the slaves of Jews, with some very high-ranking rabbis occasionally stating this well-known fact. In 2010, Israel's top Sephardic rab-

bi **used his weekly sermon to declare** that the only reason for the existence of non-Jews is to serve Jews and do work for them. The enslavement or extermination of all non-Jews seems an ultimate implied goal of the religion.

Jewish lives have infinite value, and non-Jewish ones none at all, which has obvious policy implications. For example, in a published article a prominent Israeli rabbi explained that if a Jew needed a liver, it would be perfectly fine, and indeed obligatory, to kill an innocent Gentile and take his. Perhaps we should not be too surprised that today Israel is widely regarded as **one of the world centers of organ-trafficking**...

My encounter a decade ago with Shahak's **candid description** of the true doctrines of traditional Judaism was certainly one of the most world-altering revelations of my entire life. But as I gradually digested the full implications, all sorts of puzzles and disconnected facts suddenly became much more clear. There were also some remarkable ironies, and not long afterward I joked to a (Jewish) friend of mine that I'd suddenly discovered that Nazism could best be described as "Judaism for Wimps" or perhaps Judaism as practiced by Mother Teresa of Calcutta.

It is important to keep in mind that nearly all of Israel's top leaders have been strongly secular in their views, with none of them being followers of traditional Judaism. Indeed, many of the early Zionists were rather hostile to religion, which they despised due to their Marxist beliefs. However, I have noted that these underlying religious doctrines may still exert considerable real-world influence:

> Obviously the Talmud is hardly regular reading among ordinary Jews these days, and I would suspect that except for the strongly Orthodox and perhaps most rabbis, barely a sliver are aware of its highly controversial teachings. But it is important to keep in mind that until just a few generations ago, almost all European Jews were deeply Orthodox, and even today I would guess that the overwhelming majority of Jewish adults had Orthodox grand-parents. Highly distinctive cultural patterns and social attitudes can easily seep into

a considerably wider population, especially one that remains ignorant of the origin of those sentiments, a condition enhancing their unrecognized influence. A religion based upon the principal of "Love Thy Neighbor" may or may not be workable in practice, but a religion based upon "Hate Thy Neighbor" may be expected to have long-term cultural ripple effects that extend far beyond the direct community of the deeply pious. If nearly all Jews for a thousand or two thousand years were taught to feel a seething hatred toward all non-Jews and also developed an enormous infrastructure of cultural dishonesty to mask that attitude, it is difficult to believe that such an unfortunate history has had absolutely no consequences for our present-day world, or that of the relatively recent past.

Countries practicing a variety of different religious and cultural beliefs have sometimes undertaken military attacks involving massive civilian casualties or employed assassination as a tactic. But such methods are considered abhorrent and immoral by a society founded upon universalist principles, and although these ethical scruples may sometimes be overwhelmed by political expediency, they might act as a partial restriction against the widespread adoption of those practices.

By contrast, actions that lead to the suffering or death of unlimited numbers of innocent Gentiles carry absolutely no moral opprobrium within the religious framework of traditional Judaism, with the only constraints being the risk of detection and retaliatory punishment. Only a fraction of today's Israeli population may explicitly reason in such extremely harsh terms, but the underlying religious doctrine implicitly permeates the entire ideology of the Jewish state.

The Past Perspective of American Military Intelligence

The major historical events discussed in this long article have shaped our present-day world, and the 9/11 attacks in particular may have set America on the road to national bankruptcy while leading to the loss of many of our traditional civil liberties. Although I think that my interpretation of these various assassinations and terrorist attacks is probably correct, I do not doubt that most present-day Americans would find my controversial analysis shocking and probably respond with extreme skepticism.

Yet oddly enough, if this same material were presented to those individuals who had led America's nascent national security apparatus in the early decades of the twentieth century, I think they would have regarded this historical narrative as very disheartening but hardly surprising.

Last year I happened to read a fascinating volume published in 2000 by historian Joseph Bendersky, a specialist in Holocaust Studies, and discussed his remarkable findings **in a lengthy article:**

> Bendersky devoted ten full years of research to his book, exhaustively mining the archives of American Military Intelligence as well as the personal papers and correspondence of more than 100 senior military figures and intelligence officers. *The "Jewish Threat"* runs over 500 pages, including some 1350 footnotes, with the listed archival sources alone occupying seven full pages. His subtitle is "Anti-Semitic Politics of the U.S. Army" and he makes an extremely compelling case that during the first half of the twentieth century and even afterward, the top ranks of the U.S. military and especially Military Intelligence heavily subscribed to notions that today would be universally dismissed as "anti-Semitic conspiracy theories."
>
> Put simply, U.S. military leaders in those decades widely believed that the world faced a direct threat from organized Jewry, which had seized control of Russia and similarly sought to subvert and gain mastery over America and the rest of Western civilization...
>
> Although Bendersky's claims are certainly extraordinary ones, he provides an enormous wealth of compelling evidence to support them, quoting or summarizing thousands of declassified Intelligence files, and further supporting his case by drawing from the personal correspondence of many of the officers involved. He conclusively demonstrates that during the very same years that Henry Ford was publishing **his controversial series** *The International Jew,* similar ideas, but with a much sharper edge, were ubiquitous with-

in our own Intelligence community. Indeed, whereas Ford mostly focused upon Jewish dishonesty, malfeasance, and corruption, our Military Intelligence professionals viewed organized Jewry as a deadly threat to American society and Western civilization in general. Hence the title of Bendersky's book...

The **Venona Project** constituted the definitive proof of the massive extent of Soviet espionage activities in America, which for many decades had been routinely denied by many mainstream journalists and historians, and it also played a crucial secret role in dismantling that hostile spy network during the late 1940s and early 1950s. But Venona was nearly snuffed out just a year after its birth. In 1944 Soviet agents became aware of the crucial code-breaking effort, and soon afterwards arranged for the Roosevelt White House to issue a directive ordering the project shut down and all efforts to uncover Soviet spying abandoned. The only reason that Venona survived, allowing us to later reconstruct the fateful politics of that era, was that the determined Military Intelligence officer in charge of the project risked a court-martial by directly disobeying the explicit Presidential order and continuing his work.

That officer was Col. Carter W. Clarke, but his place in Bendersky's book is a much less favorable one, being described as a prominent member of the anti-Semitic "clique" who constitute the villains of the narrative. Indeed, Bendersky particularly condemns Clarke for still seeming to believe in the essential reality of the *Protocols* as late as the 1970s, quoting from a letter he wrote to a brother officer in 1977:

> If, and a big—damned big IF, as the Jews claim the Protocols of the Elders of Zion were f—- cooked up by Russian Secret Police, why is it that so much they contain has already come to pass, and the rest so strongly advocated by the *Washington Post* and the *New York Times*.

Our historians must surely have a difficult time digesting the remarkable fact that the officer in charge of the vital Venona Project, whose selfless determination saved it from destruction by the Roosevelt Administration, actually remained a lifelong believer in the importance of the *Protocols of the Elders of Zion*.

Let us take a step back and place Bendersky's findings in their proper context. We must recognize that during much of the era covered by his research, U.S. Military Intelligence constituted nearly the entirety of America's national security apparatus—being the equivalent of a combined CIA, NSA, and FBI—and was responsible for both international and domestic security, although the latter portfolio had gradually been assumed by J. Edgar Hoover's own expanding organization by the end of the 1920s.

Bendersky's years of diligent research demonstrate that for decades these experienced professionals—and many of their top commanding generals—were firmly convinced that major elements of the organized Jewish community were ruthlessly plotting to seize power in America, destroy all our traditional Constitutional liberties, and ultimately gain mastery over the entire world.

This article is available online at:
https://www.unz.com/runz/american-pravda-mossad-assassinations/

Seeking 9/11 Truth After Twenty Years
Who Attacked America in 2001...and Why?
The Unz Review, September 7, 2021

Twenty Years After the 9/11 Attacks

The twentieth anniversary of the 9/11 Attacks is almost upon us, and although their immediacy has been somewhat reduced by the events of the last eighteen months, we must recognize that they have drastically shaped the world history of the last two decades, greatly changing the daily lives and liberties of most ordinary Americans.

The widespread doubts about the reality of the official story provided by our government and almost universally promoted by our media has severely diminished popular faith in the credibility of those two crucial institutions, with consequences that are still very apparent in today's highest profile issues.

Over the years, diligent researchers and courageous journalists have largely demolished the original narrative of those events, and have made a strong, perhaps even overwhelming case that the Israeli Mossad together with its American collaborators played the central role. My own reconstruction, substantially relying upon such accumulated evidence, came to such conclusions, and I am therefore republishing it below, drawn from my previous articles which had appeared in **late 2018** and **early 2020**, with the later material making heavy use of Ronen Bergman's **authoritative 2018 history of the Mossad**, which ran more than 750 pages.

Immediately following my own analysis is a link to a particularly noteworthy article along the same lines by French writer Laurent Guyénot, which we had originally released simultaneously with my own, then followed by more than a dozen other significant articles of the previous decade, all published or republished on this website. In coming days, some of these may also be separately featured as part of the twenty-year commemoration.

The 9/11 Attacks – What Happened?

Although somewhat related, political assassinations and terrorist attacks are distinct topics, and Bergman's comprehensive volume explicitly focuses on the former, so we cannot fault him for providing only slight coverage of the latter. But the historical pattern of Israeli activity, especially with regard to false-flag attacks, is really quite remarkable, as I noted in **a 2018 article**:

One of history's largest terrorist attacks prior to 9/11 was **the 1946 bombing of the King David Hotel in Jerusalem** by Zionist militants dressed as Arabs, which killed 91 people and largely destroyed the structure. In the famous **Lavon Affair of 1954**, Israeli agents launched a wave of terrorist attacks against Western targets in Egypt, intending to have those blamed on anti-Western Arab groups. There are **strong claims** that in 1950 Israeli Mossad agents began a series of false-flag terrorist bombings against Jewish targets in Baghdad, successfully using those violent methods to help persuade Iraq's thousand-year-old Jewish community to emigrate to the Jewish state. In 1967, Israel launched **a deliberate air and sea attack against the *U.S.S. Liberty***, intending to leave no survivors, killing or wounding over 200 American servicemen before word of the attack reached our Sixth Fleet and the Israelis withdrew.

The enormous extent of pro-Israel influence in world political and media circles meant that none of these brutal attacks ever drew serious retaliation, and in nearly all cases, they were quickly thrown down the memory hole, so that today probably no more than one in a hundred Americans is even aware of them. Furthermore, most of these incidents came to light due to chance circumstances, so we may easily suspect that many other attacks of a similar nature have never become part of the historical record...

Of these famous incidents, Bergman only includes mention of the King David Hotel bombing. But much later in his narrative, he describes the huge wave of false-flag terrorist attacks unleashed in 1981 by Israeli Defense Minister Ariel

Sharon, who recruited a former high-ranking Mossad official to manage the project.

Under Israeli direction, large car bombs began exploding in the Palestinian neighborhoods of Beirut and other Lebanese cities, killing or injuring enormous numbers of civilians. A single attack in October inflicted nearly 400 casualties, and by December, there were eighteen bombings per month, with their effectiveness greatly enhanced by the use of innovative new Israeli drone technology. Official responsibility for all the attacks was claimed by a previously unknown Lebanese organization, but the intent was to provoke the PLO into military retaliation against Israel, thereby justifying Sharon's planned invasion of the neighboring country.

Since the PLO stubbornly refused to take the bait, plans were put into motion for the huge bombing of an entire Beirut sports stadium using tons of explosives during a January 1st political ceremony, with the death and destruction expected to be "of unprecedented proportions, even in terms of Lebanon." But Sharon's political enemies learned of the plot and emphasized that many foreign diplomats including the Soviet ambassador were expected to be present and probably would be killed, so after a bitter debate, Prime Minister Begin ordered the attack aborted. A future Mossad chief mentions the major headaches they then faced in removing the large quantity of explosives that they had already planted within the structure.

I think that this thoroughly documented history of major Israeli false-flag terrorist attacks, including those against American and other Western targets, should be carefully kept in mind when we consider the 9/11 attacks, whose aftermath has massively transformed our society and cost us so many trillions of dollars. I analyzed the strange circumstances of the attacks and their likely nature at considerable length in **my 2018 article**:

Oddly enough, for many years after 9/11, I paid very little attention to the details of the attacks themselves. I was entirely preoccupied with building **my content-archiving software system**, and with the little time I could spare for public policy matters, I was totally focused on the ongoing Iraq War disaster, as well as my terrible fears that Bush might at any moment suddenly extend the conflict to Iran. Despite Neocon lies shamelessly echoed by our corrupt media, neither Iraq nor Iran had had anything whatsoever to do with the 9/11 attacks, so those events gradually faded in my consciousness, and I suspect the same was true for most other Americans. Al Qaeda had largely disappeared and Bin Laden was supposedly hiding in a cave somewhere. Despite endless Homeland Security "threat alerts," there had been no further Islamic terrorism on American soil, and relatively little anywhere else outside of the Iraq charnel house. So the precise details of the 9/11 plots had become almost irrelevant to me.

Others I knew seemed to feel the same way. Virtually all the exchanges I had with my old friend Bill Odom, the three-star general who had run the NSA for Ronald Reagan, had concerned the Iraq War and risk it might spread to Iran, as well as the bitter anger he felt toward Bush's perversion of his beloved NSA into an extra-constitutional tool of domestic espionage. When the *New York Times* broke the story of the massive extent of domestic NSA spying, Gen. Odom declared that President Bush should be impeached and NSA Director Michael Hayden court-martialed. But in all the years prior to **his untimely passing in 2008**, I don't recall the 9/11 attacks themselves even once coming up as a topic in our discussions…

Admittedly, I'd occasionally heard of some considerable oddities regarding the 9/11 attacks here and there, and these certainly raised some suspicions. Most days I would glance at the *Antiwar.com* front page, and it seemed that some Israeli Mossad agents had been caught while filming the plane attacks in NYC, while **a much larger Mossad "art student" spy operation around the country** had also been broken up around the same time. Apparently, *FoxNews* had even broadcast **a multi-part series on the latter topic** before that expose was scuttled and "disappeared" under ADL pressure.

Although I wasn't entirely sure about the credibility of those claims, it did seem plausible that Mossad had known of the attacks in advance and allowed them to proceed, recognizing the huge benefits that Israel would derive from the anti-Arab backlash. I think I was vaguely aware that *Antiwar. com* editorial director Justin Raimondo had published ***The Terror Enigma***, a short book about some of those strange facts, bearing the provocative subtitle "9/11 and the Israeli Connection," but I never considered reading it. In 2007, ***Counterpunch*** itself published **a fascinating follow-up story** about the arrest of that group of Israeli Mossad agents in NYC, who were caught filming and apparently celebrating the plane attacks on that fateful day, and the Mossad activity seemed to be far larger than I had previously realized. But all these details remained a little fuzzy in my mind next to my overriding concerns about wars in Iraq and Iran.

However, by the end of 2008 my focus had begun to change. Bush was leaving office without having started an Iranian war, and America had successfully dodged the bullet of an even more dangerous John McCain administration. I assumed that Barack Obama would be a terrible president and he proved worse than my expectations, but I still breathed a huge sigh of relief every day that he was in the White House.

Moreover, around that same time I'd stumbled across an astonishing detail of the 9/11 attacks that demonstrated the remarkable depths of my own ignorance. In a *Counterpunch* article, I'd discovered that immediately following the attacks, the supposed terrorist mastermind **Osama bin Laden had publicly denied any involvement**, even declaring that no good Muslim would have committed such deeds.

Once I checked around a little and **fully confirmed that fact**, I was flabbergasted. 9/11 was not only the most successful terrorist attack in the history of the world, but may have been greater in its physical magnitude than all past terrorist operations combined. The entire purpose of terrorism is to allow a small organization to show the world that it can inflict serious losses upon a powerful state, and I had never previously heard of any terrorist leader denying his role in a successful operation, let alone the greatest in history. Something seemed extremely wrong in the media-generated narrative that I had previously accepted. I began to wonder if I had been as deluded as the tens of millions of Americans in 2003 and 2004 who naively believed that Saddam had been the mastermind behind the September 11th attacks. We live in a world of illusions generated by our media, and I suddenly felt that I had noticed a tear in the paper-mache mountains displayed in the background of a Hollywood sound-stage. If Osama was probably not the author of 9/11, what other huge falsehoods had I blindly accepted?

A couple of years later, I came across a very interesting column by Eric Margolis, a prominent Canadian foreign policy journalist purged from the broadcast media for his strong opposition to the Iraq War. He had long published a weekly column in the *Toronto Sun* and when that tenure ended, he used his closing appearance to run a double-length piece expressing **his very strong doubts about the official 9/11 story**, even noting that the former director of Pakistani Intelligence insisted that Israel had been behind the attacks...

I eventually discovered that in 2003 former German Cabinet Minister Andreas von Bülow had published **a best-selling book strongly suggesting** that the CIA rather than Bin Laden was behind the attacks, while in 2007 former Italian President Francesco Cossiga had **similarly argued** that the CIA and the Israeli Mossad had been responsible, claiming that fact was well known among Western intelligence agencies.

Over the years, all these discordant claims had gradually raised my suspicions about the official 9/11 story to rather strong levels, but it was only very recently that I finally found the time to begin to seriously investigate the subject and read eight or ten of **the main 9/11 Truther books**, mostly those by Prof. David Ray Griffin, the widely acknowledged leader in that field. And his books, together with the writings of his numerous colleagues and allies, revealed all sorts of very telling details, most of which had previously been unknown to me. I was also greatly impressed by the sheer number of seemingly reputable individuals of no apparent ideological bent who had become adherents of the 9/11 Truth movement over the years...

When utterly astonishing claims of an extremely controversial nature are made over a period of many years by **numerous seemingly reputable academics and other experts**, and they are entirely ignored or suppressed but never effectively rebutted, reasonable conclusions seem to point in an obvious direction. Based on my very recent readings in this topic, the total number of huge flaws in the official 9/11 story has now grown extremely long, probably numbering in the many dozens. Most of these individual items seem reasonably likely and if we decide that even just two or three of them are correct, we must totally reject the official narrative that so many of us have believed for so long...

Now I am merely just an amateur in the complex intelligence craft of extracting nuggets of truth from a mountain of manufactured falsehood. Although the arguments of the 9/11 Truth Movement seem quite persuasive to me, I would obviously have felt much more comfortable if they were seconded by an experienced professional, such as a top CIA analyst. A few years ago, I was shocked to discover that was indeed the case.

William Christison **had spent 29 years at the CIA**, rising to become one of its senior figures as Director of its Office of Regional and Political Analysis, with 200 research analysts serving under him. In August 2006, he published **a remarkable 2,700 word article** explaining why he no longer believed the official 9/11 story and felt sure that the 9/11 Commission Report constituted a cover-up, with the truth being quite different. The following year, he provided a forceful endorsement to **one of Griffin's books**, writing that "[There's] a strong body of evidence showing the official U.S. Government story of what happened on September 11, 2001 to be almost certainly a monstrous series of lies." And Christison's extreme 9/11 skepticism was seconded by that of **many other highly regarded former US intelligence professionals.**

We might expect that if a former CIA intelligence officer of Christison's rank were to denounce the official 9/11 report as a fraud and a cover-up, such a story would constitute front-page news. But it was never reported anywhere in our mainstream media, and I only stumbled upon it a decade later.

Even our supposed "alternative" media outlets were nearly as silent. Throughout the 2000s, Christison and his wife Kathleen, also a former CIA analyst, had been regular contributors to *Counterpunch*, publishing **many dozens of articles there** and certainly being its most highly credentialed writers on intelligence and national security matters. But editor Alexander Cockburn refused to publish any of their 9/11 skepticism, so it never came to my attention at the time. Indeed, when I mentioned Christison's views to current *Counterpunch* editor Jeffrey St. Clair a couple of years ago, he was stunned to discover that the friend he had regarded so very highly had actually become a "9/11 Truther." When media organs serve as ideological gatekeepers, a condition of widespread ignorance becomes unavoidable...

With so many gaping holes in the official story of the events of seventeen years ago, each of us is free to choose to focus on those we personally consider most persuasive, and I have several of my own. Danish Chemistry professor Niels Harrit was one of the scientists who analyzed the debris of the destroyed buildings and detected the residual presence of nano-thermite, a military-grade explosive compound, and I found him quite credible during **his hour-long interview** on *Red Ice Radio*. The notion that an undamaged hijacker passport was found on an NYC street after the massive, fiery destruction of the skyscrapers is totally absurd, as was the claim that the top hijacker conveniently lost his luggage at one of the airports and it was found to contain a large mass of incriminating information. The testimonies of the dozens of firefighters **who heard explosions** just before the collapse of the buildings seems totally inexplicable under the official account. The sudden total collapse of Building Seven, never hit by any jetliners is also extremely implausible.

The 9/11 Attacks — Who Did It?

Let us now suppose that the overwhelming weight of evidence is correct, and concur with high-ranking former CIA intelligence analysts, distinguished academics, and experienced professionals that the 9/11 attacks were not what they appeared to be. We recognize the extreme implausibility that three huge skyscrapers in New York City suddenly collapsed at free-fall velocity into their own footprints after just two of them were hit by airplanes, and also that a large civilian jetliner probably did not strike the Pentagon leaving behind absolutely no wreckage and only a small hole. What actually did happen, and more importantly, who was responsible?

The first question is obviously impossible to answer without an honest and thorough official investigation of the evidence. Until that occurs, we should not be surprised that numerous, somewhat conflicting hypotheses have been advanced and debated within the confines of the 9/11 Truth community. But the second question is probably the more important and relevant one, and I think it has always represented a source of extreme vulnerability to 9/11 Truthers.

The most typical approach, as generally followed in the numerous Griffin books, is to avoid the issue entirely and focus solely on the gaping flaws in the official narrative. This is a perfectly acceptable position but leaves all sorts of serious doubts. What organized group would have been sufficiently powerful and daring to carry off an attack of such vast scale against the central heart of the world's sole superpower? And how were they possibly able to orchestrate such a massively effective media and political cover-up, even enlisting the participation of the U.S. government itself?

The much smaller fraction of 9/11 Truthers who choose to address this "whodunit" question seem to be overwhelmingly concentrated among rank-and-file grassroots activists rather than the prestigious experts, and they usually answer "inside job!" Their widespread belief seems to be that the top political leadership of the Bush Administration, probably including Vice President Dick Cheney and Defense Secretary Donald Rumsfeld, had organized the terrorist attacks, either with or without the knowledge of their ignorant nominal superior, President George W. Bush. The suggested motives included justifying military attacks against various countries, supporting the financial interests of the powerful oil industry and military-industrial complex, and enabling the destruction of traditional American civil liberties. Since the vast majority of politically-active Truthers seem to come from the far left of the ideological spectrum, they regard these notions as logical and almost self-evident.

Although not explicitly endorsing those Truther conspiracies, filmmaker Michael Moore's leftist box office hit *Fahrenheit 9/11* seemed to raise such similar suspicions. His small budget documentary earned an astonishing $220 million by suggesting that the very close business ties between the Bush family, Cheney, the oil companies, and the Saudis were responsible for the Iraq War aftermath of the terrorist attacks, as well as the domestic crackdown on civil liberties, which was part-and-parcel of the right-wing Republican agenda.

Unfortunately, this apparently plausible picture seems to have almost no basis in reality. During the drive to the Iraq War, I read *Times* articles interviewing numerous top oil men in Texas who expressed total puzzlement at why America was planning to attack Saddam, saying that they could only assume that President Bush knew something that they themselves did not. Saudi Arabian leaders were adamantly opposed to an American attack on Iraq, and made every effort to prevent it. Prior to his joining the Bush Administration, Cheney had served as CEO of Halliburton, an oil services giant, and his firm had heavily lobbied for the lifting of U.S. economic sanctions against Iraq. Prof. James Petras, a scholar of strong Marxist leanings, published an excellent 2008 book entitled ***Zionism, Militarism, and the Decline of US Power*** in which he conclusively demonstrated that Zionist interests rather than those of the oil industry had dominated the Bush Administration in the wake of the 9/11 attacks, and promoted the Iraq War.

As for the Michael Moore film, I remember at the time sharing a laugh with a (Jewish) friend of mine, both of us finding it ridiculous that a government so overwhelmingly permeated by fanatically pro-Israel Neocons was being portrayed as being in thrall to the Saudis. Not only did the plotline of Moore's film demonstrate the fearsome power of Jewish Hollywood, but its huge success suggested that most of the American public had apparently never heard of the Neocons.

Bush critics properly ridiculed the president for his tongue-tied statement that the 9/11 terrorists had attacked America "for its freedoms" and Truthers have reasonably branded as implausible the claims that the massive attacks were organized by a cave-dwelling Islamic preacher. But the suggestion that they were led and organized by the top figures of the Bush Administration seems even more preposterous.

Cheney and Rumsfeld had both spent decades as stalwarts of the moderate pro-business wing of the Republican Party, each serving in top government positions and also as CEOs of major corporations. The notion that they capped their careers by joining a new Republican administration in early 2001 and almost immediately set about organizing a gigantic false-flag terrorist attack upon the proudest towers of our largest city together with our own national military headquarters, intending to kill many thousands of Americans in the process, is too ridiculous to even be part of a leftist political satire.

Let's step back a bit. In the entire history of the world, I can think of no documented case in which the top political leadership of a country has launched a major false-flag attack upon its own centers of power and finance and tried to kill large numbers of its own people. The America of 2001 was a peaceful and prosperous country run by relatively bland political leaders focused upon the traditional Republican goals of enacting tax-cuts for the rich and reducing environmental regulations. Too many Truther activists have apparently drawn their understanding of the world from the caricatures of leftist comic-books in which corporate Republicans are all diabolical Dr. Evils, seeking to kill Americans out of sheer malevolence, and Alexander Cockburn was absolutely correct **to ridicule them** at least on that particular score.

Consider also the simple practicalities of the situation. The gigantic nature of the 9/11 attacks as postulated by the Truth movement would have clearly required enormous planning and probably involved the work of many dozens or even hundreds of skilled agents. Ordering CIA operatives or special military units to organize secret attacks against civilian targets in Venezuela or Yemen is one thing, but directing them to mount attacks against the Pentagon and the heart of New York City would be fraught with stupendous risk.

Bush had lost the popular vote in November 2000 and had only reached the White House because of a few dangling chads in Florida and the controversial decision of a deeply divided Supreme Court. As a consequence, most of the American media regarded his new administration with enormous hostility. If the first act of such a newly-sworn presidential team had been ordering the CIA or the military to prepare attacks against New York City and the Pentagon, surely those orders would have been regarded as issued by a group of lunatics, and immediately leaked to the hostile national press.

The whole scenario of top American leaders being the masterminds behind 9/11 is beyond ridiculous, and those 9/11 Truthers who make or imply such claims—doing so without a single shred of solid evidence—have unfortunately played a major role in discrediting their entire movement. In fact, the common meaning of the "inside job" scenario is so patently absurd and self-defeating that one might even suspect that the claim was encouraged by those seeking to discredit the entire 9/11 Truth movement as a consequence.

The focus on Cheney and Rumsfeld seems particularly ill-directed. Although I've never met nor had any dealings with either of those individuals, I was quite actively involved in DC politics during the 1990s, and can say with some assurance that prior to 9/11, neither of them were regarded as Neocons. Instead, they were the archetypical examples of moderate business-type mainstream Republicans, stretching all the way back to their years at the top of the Ford Administration during the mid-1970s.

Skeptics of this claim may note that they signed the **1997 declaration issued by the Project for the New American Century** (PNAC), a leading Neocon foreign policy manifesto organized by Bill Kristol, but I would regard that as something of a red herring. In DC circles, individuals are always recruiting their friends to sign various declarations, which may or may not be indicative of anything, and I remember Kristol trying to get me to sign the PNAC statement as well. Since my private views on that issue were absolutely 100% contrary to the Neocon position, which I regarded as foreign policy lunacy, I deflected his request and very politely turned him down. But I was quite friendly with him at the time, so if I had been someone without strong opinions in that area, I probably would have agreed.

This raises a larger point. By 2000, the Neocons had gained almost total control of all the major conservative/Republican media outlets and the foreign policy wings of nearly all the similarly aligned thinktanks in DC, successfully purging most of their traditional opponents. So although Cheney and Rumsfeld were not themselves Neocons, they were swimming in a Neocon sea, with a very large fraction of all the information they received coming from such sources and with their top aides such as "Scooter" Libby, Paul Wolfowitz, and Douglas Feith being Neocons. Rumsfeld was already somewhat elderly while Cheney had suffered several heart-attacks starting at age 37, so under those circumstances it may have been relatively easy for them to be shifted toward certain policy positions.

Indeed, the entire demonization of Cheney and Rumsfeld in anti-Iraq War circles has seemed somewhat suspicious to me. I always wondered whether the heavily Jewish liberal media had focused its wrath upon those two individuals in order to deflect culpability from the Jewish Neocons who were the obvious originators of that disastrous policy; and the same may be true of the 9/11 Truthers, who probably feared accusations of anti-Semitism. Regarding that former issue, a prominent Israeli columnist was characteristically blunt on the matter in 2003, strongly suggesting that **25 Neocon intellectuals**, nearly all of them Jewish, were primarily responsible for the war. Under normal circumstances, the president himself would have surely been portrayed as the evil mastermind behind the 9/11 plot, but "W" was too widely known for his ignorance for such accusations to be credible.

It does seem entirely plausible that Cheney, Rumsfeld, and other top Bush leaders may have been manipulated into taking certain actions that inadvertently fostered the 9/11 plot, while a few lower-level Bush appointees might have been more directly involved, perhaps even as outright conspirators. But I do not think this is the usual meaning of the "inside job" accusation.

So where do we now stand? It seems very likely that the 9/11 attacks were the work of an organization far more powerful and professionally-skilled than a rag-tag band of nineteen random Arabs armed with box-cutters, but also that the attacks were very unlikely to have been the work of the American government itself. So who actually attacked our country on that fateful day seventeen years ago, killing thousands of our fellow citizens?

Effective intelligence operations are concealed in a hall of mirrors, often extremely difficult for outsiders to penetrate, and false-flag terrorist attacks certainly fall into this category. But if we apply a different metaphor, the complexities of such events may be seen as a Gordian Knot, almost impossible to disentangle, but vulnerable to the sword-stroke of asking the simple question "Who benefited?"

America and most of the world certainly did not, and the disastrous legacies of that fateful day have transformed our own society and wrecked many other countries. The endless American wars soon unleashed have already cost us many trillions of dollars and set our nation on the road to bankruptcy while killing or displacing many millions of innocent Middle Easterners. Most recently, that resulting flood of desperate refugees has begun engulfing Europe, and the peace and prosperity of that ancient continent is now under severe threat.

Our traditional civil liberties and constitutional protections have been drastically eroded, with our society having taken long steps toward becoming an outright police state. American citizens now passively accept unimaginable infringements on their personal freedoms, all originally begun under the guise of preventing terrorism.

I find it difficult to think of any country in the world that clearly gained as a result of the 9/11 attacks and America's military reaction, with one single, solitary exception.

During 2000 and most of 2001, America was a peaceful prosperous country, but a certain small Middle Eastern nation had found itself in an increasingly desperate situation. Israel then seemed to be fighting for its life against the massive waves of domestic terrorism that constituted the Second Palestinian Intifada.

Ariel Sharon was widely believed to have deliberately provoked that uprising in September 2000 by marching to the Temple Mount backed by a thousand armed police, and the resulting violence and polarization of Israeli society had successfully installed him as Prime Minister in early 2001. But once in office, his brutal measures failed to end the wave of continuing attacks, which increasingly took the form of suicide-bombings against civilian targets. Many believed that the violence might soon trigger a huge outflow of Israeli citizens, perhaps producing a death-spiral for the Jewish state. Iraq, Iran, Libya, and other major Muslim powers were supporting the Palestinians with money, rhetoric, and sometimes weaponry, and Israeli society seemed close to crumbling. I remember hearing from some of my DC friends that numerous Israeli policy experts were suddenly seeking berths at Neocon thinktanks so that they could relocate to America.

Sharon was a notoriously bloody and reckless leader, with a long history of undertaking strategic gambles of astonishing boldness, sometimes betting everything on a single roll of the dice. He had spent decades seeking the Prime Ministership, but having finally obtained it, he now had his back to the wall, with no obvious source of rescue in sight.

The 9/11 attacks changed everything. Suddenly the world's sole superpower was fully mobilized against Arab and Muslim terrorist movements, especially those connected with the Middle East. Sharon's close Neocon political allies in America used the unexpected crisis as an opportunity to seize control of America's foreign policy and national security apparatus, with an NSA staffer later reporting that Israeli generals freely roamed the halls of the Pentagon without any security controls. Meanwhile, the excuse of preventing domestic terrorism was used to implement newly centralized American police controls that were soon employed to harass or even shut down various anti-Zionist political organizations. One of the Israeli Mossad agents arrested by the police in New York City as he and his fellows were celebrating the 9/11 attacks and producing a souvenir film of the burning World Trade Center towers told the officers that "We are Israelis... Your problems are our problems." And so they immediately became.

General Wesley Clark reported that soon after the 9/11 attacks he was informed that a secret military plan had somehow come into being under which **America would attack and destroy seven major Muslim countries over the next few years**, including Iraq, Iran, Syria, and Libya, which coincidentally were all of Israel's strongest regional adversaries and the leading supporters of the Palestinians. As America began to expend enormous oceans of blood and treasure attacking all of Israel's enemies after 9/11, Israel itself no longer needed to do so. Partly as a consequence, almost no other nation in the world has so enormously improved its strategic and economic situation during the last seventeen years, even while a large fraction of the American population has become completely impoverished during that same period and our national debt has grown to insurmountable levels. A parasite can often grow fat even as its host suffers and declines.

I have emphasized that for many years after the 9/11 attacks I paid little attention to the details and had only the vaguest notion that there even existed an organized 9/11 Truth movement. But if someone had ever convinced me that the terrorist attacks had been false-flag operations and someone other than Osama had been responsible, my immediate guess would have been Israel and its Mossad.

Certainly no other nation in the world can remotely match Israel's track-record of remarkably bold high-level assassinations and false-flag attacks, terrorist and otherwise, against other countries, even including America and its military. Furthermore, the enormous dominance of Jewish and pro-Israel elements in the American establishment media and increasingly that of many other major countries in the West has long ensured that even when the solid evidence of such attacks was discovered, very few ordinary Americans would ever hear those facts...

Once we accept that the 9/11 attacks were probably a false-flag operation, a central clue to the likely perpetrators has been their extraordinary success in ensuring that such a wealth of enormously suspicious evidence has been totally ignored by virtually the entire American media, whether liberal or conservative, left-wing or right-wing...

In the particular case at hand, the considerable number of zealously pro-Israel Neocons situated just beneath the public surface of the Bush Administration in 2001 could have greatly facilitated both the successful organization of the attacks and their effective cover-up and concealment, with Libby, Wolfowitz, Feith, and Richard Perle being merely the most obvious names. Whether such individuals were knowing conspirators or merely had personal ties allowing them to be exploited in furthering the plot is entirely unclear.

Most of this information must surely have long been apparent to knowledgeable observers, and I strongly suspect that many individuals who had paid much greater attention than myself to the details of the 9/11 attacks may have quickly formed a tentative conclusion along these same lines. But for obvious social and political reasons, there is a great reluctance to publicly point the finger of blame towards Israel on a matter of such enormous magnitude. Hence, except for a few fringe activists here and there, such dark suspicions remained private.

Meanwhile, the leaders of the 9/11 Truth movement probably feared they would be destroyed by media accusations of deranged anti-Semitism if they had ever expressed even a hint of such ideas. This political strategy may have been necessary, but by failing to name any plausible culprit, they created a vacuum that was soon filled by "useful idiots" who shouted "inside job!" while pointing an accusing finger toward Cheney and Rumsfeld, and thereby did so much to discredit the entire 9/11 Truth movement.

This unfortunate conspiracy of silence finally ended in 2009 when Dr. Alan Sabrosky, former Director of Studies at the US Army War College, stepped forward and **publicly declared** that the Israeli Mossad had very likely been responsible for the 9/11 attacks, writing a series of columns on the subject, and eventually presenting his views in a number of media interviews, along with **additional analyses**.

Obviously, such explosive charges never reached the pages of my morning *Times*, but they did receive considerable if transitory coverage in portions of the alternative media, and I remember seeing the links very prominently featured at *Antiwar.com* and widely discussed elsewhere. I had never previously heard of Sabrosky, so I consulted my archiving system and immediately discovered that **he had a perfectly respectable record** of publication on military affairs in mainstream foreign policy periodicals and had also held a series of academic appointments at prestigious institutions. Reading one or two of his articles on 9/11, I felt he made a rather persuasive case for Mossad involvement, with some of his information already known to me but much of it not.

Since I was very busy with my software work and had never spent any time investigating 9/11 or reading any of the books on the topic, my belief in his claims back then was obviously quite tentative. But now that I have finally looked into the subject in much greater detail and done a great deal of reading, I think it seems quite likely that his 2009 analysis was entirely correct.

I would particularly recommend his long 2011 interview on Iranian Press TV, which I first watched just a couple of days ago. He came across as highly credible and forthright in his claims:

- ***Dr. Alan Sabrosky Blows the Lid Off Zionist Involvement in 9/11 Terror Attacks* • 24:11**
  https://www.bitchute.com/video/tpYjyFbJzPZh/

He also provided a pugnacious conclusion in **a much longer 2010 radio interview:**

- ***"They Did It" - Alan Sabrosky* • 2:58**
  https://www.bitchute.com/video/BigWEQyw6Cb7/

Sabrosky focused much of his attention upon a particular segment of a Dutch documentary film on the 9/11 attacks produced several years earlier. In that fascinating interview, a professional demolition expert named Danny Jowenko who was largely ignorant of the 9/11 attacks immediately identified the filmed collapse of WTC Building 7 as a controlled-demolition, and the remarkable clip was broadcast worldwide on *Press TV* and widely discussed across the Internet.

- ***911 - Danny Jowenko on WTC7 Controlled Demolition*** •
  2:36
  https://www.youtube.com/watch?v=Sl2RIqT-4bk

And by a very strange coincidence, just three days after Jowenko's broadcast video interview had received such heavy attention, **he had the misfortune to die in a frontal collision with a tree in Holland.** I'd suspect that the community of professional demolition experts is a small one, and Jowenko's surviving industry colleagues may have quickly concluded that serious misfortune might visit those who rendered controversial expert opinions on the collapse of the three World Trade Center towers.

Meanwhile, **the ADL soon mounted a huge and largely successful** effort to have *Press TV* banned in the West for promoting "anti-Semitic conspiracy theories," even persuading YouTube to entirely eliminate the huge video archive of those past shows, notably including Sabrosky's long interview.

Most recently, Sabrosky provided an hour-long presentation at this June's **Deep Truth video panel conference,** during which he expressed considerable pessimism about America's political predicament, and suggested that the Zionist control over our politics and media had grown even stronger over the last decade.

His discussion was **soon rebroadcast by** *Guns & Butter*, a prominent progressive radio program, which as a consequence **was soon purged from its home station** after seventeen years of great national popularity and strong listener support.

The **late Alan Hart,** a very distinguished British broadcast journalist and foreign correspondent, also **broke his silence in 2010** and similarly pointed to the Israelis as the likely culprits behind the 9/11 attacks. Those interested may wish to listen to **his extended interview.**

Journalist Christopher Bollyn was one of the first writers to explore the possible Israeli links to the 9/11 attacks, and the details contained in his long series of newspaper articles are often quoted by other researchers. In 2012, he gathered together this material and published it in the form of a book entitled ***Solving 9-11***, thereby making his information on the possible role of the Israeli Mossad available to a much wider audience, with **a version being available online**. Unfortunately his printed volume severely suffers from the typical lack of resources available to the writers on the political fringe, with poor organization and frequent repetition of the same points due to its origins in a set of individual articles, and this may diminish its credibility among some readers. So those who purchase it should be forewarned about these serious stylistic weaknesses.

Probably a much better compendium of the very extensive evidence pointing to the Israeli hand behind the 9/11 attacks has been more recently provided by French writer Laurent Guyénot, both in his 2017 book ***JFK-9/11: 50 Years of the Deep State*** and also his 8,500 word article "**9/11 was an Israeli Job**", published concurrently with this one and providing a far greater wealth of detail than is contained here. While I would not necessarily endorse all of his claims and arguments, his overall analysis seems fully consistent with my own.

These writers have provided a great deal of material in support of the Israeli Mossad Hypothesis, but I would focus attention on just one important point. We would normally expect that terrorist attacks resulting in the complete destruction of three gigantic office buildings in New York City and an aerial assault on the Pentagon would be an operation of enormous size and scale, involving very considerable organizational infrastructure and manpower. In the aftermath of the attacks, the US government undertook great efforts to locate and arrest the surviving Islamic conspirators, but scarcely managed to find a single one. Apparently, they had all died in the attacks themselves or otherwise simply vanished into thin air.

But without making much effort at all, the American government did quickly round up and arrest **some 200**

Israeli Mossad agents, many of whom had been based in exactly the same geographical locations as the purported 19 Arab hijackers. Furthermore, **NYC police arrested some of these agents while they were publicly celebrating the 9/11 attacks**, and others were caught driving vans in the New York area containing explosives or their residual traces. Most of these Mossad agents refused to answer any questions, and many of those who did failed polygraph tests, but under massive political pressure all were eventually released and deported back to Israel. A couple of years ago, much of this information was very effectively presented in a short video available on YouTube.

There is another fascinating tidbit that I have very rarely seen mentioned. Just a month after the 9/11 attacks, two Israelis were caught sneaking weapons and explosives into the Mexican Parliament building, a story that naturally produced several banner-headlines in leading Mexican newspapers at the time but which was greeted by total silence in the American media. Eventually, under massive political pressure, all charges were dropped and the Israeli agents were deported back home. This remarkable incident was only reported on **a small Hispanic-activist website**, and discussed in **a few other places**. Some years ago I easily found the scanned front pages of the Mexican newspapers reporting those dramatic events on the Internet, but I can no longer easily locate them. The details are obviously somewhat fragmentary and possibly garbled, but certainly quite intriguing.

One might speculate that if supposed Islamic terrorists had followed up their 9/11 attacks by attacking and destroying the Mexican parliament building a month later, Latin American support for America's military invasions in the Middle East would have been greatly magnified. Furthermore, any scenes of such massive destruction in the Mexican capital by Arab terrorists would surely have been broadcast non-stop on *Univision*, America's dominant Spanish-language network, fully solidifying Hispanic support for President Bush's military endeavors.

Although my growing suspicions about the 9/11 attacks stretch back a decade or more, my serious investigation of the topic is quite recent, so I am certainly a newcomer to the field. But sometimes an outsider can notice things that may escape the attention of those who have spent so many years deeply immersed in a given topic.

From my perspective, a huge fraction of the 9/11 Truth community spends far too much of its time absorbed in the particular details of the attacks, debating the precise method by which the World Trade Center towers in New York were brought down or what actually struck the Pentagon. But these sorts of issues seem of little ultimate significance.

I would argue that the only important aspect of such technical issues is whether the overall evidence is sufficiently strong to establish the falsehood of the official 9/11 narrative and also demonstrate that the attacks must have been the work of a highly sophisticated organization with access to advanced military technology rather than a rag-tag band of 19 Arabs armed with box-cutters. Beyond that, none of those details matter.

In that regard, I believe that the volume of factual material collected by determined researchers over the last seventeen years has easily met that requirement, perhaps even ten or twenty times over. For example, even agreeing upon a single particular item such as the clear presence of nano-thermite, a military-grade explosive compound, would immediately satisfy those two criteria. So I see little point in endless debates over whether nano-thermite was used, or nano-thermite plus something else, or just something else entirely. And such complex technical debates may serve to obscure the larger picture, while confusing and intimidating any casually-interested onlookers, thereby being quite counter-productive to the overall goals of the 9/11 Truth movement.

Once we have concluded that the culprits were part of a highly sophisticated organization, we can then focus on the *Who* and the *Why*, which surely would be of greater importance than the particular details of the *How*. Yet currently all the endless debate over the *How* tends to crowd out the *Who* and the *Why*, and I wonder whether this unfortunate situation might even be intentional.

Perhaps one reason is that once sincere 9/11 Truthers do focus on those more important questions, the vast weight of the evidence clearly points in a single direction, implicating Israel and its Mossad intelligence service, with the case being overwhelmingly strong in motive, means, and opportunity. And leveling accusations of blame at Israel and its domestic collaborators for the greatest attack ever launched against America on our own soil entails enormous social and political risks.

But such difficulties must be weighed against the reality of three thousand American civilian lives and the subsequent seventeen years of our multi-trillion-dollar wars, which have produced tens of thousands of dead or wounded American servicemen and the death or displacement of many millions of innocent Middle Easterners.

The members of the 9/11 Truth movement must therefore ask themselves whether or not "Truth" is indeed the central goal of their efforts.

Other Noteworthy 9/11 Articles Available on this Website

- **9/11 Was an Israeli Job**
  How America was neoconned into World War IV
  Laurent Guyénot • *The Unz Review*
  September 10, 2018 • 8,500 Words

- **What Did Israel Know in Advance of the 9/11 Attacks?**
  Cheering Movers and Art Student Spies
  Christopher Ketcham • *Counterpunch*
  March 1, 2007 • 6,900 Words

- **Fifty Questions on 9/11**
  Pepe Escobar • *Asia Times*
  September 12, 2009 • 2,000 Words

- **More Questions on 9/11**
  Pepe Escobar • *Asia Times*
  September 18, 2009 • 1,300 Words

- **9/11: the Mother of All Coincidences**
  Eric Margolis • *Toronto Sun Media*
  September 10, 2010 • 1,700 Words

- **9/11 Sounds from the Ground**
  Alan Sabrosky • *Veterans Today*
  March 11, 2011 • 300 Words

- **Demystifying 9/11: Israel and the Tactics of Mistake**
  Alan Sabrosky • *Veterans Today*
  June 27, 2011 • 5,100 Words

- **Riposte Against Zionism: Go Tell It to the People**
  Alan Sabrosky • *Veterans Today*
  July 4, 2011 • 4,800 Words

- **The 11th Anniversary of 9/11**
  Paul Craig Roberts • *PaulCraigRoberts.org*
  September 11, 2012 • 3,200 Words

- **The 9/11 Truth Movement 15 Years Later**
  Where Do We Stand?
  The Saker • *The Vineyard of the Saker*
  September 11, 2016 • 2,800 Words

- **9/11 Truth?**
  Was it an "American coup?"
  Philip Giraldi • *The Unz Review*
  October 25, 2016 • 1,600 Words

- **Obscured American: Rudy Dent a 9-11 First Responder**
  Linh Dinh • *The Unz Review*
  April 9, 2017 • 2,900 Words

- **Alan "Israel Did 9/11" Sabrosky: Most Censored Man in America**
  Kevin Barrett • *The Unz Review*
  March 24, 2019 • 1,400 Words

- **Israel's Role In 9/11**
  FBI evidence supports prior knowledge or complicity
  Philip Giraldi • *The Unz Review*
  May 28, 2019 • 2,100 Words

- **The Dancing Israelis: FBI Docs Shed Light on Apparent Mossad Foreknowledge of 9/11 Attacks**
  Whitney Webb • *Mint Press News*
  September 10, 2019 • 3,900 Words

- **More Americans Questioning Official 9/11 Story As New Evidence Contradicts Official Narrative**
  Whitney Webb • *Mint Press News*
  September 11, 2019 • 2,200 Words

This article is available online at:
https://www.unz.com/runz/seeking-9-11-truth-after-twenty-years/

Remembering the Liberty
President Lyndon Johnson and World War III?
The Unz Review, October 18, 2021

Concealing the Deliberate Israeli Attack

I'm not exactly sure when I first heard of the *Liberty* incident of 1967. The story was certainly a dramatic one, the attack upon an almost defenseless American intelligence ship by Israel's air and naval forces late in the Six Day War fought against several Arab states. Over 200 American servicemen were killed or wounded by Israeli machine-guns, rockets, napalm, and torpedoes, representing our greatest naval loss of life since World War II. Only tremendous luck and the heroic actions of the sailors prevented the *Liberty* from being sunk with all hands lost.

The Israeli government quickly claimed that the attack had been accidental, a consequence of mistaken identification and the fog of war, but none of the survivors ever believed that story, nor did many of America's top political and military leaders, notably Secretary of State Dean Rusk, CIA Director Richard Helms, and numerous top officers, including a later Chairman of the Joint Chiefs of Staff.

Although a brief investigation ordered by President Lyndon Johnson quickly endorsed the Israeli account, over the next half-century the *Liberty* survivors regularly condemned that official verdict as a cover-up and a whitewash. Their deep outrage was only slightly assuaged by the flood of medals they had received from our guilt-ridden government, which established the *Liberty* as perhaps the most highly-decorated ship in American naval history, at least with regard to a single engagement.

The real-life events of that day almost seem like a script out of Hollywood. The first wave of unmarked attacking jets had targeted and destroyed all of the *Liberty*'s regular transmission antennas while also trying to jam all standard American broadcast frequencies to prevent any calls for help. A flotilla of torpedo boats later machine-gunned the life-rafts to ensure there would be no survivors. These relentless attacks lasted for more than an hour and completely perforated the vessel, with the sides and the decks being pitted by more than 800 holes larger than a man's fist, including 100 rocket-hits that were six to eight inches wide, and a 40 foot hole below the waterline produced by a torpedo strike. Only a miracle kept the ship afloat.

But the desperate sailors braved constant enemy fire to jury-rig a single transmission antenna, allowing them to send out an urgent plea for help. Their SOS was finally received by our nearby Sixth Fleet, whose commanders immediately dispatched two waves of jet fighters to rescue the *Liberty* and drive off the attackers, only to have both flights recalled by order of America's highest political leadership, which chose to abandon the *Liberty* and its crew to their fate. At the end, two large helicopters filled with commandos dressed in full battle gear and armed with assault weapons were preparing to board the *Liberty*, sweep its decks clear of any resistance, and sink it. But at that moment their headquarters apparently discovered that the ship had managed to report its plight to other American military forces, so the enemy broke off the attack and retreated. The first American assistance finally arrived seventeen hours after the first shots had been fired, as two destroyers reached the stricken vessel, which was still desperately trying to stay afloat.

This story combined so many elements of exceptional military heroism, political treachery, and success against all odds that if the *Liberty* had been attacked by any nation on earth except Israel, the inspirational events of June 8, 1967 might have become the basis for several big-budget, Oscar-nominated movies as well as a regular staple of television documentaries. Such a patriotic narrative would have provided very welcome relief from the concurrent military disaster our country was then facing in its Vietnam War debacle. But events involving serious misdeeds of the Jewish State are hardly viewed with great favor by the leading lights of our entertainment industry, and the story of the *Liberty* quickly vanished from sight so that today I doubt whether even one American in a hundred has ever heard of it.

Our news media has been almost as silent on the subject. In the immediate aftermath of the attack, there was naturally some coverage in our major newspapers and magazines, with several of the reports expressing considerable skepticism of the Israeli claims of having made an innocent mistake. But the Johnson Administration quickly imposed an extreme clampdown to suppress any challenges to the official story.

An American admiral soon met with all of the survivors in small groups, including the many dozens still hospitalized from their serious injuries, and he issued fearsome threats to those terrified young sailors, most of whom were still in their teens or early twenties. If any of them ever mentioned a word of what had happened—even to their mothers, fathers, or wives, let alone the media—they would immediately be court-martialed and end their lives in prison "or worse."

With our journalists having great difficulty finding any eyewitnesses willing to talk and our government firmly declaring that the attack had been an unfortunate instance of accidental "friendly fire," the newsmen quickly lost interest and the story faded from the headlines. Our government still remained so concerned about the smoldering embers of the incident that the surviving sailors were distributed across the other ships of our navy, apparently with efforts made to avoid having any of them serve together, which would have allowed them an opportunity to discuss the events they had barely survived.

The ensuing decade of the 1970s saw the Watergate Scandal unfold, culminating in the impeachment and resignation of a president, and numerous other sordid governmental scandals and abuses of power came to light in the years that followed, greatly eroding popular faith in the honesty of our government.

These changed circumstances helped provide an opening to James M. Ennes, Jr., one of the young surviving *Liberty* officers, who defied the threats of prosecution and imprisonment in order to reveal to the world what had happened. Working closely with many of his fellow survivors, he spent years preparing a powerful manuscript and was introduced to a major publishing house by star *New York Times* reporter Neil Sheehan, who had written one of the earliest news accounts of the attack. His book **Assault on the Liberty** was released in 1979, producing the first major crack in the continuing wall of silence. Admiral Thomas Moorer, former Chairman of the Joint Chiefs of Staff, contributed a Foreword to a later edition, and the facts and gripping eyewitness testimony almost conclusively established that the Israeli attack had been entirely intentional. There were quite a number of favorable early reviews and interviews, leading to strong initial sales and further media coverage.

But organized pro-Israel groups soon counterattacked with a widespread campaign of suppression, working to prevent book sales and distribution while pressuring such influential television shows as ABC's *Good Morning America* and CBS's *Sixty Minutes* into canceling their planned segments. Successful books may sell tens of thousands of copies, but popular television programs reach tens of millions, so only a sliver of the American public ever learned the story of the *Liberty*. However, those who were politically aware and interested in the topic now had a solid reference source to cite and distribute, and the book also sparked the creation of the Liberty Veterans Association, which began to demand a reopening of the case and an honest investigation of what had happened that day.

The Israelis always claimed that the *Liberty* had been attacked because it was misidentified as a particular Egyptian naval vessel, and the official report of the American investigation had concurred. But Ennes' book demolished that possibility.

- As America's most advanced electronic surveillance ship, the *Liberty* had one of the most unique profiles in any navy, with its topside covered by an enormous array of different communications antennas, even including a 32-foot satellite-dish used to bounce signals off the Moon. By contrast, the Egyptian vessel was a decrepit old horse-transport just a fraction of the size, which was then rusting away in the port of Alexandria.

- By nearly all accounts, the air and naval forces deployed against the *Liberty* were completely unmarked, thus disguising their origins. None of the calls for help sent out mentioned the identity of the attackers, which the victims only discovered near the very end of the sustained engagement. If the Israeli forces had merely been striking against an assumed Egyptian military vessel, why would they have bothered to conceal their nationality?

- Despite repeated Israeli claims to the contrary, the *Liberty* had a large and very visible American flag flying at all times, and when the first one was shot down and destroyed early in the attack, an even larger Stars and Stripes was quickly hoisted as a replacement. The name of the ship was written in large English letters on its side, instead of the Arabic used by Egyptian vessels. The clear, bright weather that day provided perfect visibility.

- Israeli surveillance planes had repeatedly over-flown the *Liberty* all that morning, sometimes flying so low that the faces of the pilots could be seen, so the ship would have been easily identified.

- From the moment the attack began, Israeli electronic jamming had been employed to blanket all regular American communication channels, proving that the attackers knew the nationality of the ship they were targeting.

- The Israelis claimed that they initially assumed that the *Liberty* was a warship because it was traveling at a high speed of nearly 30 knots, but the ship's speed during that entire period had merely been 5 knots, slower by a factor of six.

- The attack on the *Liberty* was a massive and coordinated action, lasting one to two hours, and involved waves of jet fighters, three torpedo boats, and a couple of large helicopters loaded with commandos. The initial strike destroyed all communications antennas in order to prevent the ship from calling for help, and later all the lifeboats were machine-gunned. The obvious goal was to sink the ship, leaving no survivors to report what had happened.

- After the attack ended, the Israelis steadfastly refused to admit any serious error on their part, with none of their commanders being prosecuted or even reprimanded, and instead placed the entire blame for the incident upon the Americans. Trophies from the *Liberty* attack still occupy a place of honor in Israel's war museum. Financial compensation was only paid to the seriously wounded survivors after a long battle in American courts.

Confirming the Facts But Seeking a Motive

At the time, America was Israel's primary international backer and ally, so the motive has always greatly puzzled observers—a deadly, unprovoked attack upon an American military vessel sailing in international waters, something which certainly constituted a major war-crime. Ennes had no clear answer to that question, and his carefully factual book closed with an Epilogue entitled "Why Did Israel Attack?" which provided a few pages of speculation. He suggested that the Israelis may have feared that the *Liberty*'s electronic surveillance equipment might have revealed their plans to invade Syria and conquer the Golan Heights against American wishes, and indeed that attack occurred soon after the *Liberty* was crippled. The Syrian invasion was ordered by Israeli Defense Minister Moshe Dayan, and a declassified CIA intelligence report later claimed that Dayan had ordered the attack on the *Liberty* against the opposition of some of his generals. This explanation seemed somewhat plausible but far from solidly established.

With the Ennes book having blazed a trail, other authors gradually followed. As an electronic surveillance platform, the *Liberty* operated under the auspices of the NSA, an organization then so secret that its employees sometimes joked that the initials stood for "No Such Agency." In 1982, those shrouds of mystery were finally pierced when journalist James Bamford published ***The Puzzle Palace***, presenting the agency's history and activities, which soon became a national bestseller and launched him on a career as one of America's premier authors on national security matters.

From the very first, the NSA had been absolutely certain that the Israeli attack on the *Liberty* was deliberate, and the death or grievous injury of so many of its communication technicians and other employees together with an American cover-up deeply rankled the top leadership. So Bamford's book included more than a dozen pages on the *Liberty* incident, revealing some of the secret intelligence evidence that had demonstrated Israel's clear intent.

Two years later in 1984, foreign policy writer Stephen Green published a highly-regarded analysis of Israeli-American relations entitled ***Taking Sides***, which drew glowing praise from former Sen. William Fulbright, who had chaired the Foreign Affairs Committee, international legal scholar Richard Falk of Princeton, and former Undersecretary of State George Ball. Green devoted his penultimate chapter to the *Liberty* incident, effectively summarizing the facts across those 30 pages and strongly endorsing most of Ennes' conclusions, while providing additional evidence that the attack was deliberate, some of it based upon newly declassified documents. He also pointed out that if the operation had succeeded and the *Liberty* had been sunk with no survivors, America might have easily blamed Egypt for the attack, with major geopolitical consequences. Since the ship's survival was little short of a miracle, that might have been the primary motive.

I was just a young child in 1967, and never heard a word about the attack at the time nor for long afterward. Even once the Ennes book appeared a dozen years later, I don't remember seeing anything about it, nor was I aware of the accounts contained in the specialized volumes by Bamford and Green that soon followed. At some point, I think I did vaguely hear something about an American ship that had been accidentally attacked by Israel during the 1960s, but that was probably the limit of my knowledge.

In 1991 the subject finally did get some national attention in the aftermath of America's victorious Gulf War against Saddam Hussein, as President George H.W. Bush became embroiled in a political battle with the Israeli government over the expansion of their illegal Jewish settlements in the Occupied West Bank and Gaza.

At that time, the Evans & Novak column by conservatives Rowland Evans and Robert Novak was among the most widely syndicated and influential in America, running in many hundreds of newspapers, and with Novak also having a large presence on the weekly political television shows. Their November 6, 1991 column dropped **a major bombshell**, reporting that radio transmissions proved the Israeli pilots had been fully aware that they were attacking an American ship and despite their frantic protestations had been ordered to go ahead and sink the *Liberty* regardless. These communications had been intercepted and decrypted by the intelligence staff at our Beirut Embassy, and the shocking transcripts were immediately provided to our ambassador, Dwight Porter, a highly esteemed diplomat, who had finally broken his self-imposed silence after 24 years. Moreover, these same facts were also confirmed by an American-born Israeli military officer who had been present at IDF headquarters that day, and who said that all the commanders there were sure that the ship being attacked was American. This may have been the first time I learned the true details of the 1967 incident, probably from one of Novak's many television appearances.

Pro-Israel elements of the media and their numerous activist supporters immediately launched a fierce counter-attack, spearheaded by former *New York Times* Executive Editor Abe Rosenthal, a fervent partisan of Israel, **who denounced the Evans & Novak column** as biased, misinterpreted, and fraudulent. When I read Novak's memoirs last year, he described how Israel's partisans had spent many years pressuring newspapers into dropping his column, which substantially reduced its reach as the years went by. The columnists were punished for crossing red-lines, their future influence diminished, and other journalists were given a powerful warning message against ever doing anything similar.

The story of the *Liberty* and especially the subsequent decades of political and media battles surrounding the case soon became the focus of scholarly research, with John E. Bourne making it the subject of his 1993 doctoral dissertation in history at NYU, then publishing the work through a small press two years later under the title ***The USS Liberty: Dissenting History Vs. Official History***. Bourne's coverage seemed meticulous and scrupulously fair, breaking little new ground but gathering together and conveniently referencing a great deal of the underlying information, including the surprising success of the *Liberty* survivors in getting their account of the attack into the public arena despite the overwhelmingly greater political and financial resources of their determined opponents.

One important point emphasized by Bourne is that while the version of events provided by the *Liberty* crewmen has been almost completely consistent and unchanging from the first day, the Israeli government and its partisans had promoted numerous contrary narratives, most of them mutually contradictory, with pro-Israel advocates making absolutely no effort to reconcile these, and instead merely ignoring such severe discrepancies. This surely relates to the fact that although there can only be one true account of a historical event, invented falsehoods may diverge in a wide variety of different directions.

A couple of years later in 1995, the front page of the *New York Times* broke a seemingly unrelated story, which certainly captured my attention at the time. Our national newspaper of record revealed that during both the 1956 and 1967 wars, the Israeli military **had brutally massacred** large numbers of Egyptian POWs, with the evidence coming from the detailed research of Israeli military historians, eyewitness testimony including that of a retired Israeli general, and the discovery of mass graves in the Sinai desert.

Then in 2001, James Bamford published ***Body of Secrets***, a much longer and more detailed sequel to his earlier history of the NSA, which once again became a national bestseller. This time the author devoted one of his longest chapters entitled "Blood" entirely to the story of the *Liberty*, and provided many new revelations. Among other things, he suggested that the ship had been targeted for destruction because the Israeli leadership feared that its extensive electronic surveillance equipment might record evidence of the enormous war-crimes they had then been committing along the neighboring coast, now believed to involve the execution of some 1,000 helpless Egyptian captives and local civilians, certainly one of the largest such atrocities committed by any Western army since World War II. This now provided an additional possible motive for the seemingly inexplicable Israeli attack.

Bamford's book also contained an even more momentous disclosure. After 35 years of NSA silence, he revealed that the entire *Liberty* incident had been monitored in real-time by an American electronic spy plane cruising far overhead, which intercepted and rapidly translated all the radio communications between the attacking Israeli forces and their Tel Aviv controllers, information long regarded as "among NSA's deepest secrets." This helped explain why the senior leadership of the NSA had always been virtually unanimous that the attack was deliberate and intended to leave no survivors.

These intercepted conversations from the Israeli planes and torpedo boats had repeatedly mentioned seeing the *Liberty*'s large American flag, putting the lie to decades of emphatic denials. In Washington, DC, the top leadership of the NSA had been outraged by this information, especially once they realized that the Johnson Administration intended to protect Israel from any embarrassment, and had even considered sinking the *Liberty* after the attack to prevent journalists from photographing the severe damage. Indeed, the *Liberty* was strangely ordered to sail to distant Malta rather than the much closer port in Crete, perhaps in hopes that the limping vessel with a large hole in its hull would sink along the way, thereby permanently hiding the visual evidence.

Bamford's book also provided new information on the strange circumstances of the recall of two flights of carrier jets dispatched to rescue the *Liberty* during the attack, a development that had always been a source of puzzlement. The *Liberty*'s senior intelligence officer revealed that he was later informed by the Sixth Fleet's carrier admiral that the recall had been ordered by a direct phone call from Secretary of Defense Robert McNamara, with President Lyndon Johnson himself allegedly even getting on the line to demand that the order be obeyed and the *Liberty* left to its fate.

Bamford also noted that Israel's brutal and unprovoked attack on the American ship was hardly inconsistent with that country's other behavior. Not only had the Israelis been concurrently massacring so many hundreds of Egyptian POWs, but just a day or two earlier an Israeli tank column had attacked a convoy of unarmed UN peacekeepers flying their blue flag, brutally killing more than a dozen of them, while also blasting the local UN headquarters.

Bamford's text ran more than 700 pages, with his discussion of the *Liberty* incident amounting to less than 10% of the total, but that chapter attracted a hugely disproportionate share of the press interest, with the *New York Times* even running **a major news story** on the important new evidence he provided. The book's **very favorable *Times* review** also devoted quite a lot of space to his *Liberty* coverage, even though the reviewer strongly questioned the theory that the attack might have been motivated by Israel's desire to conceal its concurrent war crimes. Although most such reviews were quite laudatory, the notoriously pro-Israel *New Republic* **launched a fierce attack**, authored by an American-born Israeli historian who had renounced his U.S. citizenship in order to enter Israeli government service, and I hardly considered it convincing at the time, even before I recently discovered Bamford's **very effective rebuttal**.

Although I only read Bamford's book itself a couple of years ago, I had seen the *Times* pieces and many of the other reviews when they originally appeared, and taken together all of this material further strengthened my conviction that the *Liberty* attack had been no accident.

Revealing the American Cover-Up After 40 Years

Up until this point, Israel's partisans had mostly operated on defense, emphasizing the original verdict of accident issued by America's official 1967 inquiry panel, while working to suppress the reach of books or articles that challenged this established position. Given this situation, Bourne's thorough media research suggested that they probably believed that silence was the best strategy to follow. The longest piece actively promoting the accidental attack theory had been **a 6,000 word article** in the September 1984 issue of *The Atlantic Monthly*, possibly written in response to the Ennes or Green books. The two authors had been Israeli journalists who relied almost entirely upon Israeli sources, mostly official ones, and the piece was hardly likely to sway the growing number of skeptics.

But in 2002, A. Jay Cristol, a Jewish bankruptcy judge in Florida who had served nearly four decades in our naval reserves, released *The Liberty Incident*, arguing that the attack had been purely accidental. Cristol's Preface emphasized his pro-Israel views and numerous Israeli friends, who encouraged and assisted this project, which he had begun some fifteen years earlier as an adult education masters thesis.

Although heavily promoted by Israel's numerous partisans, who used the occasion to loudly declare "Case Closed," I never heard of the book at the time, and was quite unimpressed when I recently read it, since it seemed to largely ignore or dismiss the mountain of evidence contrary to its thesis of Israeli innocence.

Indeed, the publication of Cristol's book provoked a particularly important reaction. One of the individuals whom the author had favorably cited as "a man of integrity," was retired Captain Ward Boston, Jr., the Navy attorney who had actually authored the official inquiry report in 1967. After having kept silent for nearly four decades, Boston was so outraged by Cristol's analysis that he came forward and signed **a legal affadivit** revealing the true facts of the original investigation.

According to Boston, both he and his superior, Admiral Isaac C. Kidd, the presiding judge, had been absolutely convinced at the time that Israel had deliberately attacked the *Liberty* and murdered our sailors, but they had been ordered by their political and military superiors, including Admiral John S. McCain, Jr., father of the late senator, to absolve the Jewish State of any blame. Moreover, major elements of their written report were deleted or altered before release, in further efforts to conceal the clear evidence of Israel's guilt. Considering that for over 35 years, Boston's official handiwork had been cited as the primary bulwark supporting Israeli innocence, his signed January 9, 2004 affidavit constituted a very powerful declaration to the contrary. Aside from condemning Cristol as a fraud and a liar and reporting that Admiral Kidd believed the author "must be an Israeli agent," Boston's statement closed with the following paragraph:

> Contrary to the misinformation presented by Cristol and others, it is important for the American people to know that it is clear that Israel is responsible for deliberately attacking an American ship and murdering American sailors, whose bereaved shipmates have lived with this egregious conclusion for many years.

A few years later, **a major expose** in the *Chicago Tribune* finally demolished the remaining shards of the decades-long cover-up. Written by a senior *Tribune* journalist who had previously won a Pulitzer Prize at the *New York Times* and drawing upon dozens of interviews and a large cache of official government documents newly declassified after four decades, the 5,400 word article was probably the longest piece on the *Liberty* incident ever to appear in the mainstream American news media. Much of the material presented was extremely damning, fully confirming crucial elements of previous accounts and demonstrating the extent of the ensuing cover-up.

Tony Hart, a former communications operator at a relay station remembers listening to the words of Secretary of Defense McNamara as he personally ordered the recall of the jets sent to rescue the *Liberty*: "President [Lyndon] Johnson is not going to go to war or embarrass an American ally over a few sailors." This independently confirmed the account reported by a *Liberty* officer a few years earlier in Bamford's book.

Aside from McNamara, nearly all the other senior members of the Johnson administration agreed with top intelligence advisor Clark Clifford that it was "inconceivable" that the attack had been a case of mistaken identity. NSA Director Lt. Gen. Marshall Carter later secretly testified to Congress that the attack "couldn't be anything else but deliberate," and numerous other former top national security officials provided similar statements to the *Tribune,* finally going on the record after forty years.

For decades, a crucial point of contention had been whether the *Liberty* was flying an American flag visible to the attacking Israeli forces. At the time, the Israeli court of inquiry had firmly declared that "Throughout the contact, no American or any other flag appeared on the ship." As recently as 2003, the *Jerusalem Post* had interviewed the first Israeli pilot to attack, and he once again declared that he had circled the ship twice, slowing down and looking carefully, and "there was positively no flag."

By contrast, declassified NSA documents stated that all the surviving crew members interviewed had uniformly agreed that their ship had been flying a large flag before, during, and after the attack, except for a brief period when it had been shot down, quickly replaced by their largest American flag, measuring 13 feet long.

NSA transcripts affirmed the claims of the Americans and proved that the Israelis were lying. As numerous sources had claimed over the years, the intercepted transmissions of the Israeli pilots had been immediately translated into English, with transcripts of their conversations rolling off the teletype machines at our intelligence offices around the world. These proved beyond any doubt that the pilots reported the ship was American and they had been ordered to sink it regardless, with the content of the transcripts confirmed by separate interviews with American intelligence specialists based in Nebraska, California, and Crete, while several other former American officials also confirmed the existence of those transcripts.

Five days later the Israeli Ambassador secretly warned his government that the Americans had "clear proof" that the attack had been deliberate. But according to a former CIA officer, the transcripts "were deep-sixed because the administration did not wish to embarrass the Israelis." This official cover-up was partially circumvented by some shrewd intelligence officials who had those transcripts assigned for official training purposes at the U.S. Army's intelligence school. W. Patrick Lang, who later spent eight years as Chief of Middle East intelligence for the DIA, vividly remembers seeing them in his coursework, and they left absolutely no doubt that the Israeli attack had been deliberate.

Although some tapes had been released, several of the personnel originally involved in recording and translating the transmissions agree that at least two of the key tapes have now gone missing or at least have not yet been declassified, and this is supported by gaps in the numbering of those that have been released.

- **New revelations in attack on American spy ship**
  John Crewdson • *The Chicago Tribune*
  October 2, 2007 • 5,400 Words

A couple of years later in 2009, James Scott, a young, award-winning journalist and son of a *Liberty* survivor, published **Attack on the Liberty**, a book that seemed likely to become the final major account of the incident. Released by a prestigious mainstream press, the text ran more than 350 pages with copious notes and numerous photographs. When I read it six or seven years ago, I didn't think it broke much new ground, but the work seemed to very effectively summarize all of the main material from more than four decades of research and debate, probably becoming that standard text on the topic.

A great deal of information is also now easily available on the Internet. Alison Weir runs *If Americans Knew*, an activist organization focused on the Israel-Palestine conflict, and **a section of her website** provides a convenient repository of numerous primary source documents regarding the U.S.S. Liberty incident. A **U.S.S. *Liberty* Memorial** website also provides considerable material on the event.

In recent years, our own Philip Giraldi, a former CIA officer, has become one of the most regular writers on the story of the *Liberty*, producing half a dozen articles focused directly on that topic:

- **Sinking Liberty**
  Who will write the final chapter on Israel's 1967 confrontation with the U.S. Navy?
  Philip Giraldi • *The American Conservative*
  March 17, 2011 • 1,600 Words

- **The USS Liberty Must Not be Forgotten**
  Forty-eight years is too long to wait for justice
  Philip Giraldi • *The Unz Review*
  June 9, 2015 • 1,200 Words

- **Remembering the U.S.S. Liberty**
  The power of the Israel Lobby
  Philip Giraldi • *The Unz Review*
  June 14, 2016 • 1,600 Words

- **Remembering the U.S.S. Liberty**
  The 50 year cover-up of a mass murder of U.S. servicemen orchestrated by Israel and its friends
  Philip Giraldi • *The Unz Review*
  June 6, 2017 • 1,600 Words

- **The USS Liberty Wins One!**
  The American Legion finally calls for a congressional inquiry
  Philip Giraldi • *The Unz Review*
  September 5, 2017 • 2,300 Words

- **Israel's War Crimes Have Killed Americans**
  If the president loves to honor the military, start with the U.S.S. Liberty
  Philip Giraldi • *The Unz Review*
  May 5, 2020 • 2,300 Words

President Lyndon Johnson and a Planned Attack on Egypt?

Over the last few years **my understanding of many major historical events has undergone a radical transformation**, but the *Liberty* incident was not among them. Since I first encountered the story almost thirty years ago, my views had merely solidified rather than changed in any significant respect. I'd immediately been persuaded that the attack was intentional, soon followed by a disgraceful American cover-up, and the three or four books I eventually read on the topic had merely filled in some blanks, while casting my original conclusions into solid concrete. The only remaining mystery was the Israeli motive for such an apparently reckless undertaking, and with three or four somewhat plausible possibilities having been suggested, there seemed to be no way of deciding between them. Not only did I regard the topic as closed, but I believed it had been closed for at least a decade or two. And that was my settled opinion until a month ago.

The story of a deadly Israeli attack upon America's own military and a long and shameful cover-up naturally provoked all sorts of wild speculation from conspiracy-minded individuals, who regularly expounded the most bizarre ideas on the comment-threads of any article discussing the topic. A couple of years ago, I noticed a flurry of such chatter, including claims of a diabolical plot by President Johnson to treacherously arrange the attack on his own ship as an excuse for starting World War III, with the theory having apparently been promoted by some recently published book.

At first I paid no attention to such nonsense, but I eventually took a look at the Amazon page of **Blood in the Water** by Joan Mellen, an author entirely unknown to me, and was shocked to discover lavish praise by Prof. Richard Falk of Princeton, an eminent international legal scholar. Thinking that the theory might be less absurd than it seemed, I clicked a button, bought it, and suspended my disbelief during the two days it took me to read the text.

Unfortunately, the contents were almost exactly as I had originally assumed, filled with implausible speculations, unwarranted assertions, and huge leaps of logic. Unsubstantiated claims were endlessly repeated, apparently in hopes of bludgeoning the reader into eventual acceptance. And although the text was purportedly written by a tenured professor of English at a small university, the editing was among the worst of any professionally-published book I had ever encountered, with the same sentence—or even the same short paragraph—sometimes duplicated on consecutive pages; such severe stylistic flaws merely deepened my skepticism about the credibility of the substantive material presented. Prof. Falk was an esteemed scholar, but he had also been in his late 80s when the book was released, and I assumed that he hadn't actually read the text apart from a few small extracts, while his outrage at a half-century of governmental injustice had secured his endorsement of such a poor quality expose. I felt that my time reading it had been wasted, and I became more firmly convinced than ever that the story of the *Liberty* was closed.

Then earlier this year I once more began seeing some chatter about a very similar theory regarding the *Liberty*, again advanced by an author totally unknown to me and presented in a book bearing an especially lurid title. I naturally dismissed such nonsense under the principle of "once bitten, twice shy."

However, a month or two ago, I happened to be reading a work by Michael Collins Piper, a conspiracy-researcher who had earned my considerable respect, and in a couple of sentences he alluded to the book in question, greatly praising its "astonishing" findings. So I looked it up on Amazon and found that it had been released in 2003. A book published 18 years ago by a tiny press that made such wild charges but had never attracted any attention nor reviews was hardly likely to be very persuasive, but since I had some time on my hands, I ordered a copy and a few days later took a look.

I had never heard of Peter Hounam and a book entitled **Operation Cyanide** containing wild talk of World War III in the subtitle certainly multiplied my doubts, but the cover carried a glowing endorsement by the BBC World Affairs Editor, hardly the sort of individual likely to lend his name to crackpots. Moreover, according to the back flap, Hounam had spent thirty years in mainstream British journalism, including a long stint as Chief Investigative Journalist at the *London Sunday Times*, so he obviously possessed serious credentials.

A bit of casual Googling confirmed these facts and also revealed that in 1987 Hounam had led the *Sunday Times* team that broke the huge story of Israel's nuclear weapons program, with the evidence provided by Israeli technician Mordechai Vanunu, just before he was kidnapped by Mossad, returned to Israel, and given a twenty year prison sentence. Hounam certainly had a much more impressive background than I had initally assumed.

The book itself was of moderate length, running perhaps 100,000 words, but quite professionally written. The author carefully distinguished between solid evidence and cautious speculation, while also weighing the credibility of the various individuals whom he had interviewed and the other material used to support his conclusions. He drew upon most of the same earlier sources with which I was already familiar, as well as a few others that were new to me, generally explaining how he reached his conclusions and why. The overall text struck me as having exactly the sort of solid workmanship that one might expect from someone who had spent three decades in British investigative journalism, including a position near the top of the profession.

As Hounam explained on the first page, he had been approached in 2000 by a British television producer, who recruited him for a project to uncover the truth of the attack on the *Liberty*, an incident then entirely unfamiliar to him. His research of the history occupied the next two years, and included travels throughout the United States and

Israel to interview numerous key figures. The result was an hour-long BBC documentary *Dead in the Water*, eventually shown on British television, as well as the book he concurrently produced based upon all the research he had collected.

As I began the text, the first pages of the Introduction immediately captured my attention. In late 2002, with the book almost completed, Hounam was contacted by Jim Nanjo, a 65-year-old retired American pilot with an interesting story to tell. During the mid-1960s he had served in a squadron of strategic nuclear bombers based in California, always on alert for the command to attack the USSR in the event of war. On three separate occasions during that period, he and the other pilots had been scrambled into their cockpits on a full-war alert rather than a training exercise, sitting in the planes for hours while awaiting the signal to launch their nuclear attack. Each time, they only discovered the event that had triggered the red alert after they received the stand-down order and walked back to their base. Once it had been the JFK assassination and another time the North Korean seizure of the U.S.S. *Pueblo*, with the third incident being the 1967 attack upon the *Liberty*.

All of this made perfect sense, but when Hounam checked the pilot's reported chronology, he discovered that the squadron had actually been put on full war-alert status at least an hour *before* the *Liberty* came under Israeli attack, an astonishing logical inconsistency if correct.

Memories may easily grow faulty after 35 years, but this strange anomaly was merely one of many that Hounam encountered during his exhaustive investigation and the facts that he uncovered gradually resolved themselves into the outline of a radically different reconstruction of historical events. Although more than half the book recounts the standard elements of the *Liberty* story that I had already read many times before, the other material was entirely new to me, never mentioned elsewhere.

President Johnson was a notorious micro-manager, very closely monitoring daily casualties in Vietnam, as well as the sudden new outbreak of war in the Middle East, and he always demanded to be told immediately of any important development. Yet when America's most advanced spy ship with a crew of nearly 300 reported that it was under deadly attack by unknown enemy forces, he seems never to have been informed, at least according to the official White House logs. Instead, he supposedly spent the morning casually eating his favorite breakfast and then mostly engaging in domestic political chit-chat with various senators.

Declassified documents from the CIA, the NSA, and the Pentagon prove that red-alert messages had been sent to the White House Situation Room almost immediately, and American military policy is that any flash message reporting an attack on a U.S. naval vessel must be immediately passed to the president, even if he is asleep. Yet according to the official records, Johnson—wide awake and alert—received no notice until almost two hours later, after the assault on the *Liberty* had ended. Moreover, even when finally informed, he seemed to pay little attention to the most serious naval attack our country had suffered since World War II, instead focusing upon minor domestic political issues. Johnson did put in two calls to Secretary of Defense Robert McNamara, who according to naval logs minutes later ordered the recall of the carrier planes sent to rescue the *Liberty*, and Secretary of State Dean Rusk later stated that McNamara would never have made that decision without first discussing it with his president. But based upon the official records Johnson himself had not yet been informed that any attack had occurred.

Indeed, according to the later recollections of Rusk and top intelligence advisor Clark Clifford, during the morning Situation Room meeting two hours later, the Soviets were still believed responsible for the attack, and the participants had a sense that war might have already broken out. Although the Israeli identity of the attackers had been known for more than an hour, most of our top government leaders still seemed to be contemplating World War III with the USSR.

Hounam believes that these numerous, glaring discrepancies indicated the official logs had been altered in potentially very serious ways, apparently with the intent of insulating President Johnson from having learned of the attack and its crucial details until long after that had occurred. The author's analysis of these severe chronological discrepancies seems quite meticulous to me, covering several pages, and should be carefully read by anyone interested in these highly suspicious events and the seemingly doctored record.

Hounam also focused upon several unexplained elements presented in the books by Ennes and others. There does seem solid if very fragmentary evidence that the *Liberty*'s positioning off the Egyptian coast was part of some broader American strategic plan, whose still classified details remain largely obscure to us. Ennes' book briefly mentioned that an American submarine had secretly joined the *Liberty* as it traveled to its destination, and had actually been present throughout the entire attack, with some of the sailors seeing its periscope. Although one of the crew had been privy to the classified details, he later refused to divulge them to Ennes when asked. According to some accounts, the sub had even used a periscope camera to take photographs of the attack, which various individuals later claimed to have seen. The official name for that secret submarine project was "Operation Cyanide," which Hounam used for the title of his book. One heavily-redacted government document obtained by Hounam provides tantalizing clues as to why the *Liberty* had officially been sent to the coast, but anything more than that is speculation.

There were other strange anomalies. A senior NSA official had been strongly opposed to sending the *Liberty* into a potentially dangerous war-zone but had been overruled, while the ship's request for a destroyer escort from the Sixth Fleet had been summarily refused. The day before the attack, top NSA and Pentagon officials had recognized the obvious peril to the ship, even receiving a CIA intelligence report that the Israelis planned to attack, and this led to several urgent messages being sent from Washington, ordering the captain to withdraw to a safe distance 100 miles from the coast; but through a bizarre and inexplicable series of repeated routing errors, none of those messages had ever been received. All of these seemingly coincidental decisions and mistakes had ensured that the *Liberty* was alone and defenseless in a highly vulnerable location, and that it remained there until the Israeli attack finally came.

Hounam also sketched out the broader geopolitical context to the events he described. Although originally open to friendly relations with America, Egyptian leader Gamal Nasser had been denied promised US assistance due to the pressure of our powerful Israel Lobby and was therefore pushed into the arms of the USSR, becoming a key regional ally, arming his military forces with Soviet weaponry and even allowing nuclear-capable Soviet strategic bombers to be based on his territory. As a consequence, Johnson became intensely hostile towards Nasser, regarding him as "another Castro" and seeking the overthrow of his regime. This was one of the major reasons his administration offered a green-light to Israel's decision to launch the Six Day War.

In the opening hours of that conflict, Israel's surprise attack had destroyed the bulk of the Egyptian and Syrian air forces on the ground, and these devastating losses soon led Nasser and other Arab leaders to publicly accuse the American military of having entered the war on Israel's side, charges almost universally dismissed as ridiculous both by journalists at the time and by later historians. But Hounam's detailed investigation uncovered considerable evidence that that Nasser's claims may have been true, at least with regard to aerial reconnaissance and electronic communications.

According to the statements of former American airman Greg Reight, he and his aerial photo reconnaissance unit were secretly deployed to Israel, assisting the attack by determining enemy losses and helping to select subsequent targets. This personal account closely matched the details of the overall operation previously described in Green's book almost two decades earlier. All these claims were supported by the extremely sharp photos of destroyed Egyptian airfields later released by Israel and published in American news magazines since experts agreed that the Israeli air force did not then possess any of the necessary camera equipment.

A successful Florida businessman named Joe Sorrels provided a very detailed account of how his American intelligence unit had been infiltrated into Egypt's Sinai Peninsula before hostilities began and set up electronic monitoring and "spoofing" equipment, which may have played a crucial strategic role in enabling the sweeping Israeli victory. There were even claims that American electronic expertise helped locate the crucial gaps in the radar defenses of the Egyptian airfields that allowed Israel's surprise attack to become so successful.

Hounam also emphasized the likely political motive behind Johnson's possible decision to directly back Israel. By 1967 the Vietnam War was going badly, with mounting American losses and no victory in sight, and if this quagmire continued, the president's reelection the following year might become very difficult. But if the Soviets suffered a humiliating setback in the Middle East, with their Egyptian and Syrian allies crushed by Israel, perhaps culminating in Nasser's overthrow, that success might compensate for the problems in Southeast Asia, diverting public attention toward much more positive developments in a different region. Moreover, the influential Jewish groups that had once been among Johnson's strongest supporters had lately become leading critics of the continuing Vietnam conflict; but since they were intensely pro-Israel, success in the Middle East might bring them back into the fold.

This provides the background for one of Hounam's most controversial suggestions. He notes that in 1964, Johnson had persuaded Congress to pass the Tonkin Gulf Resolution by a near-unanimous vote, authorizing military strikes against North Vietnam, but based upon an alleged attack upon American destroyers that most historians now agree was fictional. Although the resulting Vietnam War eventually became highly unpopular, Johnson's initial "retaliatory" airstrikes just three months before the 1964 election rallied the country around him and helped ensure his huge landslide reelection victory against Sen. Barry Goldwater. And according to Ephraim Evren, a top Israeli diplomat in the U.S., just a few days before the outbreak of the Six Day War Johnson met with him privately and emphasized the urgent need "to get Congress to pass another Tonkin resolution," but this time with regard to the Middle East. An excuse for direct, successful American military intervention on Israel's behalf would obviously have solved many of Johnson's existing political problems, greatly boosting his otherwise difficult reelection prospects the following year.

We must always keep in mind that only a miracle kept the *Liberty* afloat, and if it had been sunk without survivors as expected, almost no one in American media or government would have dared accuse Israel of such an irrational act. Instead, as Stephen Green had first suggested in 1984, Egyptian forces would very likely have been blamed, producing powerful demands for immediate American retaliation, but probably on a vastly greater scale than the fictional Tonkin Gulf attack, which had inflicted no injuries.

Indeed, Hounam's detailed investigation discovered strong evidence that a powerful American "retaliatory" strike against Egypt had already been put into motion from almost the moment that the *Liberty* was first attacked. Paul Nes then served as charge d'Affaires at the U.S. Embassy in Cairo, and in a taped interview he recalled receiving an urgent flash message alerting him that the *Liberty* had been attacked, presumably by Egyptian planes, and that bombers from an American carrier were already on their way to strike Cairo in retaliation. With an American-Egyptian war about to break out, Nes and his subordinates immediately began destroying all their important documents. But not long afterward, another flash message arrived, identifying the attackers as Israeli and saying that the air strike had been called off. According to some accounts, the American warplanes were just minutes from Egypt's capital city when they were recalled.

Let us consider this. In a taped interview a former top American diplomat revealed that in 1967 America came very close—perhaps even within minutes—of attacking Egypt in retaliation for the *Liberty*. Surely a revelation of this magnitude from such a credible source might be expected to reach the front page of the *New York Times* and other leading world newspapers. But instead I had never heard a word about it during the past 18 years, and a little Googling suggests that it has received virtually no discussion anywhere, except within the most obscure fringes of the Internet.

Most of this seems like very solid factual material, and although the resulting interpretations may differ, I think the hypothesis advanced by Hounam is quite plausible. He suggested that President Johnson helped arrange the attack on the *Liberty*, hoping to orchestrate a new Tonkin Gulf Resolution but on a much grander scale, allowing him to attack and oust Nasser in retaliation. An American military assault against such an important regional Soviet ally would certainly have raised the risk of a much broader conflict, so our strategic bomber force had been put on full war-alert an hour or more before the *Liberty* incident unfolded. However, the *Liberty* and its crew of eyewitnesses somehow managed to stay afloat and survive, and eventually word that their attackers had been Israeli rather than Egyptian reached our top political and military leadership ranks, so the plan had to be abandoned.

Our mainstream media has spent decades scrupulously avoiding the slightest hint that the attack on the Liberty had been part of a broader plot to unseat Nasser, one that probably involved President Johnson. But as the testimony of several eyewitnesses above indicates, many of these facts would have been known at least to the circle of military men and intelligence operatives involved in the project. So we should not be entirely surprised that elements of the story gradually leaked out, though often in garbled, inaccurate, and disjointed fashion.

Indeed, the first substantial account claiming that the *Liberty* attack had been intentional rather than accidental appeared in the writings of independent journalist Anthony Pearson, who in 1976 published a couple of long articles in *Penthouse*, allegedly based upon British intelligence sources, and he later incorporated these into his 1978 book **Conspiracy of Silence**. His account lacked any references, was written in a breathlessly conspiratorial fashion, and contained a number of glaring errors, so it was hardly reliable and usually dismissed. But it did seem to also contain a good deal of material that was only later confirmed by more reliable research, demonstrating that he had access to some knowledgeable individuals. And in his account, Pearson claimed that the attack had been part of a much broader American plan to overthrow Nasser, which suggests such rumors were circulating among his sources.

Bourne's very thorough research mentioned that similar claims suggesting that the *Liberty* fell victim to an American-Israeli plan to bring down Nasser had also appeared in two books on intelligence matters published in 1980, Richard Deacon's **The Israeli Secret Service** and Stewart Steven's **The Spymasters of Israel**. These accounts similarly provided no sources and since they appeared too early to make use of Ennes' detailed narrative, contained numerous factual errors, but they do further suggest that such theories, whether correct or not, had become quite widespread within intelligence circles.

A Nuclear Strike Against Egypt?

If this were the extent of the historical hypothesis advanced in Hounam's relatively short book, his work would certainly rank as a remarkable piece of investigative journalism, possibly overturning decades of assumptions about the *Liberty* incident, and perhaps uncovering one of the most shocking examples of government treachery in American history. But there are additional elements, and although they are far less solidly established, they should not be ignored.

Recollections can easily fade over more than three decades, but some memories remain indelible. Hounam provides a great deal of testimony indicating that the bombers dispatched to strike Egypt in retaliation for its assumed attack on the *Liberty* may have been armed with nuclear warheads.

Mike Ratigan, a catapult operator on board the U.S.S. *America*, recalls that his entire ship was put into "Condition November," a top alert status only used in connection with armed nuclear warheads, and that the special bombs being loaded onto the A-4 Skyhawk bombers were unlike any he had previously seen, while also being escorted by Marine guards, another very unusual situation. There was a widespread belief on the ship that a nuclear attack was about to be launched. For obvious reasons, the Navy had absolute rules that bombers carrying armed nuclear warheads were prohibited from landing on carriers, and after the flight was dispatched and then recalled, the planes were all diverted to a land airbase to be off-loaded, not returning to their carrier for four or five days.

That same carrier had been hosting 28 journalists from British and American media outlets, and some of these individuals also had strong recollections. Jay Goralski, a U.S. reporter, remembered that the bombers were launched in a retaliatory strike against shore targets and that they were only recalled and the strike aborted "at the last moment, just before they would have lost radio contact." A UPI reporter named Harry Stathos saw the nuclear-armed aircraft being launched, and was told by the deck crew that the strike was targeting Cairo, though he agreed at the time not to disclose any of this information.

Liberty survivor Chuck Rowley later spoke to a carrier pilot who claimed he had flown one of the jets that day, saying he had been carrying nuclear weapons and had been ordered to target Cairo. Other *Liberty* survivors heard similar stories over the years from naval personnel who described the special alert status that day, as nuclear warheads were armed and loaded onto the bombers preparing to launch. Moe Shafer had been transferred to the Sixth Fleet flagship for treatment of his injuries, and he claimed that the commanding admiral mentioned to him that several of his bombers had been three minutes away from a nuclear attack on Cairo when they were recalled.

Joe Meadors, another former *Liberty* crewman, later heard from military personnel on Crete their astonishment at having to unload the armed nuclear warheads of bombers that had been diverted there rather than allowed to directly return to the carrier, and they were told that the planes had been sent to strike Cairo in retaliation for the *Liberty*.

All of this evidence is merely circumstantial, with much of it amounting to hearsay, often reported second or third hand by ordinary servicemen rather than by trained journalists or researchers. But there does seem to be quite a lot of it. Hounam remains somewhat agnostic about whether Cairo had indeed been targeted for a nuclear attack in retaliation for the *Liberty*, but he does not believe that the possibility can be entirely disregarded.

We must also keep in mind that a nuclear strike against Cairo would not necessarily mean the destruction of the densely populated urban center. The author notes that a squadron of nuclear-capable Soviet strategic bombers were based at a West Cairo airfield far from the urban core, and their presence in the Middle East had aroused great American concerns. He speculates that their destruction in a nuclear attack might have been seen as a very potent demonstration of supreme American power across the entire region but without inflicting the massive casualties of a bombing closer to the center of the city. Admittedly, all of this is pure conjecture, and until additional documents are declassified and made available, we lack the necessary means of forming any solid conclusions.

It is a truism that extraordinary claims require extraordinary evidence, and while the hypothesis that America in 1967 came very close to launching a nuclear attack against Nasser's Egypt certainly falls into the former category, the evidence that Hounam has accumulated does not come close to meeting the requirements of the latter. However, while a month ago I would have regarded such a theory as utterly preposterous lunacy, not warranting a moment's thought, I now view it as a serious possibility worth considering.

The absolute and total blackout that seems to have immediately enveloped Hounam's remarkable book hardly increased the likelihood that many new sources would come forward, but the accompanying BBC documentary *Dead in the Water* was released and aired, becoming the first and only professional media treatment of that important historical episode.

As was appropriate, the bulk of the film covered the basic elements of the *Liberty* story, though including the suggestion that the motive of the Israeli action had been to provoke an American attack against Egypt and even raising the possibility that the use of nuclear weapons might have been planned. However, any speculation that President Johnson had been involved in the plot was left on the cutting-room floor, and perhaps this was the correct decision to make. The first serious documentary on a highly controversial but almost ignored historical event should probably stick close to the basics and not overly challenge its previously uninformed audience.

Although the documentary was never broadcast on American television, the rights were eventually transferred to the Liberty Veterans Association, which for many years sold the videocassette. A version of adequate quality is now available on Youtube, so those interested in the story of the *Liberty* may watch it and decide for themselves.

- **USS Liberty Dead In The Water BBC Documentary** • 1:07:14
  https://www.youtube.com/watch?v=3PDK4Ev-h8U

There is also an intriguing backstory both to Hounam's book and to the British documentary that had originally brought the author into the topic. The entire project apparently came about through the efforts of Richard Thompson, a former American Intelligence officer, who later became a highly successful international businessman. For years he had been a determined champion of the *Liberty* issue and the surviving crew members, and he organized and funded the film project, investing a total of $700,000 of his own money to bring it to fruition. After the documentary was complete, Jewish groups in Britain went to court to block its release, forcing Thompson to spend $200,000 in legal fees to overcome their challenge and allow the broadcast. And although Thompson's name is not listed on the cover of the accompanying book, he seems to have played a major role in providing some of the underlying research and he shared the copyright with Hounam.

Thompson had regularly attended annual *Liberty* reunions, and at the 40th in 2007, he arranged to meet with Mark Glenn, a journalist for *American Free Press*, an alternative tabloid newsweekly, known for its willingness to cover controversial issues, including those portraying Israel in a negative light. Thompson claimed to have important new information about the backstory to the *Liberty* incident, facts that further extended Hounam's findings, and he promised to provide the material to Glenn in a series of interviews. However, while driving home from Washington the following morning, **Thompson died in a strange one-car accident**, as his vehicle crossed the dividing meridian of the interstate highway and collided with a tree. Although aged 76, Thompson had seemed in perfect health and he had previously reported being stalked by individuals apparently connected to Israel, so Glenn found his death suspicious, **as did Michael Collins Piper**, a noted conspiracy-researcher. More of Thompson's background was provided in a fairly lengthy obituary that appeared in the **Washington Report on Middle East Affairs**, a well-regarded and somewhat establishmentarian publication critical of Israel.

This possibly suspicious death was not the only one associated with the *Liberty* issue. Anthony Pearson's articles in *Penthouse* and his subsequent book had been the first to claim that the Israeli attack was deliberate, and a few years later he began to complain of persecution by the Mossad; soon afterwards, he was dead, allegedly having been poisoned. Bourne's research reported that a rather dubious individual involved in numerous unsuccessful attempts during the mid-1980s to raise funding for a film on the *Liberty* was found shot to death in his Pasadena home in 1988, though the motive for the unsolved homicide may have been entirely unconnected.

Means, Motive, and Opportunity

The especially controversial elements of the theories propounded in Hounam's 2003 book probably precluded any discussion by most others writing on the *Liberty* incident, which is why the work never came to my attention until quite recently. In his comprehensive 2009 book, Scott thanked Thompson for having provided him with numerous out-takes from his *Dead in the Water* documentary, but neither Thompson's name nor that of Hounam appeared anywhere else in the text, perhaps because such a reference might have alarmed the very mainstream publisher, Simon and Schuster. Hounam's name also is nowhere to be found on Alison Weir's website nor that of the U.S.S. *Liberty* memorial organization. Even individuals who had published several articles on the *Liberty* were completely unfamiliar with Hounam's ground-breaking research when I queried them.

However during the last few years, this situation has begun to change. Mellen's 2018 book had developed a theory quite similar to the one that Hounam had published fifteen years earlier, and she repeatedly referenced him. As I now reread her work, all the severe flaws I had previously noticed were still just as apparent, but I also recognized that she did provide a considerable amount of additional useful information, supplementing Hounam.

The previous year had been the 50th anniversary of the *Liberty* incident and noted conspiracy researcher Phillip F. Nelson had marked the occasion by releasing a far stronger book on the incident. The author fully acknowledged that he was closely following the trail blazed by Hounam, whose work he repeatedly characterized as "seminal." **Remember the Liberty!** was written in association with several of the *Liberty* survivors and included a Foreword by highly-regarded former CIA analyst Ray McGovern.

Nelson was an especially harsh critic of Lyndon Johnson, probably best known for his 2010 and 2014 books marshaling the considerable evidence implicating LBJ in the assassination of his predecessor John F. Kennedy, and at certain points he seemed insufficiently cautious about accepting some of less solidly-attested accusations in the case of the *Liberty*. But the author does provide a great deal of important information on the president's very difficult political situation in 1967, persuasively extending Hounam's argument that a new Tonkin Gulf type event in the Middle East and a sweeping American military victory might have been crucial to Johnson's prospects for reelection in 1968.

During the three generations since World War II, America has ranked as the world's leading superpower, with its military possessing unmatched global reach and strength. Although the *Liberty* was a nearly defenseless intelligence ship sailing international waters, our powerful Sixth Fleet was nearby, so the deadly attack upon the vessel was not merely an obvious war-crime, but a very strange one, perhaps the most serious that our forces had suffered in decades, yet still entirely unpunished even today.

Solving such a crime usually involves a careful consideration of means, motive, and opportunity. There is no doubt that Israel's military deliberately attacked our ship, but the other two legs of the tripod remain puzzling. The risks that Israel took in its unprovoked attack against the ship of its sole ally were enormous. And the opportunity to sink the *Liberty* only came about due to a long and very strange series of supposed American communication errors. But if we accept the framework proposed by Hounam, Nelson, Mellen, and their adherents and postulate the secret involvement of President Lyndon Johnson, both these difficulties immediately disappear.

Planning to sacrifice a few hundred American lives and risk World War III to bolster his reelection chances would obviously add a very black mark to the reputation of our 36th president. But based upon my extensive historical research, I do not think he would have been the first American leader to have followed this sort of callous political calculus, although such decisions were afterward concealed by later generations of historians. Indeed, a couple of years ago, **I came to very similar conclusions** regarding the primary architect behind the outbreak of World War II:

> During the 1930s, John T. Flynn was one of America's most influential progressive journalists, and although he had begun as a strong supporter of Roosevelt and his New Deal, he gradually became a sharp critic, concluding that FDR's various governmental schemes had failed to revive the American economy. Then in 1937 a new economic collapse spiked unemployment back to the same levels as when the president had first entered office, confirming Flynn in his harsh verdict. And as **I wrote** last year:
>
> Indeed, Flynn alleges that by late 1937, FDR had turned towards an aggressive foreign policy aimed at involving the country in a major foreign war, primarily because he believed that this was the only route out of his desperate economic and political box, a stratagem not unknown among national leaders throughout history. In **his January 5, 1938 *New Republic* column**, he alerted his disbelieving readers to the looming prospect of a large naval military build-up and warfare on the horizon after a top Roosevelt adviser had privately boasted to him that a large bout of "military Keynesianism" and a major war would cure the country's seemingly insurmountable economic problems. At that time, war with Japan, possibly over Latin American interests, seemed the intended goal, but developing events in Europe soon persuaded FDR that fomenting a general war against Germany was the best course of action. Memoirs and other historical documents obtained by later researchers seem to generally support Flynn's ac-

cusations by indicating that Roosevelt ordered his diplomats to exert enormous pressure upon both the British and Polish governments to avoid any negotiated settlement with Germany, thereby leading to the outbreak of World War II in 1939.

The last point is an important one since the confidential opinions of those closest to important historical events should be accorded considerable evidentiary weight. In **a recent article** John Wear mustered the numerous contemporaneous assessments that implicated FDR as a pivotal figure in orchestrating the world war by his constant pressure upon the British political leadership, a policy that he privately even admitted could mean his impeachment if revealed. Among other testimony, we have the statements of the Polish and British ambassadors to Washington and the American ambassador to London, who also passed along the concurring opinion of Prime Minister Chamberlain himself. Indeed, the German capture and publication of secret Polish diplomatic documents in 1939 had already revealed much of this information, and William Henry Chamberlin confirmed their authenticity in his 1950 book. But since the mainstream media never reported any of this information, these facts remain little known even today.

Postscript: Someone brought to my attention an outstanding four-part documentary series on the story of the Liberty directed by Matthew Skow that was released last year, based upon extensive interviews with the surviving crew members and having very high production values. The overall feature runs nearly five hours, with the last segment focusing primarily on the controversial issues raised in Hounam's book. It's available for purchase or rent, and I'd highly recommend it.

- **Sacrificing Liberty**
  A Four Episode Docuseries
  Matthew Skow • ***TruHistory Films*** • 2000 • 4 hours 44 minutes

This article is available online at:
https://www.unz.com/runz/american-pravda-remembering-the-liberty/

Made in the USA
Monee, IL
22 December 2023